11 September and Its Aftermath

Books of Related Interest

Constructing Post-Soviet Geopolitics in Estonia
Pami Aalto, University of Tampere

From Geopolitics to Global Politics: A French Connection
Jacques Lévy, Reims University (ed.)

Geopolitics at the End of the Twentieth Century: The Changing World Political Map
Nurit Kliot, Haifa University and David Newman, Ben Gurion University of the Negev (eds)

The Changing Geopolitics of Eastern Europe
Andrew H. Dawson and Rick Fawn, University of St Andrews (eds)

Boundaries, Territory and Postmodernity
David Newman, Ben Gurion University of the Negev (ed.)

The Marshall Plan Today: Model and Metaphor
John Agnew and J. Nicholas Entrikin, University of California, Los Angeles (eds)

Geopolitics and Strategic History, 1871–2050
Colin S. Gray, University of Reading and Geoffrey Sloan, Britannia royal Naval College

Globalisation and the Future of Terrorism: Patterns and Prediction
Brynjar Lia and Annika S. Hansen, Norwegian Defence Research Establishment

11 SEPTEMBER AND
ITS AFTERMATH
THE GEOPOLITICS OF TERROR

Editor

STANLEY D. BRUNN

FRANK CASS
LONDON • PORTLAND, OR

First Published in 2004 in Great Britain by
FRANK CASS PUBLISHERS
Crown House, 47 Chase Side, Southgate
London, N14 5BP

and in the United States of America by
FRANK CASS PUBLISHERS
c/o ISBS, Suite 300, 920 NE 58th Avenue,
Portland, Oregon, 97213-3786

Website: www.frankcass.com

British Library Cataloguing in Publication Data

11 September and its aftermath : the geopolitics of terror.
  – (Cass studies in geopolitics ; no. 7)
  1.World politics – 21st century 2.September 11 Terrorist
Attacks, 2001 3.Terrorism 4.International relations
5.Geopolitics 6.United States – Foreign relations – 21st
century
  I.Brunn, Stanley D. II.Eleven September and its aftermath
909.8'3

ISBN 0714655724

ISBN 0-7146-5572-4 (cloth)
ISBN 0-7146-8454-6 (paper)

Library of Congress Cataloging-in-Publication Data

11 September and its aftermath : the geopolitics of terror / editor
Stanley D. Brunn.
    p. cm.
"First appeared as a special issue of Geopolitics, ISSN 1465-0045, vol.
8, no. 3 (autumn 2003)."
Includes bibliographical references and index.
    ISBN 0-7146-5572-4 (alk. paper) -- ISBN 0-7146-8454-6 (pbk. : alk.
paper)
1. September 11 Terrorist Attacks, 2001. 2. World politics--21st
century. 3. Geopolitics. I. Title: Eleventh September and its
aftermath. II. Brunn, Stanley D. III. Geopolitics.
    HV6432.7.A15 2003
    973.931--dc22
                          2003015184

This group of studies first appeared as a special issue of *Geopolitics*, ISSN 1465-
0045, Vol.8, No.3 (Autumn 2003) published by Frank Cass and Co. Ltd.

Printed in Great Britain by Antony Rowe Ltd., Chippenham, Wiltshire

Contents

vi

Introduction

STANLEY D. BRUNN

11 September 2001 at 8:48 AM (Eastern Standard Time) will be a memorable moment in the minds of many citizens of the planet, whether they lived in New York City, suburban Europe, rural Central Asia or insular South Pacific. The events of that day are forever imprinted on young and old, women and men, the powerful and powerless, the able and disabled, the working and retired, those who were at home or were in transit, America's friends and foes, those who govern and those governed. Those morning minutes in the eastern United States occurred at different times of the day and night elsewhere in the world. While some were awakening to the day, others were traveling to work or coming home from work, while still others were in hospitals, visiting friends, shopping or sleeping. There were residents of New York who witnessed these destructive events firsthand. Hundreds of thousands of others saw the second attack on the World Trade Center, and its collapse, on television, and millions of others heard about these events immediately, soon thereafter, or throughout the day. The events of that Tuesday, which were reported repeatedly on thousands of radio stations and shown on national and international television networks, were relayed to homes, farms, mines, industries, offices, airports, schools and government offices many times that day and in the days following.

In short, 11 September has become part of 'a global memory', a date and time when almost everyone precisely knew where she/he was and what she/he was doing. Because of this event 'we all became New Yorkers', as more than one commentator stated about the collective sympathy for those affected. Many Americans had friends and relatives or friends of friends who knew someone who was killed in the Trade Center Towers or the Pentagon or who lost their lives in the crash in rural Southeast Pennsylvania or as a result of rescue efforts. That this event contributed to a global memory and membership in a universal community has also meant that in the days, weeks and months following the emotions surrounding the tragedy attained global proportions as well.

The responses to the events of 11 September and the provision of meaning to 'what happened and why' remain of great concern to members of many scholarly communities. Scholars by their very nature seek answers to questions, that is, they seek to interpret and analyze 'what happened and why' through their own disciplinary lenses, models, theories and paradigms, but also through some new interdisciplinary or transdisciplinary perspectives. Since the events of that September day touched the lives, livelihoods, economies and social and political institutions of so many peoples and places inside and outside the United States, it is understandable that many questions about the specific targets and the persons responsible became the subject of inquiry and discussion. These included the responses of the print and visual media, whether in editorials, cartoons, photographs, letters to editors or continuous and extensive television coverage of events or constant (nearly 24-hour) replays of the heinous acts as well as interviews with political leaders, panel discussions with veteran military leaders and scholars, leaders of faith communities, members of disaster response teams or ordinary citizens around the world. The unprecedented events of 11 September themselves resulted in a certain amount of 'ad hocracy' among the elected, the media and the powerful and influential, that is, not being exactly sure how to express sympathy for those grieving at the loss of family members and friends, how the United States might respond militarily and diplomatically, whether the acts could have been prevented, and who was at fault. Also, what did these events say about America, Americans, American leaders, the rich world, capitalism, military might and international order?

In the discussion below I address three main themes, first, how the events of 11 September impacted the geopolitics of daily life of Americans, including the operations of local, state and federal governments; second, how members of scholarly and reporting communities (including the contributors to this volume) responded to the events; and third, what are some research topics that await our disciplinary and interdisciplinary inquiries?

Geopolitics of Daily Life

We acknowledge that there are some stark differences in the worlds 'before 11 September' and those 'after 11 September'. Those differences are evident in individual behaviours, the legislative agendas of democratic and closed societies, the funding of government programmes (especially for increased security and surveillance) and the daily operations of law enforcement, judicial and military branches. There are also differences in the speeches and rhetoric of many political leaders and in the immediate priorities of regional economic, military and political organisations. These 'before and after' worlds are evident in the United States, but also in new and old states in Europe, Asia, Africa and Central and South America. In short, every continent and country to some extent feels the impacts of the 11

September events. Keen and even casual observers and analysts almost anywhere could document changes in the economic, cultural, security and legal landscapes of their hometowns, capital cities, industrial centres, transportation and telecommunications centres.

Within the United States, there were immediate differences in human behaviour and institutional and organisational responses, especially in New York City and Washington, DC. But places distant from the crash sites were also affected. Immediately following the events that September morning, daily life was different. Businesses, schools and government offices closed; the skies became silent; military and defence installations were placed on high alert; faith communities formed (some ad hoc); attendance at interfaith religious services and events increased; community and political leaders took to the 'air or sound waves' to ensure calmness, patience, tolerance and understanding of those 'others' who were perceived as being related to or somehow sympathetic to those responsible for the terrorist acts. Calls went out around the country for volunteers to assist those cities and families affected directly. While some volunteers traveled to New York, Washington, and southeastern Pennsylvania in the days immediately following 11 September, others donated their time and resources to assist members of extended families who lost their family members and friends or were waiting for news about loved ones, friends and colleagues. Instant heroines and heroes were those who unselfishly volunteered; they included firefighters and law enforcement officers and those who risked their lives for public safety or a larger public good.

But not all that happened in American society immediately after 11 September was constructive. There were personal verbal and physical attacks against Muslims, Muslim Americans and those who 'looked' Arab or Muslim. And there were attacks on mosques and Islamic centres and those Arab Americans who owed shops and stores. Distrust and suspicion were also cast on recent arrivals who entered the United States, legally or illegally, from Mexico, Bosnia, Somalia, Russia and eastern European countries. Suspicion was cast on those who attended 'flight schools' or those international students, visitors and workers who were delinquent in reporting their immigration status. The 'search' for enemies, old or new, became part of this post-11 September world. On a global scale, former global enemies became friends, as long as they supported a 'war on terrorism'; new enemies were created, some states (the 'axis of evil') or those networks of terrorists which operate across state lines.

Many of the impacts described above soon reverberated throughout American society and the economy. Some workers (from cooks to corporate executives) lost jobs, some businesses lost sales and were forced to close or file for bankruptcy. Business and industry groups, especially in the airline and travel/tourism sectors, lobbied vigorously for bailout packages or stimulus packages to generate revenue. State and local governments as well as the US Congress debated how best and fast to respond to the impacts of these unprecedented events. Communities large and small, especially along United States–Mexico and United States–Canada borders and major ports of entry, sought quick-fix ways to improve and tighten their security. Military and defence installations around the United States and embassies and military bases around the world were placed on high alert as possible follow-up targets for domestic or international terrorists and quickly geared up for massive offensive operations against the Taliban and Al Qaeda in Afghanistan. Terrorism became a word on the lips of those in powerful and low-level political positions and those who previously only associated the word with places distant from US shores. The public, overwhelmed by the events and aftermath, quickly acquired an entirely new lexicon, which included Al Qaeda cells, the war on terrorism, bioterrorism, homeland surveillance, state-sponsored terrorism and the Axis of Evil.

A check of the Google search engine in mid-March 2003 yielded these numbers for websites for the following key words: '9/11' 5.3 million; 'September 11, 2001' 4.1 million; 'Afghanistan' 3.6 million; 'Taliban' 925,000; 'Osama bin Laden' 686,000; 'Al Qaeda' 394,000; 'Muslims in America' 314,000; and 'Al Jazeera' 58,000. In regards to specific subjects, these were the number of linkages: 'World Trade Center' 2.7 million; 'terrorism' 3.1 million; 'war on terrorism' 1.3 million; 'homeland security' 608,000; 'God Bless America' 493,000; 'patriotism' 390,000; 'bioterrorism' 237,000, 'anthrax scare' 43,100; and 'Axis of Evil' 34,500. As for other countries in diplomatic and military reporting, the results were: 'Iraq' 5.8 million; 'Pakistan' 5 million; 'Kuwait' 2.4 million; 'Syria' and 'North Korea' 2 million each, 'Palestinian National Authority' 160,000, and 'Israel' 10.5 million.

The *Christian Science Monitor* in its 10 September 2002 issue provided its readers, in a series of graphics and factoids, with a snapshot of some of the changes that had occurred over the previous twelve months.[1] For example, the terrorist attacks generated more than 300 books, Peace Corps applications were slightly over 10,000, compared to about 8,600 in the previous year, flag sales by Wal-Mart in the first seven months after 11 September were 4.96 million compared to 1.18 million the previous year, the number of violent incidents against Arab Americans (or those perceived as such) was 172 in the year before 11 September and over 600 the following year, the largest American publisher of Korans sold 1,300 copies each week before 11 September but saw an 800 per cent increase in sales in the weeks immediately following, the largest Bible publisher sold 140,000 copies a week before the attacks but experienced a 30 per cent increase shortly after 11 September. In addition, one could document the rise in unemployment (New York City was especially hard hit), declines in the stock markets, increased bomb shelter sales and increases in radio and TV broadcasts playing God Bless America (1,952 in 2000 vs 8,915 in 2001). Americans donated $2.25 billion in 11 September-related giving. The top four recipients were the American Red Cross, the September 11 Fund, the New York Firefighters Disaster Relief Fund and Twin Towers Fund (total $1.4 billion). The United States issued a postage stamp called the 'Heroes of 2001' on 7 June 2002, a semipostal issue that depicted three New York firefighters hoisting the American flag on a pile of World Trade Center rubble. Within five months more than 65 million stamps had been sold, for a revenue of nearly $30 million.

The cultural landscape, especially the visible landscape, was also altered. The 11 September events provided an opportunity to instil and demonstrate patriotism, especially in its visible forms. Flags became a distinguishing and signature feature of the everyday political landscape. Flags large and small appeared on and in buildings, in front yards of homes, on automobiles, on bumper stickers and on huge outdoor advertising spaces. Often flags (many made in China) became part of other patriotic promotions, along with the American eagle, the Statue of Liberty and words about God blessing America. The juxtaposition of religion and patriotism became a part of the national political culture, a combination one might have associated only with certain regions and states in the past. Displaying the US flag in places of worship became a controversial issue for some congregations. Displaying patriotism on one's sleeves or on one's SUV was so pervasive that these symbols of nationhood became more popular than exercising one's right to disagree with positions taken by the nation's elected leaders. For several months following 11 September those commentators, cartoonists, syndicated columnists and critical analysts of US domestic policies (privacy concerns, the USA Patriot Act surveillance or thwarting continued anthrax attacks) or of US foreign policies (unwarranted heavy bombardment of Afghanistan, labeling countries as 'evil', or hard-line Israeli military retaliation against Palestinian violence) were effectively silenced by those calling for bipartisan and unqualified support by US leaders for the 'war on terrorism'.

Other changes in daily life were evident as well, especially traveling in the days and weeks immediately following 11 September. Some Americans developed a fear of flying, even short distances. Airport security was, and still is, much tighter, as was security at international borders and entering major federal office buildings and installations, including national parks and monuments. Transferring money abroad, especially to southwest Asian countries, became more difficult; as did receiving money. Public events (concerts, sports, etc.) were cancelled or postponed. All public airports established tighter security for passenger screening and baggage check-in, even if the procedures were lax before. Joking was at a standstill. People cancelled long-distance holiday vacations and decided instead to spend time with families and in familiar locales. Consumers purchased a variety of security devices (alarm systems, light detectors, cell phones) for automobiles, apartments and houses. The federal government issued warnings (colour coded) about potential terrorist threats on major holidays and potential targets (bridges and tunnels linking metropolitan areas, sporting and entertainment events, and major airports). The anthrax scare soon after 11 September further jolted many Americans from any lingering complacency. International students, whether in the United States legally or not, were required to register with the federal government; those on campuses illegally, not enrolled full time or with expired visas and permits faced possible deportation. Family life was disrupted, not only for those who lost family members in the terrorist acts themselves, but those who were out of work, whether in high- or low-paying jobs. Many families were also left without one parent when women and men were called up for National Guard duty or as reserves for military duty in Afghanistan.

Other changes are less visible, but still evident. These include increased restrictions on sending letters and packages to international addresses, loss of privacy – for example, regarding one's possessions while travelling (by plane, bus, train), restrictions on sending monies electronically, requirements to register as a international student or visitor, monitoring of bank accounts, credit records, email and regular mail. In the months following 11 September there were proposals about issuing national identity cards, what information they should contain, who would have access to the data, and the registration of firearms and sales. The balance between civil liberties and a government's right to know information about its citizens was and still is hotly debated. And there were larger questions that surfaced in professional, business and government communities about businesses relocating to smaller cities, designing lower profile office towers and decentralising government offices and laboratories. Conversations were about spending priorities, including the budget to fight the war in Afghanistan. To this list one might add that the world of humour changed as well; how could one possibly find a light side to what happened and what was happening? A certain somberness and seriousness about the 11 September events pervades much of the American conscience twenty months later. Many Americans sought hard to understand 'what happened and why' and found the ensuing political rhetoric void of answers to these soul wrenching questions about America as a superpower, its massive military might, cultural arrogance, disregard for environmental quality and corporate greed linked to excesses of globalisation.

Members of academic communities responded to the events of 11 September in various ways. In many cities and towns there were public forums sponsored by businesses, universities and interfaith communities that were devoted to domestic security, international terrorism, military preparedness, the Middle East, South and Central Asia and post-Cold War geopolitics. Many professors deviated from their course structure to devote several days to discussing the above topics. Other professors changed their course syllabi significantly and encouraged their students in seek explanations and interpretations of what transpired through domestic and international newspaper editorials, letters to editors, photographs, music and art, new web sites, presentations by visiting professionals from the private and public sectors and surveys of businesses and the public. Some universities used the events to reach out to their international students and faculty by offering courses on Islam and interfaith perspectives on globalisation; still others invited members of 'other' communities to speak to student bodies and community gatherings.

A frequent question asked in the weeks and months after 11 September was 'Who are the "winners" and "losers"?' In a US context the most obvious losers included those who lost families and friends in the attacks and those who lost their livelihoods. As noted above, the rich and poor, powerful and powerless were affected. Other losers were companies and corporations which lost personnel, memories, revenues and data, as well as those states which lost expected revenues which they expected to finance education, health, transportation and housing programmes. Small towns and cities, large and small states found it difficult to fund needed security programmes. Even 20 months later the economic losses continue to mount, not only in the United States, Europe and Japan, but also in places subjected to reported terrorist attacks since 11 September. These include Russia, Indonesia, the Philippines, Pakistan, India, Kuwait, Yemen, Palestine and Israel. We also might count as 'losses' the fact that the academic community did not know and still does not know much about South Asia, Southwest Asia and Central Asia. We have too few students and scholars in our academic, intelligence and corporate communities who have studied the histories, cultures, economies and languages (minor and major) of these regions. Translators of Southwest and Central Asian and North African languages were and remain in short supply, as do colleges and universities offering courses, seminars and degree programmes specialising in these regions' cultures, economies, histories, geopolitics and environments. While the superpower states may have sophisticated weaponry and technology that can 'see' cities, rivers, valleys and human movements from the skies, we know too little about the ground truth geographies in these highly multicultural regions.

The 'winners', if indeed such a term is appropriate, would be those in Afghanistan who opposed the Taliban; women might be included, but even a year later not all women are free and liberated. Patriarchy dies hard, even in secular Islamic states with strong tribal traditions, and rival clans. Returning exiles to help rebuild the country might also be declared winners. The monetary winners in a US context would be those companies which lobbied successfully for stimulus packages to help them during stock market downturns, and surviving airlines and travel/tourist industries. Other winners would have to be firms training private security personnel, manufacturers and promoters of various consumer security products including alarm systems, fences and gates, providers of personal and residence insurance, and the architects who developed tighter securityscapes around airports, government office buildings, corporate offices, nuclear power plants and military bases. These continue to do a booming business, with some federal support.

The events of 11 September and afterwards revealed a number of serious 'knowledge gaps' in American culture, society and politics. The gaps included lapses in security, as it became acknowledged that forged passports were used or could be used to enter the United States. Also, contributions to some domestic charity organisations with international funding went unchecked, even though some monies originated from counties suspected of harbouring terrorist cells and strong anti-American sentiments. Not only was it evident that the United States had little knowledge about clandestine terrorist networks operating in South and Central Asia and elsewhere, but, as noted above there were few area specialists. A profound lack of professionals who knew the languages, cultures, and politics of Southwest, South and Central Asia became evident in both the US military and State Department. Universities have not been training specialists with the requisite language, cultural, economic and diplomatic/negotiating skills. Research by those in the academic community with interests in these regions had low priority and offered few rewards.

Reporting on the Events of 11 September

Some professional societies devoted sessions, panel and plenary presentations at regional and national meetings in late 2001, 2002 and 2003 to the events of 11 September. The National Science Foundation encouraged the submission of proposals from scholarly communities to promote learning about the events through conferences, workshops and publications. Other foundations and organisations also used the events to promote increased international awareness through foreign language programmes, intercultural exchanges and youth programmes. The Association of

American Geographers held a workshop in early 2002 devoted to studying the geographical dimensions of terrorism. An outgrowth of this workshop is a volume, forthcoming mid-2003, devoted to this theme.[2] The 27 chapters address a number of major themes under these chapter headings: The Changing Landscape of Fear, Societal Response to Threats, Understanding the Root Causes of Terrorism, Geospatial Data and Technologies in Times of Crisis, Vulnerability of Lifelines, The Built Environment and People, Bioterrorism, and Building a Safer but Open Society. It concludes with a research and action agenda.

Academic and commercial publishers sought ways to ensure that the 11 September events were covered in forthcoming texts and journals. A multiauthored volume, edited by Mary Buckley and Rick Fawn (forthcoming 2003), contains 26 chapters on the twin themes of terrorism and international relations; the authors come from different disciplines, nationalities and backgrounds, but all discussing the new security and political challenges facing states.[3] The chapters in the Buckley and Fawn volume not only discuss global dimensions of these issues, but also how the events of 11 September are impacting the domestic and international politics of regions, including Africa, Southeast Asia and Central Asia, but also a number of countries, including China, Russia, Indonesia, Israel, Saudi Arabia, France, Germany, the United Kingdom, Canada and the US, as well as NATO, the United Nations and the European Union. Editors of academic journals also sought statements by leading experts on the impacts of 11 September. One example was *The Arab World Geographer*, which in its final issue of 2001 included eight statements, mostly by US geographers, on how they interpreted the events.[4] Two articles appeared in the May 2003 issue of *The Professional Geographer*; one proposed a research agenda for those interested in political geography and peace and conflict studies, the other on the uses of environmental remote sensing and GIS as tools for combatting terrorism in Afghanistan.[5] Another example was the third 2001 issue of *International Security*, which contained six articles on terrorism, including the threats of terrorism to US foreign policy after 11 September and combating terrorism in Southwest and South Asia.[6] A forthcoming issue of *Journal of Travel and Tourism Marketing* (2003), an international and interdisciplinary journal, will be devoted to the risk and security issues following the 11 September events and especially how tourist economies and organisations are confronting the new realities of travel and leisure.[7] Accompanying the scholarly volumes are a number of books that appeared in the following year. Some were written by well-known authors, others by journalists, and still others by individuals who participated in rescue operations in and around the World Trade Center.[8]

The mix of authors who have contributed to the current volume includes junior and senior scholars, women and men, geographers and nongeographers from Europe and North America. While a number of individual themes are addressed in these essays; there are also many essays which overlap. This overlap is anticipated, whether considering the events within the prism of critical geopolitics or existing theories advanced to explain geopolitical shifts. There are four major themes addressed in these essays.

Mansbach, in his thought-provoking discussion, on 'The Meaning of 11 September and the Emerging Postinternational World', outlines features of a new political, economic and social world. This world has a number of distinguishing features: religion and terrorism are significant elements, political boundaries are increasingly porous, physical distance in politics is of growing irrelevance, history is accelerated and new social actors emerge who use and are familiar with new information and communication technologies.

Critical geopolitics is a central thread in three essays, by Anderson, Dalby and Coleman. Anderson's discussion is entitled 'American Hegemony after 11 September: Allies, Rivals and Contradictions' and Dalby's is 'Calling 911: Geopolitics, Security, and America's New War'. Anderson examines the concepts of neo-liberalism, unilateral multilateralism and unilateral militarism and multilateralism; he sees an ideological shift in US policy from neo-lilberalism to neo-conservativism following the attacks. Dalby, on the other hand, specifically looks at events following 11 September and the assumptions made by the United States in engaging in war against Afghanistan and linking the attacks in the United States to terrorism. Both Anderson and Dalby address the consequences of US hegemony for its allies, especially in regards to emerging economic and political shifts. Coleman, in 'Iconographies of "Terrorism" and Evil Outlaws: Geopolitical Place-Making After 11 September', challenges us to consider terrorism within the context of place and place making rather our familiar linking of geopolitics with territory. He also discusses the 'place making of evil' and how that was used to justify state response against terrorism and label the terrorists as outlaws of justice and humanity.

Kleinfeld looks at how the 11 September events were used by both groups involved in Sri Lanka's civil war to justify their actions; her article is entitled 'Strategic Troping in Sri Lanka: *September Eleventh* and the Consolidation of Political Position'. An unexpected consequence of the September events was the effort by both sides in the civil war to justify their own actions and policies and to quietly seek a peaceful resolution to this prolonged conflict.

O'Lear, in her 'Environmental Terrorism: A Critique', looks at bioterrorism and issues of environmental security. She comments on the sparse literature on the geopolitics of environmental security themes and also on the failure of environmental scientists to address issues of resource politics and national security.

Four discussions in this collection examine editorials and the statements of groups and organisations. Debrix introduces the concept of 'tabloid journalism', which is used by noted conservative writers to inform others about their own views, some which often border on the sensational. His discussion is entitled 'Tabloid Realism and the Revival of American Security Culture'. Mamadouh, in her '11 September and Popular Geopolitics: A Study of Websites Run for and by Dutch Moroccans', evaluates the contents of websites of young Dutch Moroccans in the Netherlands and how they presented materials about Islam, Palestine and the events following 11 September. Her essay is especially germane given the growing numbers of Muslims in west European cities, potential clashes and anti-immigrant sentiments in Europe, and the use of electronic technologies to disseminate information about national and international politics. Taylor and Jaspero, in their essay 'Editorials and Geopolitical Explanations for 11 September', look at the editorial content of 66 newspapers in the United States, United Kingdom, Pakistan, Egypt, Israel and Japan. They use these editorials to explain the 11 September events in light of a number of theories, including clash of civilisations, imperialism, blowback (unexpected consequences of events), state decline and Islamism. And, finally, in this category of content analyses, Dahlman and Brunn ferret out the civil society literature, neglected for the most part by geopolitical analysts, and construct a framework in which to read the press releases of 23 nongovernmental organisations with American, European and global agendas. Their objective was to discern what these statements contained about the attacks and follow-up actions. They discovered that while most releases condemned the attacks and expressed sympathy to those who lost family and friends, the responses for subsequent action ranged from aggression to restraint. The discussion is entitled 'Reading Geopolitics Beyond the State: Organizational Discourses in Response to 11 September'.

What We Don't Know

There remain many issues related to 11 September that geographers and others studying national and international political communities can and will study in the years ahead. These inquiries are certain to include those looking and testing familiar theories and models and those introducing new schema. Each article suggests a number of plausible research themes for disciplinary, interdisciplinary or transdisciplinary study. To these I would add ten, which are not the singular focus of any essays in this volume.

One is to examine the role of religion in foreign policy, as Islam and Islam/Christianity have been in the forefront of news accounts, editorials, and statements of those supporting and condemning the 11 September 2001 events. Religion is a much-neglected focus in much of the critical geopolitics and political geography literatures, even though it is a crucial component of political cultures in the United States, Western Europe and the Arab/Islamic world. It is also a major component of the worldview of leaders and their domestic and foreign policy agendas. Specific studies might investigate the presentation of Islam in popular religious magazines in Europe and North America and in history and geography textbooks, as well as the depiction of Arabs, Muslims and Muslim clerics. The magazines and textbooks in the Arab world also merit critical inquiry.

A second theme relates to how the events of 11 September were used by those states with emergent nationalistic groups within their borders and how the state uses its authority to adopt and enforce measures to de-legitimise or destroy them. Examples include the Basques, Chechnyans, Kurds, Ughyrs and rebel groups in the southern Philippines, Indonesia and Colombia. A government labeling a particular group as 'terrorist' was often sufficient for building an international coalition to thwart terrorism, even if the state applied excessive military force and violated the basic human rights of its own citizens. The dicey Kashmir and Israel/Palestine conflicts might also be easily inserted into this theme.

A third theme, tangentially addressed in several essays, relates to border security. Security issues are major issues challenging not only states that share friendly borders, but those where there has been an easy flow of resources, manufactured goods and workers. That there are hundreds of thousands of workers who cross international borders daily in North America, Europe, Southwest Asia and elsewhere has meant that for many since 11 September the trip to and from work is more time consuming, costly and risky. What may have been an easy and unimpeded trip has become prolonged and potentially dangerous.

A fourth theme would examine the issues of immigration, refugee status, political asylum and political prisoners, especially with respect to the appropriate national and international legal authorities. These issues are certain to affect new regions of cross-border conflict (South and Southwest Asia) as well as open and democratic states with recent histories of new immigrant mixes.[9]

A fifth theme would look more closely at the impacts of 11 September on Arab states and Islamic cultures from North Africa to Central Asia. How were these events covered in national print and visual media, where there is often tight government censorship? How have religious, academic and political leaders used the events to call for incipient democraticisation, whether in granting women the right to vote or opposition political parties to form and field candidates?

A sixth theme that merits more attention in the geopolitical/environment arena relates to the resource bases of rich and poor countries. While access to immense oil and gas reserves may be seen as the main reason the United States has sought to build international support for bombing Afghanistan immediately after 11 September and for the huge military buildup to invade Iraq, there are other major resource issues, especially water, that are equally paramount in Arab-world geopolitics. Water geopolitics are issues between Israel and Palestine, Turkey and Iran, India and Pakistan.

A seventh theme would consider the role of the United Nations and other Asian, European and Southwest Asian regional economic and security pacts in issues regarding terrorism, military deployment, weapons inspections, post-war reconstruction in Afghanistan and Iraq, building more open and transparent governments and measuring public opinion. That these organisations have assumed some new and different roles in regards to coalition building, joint military exercises, humanitarian aid and regional diplomacy is worthy of study.

The eighth theme relates to a set of counter or silent geopolitics, that is, what pressing human and environmental problems were neglected while the United States especially, and to a lesser extent other major European and Asian powers, became preoccupied with attacking Afghanistan, lashing out against Iraq for its supposed ties to Al Qaeda and the Palestinian Authority. It would not be difficult to argue that the United Nations, NATO, the European Union and other regional bodies have been preoccupied during the past several years fighting or seeking to fight terrorism at home and abroad, all the while neglecting an ever-widening AIDS epidemic in southern Africa and emerging in China, increased environmental deterioration (air, water and land) in urban and rural areas of the rich and poor worlds, reducing civil liberties in Europe and North America, stemming spontaneous outbreaks of violence in Nigeria, Congo, Liberia, India, Pakistan and Venezuela, and struggling with global economic woes, the consequences of which affect more than the few headline countries appearing in the global news daily.

The ninth issue, which again is touched on in several of the ensuing essays, would examine how the events of 11 September have affected not only the soul and heart of America and Americans and Europe and Europeans, Asia and Asians, but also other countries that have been impacted directly and indirectly by the military attacks, military threats, terrorist attacks and retaliation against opposition or suspected-opposition groups. The list could include Afghanistan, Pakistan, Israel, Palestine, Turkey, Iraq, Saudi Arabia, Egypt, Kazakstan, Russia, China, India, the Philippines and Indonesia.

The tenth and final issue relates to the events of early 2003, viz., the US and British invasion of Iraq. This unilateral military action, considered as part of the Bush preventive war foreign policy, was taken without the military support of traditionally strong European allies and the UN Security Council. This decision may be seen in the short and immediate run as having just as much significance in further reshaping and reordering the geopolitical, geoeconomic and geocultural landscapes of Asia, Europe and elsewhere as the 11 September events. Furthermore, the consequences of the United States serving as an occupying (military or administrative) force in a strategic oil-rich Southwest Asian country where political rivalries exist are unknown. Whether the decision will thwart international terrorism, promote anti-American sentiments in the Arab media, streets and capitals, encourage more political openness in traditional societies, aid in solving a viable solution to longstanding Israel/Palestine territorial issues, or serve as a potential source for low and high level conflicts in South, Southeast and East Asia are unknown at this time.

It is recognised by many in the international political, military, economic, humanitarian and scholarly communities that we are living in worlds with varying degrees of fluidity, dynamism and flux. These call for investigations by those in the humanities, social and policy sciences. These inquiries need to investigate these worlds and world regions using some traditional models and conceptual thinking, but also to explore some new transdisciplinary models and paradigms, the components of which are suggested in many of the essays in this volume.

NOTES

1. 'September 10: Now and Then', *Christian Science Monitor*, 10 September 2001, pp.12–13.
2. Susan L. Cutter, Douglas B. Richardson and Thomas J. Wilbanks (eds), *The Geographical Dimensions of Terrorism* (New York: Routledge 2003).
3. Mary Buckley and Rich Fawn, *Global Responses to Terrorism. 9/11, Afghanistan and Beyond* (New York: Routledge 2003).
4. 'Forum', *The Arab World Geographer* 4/2 (2001), pp. 77–103.
5. Colin Flint, 'Terrorism and counter terrorism: Geographic Research Questions and Agendas', *The Professional Geographer* 55/2 (2003), pp.161–9; Richard A. Beck, 'Remote Sensing and GIs as Counterterrorism Tools in the Afghanistan War: A Case Study of the Zhawar Kili Region', *The Professional Geographer* 55/2 (2003), pp.170–79.
6. *International Security* 26/3 (2001), pp.3–116. Articles include: Editor's Note; Ashton B. Carter, 'The Architecture of Government in the Face of Terrorism'; Philip B. Heymann, 'Dealing with Terrorism: An Overview'; B.R. Posen, 'The Struggle against Terrorism:

Grand Strategy, Strategy, and Tactics'; Stephen M. Walt, 'Beyond bin Laden: Reshaping U.S. Foreign Policy'; Samina Ahmed, 'The United States and Terrorism in Southwest Asia: September 11 and Beyond'; and Brahma Chellaney, 'Fighting Terrorism in Southern Asia'.

7. David Duval (ed.), *Safety and Security in Tourism: Relationships, Management, and Marketing*, special issue of *Journal of Travel and Tourism Marketing* 11 (2003), forthcoming.

8. A number of trade books appeared in the months immediately after 11 September and in the following year. There were three major themes to these treatises. First were those that were primarily visual and photographic in content. These include CBS News and Dan Rather, *What We Saw: The Events of September 11, 2001 in Worlds, Pictures, and Video* (New York: Simon & Schuster 2002); Nancy Lee (ed.), *A Nation Challenged: A Visual History of 9/11 and Its Aftermath* (New York: Times Books 2002); Magnum Photographers and David Halberstam, *New York September 11* (New York: Powerhouse Books 2001); and Photographers of the New York City Police Department, Christopher Sweet and David Fitzpatrick, *Above Hallowed Ground: A Photographic Record of September 11, 2001* (New York: Viking 2002). Second are those that examine the disaster relief teams, especially firefighters and law enforcement officials. Books that covered these themes include: Frank McCourt, *Brotherhood* (New York: Sterling Publications 2001); David Halberstam, *Firehouse* (New York: Hyperion 2002); Richard Picciotto et al., *Last Man Down: A New York City Fire Chief and the Collapse of the World Trade Center* (New York: Berkeley Pub Group 2002); and Dennis Smith, *Report from Ground Zero: The Story of the Rescue Efforts at the World Trade Center* (New York: Viking Press 2002). Third are those books that were combinations of the above themes and also considered the events in larger contexts. Books in this genre were: Rudolph Giuliani and *LIFE Magazine*, *One Nation: America Remembers September 11, 2001* (Boston: Little Brown 2001); Richard Bernstein (ed.), *Out of the Blue: A Narrative of September 11, 2001* (New York: Times Books 2002); Jere Longman, *Among the Heroes: United Flight 93 and the Passengers and Crew Who Fought Back* (New York: HarperCollins 2002); New York Times, *9/11/01: The Collected 'Portraits of Grief' from The New York Times* (New York: Times Books 2002); and Staff of Reuters, *After September 11: New York and the World* (Boston: Pearson 2002). An interesting volume is Andrews McMeel Publishing and The Poynter Institute, *September 11, 2001* (Kansas City, MO: Andrews McMeel Publishing 2001). It contains a collection of 150 front pages of major newspapers around the world that were published in the days immediately after 11 September.

9. For a recent snapshot of the US immigration picture, see the tables and maps in James H. Johnson, Jr, 'Immigration Reform and the Future of U.S. Metropolitan Areas in the Post-9/11 Environment', in *ULI on the Future. Cities Post 9/11* (Washington, DC: Urban Land Institute 2002) pp.12–27.

The Meaning of 11 September and the Emerging Postinternational World

RICHARD W. MANSBACH

'Postinternational politics'[1] is the 'new frontier' of global political theory, and global terrorism and religious fundamentalism are entirely consonant with that framework. This article argues that the tragic events of 11 September, while not causing fundamental change in global politics, sharply reflect those changes, Those changes make much of international relations theory seem hopelessly obsolete. The destruction of New York's World Trade Center towers by suicidal fanatics associated with Osama bin Laden's Al Qaeda was a dramatic reminder of both the startling newness of the current era, as well as how much, in some respects, it resembles the past.

International politics, as it is still widely conceived, grew out of a Eurocentric tradition of scholarship dating back at least to Hobbes and Grotius in which it was assumed that interstate relations exhausted what we need to know about the political universe around us and that the seminal problem of that universe was interstate war.[2] This was made possible by the state's conquest of rival political forms and states' subsequent control of historical meaning.

During the epoch of European ascendancy, sovereign states claiming exclusive rights over territory within their boundaries and freedom from external interference dominated global politics. As a result, for centuries, theorists and practitioners of global politics have been accustomed to regarding the sovereign state as the source of citizens' security and their most important values, and the focus of humanity's highest loyalties. This model masked the fact that human beings have always lived in a variety of political communities, have identities and loyalties to a variety of political authorities, and have identity hierarchies that are in constant flux.

11 September, along with other events, forces us to reconsider whether a model that relies on an anarchic system consisting of territorial states, each of whose citizens are united in a quest for security that pits them against the citizens of other states, accounts for what is important in the world today. Our judgement is that a very different model built from 'polities' and 'identities' (individual and collective) driven by interdependent processes of centralisation (integration) and decentralisation (localisation) of political authority is more useful.[3]

It is hardly surprising that, following Europe's extension outward, state-centric theories associated with European versions of concepts such as 'power', 'sovereignty', 'territoriality' and 'sovereign frontiers' acquired global reach. Such concepts enforced and reinforced what European elites thought ought to be the dominant norms and practices of global life. The identity of 'citizen' was constructed in Europe and then imposed throughout Europe's empires. However, the continuing erosion of state authority and capacity invites us to reexamine old concepts and construct new ones that will both provide a better fit with reality and a more accurate guide to a new normative universe.

11 September invites us to redraw our mental maps and take account of the proliferation of new identities as well as new forms of governance that defy the 'sovereign' cartography of recent centuries. This confronts us with the theoretical problem posed by James Rosenau when he asks, 'How do we reconceptualise political space so that it connotes identities and affiliations (say, religious, ethnic, and professional) as well as territorialities?'[4] The very novelty of a massive attack on America's greatest city by a nationally diffuse group of fanatics with no clear territorial base, who intentionally sought to cause mass civilian deaths, suggests that something significant is underway in global politics. This 'significant something' seems to entail the transformation of international politics – an interstate world of sovereign leviathans – into a more complex postinternational universe. If such a transformation is indeed underway, fresh eyes will be necessary in order to escape what Rosenau calls 'the conceptual jails' in which many international relations theorists remain 'incarcerated'.

To date, the postinternational enterprise has been less a coherent theoretical position than a rejection of 'internationalism'; that is, the European state-centric tradition and the model of global politics derived from this tradition.[5] While the vocabulary and conceptual elements of postinternational thinking perform the critical function of 'pointing to' a different set of factors (and, therefore, ontology) in order to understand global politics, it has not yet acquired explanatory or predictive power.

Change and Continuity – The Past and Present

But how transformative have events in global politics really been? Most international relations theorists admit that, although change has taken place, such change is marginal and incremental.[6] 11 September was the first serious military attack by non-Americans on the continental United States. It dramatically altered Americans' views of themselves and of others and of the capability of their country to ensure their security. From our point of view, the event vividly reflected the degree to which the present is different from the relatively recent past. Postinternational theorising emphasises continuous change (though at different rates in different contexts and in different directions), and it rejects the static premises of neo-realism and other forms of structural determinism.

For Rosenau, the concept of postinternational 'suggests flux and transition' and 'allows for chaos'[7] Older formulations do not suffice because change 'is so pervasive in both the internal and external lives of communities and nation-states'.[8] Change, of course, is relative. In some cases, change is little more than an extension of existing patterns, not necessarily obliterating all that has gone before. At the other extreme, change may be so dramatic that it produces qualitative as well as quantitative alterations in the nature of political life. Is a new global order resting on new systemic foundations emerging, or is the existing system simply reconstituting itself to reflect shifting technological, economic and political realities?

Those in the European power tradition suggest that little is genuinely novel in contemporary global politics and that change, if it takes place at all, tends to be incremental. We are still, they believe, dealing with the same issues described by Thucydides and Machiavelli.[9] The real world is more complex – an amalgam of issues rooted in past millennia yet made almost unrecognisable by new factors like the microelectronic revolution. Thus, Islam's attitude to 'infidels', the meaning of 'jihad', and who enjoys political authority over Muslims, were never resolved and, for a variety of reasons, have reemerged in thoroughly contemporary settings.

Still, different observers may come to different conclusions about the nature of change even when looking at identical phenomena. As Rosenau argues, there are different 'temperaments' at work in theory.[10] Some theorists are predisposed to look for continuity, while others are inclined to emphasise the degree to which the present is different from the past and to point to discontinuities between epochs. This is an uncharacteristically postmodern observation for Rosenau, albeit a correct one as far as it goes. It is possible that we are all being bamboozled or are simply incapable of achieving sufficient distance from the press of current events.

The central role of change in postinternational thinking is why the study of history, despite the subjectivity so admired by constructivists inevitably involved in its interpretation, is so critical to those who engage in such thinking. At the end of the day, the present is the same and similar to the past in some respects and different in others. So *exactly* how is the present *both similar to the past and also different*? If all theorists were obliged to answer both questions and marshal evidence before writing anything else, we could have a substantive and constructive debate on the issue of change.

Like 11 September itself, the postinternational perspective emphasises fundamental change in global politics tempered by historical inheritance. This perspective breaks sharply and self-consciously with static models, which according to adherents, view global phenomena like states as timeless and universal, Change, we see, is the product of simultaneous and related processes of fusion and fission of authority, and consequent political forms are contingent rather than universal. In a state system, fusion refers to the absorption of state authority by more extensive polities such as the EU. By contrast, fission refers to the breakdown of states into smaller polities and the growth of local authority. The first process is reflected in growing regional and global authority networks that coordinate and guide people who are physically remote from one another and that centralise or consolidate governance. Just as ancient empires were almost impossible to control from a remote centre owing to the limits of transportation and communication technologies, so contemporary networks would be inconceivable in the absence of such technologies. A second tendency consists of the fracturing of existing political units into smaller and smaller islands of self-identification that localise and often specialise authority, thereby encumbering efforts to respond effectively to collective goods dilemmas.

Thus, some societies are falling apart even as others come together; 'some norms are spreading and others are receding; some multilateral projects are utter failures and others are remarkable successes.'[11] Some authorities such as the Soviet Union and Yugoslavia have fractured, whereas others like the European Union or major transnational corporations have extended the scope and domain of their authority.

The normative implications of these processes remain obscure. Political, economic and cultural integration affords greater capacity to overcome collective problems. At the same time, they may consign fragmented and less competitive parts of the world to permanently lower living standards and a permanent peripheral status. Disintegration preserves local culture and the psychological efficacy of smaller units, yet may result in marginalisation and ethnic strife over pitifully insignificant battlefields like Kosovo.

The two processes of change are related. Centralisation and growth of authority produce their opposite by provoking the desire for recognition of and respect for social, cultural and political diversity and heterogeneity and by spurring efforts to localise authority. By contrast, localised authority produces demands for greater functional capacity, efficiency and economies of scale that can only be realised through centralisation and homogeneity. The result is a complex world of overlapping local, regional, and global authority structures that sometimes cooperate, sometimes coexist, and sometimes clash.

Where we part with liberal and constructivist theorists (many of whom are the same people)[12] is in rejecting the idea that history is going 'somewhere'. The view expressed here is more complex: A richer understanding of history acknowledges that there is more to global politics than a few centuries of European experience, and the present is almost always a synthesis of old and new. Although 11 September makes clear just how far the world has moved beyond the inheritance of state-centric international politics, it is simultaneously incomprehensible to anyone without a sense of Muslim history, as President George W. Bush was chagrined to learn when he referred to 'crusade' in his initial reaction to the attack on the Trade Center.

In sum, just as we must examine the 'international' world to make sense of postinternationalism, so we must go further back and identify a preinternational world. And in some respects, that preinternational world has more in common with a postinternational one than with the relatively brief epoch in which European states dominated the world. Militant Islam or 'Islamism' can only be understood in relation to events, some of which date back to the succession struggle following the Prophet's death and to the historical failure of Islam more broadly to come to terms with secular governments in a highly complex world. Although they seek a largely mythical past, militants like those in Al Qaeda draw sustenance from the microelectronic revolution which allows them to exist, communicate and make plans in cyberspace. The militants can be found everywhere yet, in a territorial sense, they are placeless. The great threat that religious militancy poses to a globalising world is partly a consequence of rapidly evolving technology – for example, potential access to weapons of mass destruction or the tools for cyberwar – and to the vulnerability of modern global society whose complexity and interdependence creates unprecedented specialisation

The Decline of the Territorial State

The essence of a globalising world consists of increasingly porous political boundaries and the declining relevance of physical distance and the growing autonomy capacity of non-state groups.[13] Although a variety of terrorist groups are aided or even controlled by state authorities, more and more these groups are becoming the tail that wags the dog. 11 September confirmed once again that no state, not even a superpower, has impermeable borders, can control the rapid and easy movement of persons, things and ideas across those borders, or enjoys anything even remotely like a 'sovereign' monopoly of the means of coercion at home or control of its own territory – features essential to the ideology of the interstate world.

In general, the Eurocentric world of international politics is giving way to a more complex postinternational universe of diverse and often overlapping political communities characterised by processes of fission and fusion. States are becoming functionally dissimilar. Only a relatively few can successfully co-opt important groups that lie within or, increasingly, across their boundaries and stave off serious competition from transnational forces and, as we shall see, other authority networks also have boundaries. Postinternational theory recognises that the parsimonious model of a state system is no longer adequate to describe or explain the complexities of contemporary global life. Rosenau 'self-consciously breaks with ... the "state-is-still-predominant" tendency'.[14]

As Westphalian states weaken and show themselves incapable of meeting citizens' basic needs and demands, their authority diminishes. Today, there are vast areas with crucial impact on the welfare of citizens that most governments do not control or even influence to any major degree. 'Politicians everywhere', writes Susan Strange,

> talk as though they have the answers to economic and social problems, as if they really are in charge of their country's destiny. People no longer believe them. Disillusion with national leaders brought down the leaders of the Soviet Union and the states of central Europe. But the disillusion is by no means confined to socialist systems. Popular contempt for ministers and for the head of state has grown in most of the capitalist countries.[15]

While the number of sovereign states grows, their capacity declines as new ones, carved from the carcasses of once major states, increasingly resemble the hundreds of impotent polities that dotted the old Holy Roman Empire.

No longer is it politically incorrect to speak warmly of 'empires', 'mandates', 'voluntary colonies' and the like, often under the rubric of humanitarian intervention. And as state authority diminishes, so does state legitimacy and capacity, thereby producing a downward spiral in which citizens come to identify with non-state authorities who claim that they are able to cope where states cannot. States themselves no longer have much in common except their territoriality and the fact that they are recognised as such by others. They range from the superpower (United States) to the irrelevant, unknown and ultimately underwater (Vanuatu).

As fission and fusion continue, the search intensifies for new identities and the revival of old ones that can provide coherent norms. 'Fragmegration', the term Rosenau coined to denote the two processes, implies growing instability in human loyalties, and the movement 'away from loyalties focused on nation-states and toward variable foci'.[16]

A Changing Cast of Global Actors

Al Qaeda is one of what Rosenau calls 'SFAs' or authoritative 'sovereignty-free actors'[17] that may play important roles in 'governance'. 'Governance' does not require 'government' or 'hierarchy'; 'systems of rule can be maintained and their controls successfully and consistently exerted even in the absence of established legal or political authority'.[18] As Benjamin Cohen stresses, 'all that governance really needs is a valid social consensus on relevant rights and values'.[19]

Like Al Qaeda, many 'SFAs' are non-territorial – 'congeries of spheres of authority (SOAs) that are subject to considerable flux and not necessarily coterminous with the division of territorial space'. They are, nevertheless, authoritative – 'distinguished by the presence of actors who can evoke compliance when exercising authority as they engage in activities that delineate the sphere'.[20] Al Qaeda's assault on New York reflects

> a new form of anarchy ... one that involves not only the absence of higher authority, but also encompasses such an extensive disaggregation of authority as to intensify the pace at which transnational relations and cross-border spill-overs are permeating the [domestic–foreign] frontier, even as it also allows for much greater flexibility, innovation, and experimentation in the development and application of new control mechanisms.[21]

In the sharp debate about the status of prisoners seized by American forces in Afghanistan and taken to Guantánamo, Cuba, we began to confront some of the legal puzzles raised by 11 September. They are hardly trivial, but instead force us to consider conceptual puzzles of the highest importance. Whether or not Al Qaeda members or foreigners fighting for the Taliban in Afghanistan should enjoy the legal status and protections provided under the 'law of nations' is a good deal more than a simple practical or normative problem. Who are the prisoners? Whom do they represent? The captives are the citizens of more than thirty countries including the United States, Russia, Great Britain and France, but to refer to them as American, Russian, British or French would obscure far more than it would clarify. They are politically motivated fighters, but are they legal soldiers as defined by international law?

Historically, the captives do not 'fit' dominant models of global politics, although precedent suggests that they could be treated under the laws created by states for states as illegal 'irregulars' – criminals rather than soldiers. Thus, during the Peninsula War, Napoleon Bonaparte treated Spanish regulars according to the laws of war, while denying such protection to Spanish 'irregulars'; following the Battle of Culloden in 1745, the victorious English commander, the Duke of Cumberland, accorded regular French and Irish soldiers in the army of Charles Stuart all honours and protections, while ordering the execution of all Scottish clan members who had 'come out' for 'Bonnie Prince Charlie'.

Terrorist groups like Al Qaeda are only one of many types of actors that challenge states for the identities and loyalties of citizens. With the aid of new technologies, the postinternational universe is inhabited by a vast range of authorities, reflecting different identities, differentially engaged in countless issues, and vested with authority in selected contexts. The proliferation of terrorist groups along with transnational corporations and humanitarian organisations persuades us that we need to recognise that a 'worldwide crisis of authority' has 'so thoroughly undermined the prevailing distribution of global power as to alter the significance of the State as a causal agent in the course of events'. So profound is the impact of 'subgroupism' that 'it no longer seems compelling to refer to the world as a State system'.[22]

Violence, the Individual and the State

The 'legal puzzles' and the disappearing distinction between 'war' and 'crime' highlighted by global terrorism are part of the broader change in relations between collective states and individual citizens in the postinternational world.

Any discussion of the relationship between individuals and states in global politics runs up against an apparent paradox. On the one hand, individuals today are probably more fully protected by international law and humanitarian norms than at any historical moment since the Thirty Years' War, On the other hand, as 11 September illustrates, civilians may be at greater risk of violence than they have been for centuries. This leads to another paradox: on the one hand, human-rights activists seek to limit sovereign claims against domestic interference and humanitarian intervention, while, on the other, the erosion of state authority and capacity are accompanied by growing abuses against innocent civilians.

The distinction between citizenship as an identity and identification with other polities was, of course, of the greatest importance to sovereigns who wished to bring an end to the destructive violence of the Thirty Years' War. In order to preserve major dynasties and the wealth associated with them, interstate law institutionalised a difference between state-initiated collective violence (war), on the one hand, and non-state-initiated violence (crime) on the other. Centralisation of authority and the demarcation between crime and war accompanied a growing recognition of a distinction between inside and outside the state and the burgeoning state capacity relative to other political forms to mobilise resources and, therefore, to wage war: 'Princes were supposed to wage war in such a way as to minimise the harm done both to their own soldiers, who deserved humane treatment if they happened to be captured or wounded, and to the civilian population.'[23] 11 September emphasises the point that interstate war of the Westphalian epoch is giving way to new forms of violence that are increasing intrastate or transstate and that, unlike Clausewitzian warfare, are not extensions of politics by other means. What Clausewitz's formulation 'made no allowance for at all', as John Keegan explains, 'was war without beginning or end, the endemic warfare of non-state, even pre-state peoples, in which there was no distinction between lawful and unlawful bearers of arms'.[24] The so-called 'war against terrorism' recalls the distinction Steven Metz makes when he differentiates between 'informal wars' where at least one combatant is 'a nonstate entity' and 'gray area wars' which 'combine elements of traditional war fighting with those of organised crime'.[25]

The breakdown of the barrier between civilians and soldiers in both world wars suggested that the 'law of nations' provided insufficient protection for individuals in wartime. Following the Holocaust, some progress was made toward expanding the regulation of violence beyond norms pertaining to noncombatants and prisoners of war during a war to the general protection of individuals against abuses of state coercion through universal human rights. Nuremberg established the precedent of individual responsibility for actions undertaken even under the justification of superior orders or operational necessity and extended the international regulation of violence into the shielded realm of state 'domestic' jurisdiction – the use of violence by states against those within their boundaries. The creation of the category of crimes against humanity entailed recognition of the breakdown of traditional distinctions between soldiers and civilians and between war and crime. Thus, the murder of six million Jews, like more recent 'ethnic cleansing' in Bosnia and Kosovo and genocide in Rwanda, were regarded by the global community as the acts of common criminals having no legitimate military objective. Since the Second World War, United Nations conventions – especially the Genocide Convention and the Universal Declaration of Human Rights – and international and regional human rights tribunals have repeatedly reinforced the Nuremberg precedent.

In May 1996 the first international criminal court since Nuremberg – the International Criminal Tribunal for the former Yugoslavia –was convened in The Hague, followed by an international tribunal in Arusha, Tanzania to deal with the 1994 Rwandan genocide. In the summer of 1998 a treaty was concluded to establish a permanent International Criminal Court (ICC) to try individuals charged with genocide, war crimes and crimes against humanity. Although the United States continues to oppose the ICC, it has allowed foreign victims of human rights abuses to bring civil cases against alleged perpetrators in US courts.[26] In addition, the Pinochet and Milosevic cases provide precedents that even heads of state are not immune from extradition and prosecution for crimes against humanity. In sum, the principles that individuals are deserving of international protection and that those who violate human rights will be held responsible *as individuals* have become features of global law.

The 'law of nations' had been breached, and state sovereignty no longer afforded protection for human rights violations. Among the precedents, perhaps the most important was NATO's 1999 intervention in Kosovo. 'As long as I am Secretary General', declared UN Secretary General Kofi Annan, the United Nations 'will always place human beings at the center of everything we do'. Although 'fundamental sovereignty, territorial integrity, and political independence of states' continue to be a 'cornerstone of the international system', sovereignty, Annan continued, cannot provide 'excuses for the inexcusable'.[27] In this climate, there was little opposition to American intervention in Afghanistan.

Despite these precedents, legislation and norms, the incidence of violence against civilians in warfare continues to grow. In recent years, civilians have been regarded as legitimate targets and have been the main victims of violence. At least part of the answer lies in the accelerated erosion of state sovereignty, especially, but not only, in the developing world. Just as the triumph of Europe's sovereign states centuries earlier was partly the result of efforts to limit the sort of violence against civilians that had characterised Europe's wars of religion in the sixteenth and seventeenth centuries, so its erosion is ushering in an epoch of wars by people against people in which ethnicity, religion, gender and race generate passions that were largely absent in interstate wars waged before the Second World War. Thus, just as the growth of state authority, linked to its monopoly of coercion and identity, achieved the limitation and rationalisation of war, so the erosion of state authority and the proliferation of other identities and legitimating ideologies has been accompanied by an erosion of restraints on violence and its de-coupling from political purpose.

Many postinternational wars are akin to those in Europe prior to the institutionalisation of the territorial state, when 'political, social, economic and religious motives were hopelessly entangled', and 'civilians suffered terrible atrocities'.[28] This leads to a surprising conclusion. It is widely believed that sovereignty is the main obstacle to assuring human rights and fair treatment of civilians in wartime. An obstacle it is. but it is also a two-edged sword. *To the extent that sovereignty outlawed violence within states and international law limited violence among states and against civilians, they protected individuals against unrestrained violence.* The Westphalian state provided a territorial basis to fix and enforce boundaries of identity so that the distinction between 'inside' and 'outside' became defensible. But without a monopoly or near-monopoly of the means of coercion, the distinction between war and crime tends to disappear 'as is already the case today in places such as Lebanon, Sri Lanka, El Salvador, Peru, or Colombia'.[29] Just as the identity of citizen was constructed and manipulated by the rulers of states hundreds of years ago, today other identities are being constructed and reconstructed and managed by demagogues. Osama bin Laden typifies this sort of demagogue.

The Westphalian state evolved within the historical context of shifting identities and boundaries that redefined the moral community. The legitimacy of emerging European states rested in great part on their capacity to manage violence by demarcating the boundaries of legitimate/illegitimate violence, and their ability to provide subjects/citizens with security, internal and external. But the erosion of states is accompanied by the reshuffling of identity hierarchies.

Multiple Identities and Loyalties

Al Qaeda as an institution and the self-conscious status of Islamists in the United States, Europe, and elsewhere after 11 September reflected emphatically the growing importance of identity politics in general and the growing role of multiple identities.

As the postinternational model might suggest, the threat to states posed by Islamists grows out of the replacement of *citizen* collective identity by *religious* self-identity at the top of identity hierarchies. More generally, this suggests a need for renewed emphasis on individuals and recognition of multiple identities and loyalties in the way we think about global politics. The membership of Al Qaeda is nationally diverse – Saudi, Kuwaiti, Pakistani, Afghani, Algerian, Moroccan, Chinese, Turkish, British, Filipino, and so forth – but these national designations are largely irrelevant.

The case of Islamism illustrates how individuals may serve several masters. It reminds us that citizenship no longer adequately defines who we are politically and where our political loyalties lie. The question of who is inside and who is outside the boundaries of civic and moral obligation is regaining an importance for political theory and global politics not seen since the birth of the Westphalian state.

A variety of features, new and old, may serve as the bases of self identity. However, most identities are insufficiently stable or salient to provide clear cues or durable boundaries between political communities. Any definition of self is multidimensional and fluid, and for each individual the ranking of identities and therefore the intensity of loyalties may differ.

That hierarchy will change and new identities may be created as the significance attached to political relationships with others is altered and as context shifts. Thus, identities are rarely, if ever, primordial. Few Bosnians, for example, would have thought of religion as a dominant identity until Bosnian 'Turks' were subjected to collective persecution. Just as the identities of subjects were manipulated by kings to sanctify the state, so today do mullahs manipulate identities to undermine the states in which they reside.

Recent decades have witnessed the decoupling of citizen from other identities like those based on religion, owing to state fragmentation and 'neo-tribalism'. In large areas of the world, identities and loyalties that colonial authorities and commissars suppressed are resurfacing, often making a mockery of sovereign boundaries. In this sense, religious and ethnic conflict is partly a problem of shifting identity boundaries in a state system constructed by Europeans in non-European settings. The governments of many of these states, far from being the outcome of social contracts, impartial arbiters of social conflicts, or surrogates for a national interest, represent the privileges of religious, tribal or clan factions.

The decline of state authority and the unmooring of individual loyalties from traditional institutions produces what Susan Strange memorably labeled 'Pinocchio's problem'. Once Pinocchio became a real boy, he no longer had his puppet strings to guide him and, therefore, no authority to command his behaviour. Strange underlines the dilemma:

> If indeed we have now, not a system of global governance by any stretch of the imagination, but rather a ramshackle assembly of conflicting sources of authority, we too have Pinocchio's problem. Where do allegiance, loyalty, and identity lie? Not always, evidently in the same direction. Sometimes with the government of a state. But on other times, with a firm, or with a social movement operating across territorial frontiers. Sometimes with a family or a generation; sometimes with fellow-members of an occupation or a profession ... In a world of multiple, diffused authority, each of us shares Pinocchio's problem; our individual consciences are our only guide.[30]

Any category of difference presumes a category of sameness against which difference is measured. Religion is an identity category that is significant to Islamists when viewed in terms of its *difference in contrast with a privileged identity category*. Theorising about identity, therefore, reveals the cognitive underpinning of us versus them as bases for political action. Such theorising is complicated by the fact that identities demarcate psychological rather than territorial space and, unlike territory, they can be overlapping and intersecting. The significance attached to socially constructed sameness provides the foundation for moral boundaries that encompass communities of obligation based on reciprocity and fairness.

For many Muslims, Islam is an archetypal moral community. Since all such norms of reciprocal obligation share in common their basis on the bond of *sameness*, a moral community like Islam also functions to exclude 'others' and provides justification for treating non-Muslims differently than one is obliged to treat fellow Muslims. By demarcating inclusion and exclusion on the basis of sameness and difference, moral communities draw boundaries of 'inside and outside' according to which justice is distributed. Moral boundaries are also articulated authoritatively as a system of obligations and duties attaching to community membership, such as *jihad* as defined by Islamists. In this capacity, they serve to legitimate the use of coercive power by agents of the community against members who violate the terms of obligations attaching to membership such as Salman Rushdie. Thus, moral communities are also the bases for legitimating the use of (good) violence as a mechanism of enforcement against (bad) violence – violence that violates the obligations of community membership. Just as violence by European Christians against Islam was regarded as legitimate in the Middle Ages, so violence by Muslims against 'infidels' is deemed legitimate by many fundamentalists today.

The Declining Role of Distance and Acceleration of History

The long journey of Al Qaeda terrorists saw them in Singapore, Hamburg, Kabul, London, Florida and elsewhere. Their journey and their ability to strike New York and Washington emphasise the growing irrelevance of physical distance, the accelerating pace of change, and the technologies associated with these factors. The speed at and extent to which persons, things, and ideas can move are unprecedented. Microelectronic technologies such as computers. e-mail, space satellites and facsimile machines have made it possible to move messages and funds almost instantaneously, and such technologies have virtually eliminated the distinction between 'short-term' and 'long-term'.[31] In addition, these technologies have made possible actors that live largely in cyberspace rather than any fixed territory and that allow coordination among individuals physically remote from one another who seek to participate in global politics.

The Participation Explosion

Mullahs, not kings and presidents, lie behind Al Qaeda.[32] Upstarts from below and jealous failures like bin Laden threaten to become 'new princes' by creating, financing, and managing their own groups with or without the support of states. Indeed, it appears that Al Qaeda was the tail that wagged the Taliban dog in Afghanistan. Al Qaeda is one of innumerable examples of where the role of social groups is expanding at the expense of state authority. The revolutions in transportation, information, and communication, combined with the spread of education in much of the world, are having a profound impact on the willingness of people to undertake direct action with or without government sanction, and these revolution increase the overall sense of political efficacy of many 'citizens'. In Rosenau's words, the 'printing press, telephone, radio, television, and personal computer have created conditions for skill development among citizenries that governments could not totally control and that have helped make citizenries more effective in relation to the centers of authority'.[33]

At the same time as the fates of people everywhere have become linked, citizens' expectations are expanding, and the demands they place on institutions are multiplying. No longer do people meekly accept the status and destiny that come with birth. Expanding demands new forms of security tax national and global institutions, pressuring them to find new ways to cope with burgeoning claims from below. Exploding expectations and the accessibility of information, combined with weakening states and new organising techniques, mean that the proverbial person on the street may be as well equipped to understand the small-r reality of global politics as those in government. Whether as consumers, activists, protesters, or terrorists, citizens collectively create global constraints and opportunities. All this, it might be thought, are steps toward realising a liberal version of global politics.

The Threat to a Liberal World

On the one hand, 11 September reflects a variety of liberal assumptions such as the growing role of individuals and society in global politics as opposed to states, while at the same time it is also a threat to liberalism. The liberal bias of postinternational thinking predicts, among other things, the growing autonomy of individuals; the declining role of state boundaries; the growing importance of secularism, science, and rationality; and the neoliberal free movement of persons, ideas, and things. The normative bias of postinternational thinking is liberal, a vindication of the liberal faith in the malleability of humankind and the possibility for democratic control of political life – in other words, a bias toward 'agency' at the expense of 'structure.' At a minimum, individuals are transforming global politics into a participant sport. Whether as demonstrators in Leipzig and Jakarta, terrorists in Kandahar or Jerusalem, investors in New York and London, or purchasers of goods in any city, individuals are imposing their preferences on leaders, often in unorthodox and even violent ways.

The Islamism that underlies 11 September is a reaction to and rejection of the postinternational world, especially its secular and globalised features. In seeking to turn back globalisation, the Islamist want individuals to bow to traditional leaders and values (both state and nonstate), turn their backs on science and rationality, and place greater impediments to the free movement of ideas and persons. And regardless of Islamists' aims, the attacks on New York and Washington are already increasing pressure to reinvigorate national boundaries, and reduce transnational flows. Thus, in the United States and Europe, easy migration and political asylum, as well as undefended borders, are endangered by the attack. Indeed, 11 September implies that we should treat with caution the democratic implication in the idea of a participation explosion. The Arab 'street mob' and the terrorist cell are hardly democratic institutions, but they manipulate democracy and the open society for their own ends. Paradoxically, in doing so, they undermine the foundations of Arabic states, none of which are themselves democratic in form or fact. Thus, when the Saudis encourage Islamist views and provide financial assistance to Islamist groups, they are, in the long run, undermining their own survival. Democracy is further eroded by the fact that new communications technologies make it easier to maintain closed communities.

The Declining Distinction between Foreign and Domestic

A postinternational lens de-emphasises the distinction between 'domestic' and 'foreign,' although not between 'inside' and 'outside.' The former refers to the impact of sovereign boundaries, whereas the latter delineates the borders between moral communities, often rooted in dramatically contrasting definitions of the 'self' and 'other.' Thus, many observant Muslims regard themselves as 'outsiders' whether they live in Muslim or non-Muslim countries, because they regard themselves as members of a community of Islam defined by living in accordance with a strict interpretation of the *Quran*.

As 'outsiders' in relation to most modern communities, the fanatics who constitute Al Qaeda represent a new class of security threat, one that poses a transnational and collective dilemma for states. Where the central problem in international relations was often defined as interstate war, the 'war on terrorism' is something new and different. Not classic interstate war, as we observed earlier, it is difficult from a state perspective not to approach the problem of terrorism as one of crime rather than war at all.

Al Qaeda is, strictly speaking, neither a 'domestic' nor an 'international' threat but rather is both at once. It accords, then, with the postinternational claim that national and global security are merging, because in a complexly interdependent world the conditions for well-being and happiness for most people require a high degree of collective action. Just as most individuals cannot by their own effort meet their needs for food, shelter, health, and old age as their ancestors did, individual states can neither shield citizens from global threats, nor cope with globalised challenges. Overall, as interdependent individuals caught up in a variety of authorities, we are probably less secure in our collective existence than in earlier epochs when our survival depended on our own exertion and imagination. As individuals diversify and specialise their occupation and role in society, the world mimics them, and increasingly specialised collective actors, both constructive and destructive, have emerged to deal with problems. Many of these problems pose collective dilemmas that are exceedingly difficult for a world of dispersed authority to cope with.

As we observed earlier, the boundaries of states are hardly the only politically relevant boundaries in contemporary global politics. Indeed, the erosion of state capacity is closely related to the growing incompatibility of its sovereign boundaries and the boundaries of other authoritative polities ranging from economic markets and religious communities to small tribal and even clan polities.

Conclusion: Remapping Global Politics

Many of the world's societies find it difficult to cope with the forces of postinternationalism, especially globalisation. Some are in a condition of outright civil war and/or near-collapse. The political maps of neat state boxes shed little light on 11 September. Yet since 11 September is both a result of globalisation and a threat to it, we need a new cartography to make sense of it, and quickly at that.

Recent decades have witnessed a recrudescence of identities and ideologies that clash with the loyalties and obligations of individuals as citizens of sovereign states. These challenges accompany and accelerate the erosion of state capacity. Any casual survey of the world's states reveals that they are an exceedingly mixed bag. Some cannot even maintain order domestically. There are vast areas of economic and social life with crucial impact on the welfare of citizens that governments do not control or even influence to any degree.

Islamism, like other contemporary challenges, constitutes a genuine reawakening of earlier ideas and forms, as well as a reinvention of the past. There is little place for these ideas and forms in the interstate model of global politics. Despite the turbulence in contemporary global politics, many of our colleagues continue to insist that nothing much has basically changed. To some extent, in making sense of 11 September we are all travelers in relatively uncharted political space.

Thus far we have sketched a fairly bleak contrast between an increasingly complex global politics and a Mississippi mainstream in international relations theory that is less able to analyse that world than the person on the street. State-centrism is deeply embedded in the traditional disciplines, and as John Agnew points out,

> the mainstream journals, peruse *The American Political Science Review*, the *American Sociological Review*, the *American Economic Review*, the *British Journal of Political Science*, and *Sociology*, enforce disciplinary canons of methodology and subject matter. In other words, they discipline! The vested interests – the jobs, the journals, the disciplinary hierarchies – built up over a century will not easily bend either to new times or to the blast of intellectual critique.[34]

In sum, in the new millennium, a central question for scholars of global politics is what will be the long-range impact of 'the retreat of the state'. Unlike Islamic fanatics, we face growing uncertainty as to where our allegiances should and will lie. When the opportunities arise, will we resurrect or refurbish old identities and loyalties, or establish new ones? Our conceptions of ourselves and others will continually change, and the task for us political scientists is to explain what the range of choices are, which are likely to prevail and, again as always, why?

This all suggests that global terrorism is not a technical question that is amenable to a technical fix. Although 11 September reflects the erosion of state control, its initial consequences involved 'bringing the state back in'. To date, efforts have been made to re-establish control over national borders by increasing security at airports, using military aircraft to patrol the skies above cities, beefing up immigration and customs on the Canadian and Mexican borders, deploying Coast Guard vessels in American harbours, and investing large amounts of cash to increase US intelligence and military capabilities. The war in Afghanistan was initiated to reestablish public confidence in the US government, weaken Al Qaeda, and signal that states that supported or accepted Islamic terror would pay a steep price. To date, the operation has been partly successful, but no one claims that it has brought us close to resolving the problem. No doubt, too, additional economic assistance will flow to Islamic societies in order to moderate the growing gap between participants in globalisation and those left behind. Nevertheless, all of these steps are band-aids rather than cures, ad hoc responses to a continuing threat.

Indeed, while security improvements may reduce the incidence of such terrorism, they cannot promise an end to the threat. No outsider can resolve the issues that confront Islam that have festered for more than a millennium, like the relationship between the sacral and secular, We are confronting a revolt of preinternational forces against a postinternational world, a reaction against globalisation and the norms, identities and values associated with it. Although there is no inevitability to globalisatioin, turning the clock back to an epoch in which sacred values ruled men's lives is at best extremely costly and at worst quite impossible. It requires an end to an open economic system, a reversal of human rights, and probably the abandonment of new technologies. Or, it entails a dramatic revival of state capacity even as globalisation continues, another quixotic road.

NOTES

1. James N. Rosenau uses the term to describe 'an apparent trend in which more and more of the interactions that sustain world politics unfold without the direct involvement of nations or states'. James N. Rosenau, *Turbulence in World Politics A Theory of Change and Continuity* (Princeton, NJ: Princeton University Press 1990) p.6.
2. Ibid. For an definition of this tradition, see K.J. Holsti, *The Dividing Discipline: Hegemony and Diversity in International Theory* (Boston, MA: Allen & Unwin 1985) p. vii.
3. Yale H. Ferguson and Richard W. Mansbach, *Polities: Authority, Identities, and Change* (Columbia, SC: University off South Carolina Press 1996).
4. James N. Rosenau, *Along the Domestic-Foreign Frontier: Exploring Governance in a Turbulent World* (Cambridge: Cambridge University Press 1997) p. 5.
5. See Joseph Lepgold, 'An Intellectual Agenda for Students of Postinternational World Politics', in Heidi Hobbs (ed.), *Pondering Postinternationalism: A Paradigm for the Twenty-First Century?* (Albany, NY: SUNY Press 2000) pp.155–67.
6. For a differing perspective, see Stephen D. Krasner, *Sovereignty: Organized Hypocrisy* (Princeton, NJ: Princeton University Press 1999).
7. James N. Rosenau, 'Global Changes and Theoretical Challenges: Toward a Postinternational Politics for the 1990s', in Ernst-Otto Czempiel and Rosenau (eds), *Global Changes and Theoretical Challenges: Approaches to World Politics for the 1990s* (Lexington, MA: Lexington Books 1989) p. 3.
8. James N. Rosenau, 'Before Cooperation: Hegemons, Regimes, and Habit-driven Actors in World Politics,' *International Organization* 40/4 (1986) pp.849–50.
9. For example, Robert Gilpin, *War and Change in World Politics* (Cambridge: Cambridge University Press 1981) p.7.
10. James N. Rosenau, 'NGOs and Fragmented Authority in Globalizing Space', paper presented at the Joint ISA–ECPR Conference in Vienna, 16–19 September 1998.
11. James N. Rosenau, 'Multilateral Governance and the Nation-State System: A Post-Cold War Assessment', paper presented at the first meeting of a Study Group of the Inter-American Dialogue, Washington, DC, 24–25 April 1995, p.3.
12. See, for example, Friedrich V. Kratochwil, *Rules, Norms, and Decisions* (Cambridge: Cambridge University Press 1989), Andrew Moravcsik, 'Taking Preferences Seriously: A Liberal Theory of International Politics', *International Organization* 51/4 (1997) pp.513–53, and Nicholas Onuf, *World of Our Making* (Columbia, SC: University of South Carolina Press 1989).
13. Although the state erosion is most evident in the less-developed world, it is fact of life universally owing to a variety of factors ranging from globalised markets and microelectronic technologies to the resurgence of old identities and new forms of warfare. State erosion, like capitalism before it, is a form of 'uneven development'. See, for example, Yale H. Ferguson and Richard W. Mansbach, 'Global Politics at the Turn of the Millennium: Changing Bases of "Us" and "Them",' *International Studies Review*, 1:2 (1999), pp.77–107.
14. Rosenau, *Turbulence* (note 1) p.97.
15. Susan Strange, *The Retreat of the State: The Diffusion of Power in the World Economy* (Cambridge: Cambridge University Press 1996) p.3.
16. Rosenau, *Turbulence* (note 1) p.335.
17. Ibid. p.36.
18. Rosenau, *Along the Domestic-Foreign–Frontier* (note 4) pp. 146–7.

19. Benjamin J. Cohen, *The Geography of Money* (Ithaca, NY: Cornell University Press 1998) p.145.
20. Rosenau, *Along the Domestic–Foreign Frontier* (note 4) p. 39.
21. Ibid. pp.151–2.
22. Ibid. pp.263–4.
23. Martin van Creveld, *The Transformation of War* (New York: Free Press 1991) p.37.
24. John Keegan, *A History of Warfare* (New York: Knopf 1993) p.5.
25. Steven Metz, *Armed Conflict in the 21st Century: The Information Revolution and Post-Modern Warfare* (Carlisle, PA: Strategic Studies Institute 2000) p.xii.
26. See, for example, 'To Sue a Dictator', *The Economist*, 24–30 April 1999, pp.26–7.
27. Cited in Judith Miller, 'Sovereignty Isn't So Sacred Anymore', *New York Times*, 18 April 1999, Sec.4, p.4.
28. Van Creveld (note 23) p.50.
29. Ibid. p.204.
30. Strange, *The Retreat of the State* (note 15) pp.198–9.
31. See Susan Strange, *Mad Money: When Markets Outgrow Governments* (Ann Arbor, MI: University of Michigan Press 1998) pp.24–9.
32. Ironically, Osama bin Laden enjoyed American support in earlier years during the Soviet occupation of Afghanistan after 1979.
33. Rosenau, *Turbulence* (note 1) p.239.
34. John Agnew, 'Spacelessness Versus Timeless Space in State-Centered Social Science', *Environment and Planning A* 28/11 (1996) p.1930.

American Hegemony after 11 September:
Allies, Rivals and Contradictions

JAMES ANDERSON

The terrorist attack on New York's World Trade Center and the Pentagon in Washington, DC on 11 September 2001 was a defining moment for American hegemony, the first external assault on the mainland United States of America since 1812. But what exactly has it defined? The predicted 'clash of civilisations' replacing the Cold War as President Bush initially talked of a 'crusade', echoing Osama bin Laden's 'holy war'? The end of US isolationism? Or of neo-liberal globalisation – with security at a premium, the end of 'borderless world' fantasies and the need for tougher national and global governance? While much of the world shared feelings of horror and revulsion, in some quarters there was satisfaction that the United States now shared the vulnerability experienced by other countries, even that it was now 'getting some of its own medicine'. Initially it held the moral high ground as Bush assembled an international coalition for his re-labeled 'war on terrorism'. However, as the United States and allied states proceeded to make war – first in Afghanistan, then threatening war on Iraq, only to be diverted by Israel's war in occupied Palestine which threatened the coalition – the moral grounds became decidedly shaky. The objectives and consequences became increasingly contradictory, as this essay seeks to demonstrate.

When asked about the consequences of the French Revolution, the Chinese leader Chou En Lai famously replied that it was too soon to tell. By that measure it is impossibly early to assess the impact of 11 September 2001, and this account of recent and on-going developments, ones which moreover are complex and highly contentious, is inevitably provisional and wide open to debate. But debate is just what is needed. In the real world people have to make provisional judgements all the time, before 'all the facts are in', so why not in academic discussion?

Some of the main or ostensible objectives of the war on terrorism have not (yet?) been achieved, and new ones have been added by the United States and its allies. Some, like Israel, Russia and Spain, have pursued their own 'wars on terrorism' with renewed vigour, or opportunistically used the atrocities and associated fears as a pretext to curb civil liberties and human rights, and not least in the United States itself. Bin Laden and his Al Qaeda may be having a damaging impact beyond their wildest dreams, particularly considering their weak grasp of rights and liberties as traditionally cherished in the United States, and still cherished by many Americans in opposition to their present government. Much of the damage to the United States and its allies may indeed be self inflicted, the product less of the atrocities themselves than of over-reactions or inappropriate reactions to them. For America's allies there are increasing fears about the political equivalent of friendly fire; and bin Laden's action has unwittingly boosted other right-wing reactionaries and racists all too willing to defend 'Western civilisation', seeing George Bush as a traffic policeman giving them the green light. On the other hand, the left-wing anti-globalisation movement, launched in the 1999 'battle of Seattle' demonstration against the neo-liberal World Trade Organisation (WTO), was initially seen as one of the casualties of September 11 (for was not the evil bin Laden also anti-globalisation?). In fact it got a new lease of life by also becoming the anti-war movement, a very logical development as we shall see, and one which could fill 'the hole at the heart' of the cosmopolitan alternative.

The reactions to the terrorist attack are having knock-on and unintended effects with the de-stabilising potential to create yet further, as yet unimagined, problems for the USA, its allies, rivals and enemies alike. However, we can already see the outlines of some possible consequences for the trajectory of US hegemony and its often fraught relations with its allies and potential rivals, and largely because these relations and their contradictions were already to some extent in place before 11 September. They can be approached in terms of three partly overlapping themes: different strategies with respect to allies, different forms of power, and different ideologies of globalisation. These involve relationships between, respectively, multilateralism/unilateralism, civil power/military power, and neo-liberalism/neo-conservatism, their pros and cons and the shifting balance between them. Policy oscillates between these poles, combining elements of both, and the currently dominant policy might best be characterised as 'unilateral multilateralism'.

Hegemonic Strategies, Power and Ideology

In Fred Halliday's terms, the world's single remaining superpower is 'the unaccountable hegemon' (though what would an accountable one look like?). It is 'the world's dominant power and dominant model', impinging on particular conflicts and the institutions and issues of global governance in general. But how is the hegemony of this empire exercised, maintained and reproduced? As Halliday warns, 'The greatest mistake to make about America ... is to treat its foreign policy debate as unitary', and as John

Agnew and Stuart Corbridge and Peter Taylor point out, there are several different conceptions of hegemony.[1]

Historically, the American debate has swung between internationalism and isolationism, and now it swings between multilaterism and unilateralism. Initial fears that the George W. Bush presidency would be isolationist proved unfounded – in fact this was never an option in an era of US-led globalisation, despite politicians like Bush and fellow Republicans flaunting their 'all-American' insularity.[2] President Clinton had leaned toward multilateralism, believing in the need to consult and work in co-operation with allies like the European Union (EU) and through multilateral agencies of global governance such as the United Nations's Intergovernmental Panel on Climate Change. President Bush, however, has a decidedly more unilateralist bent, acting in what he says are 'America's interests' with less concern for whether allies and multilateral bodies like it or not – infamously tearing up the Kyoto agreement to halt global warming soon after he was 'elected' courtesy of the US Supreme Court rather than the voters. Certainly unilateralism got a boost both from the 'election' of Bush as president and (after contrary signs) from 11 September. However, it predated both, and the terms have long been used to label whole presidencies (e.g., Jimmy Carter's predominantly multilateralist, Bush senior and especially Ronald Reagan unilateralist). Now unilateralism/multilateralism encapsulates the contrasts between the hawkish Pentagon faction of Donald Rumsfeld and Paul Wolfowitz, along with Bush's national security adviser, Condoleezza Rice, on the one hand, and the more cautious US State Department of Colin Powell on the other. But these contrasts suggest that while useful as shorthand for complex realities, the juxtaposition of labels may sometimes conceal more than it reveals. It obscures the possibility that *both* strategies may be used in tandem or combination for the same ends, operating simultaneously and effectively in concert rather than contradiction.

For those interested in maintaining US hegemony, the contemporary debate is not so much about these as *alternative* strategies as about getting a mix in which the two tendencies are more in concert than contradiction (and of course there were such debates within previous administrations as well). Each strategy has distinct advantages and disadvantages. Multilateralism, for instance, can mobilise allies and effective action which helps ensure victory over common enemies (e.g., the Taliban's Afghanistan, 'international terrorists', and their havens in other 'rogue states' – a hold-all category for a diversity of states which the United States contemplates attacking for a diversity of reasons). But allies, such as the European Union or Russia, are also major powers or lesser imperialisms in their own right (or wrong?), with their own particular interests in foreign interventions which may constrain the freedom of manoeuvre of the United States. They are rivals capable of causing US hegemony substantial trouble or maybe, as in the case of the European Union or China, potential rivals *for* hegemony. Keeping such rivals subordinate at the same time as dealing with enemies is thus a major objective of US foreign policy, and here unilateralism has the advantage of excluding allies/rivals from key decision making, enabling the United States to set a global agenda that suits itself.

This is clearly seen in our second theme of military/civil power. Since 11 September the United States has increasingly opted for the threat and use of military power to enforce its will, rather than the force of economics, diplomacy, ideology and law. As Neil Smith observed, the World Trade Centre and the Pentagon were symbols of *global* economic and military power, albeit power disproportionately located in the United States, but the attack on these global symbols was quickly converted to a *national* (rather than a global) event and the *multi*-national World Trade Center victims from over 80 other countries were largely ignored, which served to justify the United States making war unilaterally purely on its own terms.[3] This militarism in turn relates to our third theme of a relative shift in ideology from global neo-liberalism towards neo-conservatism. These related shifts suit the United States inasmuch as it is currently unrivalled and unchallengeable in a uni-polar world as far as military capability is concerned, whereas in terms of civil power the world is decidedly multi-polar, with the European Union for instance now on a similar economic footing to the United States. Moreover, civil power also involves less tangible aspects involving transnational institutions, their ideological or normative foundations and limited democracy, as Tony McGrew shows for the WTO,[4] and here the moral authority of the United States is even more open to challenge.

On the one hand, the Bush unilateralists are sceptical of the effectiveness of global institutions such as the United Nations for achieving world peace and stability, or more particularly for achieving US interests (not necessarily the same thing). And, no doubt, especially as some of the same officials now work for Bush jr, they are encouraged by the fact that the 'second Cold War' waged by Reagan and Bush snr in the 1980s against the 'evil empire' did indeed succeed in bankrupting the USSR through an arms race it could not afford.[5] Also, for Bush jr, militarism, at least initially, has played well with a majority of the US electorate (or those who bother to vote). On the other hand, however, it is a high-risk strategy which threatens havoc elsewhere with the danger of de-stabilising or destroying allied as well as enemy regimes (e.g., Saudi Arabia and Egypt as well as Bush jr's 'axis of evil' – Iraq, Iran and North Korea). More generally, unilateralist 'going it alone' creates mass resentment, including a crude and generalised anti-

Americanism. The United States stands accused of global arrogance and of irresponsibly endangering the planet – of being *the* rogue state with much greater potential to do damage than all the other rogues combined.

But 'rogue state' is a propaganda and ultimately nonsense category, and we should beware of falling into the trap of seeing things simplistically in terms of good guys and bad guys. Establishment US figures in the multi- and uni-lateralist factions alike – the Clintons and Powells as much as the Bushs and Rumsfelds – are all seeking to further US dominance, differing mainly about means rather than ends. Moreover, critics of US multilateralism can point to the many unsavoury and ultimately counter-productive alliances it has spawned – the US building up of bin Laden to fight Russians in Afghanistan, or encouragement of Saddam Hussein's territorial aggression against Iran which Iraq then turned on Kuwait. The current war on terrorism has at least partially legitimised some previously highly questioned actions and allies – Russia's state terror against Chechnyan nationalists, now conveniently presented as part of the war on terrororism; or General Pervez Musharraf, formerly the pariah who overthrew Pakistan's democratically elected government, now a valued friend who has had himself 'democratically' confirmed as president in a referendum with only his own name on the ballot paper. However, while the real choice is therefore not between one faction of US hegemonists or another, the unilateralist faction is now in the ascendency and hence is currently the main target for anti-imperialists.

Its actions also seriously worry US multilateralists concerned that they will de-stabilise and encourage more overt opposition from would-be allies, and that the use of US military power actually undercuts US civil power. Joseph Nye suggests that the importance or effectiveness of military power is in any case declining in our 'global information age' relative to 'soft' forms of power.[6] Whether this is a significant on-going empirical tendency, a postmodern gloss or rationalisation for his normative multilateralism, or a residue of pre-11 September wishful thinking, remains an open question. The latter two interpretations are suggested by the actual behaviour of the United States under George W. Bush, particularly since 11 September. With statements from his administration apparently oscillating between uni- and multi-lateralism, the contradictions have recently been interpreted as confusion on the part of the United States, but it is also an open question whether it is the United States, or its allies or critics, who are the more confused.

A good prism for addressing such questions is provided by the spate of US foreign policy initiatives and entanglements in the eight months after September 2001. The already huge US defence budget received a 14 per cent increase. Bush imposed a massive 30 per cent tariff on steel imports to protect an out-dated US steel industry. This was not the first contravention of neo-liberal free trade orthodoxy, nor the last, but it threatened trade wars and was dramatically blatant coming from a United States which had been foisting neo-liberal market disciplines – and openness to US capital – on an often reluctant world.[7] For the same reasons, the United States has since the 1970s been propagating liberal democracy as the norm for national government – a 'thin' version of democracy, one amenable to global neo-liberal privatisation policies, and very happily co-existing with the almost complete absence of democracy in transnational arenas[8] – but nevertheless generally preferable to dictatorship and army rule. Yet when Hugo Chavez, elected president of Venezuela with a large majority, was briefly ousted by an army coup, the United States – whose own president was 'elected' (or not) by about a quarter of his electorate – had the nerve to criticise Chavez and support the anti-democrats.[9] Such nerve of course is a function of power but the hypocrisy is not lost on the less powerful, and it undermines the soft power of America's own legitimacy. As in Venezuela, the increasing US military involvement in Colombia has echoes of the 'dirty wars' of the Reagan–Bush snr era (with again some of the same officials involved), and now Colombia had the extra twist that Bush's war on terrorism could de-stabilise the peace process in Ireland.[10]

But two particular 'prisms' are perhaps especially revealing: first, the US assaults on the heads of three multilateral transnational organisations, dealing with climate change, chemical weapons and arms control, by diplomacy rather than war; and second, the seemingly ambivalent US approach to the Israel–Palestine conflict and its relations with its allies, especially its faithful follower, the United Kingdom, and a less than compliant European Union, as Ariel Sharon launched his own 'war on terrorism'/'state terror' (delete to taste) in the occupied West Bank, which delayed subsequent US moves against Iraq (not considered here). The two prisms reveal the serious rifts between the United States and the European Union as allies/rivals; increased anti-Americanism and anti-semitism; and also spurious, self-serving accusations of both in an attempt to 'smear' legitimate criticisms.

After 11 September the post-Cold War 1990s are in retrospect confirmed as a brief episode of 'false security' – akin to the even more short-lived 'new world order' of Bush snr which critics immediately dubbed the 'new world *dis*order'. Bush jr may be entitled to tell his father 'You ain't seen nothing yet.' For if the fall of the Berlin Wall in 1989 symbolised Fukuyama's 'end of history' – in the sense of the end of ideological conflict with the final triumph of liberal democracy – then 11 September symbolises the 'return of history' with a vengeance. And liberal democracy is opposed by more than bin Laden: its critics have for long been pointing to its democratic limitations, not least in transnational arenas (Anderson 2002),[11] but now it is mainly being undercut by its own putative adherents who in dealing with global problems become both less liberal and less democratic.

The rest of this essay discusses US hegemony, first in terms of globalisation and an apparent ideological shift from neo-liberalism to neo-conservatism. Then Nye's 'multilateralist-civil power model' provides a backdrop to highlight what has actually been happening, particularly the US assault on multilateral institutions of global governance, and its approach to the Israel–Palestine conflict. These prisms are used to exemplify more general dialectics of unilateralism/multilateralism: why Bush favours military force – beyond the obvious fact that 11 September provided a justification for it – and also why it can be counterproductive. But counterproductive for whom, apart from US hegemonists? We need to understand their debate, but also move beyond it to other alternatives that are more democratic and more effective at preventing war. The historical alternative to hegemonic or 'balance of power' routes to global peace was a 'liberal internationalist' emphasis on international law, transnational institutions and the multilateral exercise of civil power. Its most vibrant contemporary incarnation is 'cosmopolitan democracy' advanced by David Held, but as suggested elsewhere there is a gaping hole in cosmopolitanism[12] which at present can only be filled by the anti-globalisation/anti-war movement.

Globalisation and Ideology

Neo-liberalism, with its emphasis on civil power in the market and its playing down of the role of the state, state borders, security and military power, seems to be in retreat from a new imperialism and neo-conservatism. Two responses to 11 September suggest in their very different ways that the basis of US hegemony in neo-liberal globalisation is giving way to something else.

The End of Neo-Liberalism?

After the initial horror, my reaction to 11 September was that it spelled the end of fantasies about a 'borderless world' – the need for security would see to that – but John Gray's response went much further. He extended his familiar conservative assault on neo-liberalism to claim that the 'era of globalisation is over'.[13] In his view, the atrocities in New York and Washington, DC had shattered the utopian project of a global free market and the 'conventional view of globalisation as an irresistible historical trend'. Global conflict, rather than being largely inter-state, would now involve non-state actors and organisations which could flourish beyond the control of governments in 'collapsed states', such as Afghanistan, states whose 'collapse' was itself a function of the global free market. The result was that 'asylum-seekers and economic refugees press on the borders of every advanced country', and Gray saw a major contradiction in the present global system – 'trade and capital move freely across the globe [but] the movement of labour is strictly limited'. 11 September had exposed the weaknesses of even a superpower, revealing the power of the weak over the strong, and it underscored the destablising effects of global laissez faire capitalism. He argued that a looser 'partly de-globalised world' would be a 'safer world', and rather than being forced to conform to a single liberal universalist model, states should be free to develop their own separate versions of modernity, opting out of global markets if they wish.

Globalisation and neo-liberalism, however, are not synonymous, nor does the former necessarily have to depend on the latter. Perhaps neo-liberal ideology has been taken too seriously on its own terms. The neo-liberal market is an ideal type or fiction which could never exist in reality. Markets have always been well short of 'free' (as the US steel tariffs dramatically confirm). Nevertheless, neo-liberal ideology is used to impose competitive market disciplines on a diversity of states and economies. While it has declined somewhat since its apex in the 1980s of Reagan–Thatcher, it can still wreck weaker economies or sectors, and it remains dominant in economic globalisation as recently leaked EU bargaining demands in the WTO make clear.[14] Therefore, the separate development behind state borders implied in Gray's 'partial de-globalisation' is not likely to be tolerated by the leading powers, especially the United States, as the stances and statements of Bush since 11 September make clearer than ever before. But more than neo-liberalism is involved.

Neo-Conservatism and the New Imperialism

Neo-conservatism, rather than overt opposition to neo-liberalism, is the hallmark of a second, rather different, response to 11 Setemeber articulated by a British civil servant and foreign policy adviser of Bush's faithful ally, the British Prime Minister Tony Blair. Robert Cooper advocated a provocative 'return to empire' and 'colonialism' to maintain world order.[15] This no doubt attracted attention, but his perspective (which pre-dated '9/11') was equally interesting for what it did not say, and for its apparent contrast to what was supposedly Blair's 'ethical foreign policy'.

In Cooper's perspective, the world consists of 'postmodern', 'modern' and 'pre-modern' states, the threat to order coming from the last two and demanding intervention by the first in the form of a 'new imperialism'. His 'postmodern' states are epitomised above all by the member states of the European Union which stand for voluntary, mutual interdependence, the 'growing irrelevance of borders' (he forgets the Union's external borders), and 'moral consciousness', rather than war or threats of war, in the conduct of international relations. In contrast, 'modern' states – he mentions China, India and Pakistan – threaten stability by behaving aggressively in their own selfish interests 'as states always have'; while 'pre-modern' states – akin to Gray's 'collapsed states' – are ones such as Somalia and Chechnya where 'the state has almost ceased to exist'. Such 'failed states' (mostly former colonies and hence, according to Cooper, due to the ending of imperialism) provide the main base for the non-state actors which threaten to cross 'our' borders – 'drug, crime or terrorist syndicates'. His solution for these sources of trouble and disorder, as contradictory as his analysis, is basically that the 'postmodern' states need to re-impose 'a new kind of imperialism' coupled with 'double standards':

> Among ourselves, we operate on the basis of laws ... But when dealing with more old-fashioned kinds of states ... we need to revert to the rougher methods of an earlier era – force, pre-emptive attack, deception ... What is needed then is a new kind of imperialism, one acceptable to a world of human rights and cosmopolitan values.[16]

This contradictory recipe for peace and stability is a 'cure worse than the disease' if ever there was one (imagine 'pre-emptive attack, deception' as the way to deal with a threat of nuclear war between India and Pakistan). That it completely flouts international law and associated ethics does not appear to concern Cooper, and it is notable for two absences.

The first is that he completely ignores the long-established 'liberal internationalist' basis for securing peace when he poses only two historical means of achieving international order – balance of power and empire hegemony. As the former is not available in much of the world (and applies to states but not international terrorists or other non-state actors crossing borders), that conveniently leaves the latter imperialistic option as his only alternative.

But here he has the problem, as he half admits, that the United States is a 'doubtful case' of his caring, sharing postmodern states committed to mutual interdependence and openness. In fact the United States looks remarkably like his old-fashioned, aggressive, selfish, stability-threatening modern state, behaving 'as states always have' – neo-liberal openness and the supposed 'decline of the nation state' are apparently for everyone else. Furthermore, from its hegemonic position the United States is an example to aggressive state nationalists everywhere (e.g., encouraging similarly bellicose and de-stabilising stances from other allies, most notably Sharon in Israel, but also cases such as Spain's increasingly hard-line refusal to negotiate with Basque separatists). So we have the contradiction that the leading power in Cooper's postmodern world has not itself reached this elevated stage (but does Cooper fondly imagine that America's partnership with Blair provides its missing postmodernism?). For clearly the United States is currently the only viable 'empire' for the imposition of imperialist 'order' on the modern and pre-modern states which are allegedly the sources of trouble (whatever the delusions of empire still harboured by British civil servants and the British prime minister). Small consolation that the United States and Britain are indeed well practised in 'the rougher methods of an earlier era'.

While the United States preaches neo-liberalism, its decidedly *non*-neo-liberal steel tariffs and threatened trade war with the European Union suggest that its standards may not be double, but triple or quadruple. There is clearly one set for the United States itself; another for allies such as Britain and the other EU states, partly to ensure their role remains strictly subordinate; a third for other modern states defined as 'trouble' (e.g., Iraq); and perhaps a fourth set for pre-modern areas too weak to defend themselves with conventional armies (e.g., Afghanistan, Palestine). Not that the United States has any monopoly on multiple standards; allies such as Britain and the European Union have their own flexible approach when it suits them.

Cooper's ideological mish-mash is useful insofar as it reflects current policy thinking and attempts to justify what is already happening or being actively considered in British and US foreign policy circles – a case of theory as usual trying to catch up with reality rather than any great visionary exercise of the imagination. He alerts us to deception as a policy instrument, and not least the deception that it is only used against 'old-fashioned states' (Venezuela? Colombia?) when in fact it is also applied to allied states and domestic audiences.[17] He inadvertently exposes the deception or double (triple?) standards lurking behind the more pious utterances (the 'moral consciousness'?) of his master Blair, publicly the loud champion of international justice and the 'ethical' liberal internationalism which his adviser completely ignores. Cooper also provides a corrective to the notion that military force and war are now of only peripheral importance in a neo-liberal world.[18]

The second 'absence' in his argument is in fact neo-liberalism (his case owes nothing to it), which raises the question of the relationship between it and his neo-conservatism. Historically, liberalism and conservatism were opposed ideologies, with freedom, prioritised by the former, in obvious contradiction with authority, prioritised by the latter. However, their 'neo' versions in contemporary circumstances can have a complementary rather than necessarily conflictual relationship, as the New Right combination of liberalism and conservatism has demonstrated over the last twenty years.

We should not assume that consistency is necessary in ideology and there are indeed some ('horses for courses') advantages in having different ideologies for different contexts or purposes. Thus while neo-liberalism may be less dominant than in the past, globalisation may actually be strengthened rather than weakened. Neo-conservatism provides additional legitimations, and may counter some of the de-stabilising effects of laissez faire which Gray highlights: the threat and actuality of war more obviously supplements civil power in the market. The contradictions, as between freedom and authority, remain, but as Levitas pointed out, if political positions – in this case US hegemony – are to be undermined by their internal contradictions, it will happen not at the ideological level but only at the material level of conflicting political forces and policies.[19] And after 11 September, policy conflicts escalated across the partly overlapping polarities of civil power/military power and multilateralism/unilateralism.

Unilateral Multilateralism and Militarism

Favouring multilateralism and civil over military force, Joseph Nye has distinguished between 'hard power', military and economic, which commands and coerces by stick or carrot, and the less tangible 'soft' power of setting the political agenda and providing attractive values and examples which shape the preferences of others, working by co-operation and co-option rather than coercion. In the global information age, and partly because the greater power of non-state actors was putting 'more activities ... outside the control of even the most powerful states', as 11 September dramatised, 'the sources and distribution of power are being transformed in a profound way'.[20] Soft power, in his view, was already becoming increasingly important relative to the declining importance of military and economic power, and especially to the United States and Europe, who are best placed to benefit because of their information and cultural resources. However, with echoes of Cooper (he refers to an earlier pre-11 September version of Cooper's postmodern argument), he suggests that while power is becoming less tangible and less coercive among advanced post-industrial societies, most of the world (and the Middle East is specifically mentioned) has not yet reached this happy state and is not so amenable to the co-optive charms of his country. Hence in this 'variegated world, all three sources of power – military, economic, and soft – remain relevant, although to different degrees in different relationships'.[21] However, where Cooper argues the need to be brutal towards less advanced societies, Nye's emphasis is that '11 September 2001 also showed that there is no alternative to mobilising international coalitions and building institutions to address shared threats and challenges'.[22]

Perhaps, but the evidence since 11 September suggests otherwise. Nye is the authentic voice of the liberal internationalist or multilateralist approach to securing US hegemony, and his empirical analysis of the information age fits his normative position. This might be vindicated eventually, but it is in stark contradiction to what has actually been happening recently. The Bush administration leading by attractive example is wide of the mark, unless bellicose threats and brutality are deemed attractive. Nye's analysis does not sit well with the rampant anti-Americanism occasioned by the US bombing of Afghanistan, the behaviour of its client state Israel, the warmongering with respect to Iraq, and what many in the rest of the world and also within the United States see as unilateral global arrogance. However, rather than characterising US policy in the 'either/or' terms of two 'alternatives', there is evidence for unilateral multilateralism in its recent behaviour within multilateral institutions, towards its European allies and with respect to the Israel–Palestine conflict.

Unilateralism and Multilateral Institutions

The main themes of US foreign policy and its relations with its main allies were already in place well before 11 September. As we have seen, continuity was symbolised by Bush inheriting important officials from the presidencies of Reagan and Bush snr. Unilateralism and militarism were already strong elements in US foreign policy, if perhaps less obvious under Bill Clinton. But his administration had greatly increased military spending, systematically used aerial bombing, and continued the US tradition of undercutting the United Nations, both directly (e.g., hounding out its Sectretary General, Butros Butros-Ghali), and indirectly through its client state, Israel, defying UN resolutions to withdraw from the occupied territories. There was already an internal shift in the US 'centre of gravity' from the more internationalist, Europe-oriented east coast to the south and west and connections with Latin America and the Pacific.[23]

Unilateralism was immediately more evident with Bush's withdrawal from the Kyoto agreement on global warming, seen as putting US energy corporation interests above the future of the planet (the United States, with four per cent of the world's population, accounts for about 25 per cent of carbon dioxide emissions); his failure to ratify the Comprehensive Nuclear Test Ban Treaty; and his plans for a 'star wars' missile defence of US borders. This promised a renewed, de-stabilising 'arms race' but was justified by a discourse of threat from 'rogue states', and Defence Secretary Rumsfeld was reported as saying the United States would go ahead no matter what anyone else thought.[24] At the same time, Bush was insisting on a determining say in Europe's defence, reportedly even more determined than Clinton to stop the European Union developing its own independent military capability and accepting a European Rapid Reaction Force only if it remained subsidiary to a US-led NATO.[25] France wanted Europe to have its own autonomous system, but Britain, while favouring a joint EU force, was reportedly 'sensitive' to US concerns that NATO remain pre-eminent.[26] A strong Europe was reportedly America's 'nightmare', and the reason why Bush 'laces contempt for Blair with flattery' and insincere talk of a 'special relationship'[27] – the contempt perhaps not unconnected with the fact that Blair had been a big supporter of the Kyoto agreement which Bush had neutered. For its part, the European Union saw itself as much closer to troubled areas such as the Balkans and the Middle East, but as having been humiliated in the Kosovo conflict, where the US military had dominated. It seemed there was a highly unequal and sometimes directly contradictory division of labour between the allies: the European Union mainly contributing economic and soft power but the United States dominant thanks to its military might. Or, as some saw it, 'the US makes war and the EU cleans up the mess'. Bush was demonising countries such as North Korea, Iran and Libya, while the European Union was developing links with them (as Clinton had begun to do with Iran);[28] and America's client state was in the West Bank smashing up civil infrastructure which had been contributed by EU taxpayers.

But among the clearest examples of America's unilateral multilateralism has been its systematic re-moulding of multilateral institutions to its own design, with the threat of withdrawing or refusing to contribute financially unless it got its own way. However, if it succeeds (which usually it has), it thereby threatens the independence, legitimacy and effectiveness of multilateral global institutions in general. Allies have typically acquiesced, rationalising that they are preventing the worse alternative of US isolationism, though (given that globalisation means that isolationism is not a real option) the arguably much greater danger is compromising the framework of transnational governance and making it even less democratic than it already is. Bob Watson, head of the United Nations's Intergovernmental Panel on Climate Change, was removed at the behest of US oil interests threatened by his policies for tackling global warming, and he was replaced by an economist who has oil industry connections (as had Hamid Karzai, whom the United States installed as president of Afghanistan). Hans Blix, chief of the UN weapons inspectorate, was attacked; and Jose Bustani, head of the Organisation for the Prohibition of Chemical Weapons, was sacked in disgraceful circumstances.[29] Both these bodies were involved in trying peacefully to persuade Saddam Hussein to get rid of weapons of mass destruction, and Bush's critics believed that the option of their diplomacy undermined America's pretext for a war on Iraq.

Unilateral Militarism and Multilateralism

The other major obstacle delaying this war was the Israel–Palestine conflict. Here there are more policy contradictions, and again strong evidence of *unilateral multilateralism*, though of a different sort, with respect to America's allies in the Middle East and particularly a less than fully compliant European Union.

Given his pre-11 September unilateralism, a decisive change to multilateralism seemed to be heralded by Bush's careful building of a coalition for his 'war on terrorism'. Its very slowness, and the absence of the precipitous unilateral response which had been widely expected, reassured allies, now relieved that what they saw as the 'Texas cowboys' had been roped in. However, while the allied states were keen to get involved, there was the contradiction that a less keen United States took complete unilateral control of the actual conduct of the war in Afghanistan.[30] Bush then proceeded to argue the need for war against Iraq as a rogue state, despite the failure to establish any link between Saddam Hussein and 11 September, and the lack of coalition support except from the faithful Blair. The war on terrorism assured US support for what Sharon successfully presented as part of the same war on terrorism when he launched a massive assault on the occupied West Bank. But that in turn halted any immediate prospect of extending the war to Iraq, as outrage swept the entire Middle East and to a lesser extent Europe, and seriously compromised the allied states in the coalition. Yet again Israel, widely seen as the agent of a contradictory US imperialism in the Middle East, could also be seen as causing problems for its patron rather than solving them.

Sharon, already legally implicated in war crimes in the Palestinian refugee camps of Chabra and Shattila some twenty years before, was now accused of totally disproportionate brutality against the Palestinian people and of actions which were counterproductive for stopping Palestinian suicide bombings in Israel. The bombings, however, rallied support for Sharon, further marginalising the Israeli 'peace and negotiation' lobby (though over 200 Israeli military reservists refused to serve in the occupied Palestinian territories[31]). He was widely seen as having engineered the conflict and taking the opportunity of the war on terrorism to achieve his long-held objectives: finally destroying the failing Oslo 1993 peace process, systematically humiliating the Palestinians and physically demolishing the infrastructure of the Palestinian Authority/nascent Palestinian state (which he re-labelled the 'infrastructure of terrorism'); and with it the 'two-state solution' to the Israel–Palestine conflict, ensuring in advance that any Palestinian state would be a failed state or 'Bantustan' if it ever came into existence.[32]

Neither the Israeli right nor the US right have ever believed in or wanted a two-state solution, despite it being the official position of their governments, but the ostensible problem was how to get Sharon to withdraw his army from the West Bank (though for some it was more a question of 'whether' than 'when'). In early April 2002, an impatient Romano Prodi, president of the European Commission, said 'American mediation efforts have failed, and we need new mediation before the Israeli–Palestinian conflicts turns into a full scale regional war'.[33] He called on the US to step aside as primary peacemaker to allow a broad alliance of countries to mediate. The next day Bush responded by calling for Israeli withdrawal from the occupied territories and said Colin Powell would go to the Middle East.

Powell, not in any hurry to grasp a poisoned chalice, set off at a leisurely pace, meandering around the Mediterranean, taking in Morocco, Egypt and Spain, and arriving in Israel over a week later. This was seen as buying time for Sharon to complete his military campaign, though in Spain Powell brought his main allies, the European Union, Russia and the UN, on board in a joint call for immediate Israeli withdrawal. Meanwhile Sharon, in the course of the week had escalated the conflict, and once in Israel Powell proved no more effective in getting a withdrawal or cease-fire. Indeed when an undermined Powell returned empty handed, Bush, like Sharon, attacked Arafat for alleged 'complicity in terrorism' and (unbelievably even by his standards), Bush referred to Sharon as a 'man of peace'[34] – just after a leading English Jewish politican and lifelong friend of Israel had openly called Sharon a 'war criminal'.[35]

US policy was clearly contradictory but there were several interpretations of this sequence. Were the American administration knaves or fools? Was there deception or simply confusion? Had the United States secretly given Sharon the go-ahead, or failed to restrain him? Either way it appeared ineffectual and/or devious. Sharon had forced Bush to back down – the latter 'blinked first', according to one commentator.[36] Perhaps, but maybe there is a more plausible interpretation. We have seen the European Union was impatient to take over the lead role, and eager to develop a coherent foreign policy of its own. Here it was hampered by Britain's close support for the United States, but it had considerable economic leverage as one of Israel's main trading partners, and there were widespread calls, including from Jewish groups,[37] for it to use economic sanctions against Sharon's policy.[38] The European Union was also keen to support Powell against the more unilateral militarists of the Pentagon. However, Powell's Mediterranean meander actually blocked any separate European Union initiative, leaving it to watch impotently as Sharon demolished West Bank infrastructure. The meeting in Spain tied the European Union, the United

Nations and Russia into what would be Powell's failed project (thus spreading the loss of face). Sharon got more time; ideological cover was provided for his allies in the US militarist unilateralist faction, while Powell, or rather the multilateralism he ostensibly represented, was shown to be ineffectual. As with the multilateral institutions, it was not a simple case of unilateralism versus multilateralism. Instead, it was again a win for the unilateralist faction through their particular use of multilateralism.

Militarism and Allied Concerns

US multilateralists concerned for hegemony had other reasons to be worried. The unilateralist militarist faction appeared successful, but at what cost in terms of fuelling anti-Americanism and related anti-semitism?[39] At what cost in terms of political destabilisation, especially of allied states in the Middle East, but also in European countries where the far right has been making inroads on the back of security and immigration fears fanned by 11 September?

Israel's military aggression against the Palestinians and its successful rejection of the United Nations and the European Union are inexplicable outside the context of Israel's patron state, the United States, and the latter is therefore widely held responsible. It is inconceivable that Israel could repeatedly ignore UN resolutions and successfully block a UN investigation into possible war crimes in yet another refugee camp, Jenin, without the support of its patron state and America's own history of undermining the United Nations. With its massive economic and military aid to Israel, the United States clearly would have the leverage to compel Israel to withdraw from the occupied territories and agree a genuine two-state resolution of the conflict. But, when apparently defying the United States, and actually defying the 'international community', Sharon knew he had strong support in the Bush administration, from much of the US media, a large majority of the US Congress, the Jewish lobby and the fundamentalist Christian right – indeed some supporters more openly extreme than Sharon himself.[40] Thus Sharon is widely seen as an agent of US imperialism, and Israel is a major generator of anti-Americanism in the Middle East and elsewhere.

For the United States itself, there are advantages in unilateralism, as we have seen, and in militarism, but also serious disadvantages for itself and its allies. Domestically, war has proved popular for Bush in the wake of 11 September and may continue to do so (unless US personnel start dying in significant numbers). Why spend all those dollars on arms if they are not used? Using them helps justify the hugely increased spending on the politically important military–industrial complex (widely distributed across the United States and a major re-distributor of income). Reagan's aggressive arms race against the 'evil empire' had bankrupted the state capitalist USSR (masquerading as socialism); and the US military asserts power in the one global arena where the United States is unchallengeable, and potential rivals for hegemony such as the European Union are at their weakest (EU total military spending is about half that of the United States, is relatively uncoordinated and is much less geared to global operations). Also, it is said that enemies such as Saddam Hussein 'understand' military force, while a war and regime change in Iraq would reassert US power in the Middle East, substitute for Saudi Arabia, an increasingly unreliable ally, and get more control over Iraq's huge oil reserves (just as access to central Asian oil was a sub-plot of the war in Afghanistan).

However, militarism may cause as many problems as it solves, through its often uncontrollable knock-on effects as US aggression encourages aggression in others, and because hard military power tends to undermine what Nye argues are the increasingly important soft forms of power.[41] For instance, key US allies in the Middle East such as Saudi Arabia and Egypt are forced to become less compliant as their own populations become increasingly enraged by the US–Israeli treatment of the Palestinians. As the (generally under-reported) mass demonstrations across the Muslim world demanded effective action such as oil sanctions but did not get them, there has been political radicalisation and an increased possibility that US-friendly regimes could be toppled. Nor can Sharon's militarism deliver genuine security for Israelis. Moreover, as some of Israel's supporters both inside and outside the country increasingly realise,[42] the colonial occupation and expansion of illegal settlements in the West Bank and Gaza not only have the intended effect of blocking a viable Palestinian state, they also brutalise and degrade Israeli society from within – a clear case of 'a nation which oppresses another cannot itself be free' (and an example of the reality behind Cooper's 'colonialism to maintain world order').

Thus, for its allies as for the United States, militarism is a decidedly two-edged sword. The war on terrorism has been used as a pretext to clamp down on often legitimate opposition; and the destabilising effects of 11 September and subsequent policy responses apply more generally, even in comparatively stable Europe. To take just one area: European Muslims have been alienated, and fascist and far right parties boosted.[43] They have become newly prominent in a number of countries, such as Holland and Denmark, through cashing in on generalised concerns for security, opposition to immigration and specifically anti-Muslim racism: 'In the aftermath of 11 September the far right has become bolder ... Ms Kjaersgaard [leader of the Danish People's Party], for example, has called for a "holy war" against Islam.'[44] The alleged incompatibility or inevitable 'clash of civilisations' is a common theme, along with whipping up fears about an undifferentiated amalgam of external threats – terrorists, drugs, crime, immigrants and globalisation. Multiculturalism has been targeted as the problem, and here, as Bhikhu Parekh points out, the modern national state is peculiarly ill equipped to meet the challenges of globalisation.[45] The aggressive 'America first' nationalism of the United States (the paradigmatic national state) encourages virulent nationalism elsewhere. And the right, not for the first time, steals the left's clothes, adapting anti-globalisation rhetoric in tandem with its own traditional anti-Americanism – which makes it imperative for the left to define its own anti-globalisation more precisely.

Against Hegemony

11 September has not ushered in a 'new world' but put the pre-existing one in harsher focus. The political impact of the Al Qaeda attack does not compare in magnitude with that of the collapse of the USSR. However, with respect to the assertion of American hegemony, 11 September can perhaps be seen as sparking a 'delayed reaction' to the collapse of the USSR and the reality of the United States being the world's one remaining superpower, its military dominance over potential rivals quite unmatched by any other hegemon in history.

Yet for a safer, more democratic world, the real choice is not between one faction of US hegemonists and another, one set of double or multiple standards and another. Unilateral multilateralism may currently be dominant, but the United States simply oscillates between different combinations of uni- and multilateralism, military and civil power, neo-conservatism and neo-liberalism. Whatever moral high ground it gained from 11 September – deservedly won in the case of the New York City firemen and other rescuers who gave their own lives trying to save people in the World Trade Center – has now been well and truly lost for US hegemony.

US multilateralists such as Nye are obviously closer to a liberal internationalist alternative. But for this alternative to be genuinely internationalist (as distinct from 'US internationalist'), it would have to confront 'the unaccountable hegemon' and the ideological basis of US power in neo-liberalism and neo-conservatism, and there is little prospect of supposed liberal internationalists (such as the multilateral European Union, never mind Blair) doing that. They share many of the same presuppositions as the United States, lacking only its strength to put them into effect.[46]

This points to 'the hole at the heart of liberal cosmopolitan democracy', in theory the most developed current alternative to hegemonic and balance of power peacekeeping, yet in practice lacking the agency to become a reality. Thus in the aftermath of 11 September David Held argued cogently about the need for 'a movement for global, not American, justice ... the rule of law in place of war', to confront 'the global polarisation of wealth, income and power ... [which] cannot be left to markets to resolve'.[47] Yet a movement of whom, or by whom, is completely unclear. It is not discussed, and the air of unreality is compounded when he also talks approvingly of 'the decreasing legal and moral relevance' of state boundaries and 'the increasing significance of international law and justice', just when the former proposition is being used by US imperialism to negate the latter.[48]

In the same publication, its editor, Mark Leonard, in echoing the need for a movement to mobilise support for cosmopolitanism, argued quite implausibly that there is no alternative to liberal democracy 'on the streets of Seattle, Genoa, North Korea or in the caves of Afghanistan'; in fact these places signify a variety of alternatives, both worse and better.[49] But his point is not only to rule out the anti-globalisation movement which first emerged on the streets of Seattle and continued in Genoa, but also to smear it by association with the unsavoury North Korean and Al Qaeda/Taliban regimes. So we can only surmise that the 'hole' in well-intentioned cosmopolitanism is to be filled by 'progressive' elites. (Blair rather than Bush? And it may be significant that Blair provides the Foreword and the final chapter of Leonard's publication).

However, as Richard Falk acidly observed,

> The only elites ... likely to contemplate world government favourably in the foreseeable future are those that currently seem responsible for the most acute forms of human suffering ... Economic and political elites will not protect the general human interest on the basis of their own values or even through ... enlightened self-interest ... Only a transnational social movement animated by a vision of humane governance can offer any hope of extending the domain of democracy.[50]

Since that was written in 1995, the anti-globalisation/anti-capitalism movement, now also the anti-war movement, has emerged and can begin to fill the hole. Furthermore, as argued elsewhere,[51] it could do so in ways where it benefits from cosmopolitan democracy as well as contributing some much-needed agency to it. The movement does indeed confront the unaccountable hegemon, its neo-liberalism and its neo-conservatism. Perhaps the one good thing to be said for the bumbling Bush replacing the slick Clinton is that it makes the argument easier for anti-imperialists. However, for the movement to clearly differentiate itself from the right's chauvinistic anti-global rhetoric and crude anti-Americanism, it has to confront not only American imperialism but also the lesser imperialisms of the allied/rival and client states – of the European Union, Russia, France, Britain ... and Israel. We have seen that US hegemony and its allied and rival imperialisms are riven with contradictions and far from invulnerable. But despite these contradictions they will not conveniently self-destruct. It is still all to play for, and not too much to say that there is, perhaps literally, a world to win, or lose.

ACKNOWLEDGEMENTS

Thanks to Ian Shuttleworth and to Róise Ni Bhaoill for comments on an earlier draft; to Liam O'Dowd for comments on neo-liberalism and borders; and to two anonymous referees for encouragement and criticism.

NOTES

1. F. Halliday, *The World at 2000: Perils and Promises* (Basingstoke: Palgrave 2001) pp.90–92, 98–9. The US population, 275 million, is four per cent of the world's total, though growing much faster than the population of most advanced countries; and its defence budget now reputedly exceeds that of the next nine (or more) states put together. Since the collapse of the USSR, it thus enjoys totally unprecedented hegemony in military terms, compared to previous hegemons such as the Dutch and British (see G. Arrighi, *The Long Twentieth Century: Money, Power and the Origins of Our Times* (London: Verso 1994); P.J. Taylor, *The Way the Modern World Works: World Hegemony to World Impasse* (Chichester: Wiley 1996)). Traditionally 'hegemony' referred to the dominance of a single state over other states, but there is also its Gramscian sense of a routinised set of global practices and ideologies widely accepted as normal and maintained by consensus as well as coercion (J. Agnew and S. Corbridge, *Mastering Space: Hegemony, Territory and International Political Economy* (London: Routledge 1995) p.17). Similarly, Taylor (pp.4–25) distinguishes the traditional sense of political dominance and control over other countries from a leadership role which involves setting standards by example. As we shall see, the recent assertion of US military power is also the re-assertion of an older, more traditional conception of hegemony; and the reversion can be partly explained in terms of decades of debate about the relative decline in America's economic hegemony (with the economic rise of Germany and Japan from the 1960s, and recently the European Union) (see Taylor pp.166–76); and also US economic power being weakened by economic globalisation and neo-liberalism (Agnew and Corbridge pp.118, 205). Perhaps specifically US economic private sector power is somewhat dissipated by neo-liberal globalisation but this does not apply to its state-sector military power, which may help explain the relative growth of neo-conservatism.

2. However, Bush did personify the contradiction that the world's present hegemon is to a substantial extent inhabited and dominated by relatively insular people who are comparatively uninvolved/uninformed about external issues which they nevertheless substantially effect. For example, Trent Lott, Senate Republican leader, boasted that he does not go abroad and shows scant interest in the outside world (openly mocking the foreign names of the heads of the United Nations and International Monetary Fund) (Halliday (note 1) p.101). Yet these are not 'backwoods' non-entities, but leaders of the world's leading power. Insularity is partly a function of size, and the historical tendency for hegemons to have a progressively larger 'homebase' – compare previous hegemons, the Genoese, the Dutch and the British (Arrighi (note 1)). Around 80 per cent of US citizens do not possess passports, seeing no need to go outside their continental-scale national state – understandable if limiting; but less excusable in leading politicians (see also note 40, below), and politically important because it feeds a unilateralism and foreign policy partly driven by domestic concerns.

3. N. Smith, 'Scales of Terror and the Resort to Geography: September 11, October 7', *Environment and Planning D* 19/6 (2001) pp.631–7.

4. A. McGrew, 'Democratising Global Institutions: Possibilities, Limits and Normative Foundations', in J. Anderson (ed.), *Transnational Democracy: Political Spaces and Border Crossings* (London: Routledge 2002) pp.149–70. See also his point about some American analysts believing transnational democracy to be an impossibility. Cynics might see this as linked to the United States having only (only?) four per cent of the world's population.

5. For example, Rice, Rumsfeld and Vice-President Cheney worked as 'Cold War warriors' for Bush snr. US officials who first came to prominence in the Latin American 'dirty wars', 'death squads' and 'Contra-Irangate' scandals under Reagan and Bush in the 1980s and early 1990s – e.g., Elliot Abrams, John Negroponte (now US ambassador to the United Nations), and Otto Reich (an ex-ambassador to Venezuela who worked for the disgraced Oliver North) – have been linked with the leaders of the short-lived coup against Venezuelan President Chavez in April 2002 (see note 9, below).

6. J. Nye, 'Hard and Soft Power in a Global Information Age', in M. Leonard (ed.), *Re-Ordering the World: The Long-term Implications of September 11th* (London: The Foreign Policy Centre 2002) p.2.

7. In March 2002 Bush imposed steel tariffs which invited retaliation from the European Union and elsewhere; and in May he was planning a 70 per cent increase in subsidies to US agriculture, as the United States continued to attack EU agricultural subsidies for distorting the market (*The Independent*, 3 May 2002).

8. This argument is elaborated in J. Anderson, 'Questions of Democracy, Territoriality and Globalisation', in Anderson, *Transnational Democracy* (note 4) pp.6–38.

9. Bush, Blair and the European Union were exposed when Chavez was unexpectedly reinstated by public protests and constitutionally-minded army officers. Whereas Latin American states had immediately denounced the coup which suspended the Venezuela parliament and took over the Supreme Court as well as removing Chavez, the United States immediately recognised the new regime, a UK government minister immediately characterised the ousted Chavez as a 'ranting demagogue', and the European Union did not object to what one journalist described as a 'decaffinated re-run' of the Pinochet–CIA coup in Chile. There was evidence of US connivance and support before and after the coup, the plotters meeting US officials beforehand (see note 5, above). Venezuela is the world's fourth-largest oil producer and an important source of US supplies. Chavez had organised with Iraq, Iran and Libya in OPEC to increase oil prices; he had condemned the US bombing of Afghanistan; criticised the 'savage-neo-liberalism' of the World Bank and IMF; and supported Cuba (*The Guardian*, 16 April 2001; *The Independent*, 17 April 2001; *The Observer*, 21 April 2001).

10. As the Irish columnist, Eamonn McCann, noted (*Belfast Telegraph*, 25 April 2002), a US congressional committee had 'staggering arrogance' in expecting Sinn Fein leader Gerry Adams to go to the United States to explain what three Irish republicans were doing in Colombia, when the US army and its allies in the Colombian army and paramilitaries were directly implicated in a murder campaign against trade union and political activists, about which there had just been protests across the United States itself.

11. Anderson, Questions of Democracy (note 8).

12. On cosmopolitanism see D. Held, *Democracy and the Global Order: From the Modern State to Cosmopolitan Governance* (Cambridge: Polity Press 1995); on its limitations see Anderson, 'Questions of Democracy (note 8).

13. J. Gray, 'The Era of Globalisation is Over', *The New Statesman*, 24 September 2001. My early response to 11 September was that globalisation would proceed but with increasing border differentiations and heightened contradictions, with measures motivated or justified by fear of 'international terrorists' impeding some legitimate cross-border traffic (J. Anderson, 'Borders after 11 September 2001', *Space and Polity* 6/2 (2002) pp.227–32). I did not know it at the time, but as well as closing all its airports, America's almost instant response was to close its borders with Mexico and Canada (Smith (note 3)).

14. The European Union's demands were mainly to secure access in foreign markets for private EU firms providing a variety of services (*The Guardian*, 18 April 2002). But they included a demand for intra-corporate labour mobility across borders – essentially free movement for higher paid executives and professionals, with employers deciding who can move. This would selectively address the world system's major contradiction where, according to Gray,

relatively mobile capital contrasts with relatively immobile labour (a contradiction which 11 September exacerbates), with the European Union continuing to try to lock out and lock up migrants from poor countries.

15. R. Cooper, 'The Post-Modern State', in Leonard, *Re-ordering the World* (note 6).
16. Ibid. pp.15, 17.
17. In a weak postmodernist moment, I gave an earlier draft the naff title: 'US hegemony, (al)lies and contradictions'.
18. Given the historical tendency towards the 'informal empire of civil society', now dominated by the United States, and the global hegemony of neo-liberalism, there has been a mistaken tendency (e.g., J. Anderson, *Theorizing State Borders: 'Politics/Economics' and Democracy in Capitalism*, CIBR Electronic Working Papers WP01, <www.qub.ac.uk/cibr>) to underestimate the continuing use of force underlying globalisation, including the fact that the United States currently has a military presence in over half the states in the world.
19. R. Levitas (ed.), *The Ideology of the New Right* (Cambridge: Polity Press 1986) pp.4–10, 20.
20. Nye (note 6) p.2.
21. Ibid. p.3, 8.
22. Ibid p.2.
23. Halliday (note 1) pp.90–109.
24. *The Observer*, 25 February 2001; *The Guardian*, 12 March 2001.
25. *The Observer*, 25 February 2001.
26. *The Guardian*, 28 February 2001.
27. *The Observer*, 25 February 2001.
28. *The Guardian*, 12 March 2001.
29. In the contradictory world of US hegemony, Jose Bustani, a seconded Brazilain diplomat, got sacked for doing his job too well. He had increased the signatories against chemical weapons from 87 to 145 states, was re-elected unanimously in May 2000 for a second five-year term, and in 2001 Colin Powell thanked him for his 'very impressive' work. But in January 2002 the US asked Brazil to recall him; Brazil refused; and in March the US accused him of financial and other 'mismanagement'. Any financial problems were in fact due to the US withdrawing financial support; but it succeeded in calling a special session to oust him in April, threatening to withdraw support and collapse the organisation. 48 states voted to remove Bustani, seven were against, and 43 abstained; the United States was involved in several illegal manoeuvres and it was booed at the meeting when it failed to produce documentary evidence for its allegations against Bustani (*The Guardian*, 16 April 2002 and *23* April 2002). Seeing his organisation as independent and valuing its international credibility, Bustani had wanted to examine chemical weapons in the United States, but it (like Iraq) had refused. Given a clear opportunity to support multilateralism and credible international law, Blair choose his 'special relationship' with Bush and the option of war against Iraq, with Britain first to co-sponsor the US resolution to sack Bustani.
30. The faithful British were rewarded with the task (the greatest since the Falklands War, according one excited TV journalist) of blowing up empty caves long after the enemy had left, and apparently more in fear of 'friendly fire' from supporting US warplanes.
31. *The Irish Times*, 20 April 2002.
32. The illegal Jewish settlements on Palestinian land – a policy vigorously supported by the Israeli right (over 30 new settlements have been built since Sharon became prime minister) – together with their connecting roads and buffer zones, fragment the West Bank and Gaza into over 200 separate, militarily-controllable enclaves. They are worse in this respect than the Bantustans of apartheid South Africa, but similar in being economically dependent on Israel for employment and providing Israeli employers with cheap labour.
33. *The Irish Times*, 13 April 2002.
34. *The Irish Times*, 20 April 2002.
35. Gerald Kaufman MP condemned the Palestinian suicide bombers but went on to ask, 'How we would feel if we had been occupied for 35 years by a foreign power which denied us the most elementary human rights and decent living conditions?' (*The Guardian*, 17 April 2002).

36. *The Guardian*, 13 April 2002.
37. For example, 'Jews for Justice for Palestinians' called for an EU boycott of Israeli exports, over 40 per cent of which are to the European Union, to force Israeli withdrawal from the occupied territories (letter to *The Guardian*, 20 April 2002).
38. *The Guardian*, 16 April 2002.
39. Both are widespread prejudices, and need to be taken into account in political analysis (see note 48, below). However, critics of Bush's policy were regularly accused of 'anti-Americanism' by right-wing commentators, as critics of Israeli state actions were typically accused of 'anti-semitism'; and the two came together when American commentators accused 'Europe' in general of 'anti-semitism' (for had not the Holocaust happened in Europe). While the charges of racism were sometimes justified, they were often a cynical misuse of 'political correctness' (even by people who also attack 'political correctness'), in order to deflect perfectly proper criticism of what particular governments and groups were doing. It was conveniently ignored that the critics included many Americans and many Israelis 'at the sharp end' of conflicting views (including Israeli soldiers who bravely refused to serve in the occupied Palestinian territories). Misuse of the Holocaust in cynical justification of Israeli aggression and state assassinations ignores the fact that the Palestinians had no responsibility whatsoever for the Holocaust (but are paying for European and North American feelings of guilt). People genuinely concerned about these prejudices should realise that they are being fed by Bush and Sharon.

Regarding anti-Americanism, some people in Europe and elsewhere are too quick to assume that all Americans in the United States think and act like their leading politicians and dominant media images. Robert Fisk, a leading journalist in the Middle East and critic of US policy, was on a speaking tour in the United States during the Middle East crisis in April 2002, and he reported that:

> I was shocked. Not by the passivity of Americans – the all-accepting, patriotic notion that the 'President knows best' – nor by the dangerous self-absorption of the United States since 11 September and the constant, all-consuming fear of criticising Israel. What shocked me was the extraordinary new American refusal to go along with the official line, the growing, angry awareness among Americans that they were being lied to and deceived (*The Independent*, 17 April 2002).

40. Dick Armey, another Texan politician and the Republican majority leader in the US House of Representatives, called for the Palestinians to be expelled from the West Bank, East Jerusalem and Gaza, and for these areas – all occupied by the Israeli army since the 1967 war – to be incorporated into Israel. Even Sharon does not openly espouse this 'ethnic cleansing' option of the Israeli far right, though it is increasingly popular in Israel. Armey, another 'insular' hegemonist (note 3, above) also said: 'I've been to Europe once. I don't have to go again' (*The Guardian*, 4 May 2002).
41. Use of military force can cast a long shadow. For example, Henry Kissinger, the blatant exponent of unprincipled realpolitik, is currently being legally pursued by Spanish, French and other European justice systems over the deaths of their own citizens in the early 1970s after the CIA-backed coup in Chile (*The Independent*, 23 April 2002).
42. Personal communications; and Anthony Lewis, 'Israel Corrupted from Within by Colonial Views' (reprinted from the *New York Review of Books* in *The Guardian*, 20 April 2002).
43. British Muslims, traditionally Labour Party supporters, feel betrayed by Blair's stance on Palestine, and if they withdraw support from Labour it could ironically let in the far right in some areas (*The Guardian*, 23 April 2002). The European far right – e.g., in Austria, Belgium, Denmark, France, Germany, Holland, Italy and Portugal – has been making gains since 11 September, partly by adapting the nationalistic rhetoric of Bush; and while some North Americans may accuse 'Europe' of being anti-semitic, most of the recent anti-semitism, in America as in Europe, is in fact directed not at Jews but at Arabs, who of course are also Semites.
44. *The Independent*, 23 April 2002.
45. B. Parekh, 'Reconstituting the Modern State', in Anderson, *Transnational Democracy* (note 4) pp.39–55.
46. Michael Ignatieff might be taken as a representative of liberal internationalism. The best he

could offer was to say that 'the only solution ... [the] last chance for Middle East peace' was for Bush to send in his troops to impose a two-state solution and the European Union to help rebuild the Palestinian Authority (*The Guardian*, 19 April 2002). Aside from the dubious practicality of militarily imposing a solution, this seems to accept America's self-image of 'peace-maker' when, as we have seen, it has been the major power preventing a solution for more than three decades.

47. D. Held, 'Violence, Law and Justice in a Global Age', in Leonard, *Re-Ordering the World* (note 6) pp.66–7.
48. Ibid. pp.57–8, 61. The air of wishful thinking was reinforced by his assertion that 'there cannot be many people in the world who did not experience shock, revulsion, horror, anger and a desire for vengeance' in response to 11 September. In fact, I was in Croatia that day and some people there thought the attack on the US mainland meant it was at last getting its just deserts for bombing other people; and similar anti-American sentiments were reportedly widespread in Latin America and elsewhere, as well as in the Middle East. It is important that this reality is not glossed over, because anti-Americanism is a politically important factor, not least in assessing American hegemony.
49. M. Leonard, 'The Contours of a World Community', in idem, *Re-Ordering the World* (note 6) pp.xvi–xvii. James Goodman, 'Contesting Corporate Globalism: Sources of Power, Channels for Democratisation', in Anderson, *Transnational Democracy* (note 4), details the very heterogeneous nature of opposition to western 'corporate globalism', ranging from transnational alliances for democratisation to those confronting globalism on a localist or particularistic basis, which includes *anti*-democratic fundamentalist movements both within Islam and Christian North America.
50. R. Falk, *On Humane Governance: Towards a New Global Politics – A Report of the World Order Models Project* (Cambridge: Polity Press 1995) pp.7, 120.
51. Anderson, 'Questions of Democracy' (note 8).

Postscript (February 2003)

Contemporary history inevitably dates quickly. Originally written in April–May 2002, this article already shows its age. Things have moved on. At the start of 2003 the America's preparations for its delayed assault on Iraq are now in full swing. But this is a high-risk venture fraught with contradictions, unpredictable outcomes and criticisms from within sections of the US establishment. It is now even clearer that the main issue is not the war on terrorism; nor is it the threat from Saddam Hussein, which only the Bush and Blair regimes affect to fully believe in. There is indeed a remarkable worldwide consensus, which includes millions within the United States and a majority in Britain, that while Saddam is undoubtedly odious his regime does not constitute a threat outside his own borders. If he no longer has weapons of mass destruction (none found so far), then past failure to comply with UN resolutions is hardly sufficient grounds for launching a major war on a country whose population has already suffered a decade of blockade and bombing by the United States and Britain. And even if Iraq does retain such weapons, is it justifiable or sensible to launch a full-scale war, irrespective of whether it is approved by a United Nations browbeaten into acquiesence by the United States? After all, everyone knows that Israel has such weapons, and regularly fails to comply with UN resolutions, and on both counts is dependent on the support of the United States. And if Saddam still has weapons of mass destruction and could use them outside his borders (e.g., against Israel), then he is more likely – so the argument goes – to actually use them if there is a war. He would have little left to lose in a very one-sided contest between the hegemonic United States (population roughly 290 million, annual GDP over $10,000 billion, per capita GDP over $37,000) and a battered Iraq (population around 25 million, GDP approximately $26 billion, per capita GDP about $1,000). Even without the use of weapons of mass destruction, a war against Iraq could possibly destabilise the entire Middle East, topple the conservative regimes in Egypt and Saudia Arabia which are the main Arab allies of the United States, and stimulate terrorism to unprecedented levels, across the Islamic world and beyond. The script could have been written by Osama bin Laden.

So why attack Iraq? It is not certain that there will be a full-scale war, but given the scale of the preparations and despite contradictory messages from the Bush regime and from Bush himself, it is difficult to see at the moment how he could pull back without loss of face and damage to his chances of retaining the presidency in 2004. And despite the risks of war, there is no doubt that at least some of his 'Pentagon hawks' actually want to destabilise the Middle East so that the entire region – and its oil reserves – can be reshaped in the interests of the United States. There is, however, very little evidence that the talk of nation-building and democratisation following regime change would actually be implemented in Iraq, never mind in the region more widely. And here the present US puppet regime of Hamid Karzai in Afghanistan, with its continuing domination by the same drug-dealing (and US-bankrolled) warlords who dominated in pre-Taliban times, does not inspire confidence. The post-Second World War precedents of nation building in Germany and Japan are hardly relevant to a very different United States in completely different circumstances.

The horrors of Saddam's regime, and of Al Qaeda terrorism, are in their separate ways pretexts rather than the main issue (and Bush's associates, despite their best efforts, have completely failed to substantiate the alleged link between Al Qaeda and Iraq). The war on terrorism inaugurated after 11 September is not being properly fought, never mind won, requiring as it would an unconventional strategy against a new type of non-territorial, non-state enemy and measures which address some of the underlying motivations and causes of international terrorism. In fact this 'war' is at present being lost and the price continues to be paid by the innocent – by Australian tourists in Bali, for example, by hotel workers in Kenya, and by US innocents abroad such as the medical missionaries murdered in Yemen. Just like his Israeli surrogate Ariel Sharon, Bush is making life more, rather than less, dangerous for his own citizens. He is stimulating terrorism instead of countering it. Instead of an unconventional, new-fashioned 'war', his regime has opted for old-fashioned, conventional war. First there was the bombing war in Afghanistan which probably killed more innocent people than 11 September, but where at least the Taliban had provided a base for Al Qaeda and the former was defeated, though not the latter. And now, following on the Gulf War and the decade of US and UK bombing and blockade, a conventional war against the long-suffering Iraqis (for it is they who will suffer whether or not Saddam and his henchmen do). Why? Would anyone or anything other than an arrogant, bullying superpower get away with such apparent stupidity, cynicism and barbarity? Bush and Blair, the new barbarians?

Iraq's secular regime is actually an anathema to Al Qaeda. Iraqi Christians like Deputy Prime Minister Tariq Aziz have supported Saddam precisely because he did not come from a tradition of religious Islamic fundamentalism, but from Arab nationalism. It is not at all surprising that the alleged link with Al Qaeda is unsubstantiated. There is, however, a link of sorts, but it is to be found in the United States rather than Iraq. The terrrorism of 11 September 11 against the mainland United States has made it politically much easier for Bush to begin to implement America's grand design for world domination through war in the Middle East, and specifically against Iraq, something which was being actively considered long before September 2001.

As before, though now even clearer, the main issue is American hegemony and how it is to be maintained vis à vis allies and potential rivals. And they are not international terrorists but conventional states or groups of states, particularly the European Union, Russia and, perhaps most threatening in the longer term, China. The first anniversary of 11 September was marked by the Bush regime's new *National Security Strategy* in September 2002. For the first time it explicitly laid out and tried to justify its new aggresive global policy of: acting unilaterally if necessary; explicitly asserting a right to make pre-emptive first strikes if feeling threatened (a dangerous precedent which others could legitimately follow); and never allowing its military supremacy to be challenged by any rival superpower (a warning perhaps to China) (*The Guardian*, 21 September 2002, and <www.whitehouse.gov>).

The advance of rivals must be blocked before they get any stronger – the present hegemonic gap between the United States and all potential rivals must be made even wider – in the view of some surprisingly *un*confident US hegemonists. They believe that a window of opportunity for decisive action to widen the hegemonic gap is now provided by the combination of 11 September 11 preparing domestic opinion for war, Saddam's Iraq providing an easy target (as well as the world's second largest oil reserves), and the remaining two years of the Bush presidency. The opportunity must be grasped before the window closes: a pre-emptive stike against Iraq as part of Bush's 'axis of evil' could, they believe, substantially widen the gap and ensure Bush another four years in the White House, and presumably more opportunities for war games of world domination. At the very least it could guarantee US hegemony for another generation (the benefits comparable to, and building directly on, those from Reagan's decisive move against the 'evil empire' of the USSR – Reagan, rather than his 'one-term' father, being Bush jnr's preferred model). Already, the comparatively modest military action against Afghanistan's weak Taliban regime has been instrumental not only in opening US access to central Asian oilfields but in changing the geopolitical map of Asia to the detriment of China and Russia, with US military bases as well as commercial interests now more tightly encircling both of these potential rivals.

The concern or lack of confidence about the long-term future of US hegemony, which seems unjustified in terms of present military strength, makes more sense when hegemony is also seen as depending on relative economic strength, not only on geopolitics but also on political economy. In terms of civil power US supremacy is by no means assured, with for instance the European Union already of comparable economic weight even before its impending enlargement, and China clearly an emerging economic giant with its fast growth rate and the world's largest national population. But here it is also clear that *military* power can be used to strengthen *civil* or economic power, as well as being sometimes in contradiction to it, as we have seen. More generally, and despite the dating of contemporary history, recent developments have supported the argument that more is concealed than is revealed by counterposing the labels civil/military, neo-liberal/neo-conservative and unilateral/multilateral.

The characterisation of current US hegemonic strategy as unilateral multilateralism has been vindicated with Bush operating (so far?) through the multilateral United Nations on Iraq, but very much on his own unilateral 'take it or leave it' terms, reserving the right to act alone if necessary while at the same time undermining the United Nations by imposing his own agenda on it. In the case of the action against Afghanistan it was suggested that US access to Central Asian oil was a sub-plot, but now in the case of Iraq some see oil as the drama's main plot. They point to the fact that the US economy is increasingly reliant on imported oil – as are some of its main allies and competitors such as Japan and the European Union – and that more direct US control in the Middle East would give the US oil companies prime access to the world's main reserves and an economic advantage over competitors. It would also pre-empt the possibility of OPEC countries determining oil prices (which for instance President Chavez of Venezuela has tried to do). Thus the use of military power would directly boost the economic power of the United States and of its immediate allies.

This goes some way towards explaining Blair's support for Bush despite the latter exposing the pretentions of the Blair government's so-called 'ethical foreign policy'. British and other oil companies are already jockeying for their share of the spoils in a post-war Iraq. What we are seeing here, as in the Gulf War, is military struggle over the world's increasingly scarce natural resources. As modern capitalism continues to exploit these to destruction, such resource wars are likely to become more common – a return to 'primitive accumulation', or stealing the resources of other countries. Oil is now at the forefront of this emerging trend, and as oilfields and oil pipelines are inherently geo-political as well as geo-economic, we are seeing the return of geopolitics to centre stage and resource wars becoming perhaps the major arena for the struggle over hegemony.

With this comes the increasing prominence of neo-conservative attitudes and ideology, but again in support of the previously hegemonic neo-liberalism rather than an alternative to it. If necessary, the one true development model of liberal democracy, private property and free enterprise has to imposed by force (except of course when the United States or the European Union feel the need for some protectionism). Despite oil's undoubted importance (and the oil industry background of Bush, Cheney, Rumsfeld, Rice et al.), we cannot reduce the question of war to material interests as narrowly defined as oil companies. Other forms of capital and other interests are involved. The issue is the more general one of hegemony and it cannot be understood in purely economic terms, any more than it can explained only in terms of politics and military power. Nor can it be understood without seeing its contradictions as opportunities for its opponents. The hegemonic gap between the United States and potential rivals may be unprecedented, but so too is the global opposition to the Bush regime and to the very idea that hegemony is an acceptable way to run the global system.

Calling 911: Geopolitics, Security and America's New War

SIMON DALBY

11 September (911)

As news spread of the first airplane crash into New York's World Trade Center horror and disbelief mingled. The emergency services rushed to the scene as fast as the TV news stations turned their cameras on the first burning tower. The second plane impact and explosion apparently turned what might simply have been a disaster into an attack. Disaster and war, vulnerability and anger, insecurity and fear melded with grief and horror. War vied with disaster tropes to make sense of the video images of planes flying into buildings, collapsing towers, and desperate people. The rubble and the ominous clouds of smoke became, in a phrase that linked back to the earlier nightmare fears of nuclear war, 'ground zero'. Given the number of dead in and under the rubble of the towers the term had an undeniable tragic aptness.

In the immediate aftermath of the terrible destruction of 11 September the political assumption in presidential statements and media commentary was that America was at war. The logos on TV screens specified events as an 'Attack on America'. In the days following 11 September the Cable News Network (CNN) adopted the theme of 'America's New War' to frame its coverage. But nearly as quickly as the state of war was declared it was also supposedly clear that this is a new form of warfare. Apparently, it was obviously America's and new and war. That it was American was supposedly self-evident given the airplanes crashing into the World Trade Center and the Pentagon. That this was new was obvious in the sense that hijacking had been combined with a 'suicide' bombing, and that mode of attack had not been tried before in the mainland United States. In a tragic twist on the cultural theme of everything being bigger in America, the scale of the death and destruction was also much larger. But in what sense was this war? The category came quickly to many lips, but no other state declared war, nothing else warlike happened. A strangely ominous silence filled the discursive space where political declarations were expected. The rituals of international statecraft and above all the performance of sovereignty in the face of its violation was apparently an entirely one-sided affair.

   In the two weeks after the plane crashes, as the theme of mourning took over from the initial focus on the disaster, law enforcement officials in the United States and abroad arrested various suspects and investigated connections, accomplices, bank accounts and stock market speculations possibly connected with Al Qaeda and various other organisations whose names suddenly appeared in the media on a daily basis. Crime and law enforcement kept trying to sneak into the script just as most politicians assured the anxious public that war was indeed the overarching narrative. Pearl Harbor and the designation of 'infamy' to describe 11 September was also in circulation in a reflection of Hollywood's recent recreation of the events of fifty years earlier; *Life* magazine was conveniently selling copies of its commemorative Pearl Harbor edition.[1]

   While fighter jets were scrambled and naval ships sailed to New York, the predominant visual themes were of firefighters and rescue personnel struggling to get near the burning towers in hopes of finding people alive under the rubble. As the toll of death and injury became clear it was not always easy to see these people as casualties. No guns were fired in anger. Who precisely the enemy was remained a mystery, although speculation quickly centred on Osama bin Laden and his apparently international terror network. National security had obviously been breached in the form of the hole in the side of the Pentagon; US military personnel had died in the crash there and the subsequent fire. This attack on a military target had the look of war about it in a way that the collapsed towers of the World Trade Center didn't. But the political ambiguities left a discursive and political space open for political leaders to fill with their specifications of events and appropriate responses to this new geopolitical situation.

Geopolitics

Geopolitics is about how 'the world is actively "spatialized", divided up, labeled, sorted out into a hierarchy of places of greater or lesser 'importance' by political geographers, other academics and political leaders. This process provides the geographical framing within which political elites and mass publics act in the world in pursuit of their own identities and interests.'[2] It is both knowledge and power, a mode of making sense of the world that facilitates action, asserts identity and justifies both. The dominant themes in modern geopolitics are the view of the world as a single entity, but a politically divided whole, its presentation in terms of places ranked in terms of their similarities to Euro-American notions of development and democratic accomplishment, and a focus on the nation state as the primary political entity that matters in struggles for primacy.

   But geopolitics is also about the performance of political acts, the specifications of friends and enemies, the designations of spaces as theirs and ours, the distinctions between hostile and friendly places and peoples. These are practices of political reasoning that can be challenged and critiqued by an investigation of their implicit geographical formulations and how these structure the arguments.[3] Geopolitics is also about the construction of popular identities, of masculinities, citizenships and quotidian cultural practices which both specify cultural norms and provide the political terms that can be interpellated in political discourse in a crisis.[4] Challenging the geographical specifications of power is part of what critical geopolitics writers have been doing for some time.[5] In line with this concern in recent scholarship this essay starts with a series of comments and reflections on the dominant themes in the saturation coverage of the events of 911 in the American mass media in September 2001. It does so because precisely which geopolitical tropes are invoked in political performance in a crisis matter; these are part of the arguments for specific forms of action.[6] The title of this essay, 'calling 911', points to the importance of these political debates; how an event is 'called', to use the sporting phrase, is an important part of geopolitical practice.

In the case of 911 many of the crucial decisions were made quickly and were made public in a discursive attempt to restore the tarnished structures of American security that had been so dramatically ruptured by the spectacular violence in New York and Washington. They were also apparently a political necessity to reassure the populace that retaliation would be forthcoming; many of the popular geopolitical tropes in circulation, not least the formulation of matters as 'Attack on America' in the media, required that there be a military response. This is not to suggest either a political consensus on the part of administration officials or that the dominant script was not contested by intense debates as to what ought to be done and by whom. The rivalry between the Department of Defense and the State Department repeatedly spilled over into public discussion; whose policy was winning this struggle was also part of the daily media coverage. The subsequent debate about the 'axis of evil' and the possibilities of attacking Iraq show clearly that there were major disagreements and political struggles over the precise responses that were needed.

But nonetheless there are at least three crucial geopolitical formulations in the initial media discussion and official statements that structure the dominant narratives and the political justifications for action. The first was that war was indeed the appropriate response in the circumstances. This frequently went unquestioned in the subsequent months in the United States. The script of a violent attack requiring a violent response was assumed even if there was no obvious assailant with a territorial base that could be attacked in response. The second assumption, that it was America's war, perhaps appeared most obvious and has had repercussions for what can be and has been done, and above all for how the whole event can be understood. The predominant geographical assumption in all that has followed is that this was an external attack on America and can only be understood in these terms. But there is more to this geography, not least the argument that while the attacks were on American concrete, if not American soil, the political fight that triggered them was one that had a more specific geographical focus in Arabia. Third were the frequent and directly related arguments that such an attack requires violent and powerful responses rather than any serious attempt to investigate the causes of the 11 September violence. Indeed, discussing the causes, and inevitably the complex geographies of these, was sometimes dismissed as nigh on unpatriotic in the United States. War talk frequently silenced careful reflection, but did so on the basis of a complicit geography, a geography that specified matters as a simple spatial violation, an external attack on an innocent, supposedly safe interior.

To illustrate how these practices and performances might be read very differently the latter parts of the essay invoke a series of historical analogies on the theme of empire suggesting that there are very different spatialities that might be invoked to read the events of 911 and the significance of the political responses. The suggestion is that the modern geopolitical reasoning of political elites in America in particular, but in other states as well, constrains the interpretation of the politics precisely because they operate in terms of a political ontology of states whether understood as autonomous actors, or in a more sophisticated sociology, as a society of states.[7] In Agnew's terms the primary entities, although not the only geopolitical, actors are states.[8] The argument that follows eschews detailed analysis of the rapidly growing literature interpreting various aspects of the 911 events in favour of an analysis of the most obvious broadly articulated facets of the geopolitical reasoning invoked in the justifications for military action. The focus in what follows is explicitly on political identity and the geographical assumptions implicit in the articulation of American responses to the September events.

The key, deliberately provocative, suggestion in the latter parts of this essay is that understanding geopolitics in other terms, and specifically in terms of the theme of empire, offers a useful alternative interpretative framework for 911. Specifically, the latter sections of the essay suggest that the media and elite political framing of the events and aftermath were only partly 'American' and novel in a narrow sense only, and a perpetuation of an old pattern of American war-fighting, one that was frequently forgotten in commentary and analysis in the last few months of 2001. Above all else, the geographical specifications of the terms of the conflict are of crucial importance in assessing the appropriate response to the events of 911. But they are linked inextricably with matters of political identity, and the American identities of innocent victim, autonomous polity and virtuous world citizen are structured in ways that deny the construction of contemporary world politics in terms of empire.

Making Sense/Making War

The point here is that geopolitical scripts might have been otherwise; the events could have been specified as a disaster, an act of madness or perhaps most obviously as a crime, an act that required careful police work internationally and in the United States. Clearly there were struggles within the administration in Washington between the Department of Defense, the White House and the State Department over how precisely to handle the response. There are also ongoing conflicts between agencies in the United States over roles, mandates, jurisdictions and responsibilities which will no doubt continue, and these are influenced in some manner by American allies in NATO and elsewhere. But a solely diplomatic and police initiative would have required a different series of assumptions concerning the nature of world order and the appropriate political responses under international law. In particular, it would have required a specification of matters in terms of overarching authorities beyond the United States and consequently a specification of complex political obligations other than an immediate invocation of the right of self defence on the part of a single state and some of its allies.

Tony Blair, the British prime minister, seized the moment on 12 September in a widely reported press conference where he repeatedly used a geopolitical rhetoric that specified matters in terms of a war between democracy and the rest, portraying the death and destruction in New York as a global attack on freedom. Once the invocation of war was issued and loosely agreed to by political leaders and media commentators in the United States many things changed very quickly. Isolationist sentiments in the Bush administration collapsed as fast as the towers of the World Trade Center. From the rubble came presidential anger and a rapid rebuilding of diplomatic links to regimes in many places and assertions of American leadership in a war against terrorism. NATO invoked Article 5 of its treaty, and the French media suggested that 'we are all Americans now'; Canadians placed American flags in their windows and expressed their sympathy publicly in a huge gathering on Parliament Hill in Ottawa. The United States speedily settled its outstanding debts to the United Nations, which in turn passed a resolution supporting American actions in its own self-defence.

The world had changed, said the TV pundits and the newspaper columnists, but quite how remained a mystery as the geopolitical specification of the terrain of conflict was decidedly obscure beyond the initial invocation of external threat from terrorism.[9] Enemies that had once seemed dangerous but distant were now enlarged into global threats; Osama bin Laden's face immediately became the icon of evil and the symbol for each days' daily denunciation. The presidential discourse drew lines between those that were on America's side or those that were on the side of the terrorists, the polarisation dynamic of conflict was set in motion hastily; them and us, freedom versus terror reprised the themes of earlier American wars, both hot and cold.[10] But quite where to draw the lines was much less clear than 11 years earlier, when the previous President Bush had insisted on drawing them metaphorically in the sand somewhere between Kuwait and Iraq. Now, too, the danger seemed horribly close in comparison. Hijacked airliners over New York and Washington are not at all like Iraqi tanks in distant Kuwait. On 11 September the US military, for all its firepower and high-technology surveillance systems, had been spectacularly thwarted by boxcutters, basic pilot training and the grim determination to die for a cause.

If the world had changed, the script of war hadn't. An attack of the magnitude of 11 September demanded an enemy, as the analogy with Pearl Harbor suggested. No credible claim to responsibility emerged; the hijackers died as at least some of them had apparently planned. The threat to hunt down those responsible was lacking precisely because those who committed the act had put themselves beyond punishment. Enemies were found by the simple expedient of arguing that those who planned, and those who harboured those who planned, were all the enemy. The besieged and impoverished Taliban regime in Afghanistan quickly became the target and the centre of numerous geopolitical depictions, many of which became entangled in discussion of the history of the Cold War and American involvement in arming the Mujahedeen. Cartographers for magazines and newspapers were kept busy; tallies of tanks and airplanes, bases and weapons adorned these explanatory images.[11] This once again looked like a war with depictions of communication routes, campaign options and military capabilities. But the utility of sending million-dollar missiles to destroy empty tents seemed more than a little dubious. There was obviously more to this and yet less than the maps could depict.

Initial tropes of cowardice concerning the hijackers rapidly gave way to ones of madness. Dying for the cause is apparently difficult to depict as cowardly, even to the surviving victims of the attacks, although Susan Sontag and a number of other commentators got into trouble for expressing this obvious point. Moral denigration there might be, but insanity and obsession work better. Invocations of primitiveness in the media, and suggestions of hijackers thinking in the terms of much earlier centuries, pitted modernity against the religious obsessions of the deluded. The release, by the FBI, of at least some of the pages of the letter supposedly left behind by the perpetrators of the aircraft hijackings on 11 September emphasized the strangeness of religious martyrdom when read through the lenses of modern categories. But to those who read military history it seemed eerily familiar, a clash of mutually incomprehensible moral codes reminiscent of many confrontations between Western military forces and a non-Western warrior ethos.[12]

The practices of othering escalated quickly with 'Islamic fundamentalist' the appropriate category and the rhetoric of jihad the practice of evil. While the dangers of vigilante action in the United States, and elsewhere among those states that identified with the victims in New York, were considerable they were in part quelled by political leaders anxious to minimise the dangers of domestic disturbances which would distract police efforts. American leaders visited mosques; interfaith services tried to bridge the gaps between religions. Above all state competence to deal with 'threats' had to be obviously reasserted in the face of its dramatic and catastrophic failure on 11 September.

Globalisation and Insecurity

Insecurity in the face of threat/disaster there was in abundance on 11 September, and it is here that the link between invocations of war and practical policing meet; calling for help requires security personnel but 911 reaches emergency services rather than the military. In the short term dealing with the disaster required fire services and police, hospitals and ambulances, searcher dogs and construction crews. Insecurity connects to risks and to disasters, threats are not here a matter of traditional military action, the boundaries between civil defence, emergency preparedness and military action were blurred in a manner that suggests that things have changed, at least in so far as the conventional distinctions between civil and military, war and disaster, risk and security no longer operate in the circumstances of 11 September.

The geography had apparently changed too; the assumption that America itself was relatively immune to terrorism, despite the earlier 1993 bomb in the basement of the World Trade Center, and the Oklahoma bombing of 1995, was no longer valid. What could reach New York was apparently obviously now a 'global' threat. Ballistic missile defences seemed absurdly inappropriate when boxcutters and martyrdom would do to inflict huge damage on America's infrastructure and symbols; and yet building such a system was subsequently accelerated by the war psychosis that gripped Washington. Insecurity is now indelibly tied to the horrifying images of burning and collapsing towers. As chaos in airports in many places, not least Canada where numerous flights were diverted, subsided, 'security' for travelers became once again a matter of pressing importance. The survivalist stores and gunshops in the United States sold gas masks, guns and all sorts of supplies to an anxious public unsure as to where the danger lay or who the enemy was; insecurity was both a matter of state and a matter that was very personal as anthrax contaminated the American postal system and killed apparently at random.

Florida once again featured in American politics, this time as a pilot training ground for the would-be hijackers. External dangers are in here too; geography is no comfort from dangers from outside. But that has not stopped the impulse to reinscribe security in spatial tropes, to assume that 'homeland defence', in the new language of American thinking, is a matter primarily of border controls.[13] Clearly tropes of inside and outside are in play here as foreign dangers are invoked to try to keep illegal acts at bay. But the point that some of the hijackers were legally resident in the United States and that the weapons, training and skills needed to carry out the attacks were gained within the boundaries of the United States stretched arguments about 'keeping the bad guys out' as the most appropriate mode of dealing with the possibilities of further attacks.

'Global' threats have long been a concern in American security thinking.[14] Although quite what makes them global as opposed to threats to specific facets of American life is frequently less than clear. Worries about rogue states equipped with ballistic missiles and weapons of mass destruction were high on the second Bush administration's concerns; other threats had nonetheless been part of the policy landscape too. From concerns with the proliferation of nuclear weapons through worries about chemical and biological weapons, not to mention drugs, environmental degradation, demographic change and all manner of international crimes, the post-Cold War security discussion had extended the discussion of American national security far beyond the traditional themes of war and peace.[15]

All this can in part perhaps be explained by looking to the discussions of the geopolitics of risk society with its complex borderless technological dangers and mobile protagonists.[16] Such formulations seemed an eerily apt and unsettling summation of matters as the rescue workers struggled with the rubble in New York. The sheer inventiveness of the planning of the September hijackings suggests that technological risks are now merging into themes of political violence. The potential for sabotage and criminal acts to unleash technological disasters has been demonstrated clearly;

abstract discussions of terrorist acts on nuclear power stations or water supply systems has been eclipsed by the use of mundane everyday technologies as brutally effective weapons. The tropes of global terrorism link to the discussion of risk society in a number of ways, not least the way in which distant developments have local consequences.

Viewed in terms of the geopolitics of risk society the consequences of political actions in distant places can be presented as having come back to haunt America. Afghanistan and the support by the CIA and related agencies for those fighting the Soviet Union are part of the story of the birth of 'global' terrorism. The presence of American troops in the Gulf is part of the rationale given by bin Laden for attacks such as those of 11 September. Blowback in the classic espionage sense of the term this probably wasn't, but the interconnections between earlier conflicts and current ones are inescapable. These violate the basic geopolitical cartography that these were the kind of events that happened somewhere else, not on inviolate American soil.[17]

But the geography of these attacks was not so new as widespread assumptions that something fundamentally new had happened suggested. In so far as risk society calls into question the geopolitical cartography of borders prior episodes have also violated American borders in analogous ways. In 1993 the World Trade Center had been attacked by the use of a truck bomb in the basement. While there were casualties, the damage to the complex was relatively minor. The Oklahoma city bombing some years later had suggested that large buildings in the United States were targets of terrorist attacks, although once it became clear that Timothy McVeigh was an American, rather than a foreigner, the geographical script of America invulnerable once again became prominent. The crucial connection of McVeigh's disillusionment with American power in the aftermath of his involvement in the Gulf War suggests a connection here again with the geopolitics of the Middle East, but that theme has not been much commented upon.[18] McVeigh has been executed; that episode is closed.

Morality and Exceptionalism

Some of the outrage in New York in particular was apparently because the conventional categories didn't work; the explanatory schemes available to make sense of the events were obviously inadequate. Part of this was because of the sheer scale of the atrocity. In the absence of any alternative the invocation of war was perhaps inevitable. Once invoked the widespread cultural assumptions of what war now involved quickly suggested that retaliation was necessary. America was not invulnerable after all. Someone had to pay. Many American commentators and a substantial part of the population clearly thought so. Anger and war combined with the sense of a profound spatial violation of security. The long historical construction of American exceptionalism, of the United States as a moral, virtuous and innocent community in the face of an evil world, was added to the sense of violation to demand retribution and military action.[19]

The point about morality and justification is especially clear in the arguments from Rudolph Giuliani, the mayor of New York. When offered a donation of ten million US dollars by Saudi Prince Alwaleed bin Talal to aid the victims of 11 September, Giuliani turned the offer down because the Prince suggested that American foreign policy ought to be rethought. The Prince's statement suggested that 'at times like this one, we must address some of the issues that led to such a criminal attack. I believe the government of the United States of America should re-examine its policies in the Middle East and adopt a more balanced stance toward the Palestinian cause'. Giuliani's response was revealing: 'There is no moral equivalence to this attack. There is no justification for it. The people who did it lost any right to ask for justification for it when they slaughtered four or five thousand innocent people, and to suggest that there is only invites this happening in the future.'[20] Giuliani refused the donation, suggesting that there was no moral equivalence between the acts of the hijackers and the consequences of American foreign policy.[21]

The rhetorical move was repeated numerous times. Henry Kissinger appeared on CNN asserting that the events were 'a fundamental moral challenge to civilization'. More interesting in all this is the crucial rhetorical shift in the logic. Explanation is equated with justification in this script. The consequences might be just what Giuliani fears. And they may well be so precisely because of the formulation of these matters as exceptional, beyond the normal logics of politics and responsibility. The construction of these events as unrelated to the long history of violence in various parts of the Muslim world conveys a moral rectitude to the American war effort which is thus justified in its violence against the Taliban and Al Qaeda. The possibility that this might subsequently foment yet further attacks on the United States is discounted by the formulation of the attack on the twin towers in terms of a singular event rather than part of a long and bloody history. Thus American action, too, is excused from the possible consequences that might ensue in the future.

The scale of the event and the invocation of both novelty and evil structured the discursive terrain in ways that left little room for discussions of complexity or considerations of the reasons that might have caused the violence. Such arguments challenge the master script of the United States as innocent victim by suggesting that 11 September is part of a complex historical process in which responsibility is not so easy to assign. In response arguments suggested that moral proportionality is wrong, indeed arguments about connections across borders have been frequently dismissed as treasonous. The implication was that America has never done anything remotely as violent as the Trade Center attacks. Opportunities to learn from the episode are squandered in the angry assertion of Americanismo. Such is the polarising dynamic of war talk with its geopolitical constructions of the contrast between our place and theirs. The overarching story is one of innocence and the desire for brutal retaliation, violent acts that the American public wants and which presidential speeches quickly promised to deliver. The military obliged a few weeks later.

Geopolitical Reasoning

But as David Campbell pointed out at some length in his analysis of the Gulf war, the denial of responsibility, by in this earlier case the drawing of lines in the sand, operated to construct geographically separate entities.[22] The abrogation of responsibility is made possible by a form of geopolitical reasoning that specifies separate spheres of political life demarcated by territorial borders. Spheres that are then, in a reprise of the basic premises of international relations thinking, granted sovereignty and hence agency, the ability to act as autonomous entities and thus can be portrayed as having to accept the full responsibility for their actions.[23] Whether read as the assertion of autonomous machismo, the operation of legitimate self defence, or an appropriate move in a strategic contest, the geographical and historical isolationism works to prepare the conceptual grounds for acts of violence. It does so by invoking the most powerful geopolitical reasoning of separate spaces, of here and there, us and them.

In the aftermath of the September events themes from Samuel Huntingdon's 'Clash of Civilizations' argument were recycled in many commentaries, where the perpetrators of the violence on the World Trade towers and the Pentagon were constructed as antithetical to modernity, deluded members of a culture that was fundamentally alien to America, progress, reason, and every other good thing that reasonable Western people understood as universal values.[24] The language of battle lines and civilisations, fundamental divisions and Western superiority seemed to fit the moment, at least to some politicians, the Italian prime minister only being the most high profile.[25] Frantic attempts by coalition politicians, Tony Blair in particular, to suggest that the Islam was not the enemy, that this was a matter of democracy or freedom or law against terror, repeatedly ran into the difficulties of geopolitical specification of the sides to this dispute.

Given the record of many of the regimes in south-west Asia such logic was bound to have fragile purchase. Instabilities there require, so the rich and powerful assure their Western patrons, the activities of repression and social control. The portrayal of the military dictator of nuclear-armed Pakistan, a state under sanction for some years as a result of its nuclear activities, as a friend of the West, and a crucial coalition supporter, stretched this particular trope to amazing lengths. But such are the dynamics of polarisation, the processes of specifying friend and enemy in a crisis, that this discursive conjuring trick appeared to work, despite the commentaries and debates broadcast by Al Jazeera.

But the difficulties of defining the sides to this dispute are especially revealing because the cartographies of violence do not work very effectively in the absence of a clearly demarcated territorial enemy. Lines of distinction between friend and enemy were being drawn in various ways. The impulse to redefine internal threats in the language of homeland defence in the United States was mirrored elsewhere. Civil liberties were curtailed; American and Canadian legislation quickly worked to expand the ability of law enforcement agencies to tap phones and electronic communication. But such innovations have long been standard practices in Western Europe where 'terrorism' has been an unfortunate part of the political landscape. Nonetheless the impulse to strengthen security agencies and reassert social control over marginal populations, political dissidents and recent immigrants from places that might potentially have terrorist sympathisers has reasserted itself powerfully; justified by the rhetorics of war and security, and the crucial geopolitical trope of homeland defence. The moral panic, in the aftermath of the Columbine High School episode, over dangerous students and violence in high schools, has been rearticulated in terms of the dangers to America from all sorts of others, the connections between violence abroad now at least tentatively connected to domestic concerns within the moral order of America.[26]

The moral exceptionalism and the difficulties with appropriate geopolitical specifications made dissent difficult. The sharp dividing lines between friend and foe drawn by President Bush made opposing military actions especially difficult precisely because of the nature of the Taliban which was hard to understand as anything except theocratic or, perhaps more specifically, Pashtun fascism. The discursive field was polarised to such an extent that there were very considerable dangers of critics of American foreign policy ending up in the impossible political position of supporting the Taliban. That said, the situation was even more complicated because the Taliban and Northern Alliance were easy to portray as equally undesirable political regimes due to the intense militarisation of their populations, the revival of 'traditional' themes of violence and torture in combat and the treatment of prisoners. This point was understood by American policy makers, although their attempts to deal with the difficulties by constructing a new government in exile seemed to have borne fruit early in 2002.

The geopolitical language was further complicated when the debate about trying to make sense of the 11 September events was tied into an investigation of Osama bin Laden's statements.[27] Some of the rhetoric of the land of the 'two holy places' and the desire to remove the infidels and crusaders from this sacred soil was easy enough to translate into a territorial version of the defence of the Umma, or the community of the faithful. The Palestinian dimension was likewise not hard to render in the language of national liberation, although this gets more difficult if the whole of Palestine is the territory under consideration. Neither are references to the division of the Middle East by European powers after the demise of the Ottoman empire as the source of many contemporary political difficulties all that hard to understand in contemporary geopolitical terms.[28] But where, in bin Laden's more recent statements, all Americans are the enemy and the language of purification enters the picture; these statements read more like ethnic cleansing. These territorial specifications of absolute enemies reflect a violence beyond compromise which was a mirror image of the Bush administration rhetoric of rooting out evil; Osama bin Laden wanted dead or alive.

On a spectacular scale the lesson of 11 September may well finally be a recognition that the splendid isolation of America as a separate continent, a geopolitics of separation, is no longer tenable. The connections of globalisation are finally reaching into the geographical categories of Americans in a way that demands that they understand themselves as interconnected to the rest of the world, even if in most cases the population remains unaware of most of the details of either historical or contemporary connections. But the enemy has been specified as global terror or terror with a global reach. The specification of the world into wild zones and tame zones, with the danger to the tame zones of democratic states coming from the wild zones, a popular cartography of danger in the American security discourses of the mid 1990s, seems to have been prophetic.[29] Afghanistan is clearly a wild zone, a source of terror and danger beyond the fringes of civilisation where wanted terrorists seek refuge and friends among the warriors lurking beyond the reach of law and order.

New Wars/Old Wars

The difficulties of specifying the events of 11 September into either conventional tropes of war, or constraining them within simple categories of inside and outside, the geopolitical reasoning that provides the explanatory context for violence in Afghanistan, suggests that new languages and political strategies are necessary to make sense of current events. As noted above, the geopolitics of risk society offers some analytical help but there is more to the geographies of insecurity highlighted by 911 than are easily captured in its themes of interconnection and complex manufactured insecurity. But old habits die hard; the cartography of violence in the places that are still designated Afghanistan, despite the absence of most of the normal attributes of statehood, illustrates the continuing fixation of a simple cartographic description in circumstances where sovereignty has to be intensely simulated to render the categories of political action meaningful.[30] Hence the explicit American doctrine of targeting states that harbour terrorists. But the geography in this formulation implicitly recognises the inadequacies of such geopolitical designations. Clearly violence is not constrained to the territories of either of the protagonists.

This point about the inadequate maps of war suggests, in an ironic but apt juxtaposition with CNN's designation of contemporary events as 'America's new war', that Mary Kaldor's arguments that the post-Cold War period has produced a 'new' form of war may provide some analytical help. She argues that, on the one hand, contemporary warfare draws on the reaffirmation of particular political identities, often in violent ways, but on the other hand, does so in a globalised economy where weapons and communications freely flow across numerous boundaries.[31] The new globalised circumstances make the military cartography of clear national boundaries, as was the case during the historical period of European rivalry, and the more recent geography of nearly impermeable bloc boundaries during the Cold War confrontation, irrelevant.

Now cell phones, the Internet, offshore trading companies and international arms markets mesh with ethnic divisions. Crucially, all these connect up with local militias' struggles to monopolise control over resources in particular places, and hence gain the revenues from supplying them to global markets.[32] The crucial point in Kaldor's analysis is that the assumptions of warfare happening between mutually exclusive spatial entities, whether at the state level or, during the Cold War, the scale of geopolitical blocs, no longer holds after the Cold War. Permeable boundaries and shifting alliances mark the struggles of local militias and the local political economies of warfare in specific places. Enemies no longer so obviously control territories; violence is often constrained to particular places but its connections spill over the territorial boundaries of conventional geopolitical cartographies.

In the case of Afghanistan emeralds and heroin among other commodities were exported to provide the weapons and ammunition to keep the various factions fighting through the 1990s. The attempt by the Taliban regime to reassert a form of political order that does not rely on drugs may have been at least partly genuine in the last few years of their rule but the political economy of new wars seems inescapable. Resource flows are a major source of funding to maintain power in local areas. But in many of the cases of Kaldor's 'new wars', local particularisms, whether in the form of nationalism, ethnic identity or religious affiliation, have been supported from afar by diasporic populations, through fundraising, political contacts and weapon purchases. This is the pattern of warfare in what she calls the 'global era' where the economic connections between the wild zones and tame zones are a crucial part of what keeps the violence going.

This pattern of ongoing violence which partly explained the post-Soviet situation in Afghanistan collided with another struggle involving Al Qaeda and Osama bin Laden. But this is one that might be best understood in a geopolitical frame of reference entirely different from the specification of the events of late 2001 as 'America's New War' with a terrorism understood in 'global' tropes. Instead, it might be better understood as an internal struggle within the Islamic world, and Saudi Arabia in particular, over the future of the kingdom and who best determines the form of Islam practised at its geographical heart.[33] Viewed in these terms, the events of 11 September can be read differently if one suspends the geographical focus on the United States and thinks about other geographies of conflict. Osama bin Laden then becomes part of Saudi diasporic politics, just one more, admittedly powerful, exile plotting revenge and a return to the homeland and glory. His lieutenants in the 11 September attack, mainly Saudis and some Egyptians, who had lived as students in Germany as well as the United States, fit the pattern of diasporic politics with the important exception that they attacked in the United States rather than indirectly supporting violence in the homeland. Focusing on Afghanistan and 'global' terror networks occludes the geographical specificity of the protagonists in important ways. And this geography matters.

Understood in these terms the attack on America can be read as a strategy to involve the Americans in the struggle in the Middle East more directly in a classic strategic move of horizontal conflict escalation where an impasse triggers a strategy of broadening the conflict.[34] While bin Laden himself might not aspire to head an Islamic state after the collapse of the house of Saud, his strategy of extending the war to America might be entirely strategically rational if the object is to increase the political stresses in Riyadh between various factions in the ruling house by unleashing American-lead destabilising violence in the region. It was a reasonable military strategy to assume that such violence might well trigger a revolt within Saudi Arabia and the possibility of the overthrow of the monarchy.[35]

In this regard the complex international politics of dissidents in exile is also relevant; political actors abroad can be a serious challenge to order. The irony of Wahhabi-inspired and Saudi-funded schools training the fighters in the Taliban movement is considerable although not without historic parallel. Although Osama bin Laden's 'disappearance' at the end of 2001 lead to much speculation, it seems unlikely that anyone is going to follow the example of the German government with Lenin in 1917, and put bin Laden on a plane to Riyadh to plot the overthrow of another hopelessly corrupt monarchy. Osama bin Laden's use of video tapes to spread his message is also reminiscent of the earlier use of audio tapes by Iranian clerics in exile in Paris in the 1970s, even if the latter did not have the benefit of Al Jazeera's television coverage to further discussions of their political views. Such ironies and complexities add many dimensions to the understanding of the events of 11 September.

In the North American mainstream media 11 September was initially largely, but obviously not entirely, understood as a simple, mostly inexplicable act of violence directed at America, rather than at American foreign policy, or more particularly at its support of the Saudi regime and the presence of American troops on 'holy ground'. The war is specified as an American one, not as a struggle within the Saudi elite, or more generally in the Middle East. The geography in this scripting of events has little to do with complex diasporic politics, political economies of resource control, power and violence at distances from the metropole. The United States is, in the language of moral exceptionalism, the aggrieved victim rather than a political player in a much bigger and more complex drama.

But the geopolitical specifications of this drama matter in determining how one should act, which identity to assert and whom to drop bombs on in retaliation. Despite the fact that the hijackers on 911 were mainly Saudi citizens, Afghanistan was the target of military action.[36] Connections between the Saudi royal family and the American military were noted in the media coverage, as were discussions of Al Jazeera and the role of allies in the 'coalition', but the larger canvas and long history of oil power and privilege and the sense of grievance on the part of much of the population in the region frequently got short shrift in the specification of politics as that which the rulers of the various states do in the region.[37] Once again its seems that the most obvious geographical specifications of the world in political discourse are key to understanding how power works.

Imperial Power

All this suggests that the geopolitical specifications of power in the post-911 war situation matter in terms of how contemporary violence is rendered intelligible. Diasporas and monarchies, remote refuges attacked by technologically superior military force operating at great distances, exotic plots and elite assurances of control and security all suggest an imperial situation much more than they suggest the neat territorial boxes of sovereign states and warfare as something that states do to each other. Revolts and insurgencies, disruptions in the remote provinces, political marriages and unstable alliances with dubious fair-weather friends are the stuff of imperial drama. The cultural motifs of such understandings are obvious. 'Star wars' movies had given us the logic of empire with its ruling centre on Coruscant, the completely urban planet from where the empire is ruled, well before Ridley Scott gave us 'Gladiator' with Rome as a fragile idea worth fighting for and the figure of Maximus Decimus Meridius struggling with the precepts of Stoicism in the violent contingency of slavery. Gladiators and extreme sports fed into excess, the cultural theme of America in the 1990s; the trivial distractions of sexual indiscretions among the very powerful titillated the patricians in Washington and amused the plebeians everywhere else. Computer entertainment was dominated by games of 'Civilization' and the various 'Ages of Empire' with their explicit scripts and strategies of imperial power.

In cultural terms we in the 'West' who write geopolitical articles live in an imperial era, but the state-centric categories of American social science, coupled to the anti-imperial ethos of American exceptionalism, make this very difficult to articulate. America in its exceptionalism may be many things, but surely, so the argument goes, not an empire. That is part of the European experience, the corrupt flawed societies, that have been superseded by the enlightened republicanism of the New World. But the connections between such enlightenment, republican virtues, and the construction geopolitical views of the United States as exceptional, reprise numerous imperial tropes even if these are widely ignored.[38] World politics is about international relations and, now that the rivalry with the Soviet Union is over, it is about the much more mundane managerialism of interstate trade which so many international relations scholars study. Dangers come from failed states, rogue states and high-tech weapons in the wrong hands. At least so our scholars frequently tell us, but practical experience, and media coverage, is of globality and interconnection, power and movement, violence in the wild zones on the edges of the operation of pax Americana.[39]

The pattern of elite interconnections in the global age and the violence and poverty among those in the poor peripheries of the world economy suggest that it might be time to revisit Johan Galtung's model of imperialism formulated thirty years ago.[40] In this model he posited a series of links between the elites in the North and the South where trade arrangements are agreed upon to mutual advantage. The commonalties of elite interest were contrasted to the competing interests of labour and the poor which elite co-operation effectively allowed to be played off against each other, effectively using geography to effect exploitation. Resource extraction follows a similar pattern of elite enrichment, often at the expense of local dispossession. Empire has long been about the appropriation of peripheral wealth for the enrichment of those at the imperial centre. But, as Galtung argues, more so than many of the then-contemporaneous 'dependency' arguments, it has been a matter of complex military power arrangements and cultural incorporation that frequently use local allies to provide auxiliary forces to supplement and support imperial troops who ultimately secure the extraction of resources and the maintenance of political order.

Clearly the processes of coalition building in the immediate aftermath of 11 September suggest a network of elite co-operation, much of which may not have been seen by people 'in the street' in many places to be in their interest. Extending Mary Kaldor's insistence on thinking through the economic connections that are part of the political economy of warfare, the connections between the elites in the Gulf states and America follow Galtung's model. Their common interest in oil production may not necessarily promote the welfare or political participation of local residents and certainly not that of the migrant labourers that keep the oil pumps working and the local society functioning. The huge inequities of wealth between those with direct access to the oil revenues in the region and those without is one of the political grievances that feed potential political instabilities there. That is exactly why at least some military protection from an imperial power is a dangerous necessity for many Gulf leaders; some external help is needed in keeping dissent under control and cross border influences in check in these rentier states.

Further imperial analogies suggest themselves in many ways. Numerous media commentators noted that few conquerors have had much success in central Asia since Alexander the Great. What they have not noted is that Alexander conquered the Persian empire, and successfully marched through what is now designated Afghanistan, not only because he understood the capabilities of his troops and his enemies very well, but also because of his remarkable ability to effectively incorporate local rulers into his imperial political arrangements. Alexander's abilities as a 'coalition builder' are perhaps the most crucial but often forgotten part of his success.[41] The construction of a new coalition government in the aftermath of the defeat of the Taliban movement suggests that at least some strategists in Washington learnt this lesson.

But the imperial analogy, and its implicit suggestions of the need to drastically rethink the spatial assumptions of contemporary geopolitics, can be taken further. Might the strategy on the part of the attackers of New York and Washington now be understood in terms of an attempt, albeit a drastic and misguided one, to get the attention of imperial rulers concerning misrule by some of the provincial governors? This was a constant theme in the early Roman empire where provincial governors extracted wealth from their provinces to take back to Rome and enhance their power, wealth and prestige. Johan Galtung would also recognise the process, but does it make more sense as an understanding of the role of the Middle East in the American empire? Substituting contemporary petroleum for Roman wheat from Africa suggests a further loose analogy. Stability of grain supplies was a constant theme in Rome, might assuring petroleum supplies for the global economy be understood as the modern equivalent? At least one recent analysis suggests that oil is the most likely source of future wars in many places, not least the Middle East.[42]

Thinking about the current circumstances in terms of empires obviously does not provide either a perfect series of analogies or an obvious set of policy prescriptions and political strategies. But it does call into question the prominence of state thinking in international relations and security thinking. It directly challenges the state cartography of violence implicit in so much security thinking and the literature of international relations. Obviously the world is much more connected than was the case when either Alexander or the Caesars ruled. Economies are more interdependent, although the stability of Rome depended on regular supplies of wheat from the provinces in much the same way that the global economy under American dominance relies on a regular supply of petroleum. Americans understand themselves as a republic, modeled in part on Rome. The early history of Rome is one of accidental empire, at least prior to the rise of Marius, Sulla and Julius Caesar.[43] The analogies with America in the twentieth century, fighting defensive wars in the case of both of the world wars, and inadvertently gaining an empire in the process, follows Rome's history loosely too.

Imperial Wars

Viewed in these terms the claims to novelty in the case of the war America was involved in after September 2001 evaporate. Understanding matters in terms of the trope of empire suggests that American military power is not engaged in a new kind of warfare, but rather in a very old pattern, updated to use the latest military technologies of laser-guided bombs and satellite communication, but a very old pattern nonetheless. Understanding war in the terms of state-to-state conflict, the Second World War model, or even in its updated version the Gulf war of 1991, severely limits the understanding of warfare to a matter of pitched battles between large armies. There is another history of the use of American military power, one of the conduct of small wars in the rise of US power, a pattern of violence that Max Boot, in his recent volume on the topic, suggests might best be called '"imperial wars" – a term that, American sensitivities notwithstanding, seems apt to describe many US adventures abroad'.[44]

The other function of imperial troops has long been pacification on the frontiers of empire and maintaining control in the face of internal disturbance. American troops have been acting in garrison mode around the globe in numerous countries for the last half century. These numbers have been cut in the aftermath of the end of the Cold War, but bases abroad remain an integral part of American military operations. While phalanxes, roads, ballistas and galleys have been replaced by special forces, airlift capabilities, strategic bombers and aircraft carriers, securing communications and resource supplies in far flung parts of empire is still the task of military agencies. And they still do it in combination with local forces who provide intelligence and support as well as many of the soldiers needed for combat, scouting and policing.[45] Garrison troops frequently operate to support local political leaders in favour among imperial rulers, but in the process they can inflame opposition and local resentment. The presence of American troops supporting the Saudi regime is precisely one of Osama bin Laden's grievances.

This very different geopolitical understanding of the role of military force implies that counter-insurgency warfare at the fringes of imperial control is what is effectively occurring now under the misnomer of a new war. Understanding matters in these terms suggests a few crucial lessons. The history of counter-insurgency warfare suggests both the denial of support for guerrilla fighters and the necessity to undercut their political demands by making political reforms that remove sources of grievance.[46] Counter-insurgency wars also require stable bases from which garrison troops can deploy; the coalition members in Asia are being relied on to supply this stability, but revolt in the form of political instability in Pakistan and elsewhere remains a major concern to American planners. Counter-insurgencies are not new, but their success is in part about hearts and minds as well as the starvation of the support base of the guerrillas. Political initiatives will be needed, in many places and not just in Palestine, if effective pacification is to be coupled to long term elite co-optation.[47]

But failure to understand this necessity of empire is not new either; the history of Rome was also frequently one of reluctance to undertake the risks of warfare until a pressing military necessity presented itself. Likewise, resistance to imperial rule often underrated the power of the empire when mobilised. For Rome the crucial consideration was that its power was seen to be greater than that of its opponents, but this image required the military ability to destroy opposition:

But for the Romans, their hegemony and their very security depended on universal recognition of their empire's maiestas, its 'greaterness', Their policy depended on perceived and acknowledged military superiority, on the terror and awe of the enemy; and if this image was challenged by invasion, defeat, or revolt, the Romans reasserted it with the maximum possible brutality and ferocity.[48]

Since the end of the Second World War, American military thinking and strategy has depended on deterrence as its primary mode of security provision. The assumptions of superiority have rested on technological sophistication and the ability to reach all parts of the globe. The overwhelming capabilities of American forces have been the bedrock of deterrence for half a century; the parallel is again suggestive.

Strategic studies, and the understanding of the world in these terms, has been a crucial part of the cultural processes of American hegemony since the early days of the Cold War.[49] In the practice of strategic thinking the assumption has usually been that conflict between states is primary. This is tied into additional assumptions that opponents are rational actors who can assess relative military capabilities and the dangers to their interests and be deterred in the face of overwhelming military power. But revolts in the provinces were also about political theatre, dramatic gestures and frequently the willingness to resist in the face of ridiculous odds. More importantly for the analogy with 11 September developed in this essay, revolts and rivalries frequently drew imperial power more directly into local disputes.

Imperial Geopolitics

The imperial analogies in the preceding section could be extended in numerous ways but for the purposes of the argument here they make the point that challenging the taken-for-granted geographies of independent states, and the assumptions of territorial entities as the key actors in contemporary political struggles, is an important part of a critical analysis of the aftermath of 11 September. In particular, changing the spatial understanding of American identity from an innocent violated territorial identity to an imperial actor challenges the dominant scripts of 11 September and so reveals the invocation of taken-for-granted geopolitical tropes as a political strategy that is both efficacious in mobilising the population for war and in obscuring the larger patterns of interconnection in the global (imperial?) polity. But of course an imperial cartography is precisely the spatial rendition of events that is precluded by the operation of American exceptionalism, and of its geopolitical cartography of America as the virtuous autonomous polity facing many other polities that may not be friendly. This is supported by the peculiar practices of American military power, ones that frequently defeat enemies but do not conquer, annex or fundamentally remake the defeated polity. The resulting 'Empire of Disorder' allows American national identity to maintain its anti-imperial rationalisations while committing troops to garrison duties and counter-insurgency operations in many places.[50]

In the last few months of 2001 more critical modes of reasoning that refused the obvious geopolitical specifications of identities on offer would have been useful to avoid the immediate call to either support the United States or be accused of various moral and political inadequacies. These alternative geopolitical tropes were in short supply at the end of 2001. Imperial analogies used in this essay are a device to ask questions about the taken-for-granted specifications of identities and places that structure political discourse. What is clear from such an argument, as from many other modes of thinking, is that power cannot be simply mapped in the terms of states; its patterns deny the applicability of such a cartography.[51] But the claims to a virtuous home place and perfidious external threat remain a powerful political language intimately tied to the justifications of many varieties of political violence.

Imperial analogies also raise the questions of intervention, political responsibility and the possibilities of alternative modes of rule. They suggest the importance of understanding the antecedents of contemporary thinking in imperial histories, and the claims of nation and state as founded on an overemphasis of the possibilities of autonomy in a complex world of cross-cutting economic, political and ecological connections.[52] Such thinking also suggests that, in John Agnew's terms, the post-Cold War period might be better understood as a period in which the nineteenth-century terms of geopolitics, of civilisational specifications of world order, might be understood to be once again the more important overarching themes in geopolitical discourse. In contrast to the twentieth-century periods of inter-imperial rivalry in the first half and the Cold War ideological confrontation in the second half, once again civilisational superiority is being invoked in the clash with terrorism. As is the case with recent development discourse, it also seems now that the military dimensions of geopolitical discourse frequently conform to a fundamental division between Western power and peripheral inferiority.[53]

The events of 11 September also suggest that autonomous entities are no longer the obviously endangered subjects of security.[54] Consumers are not safely here in their cities divorced from the consequences of the political economy that provides their commodities and their identities. Interconnections across frontiers are the key to diasporic politics and the possibilities of security have to be rethought to address the impossibility of stable identities within specified boundaries. Likewise, the interconnections between what the United States or US-based corporations do in remote places is no longer a matter that does not connect, in however unlikely ways, with everyday life in America. Security requires understanding political connections to distant events; politics is also about obligations to distant strangers.

Globalisation is now the term preferred for discussions of the post-Cold War period for the cultural recognition of these processes, but common assumptions of radical novelty are less useful here than the much simpler suggestion that the cartographic imaginary of a politics of little boxes has always been inadequate as a specification of the appropriate terms for understanding world politics.[55] Indeed, it is not much of a stretch to suggest that modern political organisation owes more practically to Alexander with his complex organisational arrangements of empire than to his tutor Aristotle whose theme of the *polis* so dominates the modern political imaginary of supposedly autonomous political spaces.[56] And yet, in the face of obvious imperial interconnections, the ideal of the autonomous *polis* still underwrites the cartographical specification of virtuous autonomous states.

American political innocence, and the posture of reluctant imperialism, of the beneficent superpower intervening to fix political problems abroad, may be the most obvious casualty of the new war. While full-scale warfare between industrialized states, and especially between the democracies, seems increasingly unlikely, as this essay has suggested, political violence remains an ugly reality in many parts of the world outside the core regions of economic prosperity. It is this simple geographical point that 11 September makes abundantly clear, precisely because the attacks in New York and Washington so spectacularly violated the basic geopolitical division between supposedly wild zones and supposedly tame zones that structure the geopolitical discourses of the rich and powerful. Empire implies much more complex and messy interconnections and responsibilities than state- or bloc-based political cartographies. But so far it remains unlikely that American power, and at least its indirect dependence on petroleum supplies from the Gulf continuing to fuel the global economy that ensures its prosperity, will be rethought fundamentally, despite the spectacular destruction of that economy's most obvious artifactual symbols, the World Trade Center towers.

84 11 SEPTEMBER AND ITS AFTERMATH

NOTES

1. See Cynthia Weber, 'Flying Planes Can be Dangerous', *Millennium* 31/1 (2002) pp.129–47.
2. John Agnew, *Geopolitics: Revisioning World Politics* (London: Routledge 1998) p.2.
3. The classic statement is Gearóid Ó Tuathail, *Critical Geopolitics: The Politics of Writing Global Space* (Minneapolis: University of Minnesota Press 1996).
4. Joanne Sharp, *Condensing the Cold War: Reader's Digest and American Identity* (Minneapolis: University of Minnesota Press 2000); Gertjan Dijkink, *National Identity and Geopolitical Visions: Maps of Pride and Pain* (London: Routledge 1996).
5. Gearóid Ó Tuathail and Simon Dalby (eds), *Rethinking Geopolitics* (London: Routledge 1998).
6. Cynthia Weber, 'Performative States', *Millennium* 27/1 (1998) pp.77–95.
7. See Robert Jackson, *The Global Covenant: Human Conduct in a World of States* (Oxford: Oxford University Press, 2000).
8. John Agnew, *Reinventing Geopolitics: Geographies of Modern Statehood, Hettner Lecture 2000* (Heidleberg: University of Heidleberg 2001).
9. *The Economist*, 15–21 September 2001, front cover specified matters as 'The Week the World Changed'.
10. It also linked to more recent designations of 'wars' against crime and specifically drugs, but the invocation of a new war on terrorism suggested a larger-scale, more explicitly military-lead operation.
11. Exemplary in this regard is the *Newsweek* special pullout map of Afghanistan in its 1 October 2001 issue.
12. A matter recently addressed once again in Victor Davis Hanson, *Carnage and Culture: Landmark Battles in the Rise of Western Power* (New York: Doubleday 2001). More generally see John Keegan, *A History of Warfare* (New York: Vintage 1994).
13. Mathew Coleman, 'Iconographies and Outlaws After 9/11' *Geopolitics*, 8/3 (2003) pp.87–104.
14. As for instance in collections of essays from leading publications such as *International Security*. See Sean Lynn Jones and Steven E. Miller (eds), *Global Dangers: Changing Dimensions of International Security* (Cambridge, MA: MIT Press 1995).
15. Michael Klare and Yogesh Chandrani, (eds), *World Security: Challenges for a New Century* (New York: St Martin's 1998).
16. See Gearóid Ó Tuathail, 'De-Territorialised Threats and Global Dangers: Geopolitics and Risk Society', in David Newman (ed.), *Boundaries, Territory and Postmodernity* (London: Frank Cass 1999) pp. 17–31.
17. On American security thinking in terms of invulnerability see J. Chace and C. Carr, *America Invulnerable: The Quest of Absolute Security 1812 to Star Wars* (New York: Summit 1988).
18. See Matthew Sparke, 'Outsides inside Patriotism: The Oklahoma Bombing and the Displacement of Heartland Geopolitics', in Ó Tuathail and Dalby, *Rethinking Geopolitics* (note 5) pp.198–223.
19. John Agnew, 'An Excess of "National Exceptionalism": Towards a New Political Geography of American Foreign Policy', *Political Geography Quarterly* 2/2 (1983), pp.151–66. More generally on this construction of endangered American virtue see David Campbell, *Writing Security: United States Foreign Policy and the Politics of Identity* (Minneapolis: University of Minnesota Press 1998).
20. 'Giuliani rejects Saudi prince's $10M after pro-Palestian remarks', *The National Post*, 12 October 2001, p.A1.
21. For more on this episode see Judith Butler 'Explanation and Exoneration, or What We Can Hear', *Theory and Event* 5/4 (2002).
22. David Campbell, *Politics without Principle: Sovereignty, Ethics, and the Narratives of the Gulf War* (Boulder: Lynne Rienner 1993).
23. R.B.J. Walker, *Inside/Outside: International Relations as Political Theory* (Cambridge:

Cambridge University Press 1993).
24. Samuel Huntingdon, 'The Clash of Civilizations,' *Foreign Affairs* 72/3 (1993) pp.22–49.
25. See Edward Said, 'The Clash of Ignorance,' *The Nation*, 22 October 2001, pp.11–13.
26. On the articulations of danger in American political discourse prior to 11 September see Patricia Molloy, 'Moral Spaces and Moral Panics: High Schools, War Zones and Other Dangerous Places', *Culture Machine* 4 (2002) <http://culturemachine.tees.ac.uk..
27. On Bin Laden see Yossef Bodansky, *Bin Laden: The Man who Declared War on America* (Roseville, CA: Prima 2001) and Roland Jacquard, *In the Name of Osama Bin Laden: Global Terrorism and the Bin Laden Brotherhood* (Durham: Duke University Press 2002).
28. Berch Berberoglu, *Turmoil in the Middle East: Imperialism, War and Political Instability* (Albany: State University of New York Press 1999).
29. M. Singer and A. Wildavsky, *The Real World Order: Zones of Peace, Zones of Turmoil* (Chatham, NJ, Chatham House 1993).
30. Cynthia Weber, *Simulating Sovereignty* (Cambridge: Cambridge University Press 1995).
31. Mary Kaldor, *New and Old Wars: Organized Violence in a Global Era* (Stanford: Stanford University Press 1999).
32. In general on this theme see: Mats Berdal and David M. Malone, *Greed and Grievance: Economic Agendas in Civil Wars* (Boulder, CO: Lynne Rienner 2000).
33. Michel Feher 'Robert Fisk's Newspapers' *Theory and Event* 5/4 (2002).
34. Michael Scott Doran 'Somebody Else's Civil War', *Foreign Affairs* 81/1 (2002), pp.22–42.
35. It might also, of course, be read as a more straightforward military assault designed to convince the United States to remove its troops from the Middle East, following on from earlier, and, viewed in these terms, apparently successful attacks on US forces in Lebanon and Somalia. As such this, if it was the plan behind the 911 attacks, has obviously turned out to be a major strategic miscalculation.
36. Victor Davis Hanson's polemic in *Commentary* magazine goes so far as to specify the Saudi elite as America's enemy in 'Our Enemies, the Saudis', *Commentary*, July 2002.
37. On the history of oil and power in the Gulf see Daniel Yergin, *The Prize: The Epic Quest for Oil, Money and Power* (New York: Simon and Schuster 1990).
38. William V. Spanos, *America's Shadow: An Anatomy of Empire* (Minneapolis: University of Minnesota Press 2000).
39. Michael Shapiro, *Violent Cartographies: Mapping Cultures of War* (Minneapolis: University of Minnesota Press 1997).
40. Johan Galtung, 'A Structural Theory of Imperialism', *Journal of Peace Research* 8/2 (1971), pp.81–117.
41. J.F.C. Fuller, *The Generalship of Alexander the Great* (Ware: Wordsworth editions 1998).
42. Michael T. Klare, *Resource Wars: The New Landscape of Global Conflict* (New York: Metropolitan Books 2001).
43. Susan P. Mattern, *Rome and the Enemy: Imperial Strategy in the Principate* (Berkeley, CA: University of California Press 1999).
44. Max Boot, *The Savage Wars of Peace: Small Wars and the Rise of American Power* (New York: Basic 2002) p.xvi.
45. This is obviously a gross overgeneralization about the conduct of imperial military operations, and in the Roman case it obviously applies more obviously to earlier parts of the history of the empire. See Arther Ferrill 'The Grand Strategy of the Roman Empire', in Paul Kennedy (ed.), *Grand Strategies in War and Peace* (New Haven, CT: Yale University Press 1991) pp.71–85.
46. Caleb Carr, *The Lessons of Terror* (New York: Random House 2002).
47. Michael Howard, 'What's in a Name', *Foreign Affairs* 81/1 (2002) pp.8–13.
48. Mattern (note 43) p.210
49. Bradley S. Klein, *Strategic Studies and World Order* (Cambridge: Cambridge University Press 1994).
50. Alain Joxe, *Empire of Disorder* (New York: Semiotexte 2002).

51. John Agnew, 'Mapping Political Power Beyond State Boundaries: Territory, Identity, and Movement in World Politics', *Millennium* 28/3 (1999) pp.499–521.
52. Simon Dalby, *Environmental Security* (Minneapolis: University of Minnesota Press 2002).
53. On development and geopolitics see Simon Dalby, 'Danger, Disease and the Dark Continent: Geopolitics and "Global" Security' in P. Pagnini, V. Kolossov and M. Antonsich (eds), *Europe between Political Geography and Geopolitics* (Rome: Societa Geographica Italiana 2001), pp.403–14.
54. R.B.J. Walker, 'The Subject of Security' in K. Krause and M.C. Williams (eds), *Critical Security Studies: Concepts and Cases* (Minneapolis: University of Minnesota Press 1997), pp.61–81.
55. R.B.J. Walker 'International Relations and the Concept of the Political' in Ken Booth and Steve Smith (eds), *International Relations Theory Today* (Cambridge: Polity 1995) pp.306–27.
56. Lucian Ashworth, 'Forget Aristotle: Alexander the Great and the Military Origins of Modern Organization', unpublished paper.

The Naming of 'Terrorism' and Evil 'Outlaws': Geopolitical Place-Making After 11 September

MAT COLEMAN

Introduction: Cultural Geography and Geopolitical Research

In the mid-1980s, and particularly following the collapse of the Berlin Wall, a loose group of political geography and international relations scholars began to challenge the rigid spatial division of 'politics within' and 'relations without' featured in realist and liberal accounts of world politics.[1] Painted with a broad brush, these scholars insisted on a reformulation of geopolitics. Rather than the study of a 'fixed and objective geography constraining and directing the activities of states', geopolitics was rethought as a cultural complex of practices and representations.[2] The suggestion was that the allegedly given character of borders, boundaries and states was better understood as a question of territoriality, or of the consensual and coercive social ordering of space. The *facts* of territory were re-presented as moot *claims* made concerning the location and horizons of political space, anchored by practices of statecraft.

Recent work in political geography and international relations has followed up these initial claims with extensive research into the links between and among borders, boundaries, and what might be termed the politics of identity. For instance, Agnew has noted that from the historical complex of sometimes complementary – sometimes contradictory – political and economic territorialities, statist territorial discourse emerged as hegemonic and settled how political identity and political community could be imagined.[3] In a similar spirit, Shapiro has suggested that the state's instrumental and rational 'face' of logistical truths is buoyed by a second, hidden 'face' concerned with questions of identity and location, and with ontological services provided by the 'enemy'.[4]

In articulating the cultural work done by claims previously understood as territorial truths, these geopolitical studies draw on ideas perhaps more readily associated with the rich field of cultural geography and, in particular, work on the 'making of place' which has stressed place as a subjective center of meaning.[5] From this vantage point, place can be considered a narrativised space that grounds meaning for agents through architectures and symbolic investments, and as such, is a phenomenological geography where the material and the imaginary combine to physically and culturally locate identities in specific sites of community and memory.[6] The point is that recent critical political geographic studies, in laying bare the identity-based foundations of an often taken-for-granted world of geopolitics, suggest the centrality of cultural geographic inquiry to the worlds of statecraft, war and security.[7]

This is not simply an academic nicety: making sense of recent geopolitical events requires attending to the cultural geographies of geopolitical representation and practice. With this in mind, this essay explores recent US geopolitical articulations of place and identity. In the first section, I suggest, through Jean Gottmann's work on national iconographies, that the post-11 September naming of 'terrorism' is an instance of American geopolitical place-naming – or geo-graphing – as much as it is an objective assessment of geopolitical threat. In this sense, the US geopolitical identification of 'terrorism' works against a sense of time–space implosion implied by the September attacks by reasserting the state as a site of belonging and as the legitimate location of orderly politics. In the second section, I give consideration to how the naming of 'terrorism' invokes the abnormal character of 'terrorists', or more accurately how the naming of 'terrorism' brings evil into play. Reading the controversial political philosopher Carl Schmitt, I argue that scrutiny of contemporary designations of evil makes evident the geopolitically strategic – and potentially unjust and inhumane – constitution of state responses declared in the name of justice and humanity. This is particularly relevant given the US bombing campaign in Afghanistan, the alleged poor treatment of Taliban and Al Qaeda prisoners at Camp X-Ray in Guantánamo Bay, Cuba, and the recent detainment of suspected residents and visitors in the United States. In a third and concluding section I suggest that the place-making naming of 'terrorism' and the geopolitical designation of evil work together to erect an impossibly bordered post-11 September American homeland, reminiscent of basic Cold War mappings of civilian life and international anarchy, which impedes an adequately 'networked' understanding of contemporary world politics.

'Digging In' After 11 September: Naming 'Terrorism' and the Geopolitical Making of Place

In the wake of the horrific events in New York City and Washington, DC and near Shanksville, PA, the cover of the 24 September 2001 special edition of *Time* pronounced in a large, bold font: 'One Nation, Indivisible', and 'America Digs In – And Digs Out'. The accompanying full-page photo is of President Bush, standing on a pile of rubble amid construction and emergency response workers at 'ground zero' where the north and south World Trade Center towers once stood. President Bush, with a megaphone at his side and against a skyline of dust and debris, holds an American flag high. As those of us who watched this moment on live television might recall, the workers and rescue teams are cheering: U-S-A! U-S-A!

Inside the publication, pull-out and double-page photos capture a number of moving scenes: a human chain of emergency workers passing a stretcher draped with an American flag; a 'wall of prayers' – photos and descriptions of the missing, and presumably dead – at the entrance to the Manhattan Bellevue Hospital; a candlelight vigil in Illinois; hordes of construction workers removing debris from the World Trade Center site; a couple hanging a commemorative flag from a tree in rural America; and, among other things, a stern-looking President Bush, as the caption puts it, 'sending a message to terrorists and the world'. Flags are front and centre in almost every photo, linking otherwise different peoples and places across the country.[8] Indeed, the contents page announces the key theme: 'Showing the Flag'.

This geopolitical narrative – of waving the flag, and of 'digging in' against future attacks – is more than mere editorial license. Rather, the themes presented in the magazine neatly distil the logic of post-11 September US geopolitical practice. The language of 'digging in' against threat evidences a powerful, popular geopolitical narrative of a 'barricaded place', and mirrors the fact that borders have become significant focus points in post-11 September US security practice.[9] In the weeks following the collapse of the towers, undocumented immigration at both the Canadian and Mexican borders – those sites identified as key 'terrorist alien' entrance points – came under intense scrutiny.[10] Consequently, despite the fact that those involved in the events of mid-September entered the country legally and through non-border ports of entry, foreign policy attention turned specifically to the 'criminal alien' at America's northern and southern borders, and as a result, border patrol and policing – particularly in the US–Mexico borderlands – increased markedly.[11] For example, within hours of the attack, alert level 1 'code red' search authority technologies and procedures were called into service: density meters, laser sighters, and x-ray machines were deployed; and scores of Immigration and Naturalization Service officers and US Customs agents – as well as National Guard troops – went to work at commercial and non-commercial US–Mexico ports of entry, choking much of the cross-border traffic, legal and otherwise.[12] By the end of the month, previously non-compulsory biometric identity border crossing cards – with computerised facial recognition and fingerprint technologies, as well as machine readable information – were made mandatory travel documents,[13] and San Diego businesses began to warn of impending economic collapse due to the drastic slowdown in cross border shopping.[14]

The Uniting and Strengthening America By Providing Appropriate Tools Required to Intercept and Obstruct Terrorism Act, or the PATRIOT Act, passed on 26 October 2001, is pivotal to this rebordering focus. Described by Attorney General Ashcroft as legislation that authorises 'new weapons for us to fight the war at the borders and here at home', the act identifies US borders as particularly vulnerable, and provides for new federal immigration powers of expedited 'terrorist' arrest, detention, deportation, and extradition, without judicial oversight and constitutional review.[15] Furthermore, the act proposes the creation of a centralised border database of all non-citizens entering and exiting the US as well as the introduction of a shared North American electronic customs network to track questionable international containerised traffic. The May 2002 passage of the Enhanced US Border Security and Visa Entry Reform Act, which requires that foreign visitors to the United States carry biometric (fingerprint or retinal) identification, that US colleges and universities keep track of foreign students, and that federal (and local) law enforcement and intelligence agencies begin the long task of coordinating their activities in order to implement a 'first line of defence' at the border, suggests that this trend is not likely to dissipate in the near future. In short, attention has been focused on the territorial margins of the American state: implementing order concerns fortifying borders.

Confounding the apparent end of traditional state-based geopolitics,[16] this rebordering is best grasped as a moment of state territorialisation, a process which involves: classification by area, or the assignment of things and people by areal category; communication or the performance of conceived boundaries through gesture, statement, symbol, and marker; and, last, enforcement of control over access through the threat of sanction.[17] However, it is important to stress that such rebordering or territorialisation is not simply an organisational problem, but is also a social process underwritten by claims of community and belonging.[18] In other words, territoriality concerns a substantive articulation of identity and allegiance – a point made more generally in recent 'identities, borders, orders' (IBO) and 'territorialities, identities, movement' (TIM) studies in political geography, which, although diverse in their various outlooks, have jointly stressed that territoriality cannot be explained by an examination of boundaries in and of themselves.[19] This is because borders concern sociospatial narrative practices and processes in which 'we come to know, understand and make sense of the social world and constitute our social identities'.[20] As Albert and Brock note, borders and boundaries merely instantiate a flattened two-dimensional space of insides and outsides; it is the cultural and social constitution of borders that gives bordered places their tangible, three-dimensional shape.[21] In other words, in order to grasp the import of territoriality in the late modern world, one must look beyond the physicality of fences and checkpoints to place-making 'hedge-and-fence' stories about ourselves and others.[22]

This need to investigate self/other stories of borders and boundaries brings us back to the popularised geopolitical language and images of 'digging out' the remains of the World Trade Center towers and 'digging in' against threat, featured on the cover of the special September 2001 issue of *Time*. The claim made and depicted on the cover – of a besieged-but-indissoluble nationality – does not vindicate what might be called ethnic-genealogical 'blood and belonging' models of nationhood,[23] but instead points to the production of a state-based geography of identity/difference.[24] It is here that the popular geopolitical naming of 'terrorism' takes on great importance. 'Terrorism' – as depicted in glossy images of collapsed buildings and body bags – suggests the meltdown of the sovereign inside/outside geography central to definitions of the state: the 'inside' – understood, at least in the particular experience of the West, as the 'civilian' realm of orderly and democratic election and lobby – gives way in the presence of an 'anarchic' and 'militaristic' nonstate action whose aggressive mode of political expression is 'normally' associated with an 'anarchic' international realm of undemocratic 'anything goes' realpolitik. The identification of 'terrorism' suggests the incapacity of a statal inside/outside geography that 'usually' provides distance from such violence through, for instance, the vigorous policing of borders and the surveillance of potentially 'troublesome' domestic constituents. Once named, the threat of future 'terrorist' politicking – in conjunction with a sense of insecurity born from the failure of state policing techniques and technologies – lends an immediate and uncritical sense of urgency to the patriotic project of restoring the state to its apparently former invincibility. In short, if the popular naming of 'terrorism' signals the collapse of the state and a late modern condition of political time–space compression in which the 'civilian' mixes with the 'anarchic', then such naming also works paradoxically to reconstitute a geography of 'civilian' insides and 'anarchic' outsides through an active state-based decompression of time–space relations. In response to the collapse of state borders, America 'digs in'.

In this sense, the naming of 'terrorism' and 'terrorists' speaks more of the geo-graphing of collective identity and place than it does of an already established collectivity and location under threat: to name 'terrorism' is to write – and to right, as in to restore – legitimate state politicking through reference to a ruthless and unruly nonstate violence against which citizens must be defended.[25] In other words, the naming of 'terrorism' provides an alien other against and through which the shape and substance of the state is clarified and subsequently barricaded, thereby targeting a clearly defined enemy rather than the state's complicity in creating the conditions for violent nonstate global politicking in the first place.[26] This last point is particularly important. The act of defining and marking 'terrorism' in the name of national security makes difficult a consideration of national security as an ongoing practice directly constitutive of violent nonstate responses, and thus as a practice which provides for insecurity rather than security.[27] Here, managing a condition of 'terroristic' borderlessness – construed as a danger and a source of disorder to 'proper' rules of warfare, diplomatic conduct, and domestic sovereign politicking – trumps a more complex understanding of transboundary involvement with other peoples and places.

This 'digging in' process of identity articulation was well understood by the political geographer Jean Gottmann, who noted that anxieties born from the uncertainties of transboundary flows (*circulation*), themselves necessary for social reproduction, call forth the closure – or partitioning (*cloisonnement*) – of geopolitical space.[28] In the face of unruly political, economic and cultural movement, argued Gottmann, comes an iconographic geography of national or regional identification – of ideas, memories, principles, histories, heroes, hierarchies, and fortifications – that results in the partitioning of political space in the name of a particularly emplaced people.[29] As Muscarà notes, such iconographies, manifest in both geopolitical practice and representation, 'respond to a need of territorial identity that a community expresses in order to resist change'.[30] These socially rooted and politically appropriated barriers to movement are conservative, foundational, assimilatory, resilient and curative cultural markers that 'constitute the cement of a people and relate it to a parcel of space: a region, a territory'.[31] In other words, the defensive erection of iconographies suggests that spatial structures are the result not simply of palpable organisational projects but also of 'unconscious projections' of community, order and identity.[32] Accordingly, extending Gottmann's analysis to current events, it is not remiss to suggest that post-11 September American rebordering articulates an ordered identity-in-place through the (popular) representation and (geopolitical) practice of the iconographic metaphor of *Heimat* (i.e. homeland), constituted in relation to threatening, circulatory geographies of *Fremde* or foreignness (i.e. 'terrorism').[33]

In this light, the naming of 'terrorism' and the subsequent articulation of homeland is best grasped as a place-making grammar and practice of partition that performs the key labour of inferring a 'we' from an 'I', in relation to a 'they' – a psychosomatic projection of community Gottmann identified behind all material human geographies.[34] This is perhaps nowhere more apparent than with the Americanisation of those killed during the events of 11 September, where an American 'we' has conveniently buried the multiple nationalities and identities of those trapped in the World Trade Center towers, against the spectre of 'terrorism'.[35] Indeed, this is the popular geopolitical work done in the special issue of *Time* magazine examined above: as the stories inside uncover the destruction and danger of 'terrorism', iconographic national place-making results, and is subsequently normalised; and vice versa, as various national iconographies and practices are celebrated (i.e. flag-waving), 'terrorism' emerges as an increasingly unfathomable yet impending threat. In short, through participation in the naming of 'terrorism', the magazine popularly redraws the transgressed line between the 'civilian' and the 'anarchic' that has also been redrawn in US geopolitical practice.

'Outlaws of Humanity': the Afghan Campaign, FBI Round-ups, and Camp X-Ray

Perhaps the more challenging question in this discussion of the production of collective identity is how – and with what results – the naming of 'terrorism' turns on the consistent invocation of evil as an explanation for 11 September, and as a justification for action in the wake of the events of that day. Let us return again to the special mid-September issue of *Time* discussed above. The contents page reads:

> America's first nights of mourning and fear are giving way to a palpable anger. The entire nation joins New York and Washington in heartrending memorials even as it learns to focus on its latest enemy – and how to strike back.

In this post-mourning spirit of 'striking back', those held responsible for the attacks are made visible. Large, pixillated passport photo blow-ups of Mohammed Atta and Marwan Al-Shehhi – the suspected pilots of the two planes that brought down the World Trade Center towers – remind the reader of the banality of America's 'latest enemy'. However, the sub-title to the two photos – which encourages the reader to ponder the two men's dozen or so associates still at large in the United States, as well as the potential for future chemical, biological and 'dirty' nuclear attack – at once reinscribes their ordinariness as extraordinary.[36] Thus, while the publication puts a human face to the 'terrorists', it also suggests that their everyday familiarity masks a latent, threatening evil: looks are deceiving.[37]

An analogous invocation of evil contextualises the Bush administration's new post-11 September resolve for world order. Couching

US geopolitics in terms of humanity and justice, administration officials name not just 'terrorism', as noted above, but a 'terrorist *parasite*' whose regime of intimidation is ultimately described as incomprehensible and alien. As President Bush noted during his 2002 State of the Union Address of America's new war against terror:

> *Our cause is just*, and it continues. Our discoveries in Afghanistan confirmed our worst fears, and showed us the true scope of the task ahead. We have seen the depth of our enemies' hatred in videos, where they laugh about the loss of innocent life. And the depth of their hatred is equalled by the *madness of the destruction they design* .... *They embrace tyranny and death as a cause and a creed.* We stand for a different choice, made long ago, on the day of our founding. We affirm it again today. We choose freedom and the dignity of every life (italics added).[38]

Similarly, the Bush administration's fiscal year 2003 budget argues that 'America has evil, cold-blooded enemies capable of unprecedented acts of mass murder and terror'.[39] This looming condition of vulnerability necessitates that 'we bring justice to those responsible for the events of 11 September'.[40]

A quick review of Carl Schmitt's *The Concept of the Political* (1932) suggests why this good/evil US foreign policy mapping should be of interest to the political geographer. Schmitt argues that the principal political distinction is one between friend and enemy. The inherently antithetical relation of friend and enemy denotes 'the utmost degree of intensity of a union or separation, of an association or dissociation'.[41] Accordingly, the relation concerns the attribution of alienness and difference to an enemy such that extreme conflict is possible, in physical defence of the self. Religious, economic, moral and other various antitheses may fuel the violent group distinction of friend and enemy, but the relation itself nonetheless remains beyond such justifications:

> The political can derive its energy from the most varied human endeavors, from the religious, economic, moral, and other antitheses. [The political] does not describe its own substance, but only the intensity of an association or dissociation of human beings whose motives can be religious, national (in the ethnic or cultural sense), economic, or of another kind and can effect at different times different coalitions and separations. The real friend-enemy grouping is existentially so strong and decisive that the nonpolitical antithesis, at precisely the moment at which it becomes political, pushes aside and subordinates its hitherto purely religious, purely economic, purely

cultural criteria and motives to the conditions and conclusions of the political situation at hand.[42]

Schmitt notes that only 'an existential threat to one's own way of life' – and not a rational purpose, norm, social ideal, legality, legitimacy, program or aesthetic – justifies the killing constitutive of the political relation of friend/enemy.[43] It is a 'real enemy' – as in a group or individual that threatens physical survival – and not 'ideals or norms of justice' which justifies the warring of the political relation.[44]

Schmitt's matter-of-fact discussion of the brutality of political bloodshed, if (rightly) worrisome in the context of Schmitt's own active endorsement of German National Socialism,[45] does usefully point to the difficulty of marrying the concepts of justice and humanity with the practice of war. After all, for Schmitt, justice and humanity – as suggestive of some condition of universality in which the political group relation of friend/enemy is either deferred or eradicated in the process of identifying some *common* regulative ethical ideal or moral norm – are impossible. Consequently, those wars waged in the name of a universal justice and humanity or against some universally posited articulation of injustice and inhumanity are, rather than motivated by some higher cause, a specifically intense mode of the political relation of friend/enemy:

> When a state fights its political opponent in the name of humanity, it is not a war for the sake of humanity, but a war wherein a particular state seeks to usurp a universal concept against its military opponent. At the expense of its opponent, it tries to identify itself with humanity in the same way as one can misuse peace, justice, progress, and civilisation in order to claim these as one's own and deny the same to the enemy.[46]

Here, Schmitt argues that to fight in the name of justice and/or humanity is to tactically deny the enemy knowledge of justice and the quality of humanity. Consequently, to invoke some higher claim behind war is to make the enemy an 'outlaw of humanity', thereby preparing the ground for war against this stranger.[47] In other words, battles declared in the name of some higher appeal – and, important for our purposes here, against some mode of incomprehensible devilry or evil – indicate a *strategic exclusion* of the enemy from a 'normal' moral and ethical universe. This move dissolves an otherwise contested pluriverse of rival group projects through the naming of a universal in whose name an evil is to be eradicated. This universal deflects attention from the political reality that the so-called abnormality of the enemy could be called into question through scrutiny of the mode of warring employed by the friend against the enemy. In Schmitt's world, then, the invocation of higher justifications is ontologically meaningless but is, nonetheless, strategically noteworthy because such a move, by denying the intimacy of the friend/enemy relation, defuses a consideration of the self's warring displacement of the enemy into an extra-human realm of inexplicable evil.

The production of 'outlaws' is no more important than in a consideration of state responses to (actual and would-be) 'terrorists' (now indispensably) considered to be evil. The identification of 'terrorism', for example, not only gives a sense of official being to the state but does this through the 'moral isolation of nonstate violence'.[48] Here, 'terrorism' references the other to a condition of statehood dependent on the legitimate employment of violent warring means in the maintenance of territorial sovereignty. Subsequently, 'terrorism' is outlawed or rendered as distinct to an apparently defensible statist mode of warring, despite the fact that both state geopolitics and 'terrorism' concern the use of violence for political purpose.[49] The isolation of 'terrorism' as evil, then, allows for the violence built into state responses to 'terrorism' to be normalised – celebrated, even – as the 'normal' use of force in the defence of territorial sovereignty against a threat of somehow extra-human constitution. In the post-9/11 context, it is exactly the 'moral isolation of nonstate violence from other modalities of violence' which allows for both American outrage and support for the 'bombing' of human bodies: outrage, that is, concerning New York, and support concerning Afghanistan. One is an unwarranted and abnormal act of violence; the other is a justifiable act of self-defence and the means for the prosecution of a geographically located evil.

This problem of evil 'outlaws' also sheds light on recent attempts by the US government to claim that the treatment of the 600 or so alleged Taliban and Al Qaeda prisoners at Camp X-Ray in Guantánamo Bay is not subject to the rules of the Geneva Convention concerning the treatment of prisoners of war, which requires that detainees surrender only their name, rank and military identification number when questioned.[50] Arguing that these 'committed terrorists' are not state agents but extraordinarily unusual nonstate actors whose very being permanently threatens the system of sovereign states, and thus that the prisoners are not covered under the terms of the Geneva Convention, the Bush administration has allegedly authorised sensory deprivation techniques and other abusive modes of psychological control in order to weaken prisoners and make interrogation sessions more 'fruitful'.[51] Importantly, such techniques of interrogation are understood to be warranted due to the abnormal character of the prisoners in question. The insinuation is that those located beyond a common, universal humanity cannot themselves claim (temporary) membership so as to protest what could be termed inhumane treatment. More recently, Defense Secretary

Rumsfeld announced that the Pentagon plans to hold these detainees indefinitely in Guantánamo Bay, even if acquitted by military tribunals.[52] Arguing that acquitted prisoners are still 'sworn enemies of the United States' on the battlefield, Rumsfeld called this 'commonsensical' move 'responsible and lawful'. Despite Rumsfeld's recourse to the law, the abnormality of the detainees trumps all legal procedure. Literally, identification of the evil 'terrorist outlaw' permits the prosecutorial identity to act outside the law.

The production of outlaws also works on a domestic scale. The mounting panic concerning the unrecognisability of 'terror' – as noted above with the photos of Atta and Al-Shehhi, and particularly given the recent arrests of American citizens John Walker Lindh and Jose Padilla – has normalised otherwise unconstitutional domestic policing practices. Evidencing the amorphous and enveloping post-11 September definition of evil, the Federal Bureau of Investigation has rounded up more than 1,000 'Middle Eastern' and 'South Asian' males since mid-September 2001. Although some have been released and many deported, hundreds remain imprisoned – indefinitely, and without bail or official legal counsel – on the presumption of having violated minor immigration procedures, although the Justice Department – empowered by the PATRIOT Act – is under no compulsion to disclose case details with either the 'suspects' or their lawyers, as potential links to larger 'terrorist' networks are investigated. This has been defended as an acceptable short-term stop-gap measure – a sort of national security triage – and has generated much public conversation concerning the proper relationship of democratic freedoms to national security policing efforts. The general consensus seems to be that if the freedom provided by democracy allows for the incursion of destabilising 'terrorist' acts, then certain freedoms must be temporarily placed on hold until the conditions for democracy can be resecured. As a prominent American intellectual has argued 'police work is the first priority ... because the first obligation of the state is to protect the lives of its citizens, and American lives are now visibly and certainly at risk'.[53] On the ground this logic works itself out as the interrogation and incarceration of suspected outlaws whose ostensibly unintelligible and dangerous political motivations invalidate constitutional process. Here, the violence of the friend/enemy relation is overtly justified by the apparently latent evil of those detained.

These three brief examples are meant to draw attention to two key points. First, Schmitt's critique of the marriage of justice, humanity and war demonstrates the strategic geopolitical function of invocations of the abnormal, the delinquent, the evil, etc. The above is not intended to somehow dismiss the real horror of various historical events and the agents involved. For instance, it is clear that Al Qaeda operatives planned and executed the events of 11 September. Moreover, it seems that these events should probably, upon reflection, at least for any self-reflexive and sentient body, be horrific. In other words, I do not intend to argue in favour of a laissez-faire ethic as concerns the horrors of identity politics.[54] Nor, from a different standpoint, is the above intended to divide ethical investigation from geopolitical analysis, as Schmitt's own investigation of the marriage of justice and war suggests. Whereas Schmitt's realist discussion of the relation of friend/enemy tends towards a prioritisation of war at the expense of a plurality of otherwise provincially articulated norms of justice, the examples above are meant to provoke consideration of the injustices lodged in the naming of evil 'outlaws' and 'terrorists'.[55]

Second, the three cases noted above are meant to draw attention to the strategic value of designations of evil. The identification of evil works as a territorial remedy – as an ordering representation and a policing practice – that tips the scales towards partitioning (*cloisonnement*) and away from movement (*circulation*) in a geography that was – following Gottmann – a crossroads (*carrefour*) on 11 September, rather than a properly sovereign locale. In this sense, the identification of an evil 'terrorist parasite' beyond the realm of humanity performs a crucial therapeutic, iconographic, and partitioning logic such that insides and outsides – and members and outlaws – can be suitably mapped, differentiated, and either celebrated or punished as if housed in different moral universes. In so doing, the United States – a previously 'accessible' geography – is rendered 'secure'.

A Remainderless Homeland? Concluding Thoughts on Contemporary Geopolitical Place-Making

This essay has attempted to look critically – using the work of political geographer Jean Gottmann and political philosopher Carl Schmitt – at the events and aftermath of 11 September. Specifically, by repositioning the post-11 September naming of 'terrorism' as a geopolitical place-making practice and suggesting the potentially unjust and inhumane character of recent designations of evil central to such efforts, this essay attempts to denaturalise and question a set of dominant geopolitical signs, images and languages that turn on barricaded iconographies of homeland and on the professed incomprehensibility of evil outlaws. From this point of view, geopolitics concerns not just the military and financial 'hardware' of power politics, but also a crucial 'command of and faith in signs: the security of selected images and languages'.[56] Importantly, the contestable cultural or social constitution of both homeland and evil points to the difficulty of assuming foreign policy as an extra-normative science of objective facts, dangers, threats, and responses. Rather, 'Foreign Policy' – as in the conventional sense of state capacity – concerns a more general instance of 'foreign policy' – as in the existentially based making foreign of others designated as evil.[57] In this sense, and as alluded to in the introduction, statecraft requires interrogation as a practice – built from a set of disputable representations – that provides for a sense of self by estranging an evil other according to a normalised (cultural) geography of identity here and difference there. In sum, practices and representations of identity and place – waving the flag and 'digging in' – usually reserved for cultural geographic study seem essential to the study of geopolitics.

Important epistemological and pedagogical challenges follow from a recognition of the centrality of cultural geographic articulations of identity and place to contemporary geopolitics. At a time when scholarly investigation seems more and more willing to consider the networked and hybrid composition of world politics, and when the popular Western imagination appears caught up in the excesses of so-called 'globalisation', geopolitics remains committed to simpler geographies. In other words, despite widespread recognition of the porosity of the everyday,[58] the unbordered – or 'dilemmatic'[59] – constitution of self and community is rarely recognised in the actual world of geopolitical statecraft. Rather, a bordered politics of home without remainders – written by the relation of 'terrorism'/us and through the invocation of evil to nonstate 'outlaws' – is asserted in order to provide iconographic retreat. The construction of homeland writes a closure – a staple international relations Cold War script long thought to be outdated – in which the earth's surface is perfectly divided among compartmentalised peoples, mapped by geopolitical 'lines in the sand'. To this end, the bordered metaphor of 'global apartheid' is far more appropriate to the world of geopolitics than neoliberal accounts of the 'end of geography'.[60] Identities, in other words, continue to be 'specified within the conventional understandings of geopolitical boundaries and modern sovereign states',[61] notwithstanding the seeming inapplicability of a Clausewitzian landscape of state armies and national interests, with corresponding and well-defined territorial aims, to the contemporary world.[62]

As cultural geographers such as Tuan and Entrikin have argued, such geographical escape from a world of fears, burdens and angst – in the form of 'cultural cover' or disconnected place-making – deserves critical inspection, if nothing else because the world is built from the interconnection of places and peoples.[63] In the context of the events of 11 September, as Edward Said noted in the immediate aftermath of the attacks, this line of thinking involves a discussion of the history of US geopolitical interests and practices in the Middle East – interests and practices that render claims to innocence, territorial transgression and simple articulations of evil entirely problematic.[64]

For instance, it is important to focus on Al Qaeda as a political, religious and cultural organisation engaged in response to the abandonment of US-sponsored *mujahedeen* forces after the Soviet withdrawal from Afghanistan, to the presence of infidel US forces in Saudi Arabia following Saddam Hussein's 1990 Kuwaiti invasion, to US geopolitical support for Israel, and, among other things, to the ongoing US embargo against Iraq in the name of regional oil security. Here, Al Qaeda might be better understood as a 'combat fundamentalism' resisting the 'ostracising imperialism' of the US, which dominates some regions (of geopolitical and geoeconomic interest) while isolating others.[65] From this perspective it seems profitable to understand US foreign policy as an unbordered 'armed struggle' in the maintenance of empire,[66] or rather differently as a sort of Wilsonian global hegemony gone awry.[67]

In these contexts, the events of 9/11 are less easily described as an attack on innocents and perhaps better grasped as an instance of US foreign policy blowback,[68] and as such are less easily mapped in terms of a simple realist geography of states and anarchy. If nothing else, remembering bin Laden's history of collaboration with the United States during the Soviet occupation of Afghanistan in the 1980s – particularly in the context of the present-day drive to outlaw this one-time US geopolitical asset – underscores the dangers and dishonesties of enduring Cold War amnesiastic 'interpretive dispositions' which author an us/them geography of 'strategic international McCarthyism'.[69] Here, claims that post-11 September geopolitics requires alignment either for or against the United States in the fight against evil are readily problematised by a consideration of the impossibly remainderless – or cut and dry – quality of US foreign policy practices themselves. In this light, the task in the aftermath of 11 September is to challenge the 'expert' and 'authorised' interpretation and counsel of makers of statecraft, and in a twist on recent comments made by Der Derian, to insist on uncovering 'what is [geographically] dangerous to think and say'.[70]

ACKNOWLEDGEMENTS

I would like to thank John Agnew, Denis Cosgrove, Mustafa Dikeç, Nick Entrikin, Gerard Toal, and most of all Luca Muscarà and Kalapi Roy for the many thoughtful, provocative, and at times animated conversations that resulted in the writing of this paper. Responsibility for all errors and interpretations is mine.

NOTES

  1. In IR see: R.K. Ashley and R.B.J. Walker, 'Reading Dissidence/Writing the Discipline: Crisis and the Question of Sovereignty in International Studies', *International Studies Quarterly* 34/3 (1990) pp.367–517; D. Campbell, *Writing Security* (Minneapolis, MN:

University of Minnesota Press 1992); J. Der Derian and M. J. Shapiro (eds), *Intertextual/International Relations* (Lexington, MA: Lexington Books 1989); K. Krause and M.C. Williams (eds), *Critical Security Studies* (Minneapolis, MN: University of Minnesota Press 1997); Y. Lapid and F. Kratochwil (eds), *The Return of Culture and Identity in IR Theory* (Boulder, CO: Lynne Rienner 1996); J. G. Ruggie, 'Territoriality and Beyond: Problematizing Modernity in International Relations', *International Organization* 47/2 (1993) pp.139–74; and, among others, R.B.J. Walker, *Inside/Outside* (Cambridge: Cambridge University Press 1993). In political geography see: J.A. Agnew, *Place and Politics* (Boston, MA: Allen and Unwin 1987); S. Dalby, *Creating the Second Cold War* (London: Pinter 1990); A. Paasi, 'The Institutionalization of Regions: A Theoretical Framework for Understanding the Emergence of Regions and the Constitution of Regional Identity' *Fennia* 16/1 (1986) pp.105–46; G. Toal, *Critical Geopolitics* (Minneapolis, MN: University of Minnesota Press 1996); and, among others, P. Taylor, 'Beyond Containers: Internationality, Interstateness, Interterritoriality', *Progress in Human Geography* 19/1 (1995) pp.1–15 and 'The State as a Container: Territoriality in the Modern World-System', *Progress in Human Geography* 18/2 (1995) pp.151–62.

2. J.A. Agnew and S. Corbridge, *Mastering Space* (London: Routledge 1995) p.3.

3. J.A. Agnew, *Geopolitics* (London: Routledge 1998).

4. In this reading, IR is as much as *cosmology* as it is the study of institutional practices in the world. M. J. Shapiro, 'Warring Bodies and Bodies Politic: Tribal Warriors versus State Soldiers', in M.J. Shapiro and H.K. Alker (eds), *Challenging Boundaries* (Minneapolis, MN: University of Minnesota Press 1996) pp.457–8.

5. J.N. Entrikin, *The Betweenness of Place* (Baltimore, MD: Johns Hopkins University Press 1991) and R.J. Johnston, *A Question of Place* (Oxford: Blackwell 1991).

6. E.S. Casey, 'Between Geography and Philosophy: What Does It Mean to Be in the Place-World?' *Annals of the Association of American Geographers* 91/4 (2002) pp.670–80; J.N. Entrikin, 'Hiding Places', *Annals of the Association of American Geographers* 91/4 (2002) pp.681–4.

7. Walker, for instance, notes that international relations is as much concerned with 'entrenched discourses about political life' as it is with international relations *per se*. See Walker (note 1) p.164.

8. On the geopolitical significance of flags, see M. Billig, *Banal Nationalism* (London: Sage 1995).

9. On the importance of popular geopolitical codes, see J.P. Sharp, 'Hegemony, Popular Culture and Geopolitics: the *Reader's Digest* and the Construction of Danger', *Political Geography* 15/6–7 (1996) pp.557–70.

10. The term 'terrorist alien' is taken from J. Ashcroft, *Attorney General John Ashcroft Outlines Foreign Terrorist Tracking Task Force* (2002), available on-line at <http://www.usdoj.gov/ag/speeches/2001/agcrisisremarks 10_31.html>.

11. The recent border build-up can be placed within a larger period of US–Mexico border militarisation. See T. Dunn, *The Militarization of the US–Mexico Border 1978–1992* (Austin, TX: University of Texas Press 1996) and J. Nevins, *Operation Gatekeeper* (London: Routledge 2002).

12. On the contradiction between these security practices and free trade, see: S. Flynn, 'America the Vulnerable', *Foreign Affairs* 81/1 (2002) pp.60–67.

13. More than four million of the new credit card style 'laser visas' were issued.

14. Cross-border convenience shopping dropped drastically in San Diego's San Ysidro region during the four months following 11 September. San Ysidro businesses are approximately 90 per cent dependent on the business of border-crossing Mexican nationals – a $4 billion per year economy. Local business associations backed San Diego City's declaration of a state of emergency, and supported a drive for $20 million worth of federal funding to prop up local businesses and make ports of entry more efficient.

15. Ashcroft (note 10). A series of public laws – the Illegal Immigration Reform and Control Act of 1986, the Immigration Act of 1990, the Violent Crime and Law Enforcement Act of 1994, the Antiterrorism and Effective Death Penalty Act of 1996, and the Illegal Immigration Reform and Immigrant Responsibility Act of 1996 – have worked steadily to inflate the grounds for immigration inadmissibility by expanding the definition of 'aggravated felony' and 'criminality', and by developing definitions of 'terrorist' organizations. In this sense, although the new PATRIOT Act and the Enhanced Border

      Security Act may be novel in terms of the vast sums of money involved, their substance in
      fact is not, as both build on trends already well-cemented in congressional public law
      making in the realm of immigration.
16.   B.W. Blouet, *Geopolitics and Globalization in the Twentieth Century* (London: Reaktion
      Books 2001).
17.   R.D. Sack, *Human Territoriality* (Cambridge: Cambridge University Press 1986) p.19.
18.   See: A. Paasi, 'Classics in Human Geography Revisited: Commentary 2', *Progress in
      Human Geography* 24/1 (2000) pp.93–5 and J.A. Agnew, 'Classics in Human Geography
      Revisited: Commentary 1', *Progress in Human Geography* 24/1 (2000) pp.91–3.
19.   On 'identities, borders, and orders' see M. Albert, D. Jacobson and Y. Lapid (eds),
      Identities, Borders, Orders (Minneapolis, MN: University of Minnesota Press 2001). On
      'territorialities, identities, movements', see: L. Brock, 'Observing Change, "Rewriting"
      History: A Critical Overview', *Millennium* 28/3 (1999) pp.483–97.
20.   A. Paasi and D. Newman, 'Fences and Neighbors in the Postmodern World: Boundary
      Narratives in Political Geography', *Progress in Human Geography* 22/2 (Feb. 1998) p.195.
      For an account of boundaries as indicative of more general social processes, see: A. Paasi,
      Territories, Boundaries, and Consciousness (New York: John Wiley 1996).
21.   M. Albert and L. Brock, 'What Keeps Westphalia Together? Normative Differentiation in
      the Modern System of States', in Albert, Jacobson and Lapid (note 19) pp.29–50.
22.   Paasi and Newman (note 20).
23.   M. Ignatieff, *Blood and Belonging* (New York: Farrar, Straus and Giroux 1993).
24.   W.E. Connolly, *Identity/Difference* (Ithaca: Cornell University Press 1991).
25.   Geo-graphing refers to the authoring of spaces on the earth. For instance, geo-graphy is 'not
      something already possessed by the earth but an active writing of the earth by an expanding,
      centralizing imperial state'. See Toal, *Critical Geopolitics* (note 1) p.2.
26.   The category of 'terrorism' has purchase only in relation to the terms 'state', 'war' and
      'sovereignty'. In other words, 'terrorism' – a word invented 'to characterise nonstate
      violence by those closed out of the system of states' – is the other to a system of states, in
      which the units are expressly authorised to employ violent warring means in the securing of
      territorial sovereignty. W.E. Connolly, 'Identity and Difference in Global Politics', in Der
      Derian and Shapiro (note 1) p.334.
27.   S. Dalby, 'Contesting an Essential Concept: Reading the Dilemmas in Contemporary
      Security Discourse', in Krause and Williams (note 1) pp.3–32.
28.   J. Gottmann, 'Geography and International Relations', *World Politics* 3/2 (1951) pp.153–73
      and idem, 'The Political Partitioning of the Our World: An Attempt at Analysis', *World
      Politics* 4/4 (1952) pp.512–19. For an excellent review and discussion of Gottmann's
      geographies of 'circulation' and 'rescue' see L. Muscarà, 'Jean Gottmann's Atlantic
      Transhumance and the Development of his Spatial Theory', *Finisterra* 33/65 (1998)
      pp.159–72 and idem, 'Les Mots Justes de Jean Gottmann', *Cybergeo* 54 (1998) pp.1–15.
29.   Recent study inspired by Gottmann's political geography has focused on stamps and flags
      as important iconographic markers in the assertion of identity and place. See: S.D. Brunn,
      'Stamps as Iconography: Celebrating the Independence of New European and Central Asian
      States', *GeoJournal* 52/4 (2001) pp.315–23 and S. Matjunin, 'The New State Flags as
      Iconographic Symbols of the post-Soviet Space', *GeoJournal* 52/4 (2001) pp.311–13.
30.   L. Muscarà, 'Gottmann's Geographic Glossa', *GeoJournal* 52/4 (2001) p.290.
31.   G. Prevelakis, 'Preface', *GeoJournal* 52/4 (2001) p.281.
32.   Muscarà, 'Gottmann's Geographic Glossa' (note 30) p.286. This is most obviously the case
      when considering ethno-national claims of belonging. See, for instance, F. Eva, 'For a
      Europe of Flexible Regions and not of Region-States Divided by Ethnicity', *GeoJournal*
      52/4 (2001) pp.295–301.
33.   D. Morley and K. Robins, 'No Place Like Heimat: Images of Home(land) in European
      Culture', in E. Carter, J. Donald and J. Squires (eds), *Space and Place* (London: Lawrence
      and Wishart 1993) pp.3–32.
34.   I borrow the language from W.J.M. Mackenzie, *Political Identity* (New York: St Martin's
      Press 1978).
35.   I owe this insightful point to an anonymous reviewer. However, it is interesting to point out
      that this process of Americanisation shapes living bodies too, and sometimes in the most
      puzzling places (i.e. not in the United States). For instance, in a recent article Rosas recounts
      a 11 September interview with a group of young, male Mexicans living on the border. Once

incarcerated in the United States on immigration-related charges, and now seeking work in the *maquiladoras*, this group of men imagine out loud fighting in the US Army against Osama bin Laden in order to avenge the deaths of Mexican *paisanos* killed in the World Trade Center towers. See G. Rosas, 'Post-September 11 at the Border', *Bad Subjects – Political Education for Everyday Life* 60 (2002), available online at <http://eserver.org/bs/>.

36. This is precisely the logic employed by the Bush administration to justify a hyper-attentive domestic counter-terrorism. See: P. Passavant and J. Dean, 'Representation and the Event', *Theory and Event* 5/4 (2001) p.9.

37. This is perhaps most obvious in the publication's photos of the 'most wanted man in the world', Osama bin Laden, Emir General of *Al Qaeda*. While bin Laden is made visible and tangible, his latent evil is represented, in a particularly telling photo, by capturing his serious and scornful bearded face through a blood-red tinted lens.

38. President   Bush's   29   January   2002   Address   is   available   online   at <http://www.whitehouse.gov>.

39. Office of Management and Budget, Executive Office of the President of the United States, *Budget of the United States Federal Government, Fiscal Year 2003* (Washington, DC: US Government Printing Office 2002) p.15.

40. Ibid.

41. C. Schmitt, *The Concept of the Political* (Chicago, IL: University of Chicago Press 1996) p.26.

42. Ibid. p.38.

43. Ibid. p.49.

44. Ibid.

45. Schmitt voluntarily joined the National Socialist Party in May 1933 (one year following the original publication of *The Concept of the Political*). Schmitt's virulent and open anti-Semitism between 1933 and 1936, his generally apologetic stance with respect to Nazi practices during the Second World War, and his public defense of the Nazi treatment of Jews during the Nuremberg trials, have made Schmitt a very difficult philosophical-political personage open to extensive critique. See J. Habermas, *The Inclusion of the Other* (Cambridge, MA: MIT Press 1998). Unfortunately, as Mouffe and others note, much of this critique proceeds in an *ad hominen* manner and dismisses his philosophical insights on the basis of his politics. See C. Mouffe (ed.), *The Challenge of Carl Schmitt* (London: Verso 1999) and T. Strong, 'Dimensions of the New Debate Around Carl Schmitt', in G. Schwab (ed.), *The Concept of the Political* (Chicago: University of Chicago Press 1996) pp.ix–xxix.

46. Ibid. p.54.

47. Ibid.

48. Connolly, *Identity/Difference* (note 24) p.207.

49. Of course, some rogue states are overtly referred to as terrorist states by the US government and other western states. This conflation confounds more contemporary uses of 'terrorism' as a moral exception to statehood. See: M. Klare, *Rogue States and Nuclear Outlaws* (New York: Hill and Wang 1995) and G. Toal and T. Luke, 'Present at the (Dis)integration: Deterritorialization and Reterritorialization in the New Wor(l)d Order', *Annals of the Association of American Geographers* 84/3 (1994) pp.381–98.

50. A recent US federal judicial ruling has further suggested that these detainees are not under the jurisdiction of the US Constitution either, since Guantánamo Bay is not formally American territory, but land leased annually from the Cuban government.

51. This claim has been articulated by both the International Committee of the Red Cross and Amnesty International.

52. This is quite clearly against the Third Geneva Convention, which requires that once a conflict is over enemy combatants must either be officially charged or released.

53. M. Walzer, 'Five Questions About Terrorism', *Dissent* 49/1 (2002) pp.1–6.

54. This essay has concentrated on the US reaction to the events of 11 September in terms of 'American' politics of identity and place making. However, it seems all too clear that the same interrogation could be made of the Al Qaeda network and political campaign. For instance, it is evident that bin Laden considers America to be evil, and that his politics concerns a sense of identity and place driven by an inflated sense of American responsibility for Middle Eastern disorder. A corrective to the narrow focus of this essay would consider this area of pressing importance.

55. To follow through on Schmitt's discussion of the strategic geopolitical use of humanity and

justice in a professed pluriverse of incompatible group projects and values tends to render ethical questions surficial, so to speak, to the warring relation of friend/enemy, thereby risking – as noted in the text – a normalisation of the horrors of identity politics. My employment of Schmitt's claims concerning the tactical utility of the concepts of humanity and justice is intended to invite a decidedly different consideration of the ethical content of the friend/enemy relation, and of the injustices lodged in any identification of evil. This is in the spirit of Connolly, *Identity/Difference* (note 24). For an in-depth discussion of these issues in Connolly's work, see: K. Roy, *Political Encounters in Benevolence*, thesis, Carleton University, Canada, 2002.

56. J. Sidaway, 'Iraq/Yugoslavia: Banal Geopolitics', *Antipode* 33/4 (2001) p.601.

57. Campbell, *Writing Security* (note 1).

58. For instance, Sack urges geographers to consider modern human agents as 'geographical leviathans' whose actions are distinctly unbordered. See R. Sack, *Homo Geographicus* (Baltimore, MD: Johns Hopkins University Press 1997).

59. The language of 'dilemmatic spaces' and 'remainders' is taken from B. Honig, 'Difference, Dilemmas, and the Politics of Home' in S. Benhabib (ed.), *Democracy and Difference* (Princeton, NJ: Princeton University Press 1996) pp.257–77.

60. S. Dalby, 'Globalisation or Global Apartheid? Boundaries and Knowledge in Postmodern Times', in D. Newman (ed.), *Boundaries, Territory and Postmodernity* (London: Frank Cass 1999) p.140. For a similar assessment, see also G. Toal, 'Borderless Worlds? Problematising Discourses of Deterritorialisation', *Geopolitics* 4/2 (1999) pp.139–54 and idem, 'De-Territorialised Threats and Global Dangers: Geopolitics and Risk Society', in Newman, *Boundaries*, pp.17–31.

61. Dalby, 'Globalisation' (note 60) p.147. See also idem, 'Calling 911: Geopolitics, Security and America's New War', *Geopolitics* 8/3 (2003) pp.61–86.

62. See: M. Kaldor, *New and Old Wars: Organized Violence in a Global Era* (Cambridge: Polity Press 1999).

63. Y.F. Tuan, *Escapism* (Baltimore, MD: The Johns Hopkins University Press 1998) and idem, 'Island Selves: Human Disconnectedness in a World of Interdependence', *Geographical Review* 85/2 (1995) pp.229–39. See also Entrikin, *The Betweenness of Place* (note 5).

64. E. Said, 'Together We Must Stand', *Guardian Weekly* (20–26 September 2001) p.15. Walzer also notes the need to contextualise the events of 11 September in a larger geopolitical framework, but his conclusions are radically different from those drawn by Said. Walzer argues that American foreign policies cannot be altered in the face of 'terrorism' because they will be globally interpreted as appeasement: 'There are American policies ... that should be changed, but in politics one must not only do the right thing, one must do it for the right reasons; the attacks of September 11 are not a good reason for change'. See Walzer (note 53) p.6. Kaplan also insists on understanding the events in a geopolitically contextualised sense but, as with Walzer, takes a realist rather than a critical stance: US foreign policy is about maintaining hegemonic priorities and strategic interests, and thus cannot be faulted in the face of threats to preeminence. See: R.D. Kaplan, *Soldiers of God* (New York: Vintage 2001).

65. M. Mann, 'Globalization and September 11', *New Left Review* 12 (2001) pp.51–72.

66. N. Milner, S. Krishna and K.E. Ferguson, 'The US Response as Armed Struggle', *Theory and Event* 5/4 (2002).

67. W. Pfaff, 'The Question of Hegemony', *Foreign Affairs* 80/1 (2001) pp.221–32.

68. C. Johnson, *Blowback: The Costs and Consequences of American Empire* (New York: Metropolitan Books 2000).

69. D. Campbell, 'Time is Broken: The Return of the Past in the Response to September 11', *Theory and Event* 5/4 (2002).

70. J. Der Derian, *Before, After, and In-Between* (2001), available online at <http://www.ssrc.org/sept11/essays/der_derian.htm>.

Strategic Troping in Sri Lanka: *September Eleventh* and the Consolidation of Political Position

MARGO KLEINFELD

Introduction

On 11 September 2001,[1] people in Sri Lanka sat glued to their TV sets watching images of the New York World Trade Center towers collapsing, due to the unusual move by CNN to use its US feed to broadcast footage throughout South Asia.[2]

But once the initial shock of those images gave way to political analysis and discussion, it became clear to me while doing research in Colombo that the *September eleventh* presented in the popular American press was not the same *September eleventh* that I witnessed in Sri Lanka.[3] That *September eleventh* occurred within an existing *Sri Lankan* discourse about terror, war, national liberation, homelands, sovereignty and a host of other elements that have long been staples of Sri Lankan politics, especially as they pertain to the nearly twenty-year old civil conflict.[4]

As elsewhere in the world, *September eleventh* was also a discursive event and figure of speech or trope – 'literally a turn or deviation from literal speech or the conventional meaning and order of words', according to Hayden White.[5] In Sri Lanka, it performed a variety of political tasks for both parties to the conflict: the People's Alliance government until its parliamentary defeat in December 2001, and the Liberation Tigers of Tamil Eelam (LTTE), also referred to as the Tigers, a group that has been fighting for a separate state, Tamil Eelam, since about 1983.[6] From 11 September 2001 through the dissolution of parliament by President Chandrika Bandaranaike Kumaratunga on 10 October, and until the snap elections of 5 December 2001,[7] the PA government and the LTTE used *September eleventh* as a new opportunity to brand the other as terrorist – LTTE terrorist or state terrorist – but this time invigorated with the emotional intensity and moral certitude attached to the events in the United States and the global response. In this essay, I argue that *September eleventh* and its associated lexicon were used by both belligerents to vilify the other and to code and recode stories about the Sri Lankan war through the trope of synecdoche, and that the purpose of this troping strategy was to destabilize each adversary's legitimacy while promoting their own territorial desires and visions for the future.

Tropes, Synecdoche and Global Framing of Political Violence

Narrative has become a staple of geopolitical analysis since the body of work known as critical geopolitics, brought to prominence by John Agnew, Gerard Toal (Gearóid Ó Tuathail), Simon Dalby, Paul Routledge and others, problematised geopolitics itself as a discursive project.[8] In this literature, political narratives are connected to the production of political spaces such as states, homelands, boundaries and geopolitical world orders (e.g. East and West) through strategic representations, discourses, and metaphors. An examination of troping as such, however, that is the transformation of a chronicle of events into a story with a beginning, middle and end,[9] has not typically been employed to analyse geopolitical texts.[10] In this essay I hope to demonstrate that troping and the arrangement of events in narrative, the choice of plotlines, and the deployment of implicit relationships through tropes, can be useful to geopolitical scholars interested in uncovering meaning beyond the content of narrative.

There are four master tropes that facilitate the allegorisation of events and the emplotment of facts into narrative: metaphor, metonymy, synecdoche and irony.[11] Each of these asserts particular types of relationships within phenomena, which become the basis for narrative structure, whether in historical texts, fiction, or in discourses associated with contemporary politics. The synecdoche is best known as a signifier expressing a part for a whole relation and the 'sharing of essential qualities behind or beneath manifest attributes of two or more entities'.[12] The individual as a replica of the universe, according to Kenneth Burke, is synecdoche in its most ideal form.[13] In addition to integrating phenomena into a whole, an important function of synecdoche is 'to *justify belief* in the possibility of understanding the particular as a microcosm of a macrocosmic totality'.[14]

September eleventh in Sri Lanka has worked as a synecdoche by implying the interconnectedness of all political violence. In this way, *September eleventh* can signify an instance of global terrorism such as the US attacks, as well as an LTTE attack or a repressive action by the government of Sri Lanka. In his work on the rhetorics of landscape, Jim Duncan notes that 'synecdoches are powerful signifiers because they parsimoniously conjure up in the mind of the observer a whole narrative'.[15] One reason that *September eleventh* as synecdoche has been so powerful in the United States is that it has been able to provide unproblematic causal connections and explanations for complex and dynamic political histories and geographies, rooted in politically comfortable 'Islam versus the West' geopolitical narratives.[16]

In Sri Lanka, *September eleventh* supplied a slightly different morality tale built upon familiar tropes of unjustified violence, and easily inserted into an existing political discourse that refers back to ancient Tamil and Sinhalese narratives describing the contest for control of Sri Lanka. Since September 2001, each party to the conflict has used the trope of *September eleventh* as shorthand for terror, blind hate and evil in order to reinforce its demonisation of the other. And, importantly, alongside accusations based on these emotionally charged embedded referents was the emplotted solution – eradicate them without compromise. Terrorism in this sense can be regarded as a hegemonic signifier.[17] There is only one course of action related to it: stamp out the terror and annihilate the terrorist. This one-sided, no-options politics is a powerful instrument for identifying actors to be destroyed or disciplined, and for claiming a particular future and specific spaces – in Sri Lanka, a Sinhalese-dominated unitary state or an LTTE-controlled region in the north and the east – to be protected from harm.

September eleventh as synecdoche also provided a discursive strategy that set the scale or 'structural context' for political action.[18] What is interesting is that there are no struggles by political actors in Sri Lanka over the appropriate scale of the conflict after September 2001. Both sides used the global framework that *September eleventh* and the geopolitical actions associated with it signified, in Sri Lankan narratives about terror, war and the belligerent other. By attempting to locate themselves on the 'outside' of global terror and the other on the 'inside', the PA government and the LTTE were able to overcome their particular limitations at other scales. The PA tried to link LTTE actions to global terror, hoping to justify calls for international assistance in a failing war with the LTTE. The Tigers and their supporters, on the other hand, used *September eleventh* to argue against its status as a terrorist organization, which had resulted in the proscription of the group in several countries including India, the United States and Canada. A global context for the war in Sri Lanka effectively elevated what could be construed as a national or local struggle to international significance. Furthermore, the global scale enabled the invocation of particular actors such as 'the international community', 'the Sinhalese people', or national liberation movements throughout the world, while allowing others to fade, for example civilians affected by the government embargo of goods into the conflict area or victims caught in the crossfire of a political assassination.

Existing Plots: Contentious Nationalisms, Terror and Injustice

The many different narratives about the war in Sri Lanka indicate how historians, politicians and others pick and choose facts and their arrangement to make their stories meaningful.

> Since no given set or sequence of real events is intrinsically tragic, comic, farcical, and so on, but can be constructed as such only by the imposition of the structure of a given story type on the events, it is the choice of the story type and its imposition upon the events that endow them with meaning. The effect of such emplotment may be regarded as an explanation.[19]

As is the case with so many conflicts associated with competing nationalisms, stories of historic enmity in Sri Lanka, promulgated by nationalists from both sides, have served to naturalise complex peoples into two distinct and mutually exclusive identities.[20]

On one side of the conflict are the Sinhalese, who live mostly in the southern and central parts of Sri Lanka and make up approximately 74 per cent of the population. The Sinhalese can be differentiated according to caste, place (e.g. urban and rural, high country, low country), class and religion (e.g. Buddhist and Christian), among other things. Sinhala nationalism, fueled by the desire to preserve the island for what is considered to be one of the most sacred spaces of Buddhism, has long driven Sri Lankan politics.

On the other side are the Tamils, comprised of at least four distinct groups, including Hindu and Christian Jaffna Tamils in the north, Tamil-speaking Muslims in the east, lower-caste tea workers living in the central region of the country, and Colombo Tamils.[21] The LTTE has promoted itself as the legitimate voice of all the Tamil-speaking people from approximately 1983, despite charges that LTTE opponents have been killed, cleansed from LTTE-controlled areas or 'terrorized into silence', making alternative Tamil representation impossible.[22]

Charges of injustice, terror and genocide have served as the connective tissue in the telling of the conflict in Sri Lanka. For some, the Sri Lanka conflict dates from 1983, when a government-instigated anti-Tamil pogrom killed about 3,000 individuals, displaced hundreds of thousands, and inspired even moderate Tamils to take up arms against the government or support those who would.[23] For others, the conflict dates from 1977, when the Tamil United Liberation Front (TULF) put forth its agenda for an independent state called Tamil Eelam, which was considered to be a direct provocation against the Sri Lankan state and its territorial integrity. A. Jeyaratnam Wilson cites Sri Lanka's independence from Great Britain and the intensification of communal tensions between the majority Sinhalese and the minority Tamils as the catalyst for conflict, beginning with the government's disenfranchisement of the Tamil tea workers immediately after independence to change the balance of power that favoured the Sinhalese. The seeds of conflict are also linked to the Buddhist revivalism of the nineteenth century, and a corresponding defensive ethnonationalism on the part of the Jaffna Tamils.[24] The history of violent conflict is frequently traced back to the early chronicles of Sinhalese kings defeating Tamil ones, most notably the defeat of the South Indian Chola (Tamil), King Elara, by Dutugemunu, who re-established Sinhalese control over the island, and thereby created a safe space for Buddhism to flourish.[25]

The term 'terrorist' in Sri Lanka became popularised with the 1979 Prevention of Terrorism Act (PTA) directed at political violence in Tamil-dominated areas in the northern and eastern parts of the island.[26] Well before *September eleventh*, it was not unusual to hear the LTTE referred to only as 'the terrorists' by hardline Sinhalese nationalists as well as moderates. Cited as Tiger terrorist activities are several high-profile political assassinations, including the suicide bombings of the Indian Prime Minister Rajiv Gandhi in 1990, the President of Sri Lanka, Ranasinghe Premadasa, in 1993, and Neelan Tiruchelvam, a Tamil member of Parliament, scholar and peace activist killed in July 1999. An unsuccessful attempt to assassinate President Kumaratunga in 1999 resulted in permanent injury. Nearby civilians have also been killed as a result of these and other suicide attacks that have mostly targeted leaders opposed to the Tigers or to Tamil Eelam.

There is also a long list of LTTE attacks on economic and governmental infrastructure, including the bombing of the Central Bank in 1996, and the detonation of a truck filled with explosives at the Dalada Maligawa (Temple of the Tooth), one of Sri Lanka's holiest Buddhist shrines, which resulted in the banning of the group and its activities in the country.[27] The most recent attack was on the Bandaranaike International Airport in July 2001. For many in the government, and to repeat a popular phrase attributed to President Wijetunge in 1993, 'there is no ethnic problem in Sri Lanka, only a terrorist problem'.

Political violence in the last few decades has been well documented for both sides of the war in Sri Lanka, however. According to the LTTE, ethnically motivated, racist Sinhalese regimes have not only denied Tamils their rights and control over their lands in their desire for a Buddhist Sinhala homeland encompassing the entire island, but have had genocidal intentions as well. Early governmental actions such as the 1956 Sinhala Only Act, quotas for university admissions, and internal colonisation schemes affecting the Tamil-dominated dry zone are cited as evidence.[28]

More recently, the PTA, designed by the Jaywardena government and still in force today, has been widely criticised for its indefinite detentions and state-sanctioned torture.[29] The same Jaywardena government is thought to be responsible for the 1983 anti-Tamil pogrom referred to as the Tamil holocaust. During the 1990s, indiscriminate bombings, massacres, rape while in custody, and an economic embargo preventing medicine and food from entering the conflict areas, are part of a long list of human rights violations by the government, verified by international non-governmental organizations (INGOs) and which, according to the LTTE, indicate state terror.[30] Specific allegations have indeed been verified by INGOs, undoubtedly part of the reason for their problematic relationship with the Sri Lanka government.[31]

Political Environment Prior to *September Eleventh*

In June 2001, President Kumaratunga and the PA, her fragile coalition government, lost its parliamentary majority when Rauf Hakeem and the Sri Lanka Muslim Congress crossed over to the opposition. In order to avoid a no-confidence motion, Kumuratunga prorogued Parliament on 11 July. Two weeks later, the LTTE attacked the Bandaranaike International Airport in Katunayake; about a dozen military aircraft and half of the state's civilian fleet were damaged or destroyed. Casualties remained limited, although Western tourists caught in the crossfire were the cause of widespread international media attention.

The attack indicated that, first, the Tigers had the military intelligence, means and desire to continue attacking the South, despite government claims regarding the success of their 'war for peace strategy'; and second, that as a result of ever-increasing defence spending and the likelihood of LTTE attacks on other economic targets in the future, the economy was on a hopeless course. Western governments that had not already done so issued travel warnings about the country's unstable political situation, eroding any hope of an economic turnaround in a country dependent on tourist dollars. War risk surcharges levied soon after the attack were also a blow to the shipping industry.

Despite charges of totalitarianism and dictatorship,[32] parliament remained suspended in Sri Lanka until the first week of September 2001, when the PA government entered into an unlikely alliance with the Marxist and ultra-nationalist Janatha Vimukthi Peramuna (JVP), responsible for two bloody uprisings that resulted in approximately 80,000 dead; one in 1971 against the government of Sirimavo Bandaranaike, Kumaratunga's mother, the other in 1988.[33] In addition to the new caretaker government, many were upset by some of the JVP's conditions, especially that no peace negotiations take place with the LTTE for one year. One week after the signing of the PA–JVP Memorandum of Understanding, four planeloads of civilians were deployed against US targets.

Initial Response to *September Eleventh*

Euphoria

There was a deluge of response to *September eleventh* in the Sri Lankan press during the first week and a half after the attacks.[34] The official response from the government was certainly one of sympathy, but sympathy with a purpose – for the world to unite against terror and eradicate it wherever it strikes, especially in Sri Lanka. From Kumaratunga's first statements, highlighting the need for an 'international community to suppress terrorism',[35] the PA government, Sinhala hardliners and moderate nationalists became euphoric in light of the new global war on terrorism. George W. Bush's and Dick Cheney's sabre-rattling were front-page news in the state-run *Daily News*. Headlines optimistically declared that 'Terrorism will Face Full Wrath of US' and 'World Terrorism will Now be Wiped Out'.[36] *September eleventh* and Bush's promises to deal with terrorism in the form of a global alliance was heady stuff in Sinhalese Sri Lanka, justifying continuing the military intervention against the Tigers, with the general warning that 'unless we stand together, we will fall together'.[37]

Sri Lanka's Role

For many in the south, Sri Lanka had suffered alone with a terrorist problem for more than 18 years. Sri Lanka's plight had finally 'assumed urgent global relevance' and because of its experience with terrorism, Sri Lanka would undoubtedly be 'a frontline state in the global war on terror'.[38] These sentiments were underscored by the fear that if Sri Lanka didn't 'strike while the iron was hot' and compel foreign governments to get involved in the conflict with the LTTE, that Sri Lanka would become the weak link in the global war.[39]

But beneath the anticipation that Sri Lanka would soon have the military muscle to defeat the Tigers, there was a simmering anger that Sri Lanka's conflict had been ignored by the international community for far too long. Outrage over US double standards on terrorism filled the national press from journalists and the public at large: 'It appears by TV comments, that only Americans are real people; there's been no outrage for non-Americans who have been killed.'[40] In one letter, a citizen asks: 'Where were they when the Tigers attacked Sri Lanka?', and answers, 'only terrorism against white nations remains unacceptable ... they just send travel advisories for their own citizens.'[41]

International hypocrisy on matters related to terrorism was also chronicled in the national press as well. This included US failed promises to eradicate continuing work for the LTTE policies toward Islamic peoples; Tony Blair's terrorists demonstrated by the fact that Anton Balasingham from England, or the fact that until the events of 11 September, terrorism had not been put on the agenda of the Commonwealth Summit scheduled for October.[42]

Global Terror Networks

Newspaper reports on the 'globality' of the terror problem were common. LTTE practices, such as suicide bombings, emulated by other *terrorists* were often cited as an indication that the conflict was not Sri Lanka's alone. Sinhala nationalists argued vigorously that all terrorists were interlinked through the same financial and communication networks that crisscrossed the globe, and fueled the production of terror. The Tamil diaspora and the Western states that sheltered them were also implicated in these networks. Initially, both the LTTE and Al Qaeda were thought to be working separately through the same 'conduits of evil'; for example, both groups were allegedly collecting money at the Canadian border.[43]

September eleventh soon became an opportunity to directly link Tiger terror to *September eleventh* terror, however. From about 17 September, the LTTE and Al Qaeda were specifically associated with one each other, while the press ridiculed any 'terrorist groups that masqueraded as liberation movements' and called for the ban of all liberation movements.[44] And, following on the heals of the US 'no negotiations with terrorists' position, intensified after *September eleventh*, any sort of political settlement with the LTTE was attacked: absolutely 'no negotiations with rabid dogs'.[45] The president of the nationalist Sinhala Jathika Sangamaya mocked, 'no one has yet urged the United States of America to enter into "Peace Talks" with whatever terrorist organization it was that was responsible' for *September eleventh*.[46]

The LTTE Responds

On 15 September, when the *Daily News* published the story, 'Destruction of Pentagon, a Good Lesson say Tigers',[47] the LTTE issued a sharp statement condemning the US attacks and denying the story's charges that it had distributed leaflets in Jaffna saying the attacks 'were a good lesson for the US'. In the statement, Anton Balasingham denounced the government's story:

It is sad to note that the Sri Lanka government and its anti-LTTE ally, the EPDP,[48] are attempting to exploit the phenomenal tragedy faced by the American people to their own political advantage.

We share the profound sorrow and anguish experienced by the families, relatives and friends of those thousands of innocent victims who perished in this carnage. This is a colossal human tragedy and we condemn this brutal crime.[49]

On 19 September, a *Tamil Guardian* editorial entitled 'In Defence of Homeland: The American People's Intent of Self-Defence is Understood', affirmed support for the US war on terror by the Tamil community within and beyond Sri Lanka, particularly in the face of unjustified violence. The author acknowledged and welcomed the US no compromise position against those sworn to destroy it, and adopted *September eleventh* as a Tamil symbol for the rightful defence of homeland and the Tamil war on terror in Sri Lanka. 'Hate-filled attackers', and the terror directed at the Tamil people since 1983, became dominant metaphors used to describe the actions of the Sri Lankan government:

Over days, not hours, systematically, not abruptly, and with unannounced malice, not declared intent, the lives of several thousand people were extinguished by Sinhala mobs in a historic cataclysm which forced the Tamil community into resolute determination to remove forever the threat of ethnic pogrom that dangles over them. As we watch American youth flock to military recruitment centers across their homeland, we recognize the same outrage which drove Tamil volunteers to armed struggle in the aftermath of our holocaust.[50]

Just as the government of Sri Lanka used *September eleventh* to reframe their war with the LTTE, the LTTE and their supporters used the same trope to recode their movement as legitimate and just, and to charge the government with state terror.

The US Embassy Speaks

The euphoria and hoped for intensification of the government's military crackdown on the LTTE, constellated during the aftermath of *September eleventh,* took another turn on 23 September, when Stephen Holgate, the US Embassy spokesperson in Colombo, 'made it clear that the LTTE would not be a specific target when the US began its global assault on terrorism'.[51] Holgate's statements were front-page news in the *Sunday Times*:

> We are fighting against terrorists who are not asking anything; they are not demanding anything, and not coming for negotiations; they want only to kill Americans ...There is a distinction between the LTTE and the terrorist in the Middle East. So the U.S. has not changed its stand in calling on the Sri Lankan Government to go for peace talks.[52]

Holgate's remarks complicated the government's deployment of the trope of *September eleventh*, particularly its more explicit argument that Sri Lankan terror was global terror. Not surprisingly, the reaction to Holgate's position was intense; people were furious. The first published editorial in response, 'Forked tongue', ran alongside Holgate's remarks, and was to become one in an endless stream of indictments of US hypocrisy and double standards with respect to terror.

> The U.S. has nothing to negotiate with Osama bin Laden as he hates America full-stop. But, with LTTE terrorists, it is a different cup of tea, because they are asking for something! If Osama bin Laden demands 1/3rd of American and 2/3rds of its coast as a separate state tomorrow – does it mean that the U.S. must not then wage war but negotiate with bin Laden? ...
>
> Sri Lankans have to smirk at all of this, having lived though it for so long, as we know about terrorism first hand, having borne the brunt of a more vicious and ferocious kind of terrorism than the U.S. has just faced for so many years now.[53]

A statement released immediately after the story broke, from Lewis Amselem, US chargé d'affaires, expressed support for the PA government's position on terrorism, but reminded the restless Colombo community that negotiations were Kumaratunga's idea:

> The United States has supported and will continue to support the policy of the Government of Sri Lanka, which while resisting terrorism says that a political solution must be found to the civil conflict in this country. We have long agreed with President Kumaratunga's position that negotiation offers the best hope for long-term peace in Sri Lanka. We also reiterate our support for the position of the Sri Lankan Government against the establishment of an independent Tamil Eelam.[54]

Two days later, Amselem repeated these statements at a memorial service for the victims of *September eleventh*, this time adding that 'terror is terror' and 'mass murder is mass murder'. He emphasised his earlier remarks regarding negotiations:

We support the Government of Sri Lanka's *long-standing and repeatedly announced goal* of seeking a negotiated political solution to the conflict that has hurt this wonderful country and its people regardless of their ethnicity or religion.[55]

Anselem attempted to extricate the embassy from Holgate's comments. It appeared that his strategy, in addition to suggesting that it was Kumaratunga's idea in the first place, was to maintain the requisite moral closure now associated with terrorism (e.g. necessary to resist, causes harm), but also to uncouple the Sri Lankan situation from *September eleventh* and the snowballing issue of global terror.

The contradictions between *September eleventh* and the moral high ground raised by embassy statements needed to be reconcilled. Despite the overwhelming support for the US position against terrorism – 'Bush's speech was music to our ears'[56] – hardliners insisted that the US embassy statements should be disregarded, and that American *actions* should be emulated instead. Many thought that Sri Lanka's exclusion from the war on terror was based on flawed logic rooted in self-interest and racism. Nalin de Silva asked 'why does the USA have double standards?' and answered that terrorism for the United States only involves attacks on Western civilisation and protestant culture.[57] Implying that Western states with large Tamil communities harboured Tamil terrorists and funded LTTE operations, another headline asked sarcastically, 'Will Bush attack Britain, Norway, Canada?'[58]

The LTTE–Al Qaeda Connection

There was also a redoubling of efforts to strengthen the charge that the LTTE were directly associated with Al Qaeda. Headlines such as 'Probe on LTTE – bin Ladin Links',[59] 'U.S. has Evidence of Osama's Link'[60] and 'Osama Hand in Glove with LTTE',[61] strengthened the argument that *September eleventh* and the Sri Lanka civil war were part of the same global problem. And even though the LTTE was not considered 'terrorist' in the same way as Al Qaeda in the eyes of the US, the mere possibility of a relationship to the world's public enemy number one could be damaging. Speculations about such linkages were taken seriously, and helped to further demonise the LTTE.

The LTTE, its supporters, and those who favoured political negotiations to end the war responded to the alleged relationship by repeatedly stating that there were no connections between the LTTE and the events of *September eleventh*. LTTE sympathisers argued that the PA government would 'go to any lengths to tie the Tamil Tigers with Al-Qaida', even if it meant denials or distortions.[62] Furthermore, by attempting to link the LTTE with 'America's self-avowed enemies' the Sri Lankan government appeared to have a 'desperate need to justify its own tyrannical violence', according to the *Tamil Guardian*.[63] The government's tactic was presented as an indicator of the longtime charges by LTTE sympathisers against the state:

> State controlled information-flows will often deny non-state actors the opportunity and the means to elucidate their positions ... That such states will attempt to ingratiate themselves with the alliance against terror should also be expected. Inevitably, under the guise of 'fighting terrorism', some countries will seek to enlist U.S. military assistance in their own internal repressions.[64]

Government attempts to link the LTTE with Al Qaeda without evidence were used as a fresh opportunity to stigmatise the government and to argue that this was one more example indicative of fanaticism, hate and state terror.

Freedom Struggle

Holgate's statements had been a boon to the LTTE, despite the fury they inspired in the south. The United States favoured negotiations between what seemed to be two legitimate parties, and although the LTTE was banned in the US in 1997, they were clearly not reviled in the same way as Al Qaeda. Moreover, just as the international coalition against terror was gearing up for war, the LTTE's history of committing acts of political violence seemed of little concern to the United States and its partners. One writer even suggested that the LTTE could assist the United States in its war against terror: 'There is every possibility that the Tigers would cooperate wholeheartedly with Washington if it requires assistance.'[65]

The LTTE and its supporters exploited the opportunity to respond to long-time critics and gain political ground. The LTTE were not religious extremists like the Taliban or Al Qaeda, they suggested, nor did they have any religious agenda, as did other groups identified as terrorist. Stories discussing the difference between 'unbridled terror' and hate, and armed struggle in support of freedom, proliferated. Do not automatically condemn non-state entities that take up arms, and unfairly pin the 'terrorist label' on them, LTTE supporters argued.[66] Just as the anti-apartheid movement in South Africa was forced to respond to an unjust state, the LTTE had no choice but to take up arms and resist the government's oppressive practices.[67]

The Campaign

At midnight on 10 October 2001, Kumaratunga dissolved parliament permanently and set elections for 5 December. *September eleventh* was to become the key to election politics in what was often a bloody and chaotic campaign, amidst accusations and defections from one party to another. Two significant events indicate the significance of *September eleventh* during this time. First, the PA party alleged that its political opponent, the United National Party (UNP), headed by Ranil Wickremesinghe, had entered into a secret agreement with the LTTE. This 'secret pact' was tantamount to the support of terrorism by the UNP and its declaration was to shape the election campaign. Second, Velupillai Pirapaharan,[68] the LTTE's infamous leader, addressed his annual Maveerar or Heroes' Day speech to the Sinhala people of the south and to the international community one week before the election. The focus of the speech was terrorism.

Charges and Countercharges

The campaign for control of parliament and the government centred on terror. The PA party argued that any negotiations with LTTE terrorists would result in the destruction of the state of Sri Lanka. They also claimed that the opposition UNP party, now contesting with the Tamil National Alliance (TNA) and others who favoured peace as the path to economic recovery under the banner of the United National Front (UNF), had an illicit pact with the LTTE. Beginning with charges that the LTTE was funding parliamentary defections from the PA to the UNP, there was a crescendo of accusations by the PA leadership including the existence of a secret memorandum which promised the Tigers that the country-wide ban on their activities would be lifted if the UNF won the election.[69]

The UNP did not take these charges lightly, and sued the state-owned Associated Newspapers of Ceylon Ltd, publisher of the *Daily News*, *Dinamina* and *Silumina*.[70] The Supreme Court petition charged the publisher with rights abuses resulting from its articles that asserted a relationship between UNP candidates and the LTTE.[71] The UNP also went on a counteroffensive by taking out full page newspaper advertisements condemning the PA's fabrications, and by soliciting letters from the Mahanayakes Theras, chiefs of the Buddhist clergy and whose moral authority plays a significant role in Sri Lankan politics.[72]

None of this deterred the PA from continuing to cite links between the UNP, the LTTE and terrorism, echoing statements made directly after *September eleventh* that the Tigers were a threat both domestically and internationally. In an interview on 30 October with David Frost about

September eleventh, President Kumaratunga warned that terrorism 'will not be contained within the boundaries of one nation and can spill over ... spill over right across the globe'.[73] In the interview, apparently on the advice of a British PR firm, Kumaratunga not only identified terrorism with the LTTE, but also with previous UNP regimes.[74]

Back at home, the TNA was denounced as a puppet of the LTTE, while UNP 'acts of thuggery' from Jaywardena's times were reiterated in the state press.[75] On 4 November, campaign charges seemed to reach unprecedented heights. The *Daily News* headline read:'If the UNP is Elected, Then Prabhakaran Would Become President'.[76] In addition to these more zealous remarks, there was a liberal dose of terror talk implicating the PA's political opponents. As one commentator on the election noted, all Tamil parties were now viewed and labeled as terrorist.[77]

Although the PA attempted to capitalise on the emotional appeal of *September eleventh*, when many of their accusations linking the LTTE to Al Qaeda and UNF member parties to the LTTE went unconfirmed, and as they became increasingly impassioned, the conclusion was that the PA had little else to run on. PA tactics started to backfire, drawing contempt even from those who sympathised with the PA's anti-LTTE position, as this sarcastic comment demonstrates:

> It's not the UNP's silence on the issue that should cause voter suspicion (as one government newspaper claimed last week). It's the government's miserable cheek, letting terrorists campaign for parliament. What is stopping the police – who sometimes pounce on Tamil civilians on the merest suspicion that they are involved with the LTTE – from arresting publicly denounced terrorists like Ranil Wickremesinghe and the rest of his gang? What's more, the allegation that they are Tigers comes from the head of state.[78]

Pirapaharan Takes His Case to the People – of the South

Until 27 November, the LTTE had made no comment on the election. Pirapaharan's annual Heroes' Day address was, therefore, eagerly awaited, as much for possible 'clues' embedded in the text as to his next move, as for voting instructions to his Tamil supporters. This year, what was extraordinary was that, first, he addressed his talk to the Sinhalese voters of the south and to the international community and, second, that the focus of his talk was the status of the LTTE as a terrorist organisation.

A key theme of the speech was its call for 'a clear and comprehensive definition of the concept of terrorism'.[79] Pirapaharan described two kinds of political violence – the reactive violence of the oppressed or legitimate political violence, and illegitimate violence – the violence of the oppressor.

He lamented that because world governments were now waging a 'global war on terror', that their

> narrow definition [of terrorism] has erased the distinctions between genuine struggles for political independence and terrorist violence. This conception of terrorism has posed a challenge to the moral foundation of armed struggles waged by liberation movements for basic political rights and for the right to self-determination. This development is regrettable. As a consequence our liberation organisation is also being discredited in the international arena.[80]

Pirapaharan described the genocidal conditions that gave birth to the LTTE, the failure of non-violent struggles against the state, and argued that the desire for self-determination and control over Tamil lands was 'neither separatism nor terrorism'. A clear definition of terrorism, Pirapaharan said, would make it obvious that there was a difference between the fight for self-determination and blind terrorism. The LTTE had no choice but to take up arms – unlike those involved in the events of *September eleventh*:

> Our struggle is based on the right to self-determination, a principle endorsed by the UN Charter. We are not terrorists. We are not mentally demented as to commit blind acts of violence impelled by racist and religious fanaticism. We are fighting and sacrificing our lives for the love of a noble cause i.e. human freedom. We are freedom fighters.[81]

A clearer definition of terrorism, he contended, would also compel the international community to see the government of Chandrika Kumaratunga as fanatic and terrorist, and to reconsider their hasty inclusion of the LTTE in lists of terrorists organisations, made under pressure from the Sri Lankan 'war mongering ruling elite'. Pirapaharan urged the international community to identify terrorist states and to penalise them. His final plea to the Sinhalese people was to vote against the racist and repressive policies of the current government of 'Sinhala state terrorists'.[82]

Kadirgamar Responds to Speech

Pirapaharan's speech created a stir in the south. Lakshman Kadirgamar, Sri Lanka's foreign minister, and architect of the international anti-LTTE campaign since Kumaratunga was elected to office in 1994, reacted strongly to the speech in the *Sunday Observer*, three days before the election. In what was to be one last attempt from the PA camp to make its case against negotiations with the LTTE, Kadirgamar identified five themes in the speech and refuted each one. With regard to Pirapaharan's call for a definition of terrorism, Kadirgamar cited pre-*September eleventh* anti-terrorist legislation along with more recent international actions that followed in the wake of *September eleventh*. All of these statements and actions, he argued, unequivocally condemn

> the use of violence to promote a political cause by provoking a state of terror in the general public, a group of persons or a particular person and thereby intimidating the public or influencing the government. These various definitions of terrorism also make it clear that no cause or consideration can be invoked to justify an act of terrorism. Motivation is irrelevant.[83]

Kadirgamar made it absolutely clear in his response that the LTTE were terrorists, and should not be accorded any political legitimacy by the international community. The implication was that the same held true within the national context, and that a vote for the UNP/UNF would be a vote for political parties that condoned negotiations with terrorists. To reinforce this point further, Kadirgamar cited LTTE actions indicative of terror and described them in *September eleventh* terms:

> The bombing of the Central Bank by the LTTE in Colombo was conceptually and symbolically no different from the destruction of the World Trade Centre in New York by al-Qaida – in one case a large explosive device was driven into the building by a suicide driver, in the other a large aeroplane was converted into an explosive device and flown into the building by suicide pilots ...
> The bombing of the Dalada Maligawa by the LTTE is no different from the bombing of the Bamiyan Buddhas by the Taliban. Mr. Prabhakaran's plea is that a so-called 'freedom struggle' should be accorded a licence to commit acts of terror. This is precisely what the international community has refused to concede.[84]

On 5 December 2001, the voters elected the UNF government with Ranil Wickremasinghe as prime minister. Since then, the UNF/UNP has embarked on a fast-track peace process, signing a Memorandum of Understanding with the LTTE on 22 February 2002 for an indefinite cease-fire. Two rounds of peace talks between the Tigers and the UNP government – in September and October 2002 – have already taken place in Thailand, the first such talks in seven years. The talks are thought to have been more successful than expected. The outcome, however, is still far from decided.

Conclusion

That *September eleventh* would become the key to Sri Lankan election politics in October and November 2001 was not a surprise. Ground zero in

New York was feared to become the centre point of an economic crisis in Sri Lanka, intensifying the anxiety from the Bandaranaike Airport attacks of 23 July, as well as the centre of a military crisis, whose effects would emanate from New York to Sri Lanka via Afghanistan. But *September eleventh* also played a critical role in the narratives used by the PA and LTTE, and echoed by their supporters, which had little to do with the economic fallout Sri Lankans would likely experience from the New York and Washington attacks, or the reinvigorated antagonisms between Islam and the West. The troping of *September eleventh* in Sri Lanka was used, instead, to consolidate each party's political position and to undermine their adversary's legitimacy.

In Sri Lanka, *September eleventh* provided a global frame for narratives about terror, about war, and about each belligerent. The PA hoped that a global war would assist them in their war with the LTTE. When US embassy statements made it clear that Sri Lanka would not be of interest to the international coalition against terrorism, the PA attempted to tie the LTTE and Al Qaeda to one other through shared global terror networks, and ignored the 'local' histories and conditions that could put the LTTE and PA into a more complex relationship with one another. *September eleventh* also justified continuing the government's war, since negotiations with global terrorists – Al Qaeda or LTTE – had become unthinkable in Sri Lanka as it was elsewhere.

At the same time, the LTTE used *September eleventh* to resist the PA's charges of terror. With little evidence to demonstrate Al Qaeda's relationship to the LTTE, the LTTE were able to deflect attention designed to implicate them in global terrorism and strengthen arguments against their status as terrorists. Furthermore, under cover of the global discourse on terror that *September eleventh* as synecdoche provided, the Tigers could disengage from the local effects of their actions and deny any relationship to terrorism. Perhaps the greatest boon to the Tigers' cause was Holgate's statements urging the Sri Lankan government to negotiate. The implied logic that negotiations should only take place with non-terrorist opponents helped the Tigers make their case that LTTE political violence was legitimate and just. And, by invoking *September eleventh's* emplotted narrative of hate and fanaticism as the cause of global terror, the LTTE was able to stigmatize the government as state terrorists, showcasing the PA's unfounded allegations designed to implicate the Tigers in the events of *September eleventh.*

For me, there is a strong temptation to link the troping of *September eleventh* in Sri Lanka to the change of government in December 2001, and to the subsequent peace process. By emplotting peace in Sri Lanka through *September eleventh*, it is tempting to create my own narrative – to endow tragic events with a valuable purpose, and to create a beginning, middle and, ultimately, a happy ending for the people in Sri Lanka. I think, however, that all conflicts, the one in Sri Lanka as well as the so-called war on terror, are over-determined, and that if there is a moral to this story, it is to be wary of simple stories and especially cautious about their happy endings.

NOTES

1. In this essay I use the European dating convention, i.e. 'date month year', for example, 11 September 2001. The italicized term *September eleventh* refers to the trope or figure of speech that expresses more than simply a date, as is discussed throughout. I do not use the term '9-11' or '9/11' since this can be interpreted as a date or the expression 'nine one one,' which has connotations related to emergency service in the United States.

2. N. Subramanian, 'TV Channels Bring Disaster to your Living Room, Live', *The Hindu Business Line*, online edition, 14 September 2001, available at <http://www.hinduonnet.com/businessline/catalyst/2001/09/14/stories/1914m05c.htm>.

3. I arrived in Sri Lanka on 30 August 2001 to begin my dissertation fieldwork on the politics of war-affected children in Sri Lanka.

4. The terms 'conflict' and 'war' have loaded political meanings. War, civil or international, can imply a state of belligerency between two legitimate parties, while conflict can refer to state citizens that take up arms, suggesting that only states can make war. Motivation, scope and numbers of casualties can also signify one or the other. In this essay, I use the term 'war' and conflict interchangeably to describe the situation in Sri Lanka, following from Ingrid Detter's definition of war as 'a sustained struggle by armed force of a certain intensity between groups of a certain size, consisting of individuals who are armed, who wear distinctive insignia and who are subjected to military discipline under responsible command', and not to confer legitimacy or illegitimacy to a particular party or perspective. For a thorough review of these debates on definitions of war, see I. Detter, *The Law of War*, 2nd ed. (Cambridge: Cambridge University Press 2000) esp. p.26.

5. H. White, *Figural Realism: Studies in the Mimesis Effect* (Baltimore, MD: Johns Hopkins University Press 1999) p.104. For more on Hayden White's work, see J. M. Mellard, *Doing Tropology: Analysis of Narrative Discourse* (Urbana and Chicago, IL: University of Illinois Press 1987).

6. The demand for a separate state, first made in 1977, was dropped on 18 September 2002 by Anton Balasingham, the LTTE's chief negotiator, in the first round of peace talks between the LTTE and the current government. See 'Tigers Shelve Eelam Call', *The Daily Mirror*, 19 September 2002.

7. On 5 December 2001, the People's Alliance party lost control of the parliament and the government in national elections. The United National Front made up of the United National Party and several Tamil parties, called the Tamil National Alliance, won the majority of seats. The UNP's Ranil Wickremesinghe heads the new government as prime minister. Chandrika Bandaranaike Kumaratunga will remain president until 2005.

8. Some of these early works include J. Agnew, 'The Territorial Trap: The Geographical Assumptions of International Theory', *Review of International Political Economy* 1/1 (1994) pp.53–80; S. Dalby, 'Critical Geopolitics: Discourse, Difference and Dissent,' *Environment and Planning D: Society and Space* 9/3 (1990) pp.261–83; G. Ó Tuathail, *Critical Geopolitics: The Politics of Writing Global Space* (Minneapolis, MN: University of Minnesota Press 1996); and G. Ó Tuathail and J. Agnew, 'Geopolitics and Discourse:

Practical Geopolitical Reasoning in American Foreign Policy,' *Political Geography* 11/2 (1992) pp.190–204.

9. H. White, *The Content of the Form: Narrative Discourse and Historical Representation* (Baltimore, MD: Johns Hopkins University Press 1987) p.23.

10. One exception is D. Campbell, *National Deconstruction: Violence, Identity and Justice in Bosnia* (Minneapolis, MN: University of Minnesota Press 1998). Although not explicitly identified as tropes, one might argue that 'geographs' used in some critical geopolitical analysis could be considered as such. See, for example, Simon Dalby, 'The "Kiwi Disease": Geopolitical Discourse in Aotearoa/New Zealand and the South Pacific', *Political Geography* 12/5 (1993) pp.437–56.

11. The precise definitions of these are contested. See K. Burke, *A Grammar of Motives* (Berkeley, CA: University of California Press 1969) pp.503–17, and D. Chandler, *Semiotics: The Basics* (London: Routledge 2002) pp.132–40.

12. White, *Figural Realism* (note 5) p.104.

13. K. Burke (note 11) p.508.

14. H. White, *Tropics of Discourse* (Baltimore, MD: Johns Hopkins University Press) p. 73, emphasis added.

15. J.S. Duncan, *The City as Text: The Politics of Landscape Interpretation in the Kandyan Kingdom* (Cambridge: Cambridge University Press 1990) esp.20.

16. E.W. Said, *Covering Islam: How the Media and the Experts Determine How We See the Rest of the World* (New York: Pantheon 1981).

17. This idea is based on Lee Edelman's argument that there is only one side when it comes to narratives involving the category of the child, a hegemonic signifier. L. Edelman, 'The Future is Kid Stuff: Queer Theory, Disidentification, and the Death Drive', *Narrative* 6/1 (1998) pp.18–30.

18. L.A. Staehli, 'Empowering Political Struggle: Spaces and Scales of Resistance', *Political Geography* 13/5 (1994) pp.387–92, esp. 387. See also K. Jones, 'Scale as Epistemology', *Political Geography* 17/1 (1998) pp.25–8.

19. White, *Content of the Form* (note 9) p.44.

20. Committee for Rational Development, *Sri Lanka, The Ethnic Conflict: Myths, Realities, and Perspectives* (New Delhi: Navrang 1984); C. Manogaran, *Ethnic Conflict and Reconciliation in Sri Lanka* (Honolulu, HI: University of Hawaii Press 1987); the collection of essays in C. Manogaran and B. Pfaffenberger (eds), *The Sri Lankan Tamils: Ethnicity and Identity* (Boulder, CO: Westview 1994); G. Obeyesekere, 'The Vicissitudes of the Sinhala-Buddhist Identity Through Time and Change', in M. Roberts (ed.), *Collective Identities, Nationalisms and Protest in Modern Sri Lanka*, (Colombo: Marga Institute 1979) pp.279–313; D. Hellmann-Rajanayagam, *The Tamil Tigers: Armed Struggle for Identity* (Stuttgart: Franz Steiner 1994); K.M. de Silva, *The 'Traditional Homelands' of the Tamils of Sri Lanka: A Historical Appraisal* (Colombo: International Centre for Ethnic Studies 1987); and N. Silva (ed.), *The Hybrid Island: Culture Crossings and the Invention of Identity in Sri Lanka* (Colombo: Social Scientists' Association 2002).

21. A.J. Wilson, 'Ethnic Strife in Sri Lanka: The Politics of Space', in *Regional Politics and Policy* 3 (1993) pp.145–69; idem, 'The Colombo Man, the Jaffna Man, and the Batticaloa Man: Regional Identities and the Rise of the Federal Party,' in *The Sri Lankan Tamils: Ethnicity and Identity* (Boulder: Westview, CO 1994); and S.W.R. de A. Samarasinghe and V. Samarasinghe, *Historical Dictionary of Sri Lanka* (Lanham, MD.: Scarecrow Press 1998).

22. See for example R. Hoole et al., *The Broken Palmyra: The Tamil Crisis in Sri Lankan – An Inside Account*, 2nd ed. (Claremont, CA: Sri Lanka Studies Institute 1990).

23. S.J. Tambiah, *Sri Lanka: Ethnic Fratricide and Dismantling of Democracy* (Delhi and Oxford: University of Oxford Press 1986).

24. S. Hennayake, 'Interactive Ethnonationalism: An Alternative Explanation of Minority

Ethnonationalism', *Political Geography* 11/6 (1992) pp.526–49; D. Little, *Sri Lanka: The Invention of Enmity* (Washington, DC: United States Institute of Peace Press 1994); and S.J. Tambiah, *Leveling Crowds: Ethnonationalist Conflicts and Collective Violence in South Asia* (Berkeley, CA: University of California Press 1996).
25. S.J. Tambiah, *Buddhism Betrayed?: Religion, Politics, and Violence in Sri Lanka* (Chicago and London: University of Chicago Press 1992).
26. A good overview of the PTA can be found in S.J. Tambiah, *Sri Lanka* (note 23) pp.38–47.
27. S. Wickremasinghe, *Emergency Rule in Sri Lanka: State of Human Rights 1999* (Colombo: Law and Society Trust 1999) pp.39–42.
28. A.S. Balasingham, *Liberation Tigers and Tamil Eelam Freedom Struggle* (Madras: Political Committee Liberation Tigers of Tamil Eelam 1983).
29. During the recent peace talks in Thailand, LTTE negotiators requested that the PTA be repealed. Government negotiators refused.
30. Detter (note 4) p. 22, views state terror as violence directed against *other* states or citizens of other states. For another perspective, see Eqbal Ahmad, *Terrorism: Theirs and Ours* (New York: Seven Stories Press 2001) esp. p.17. Ahmad sees terrorism as coercive violence regardless of who commits it.
31. Human rights violations reported by Amnesty International, Human Rights Watch, and other international NGOs are part of the sometimes tense relationship with the government. International organizations and missions working in Sri Lanka, especially in the conflict area, have risked expulsion if information damaging to the government was made publicly available.
32. Kumaratunga was within her legal right to prorogue Parliament, although the ethics of this decision has been called into question. There is currently a constitutional amendment before parliament which would prevent this from happening again.
33. The JVP also allegedly assassinated Kumaratunga's husband, Vijaya Kumaratunga, in 1988.
34. The following sections are based upon my readings of the English language dailies published in Colombo, as well as Tamil expatriate websites sympathetic to the LTTE position. They are also informed by conversations with colleagues who worked or were associated with humanitarian organizations in Colombo, and with people I encountered day to day from August through November 2001. It is important to keep in mind that the story of *September eleventh* that I tell in this essay primarily reflects an elite and middle-class urban view from the Sinhala-dominated south and the Tamil diaspora. It does not necessarily represent the views of rural Sri Lankans, who comprise about 70 per cent of the country's 19 million people, nor does it specifically address Sri Lankan Muslims, who comprise about 7 per cent of the populace. Where possible, I let commentators speak for themselves through quotations.
35. *Daily News*, 12 September 2001.
36. *Daily News*, 17 September 2001; *Daily Mirror*, 22 September 2001.
37. 'Terrorism Now Everybody's Problem', *Daily News*, 14 September 2001.
38. D. Jayatilleka, 'New Barbarism in New Century', *Daily Mirror*, 18 September 2001.
39. 'Fanatical Terrorism', *The Island*, 16 September 2001.
40. R. Abeynayake, 'Moms and Dads, Brothers, Friends and Terrorists', *Sunday Times*, 16 September 2001.
41. 'Where were they when Tigers attacked Sri Lanka?', letter to the editor, *The Daily News*, 19 September 2001.
42. 'World Leaders Awakened by Attack on the U.S.', *Sunday Times*, 16 September 2001.
43. 'Boston Globe Says: Bin Laden and LTTE loyalists Raise Funds Near Border', *Daily News*, 17 September 2001.
44. 'Today's Need: A World-wide Ban on 'Liberation' Movements', *The Island*, 13 September 2001; 'Black September 2001', *Daily News*, 18 September 2001.

45. 'Bhumiputra Backs US Stance', *Daily Mirror*, 25 September 2001.
46. S.L. Gunasekara, 'Terrorism, George Bush and Sudu Menike', *The Island*, 15 September 2001.
47. *Daily News*, 15 September 2001.
48. The Eelam People's Democratic Party or EPDP is one of many armed paramilitary groups that has worked with the government and army against the LTTE.
49. 'LTTE Condemns Attack on US', available from Tamilnet, <http://www.tamilnet.com>.
50. *Tamil Guardian*, 19 September 2001.
51. 'US excludes LTTE from Global War', *Sunday Times*, 23 September 2001; and 'War and Peace: US Twin Policy in Lanka', *Sunday Times,* 30 September 2001.
52. Ibid.
53. 'Forked Tongue', *Sunday Times*, 23 September 2001.
54. 'American Support for Sri Lankan Efforts Against Terrorism', press release, US embassy, Colombo, 23 September 2001.
55. 'Statement by United States Chargé d'Affaires Lewis Amselem at Memorial Ceremony for Victims Of Terrorism', press release, US embassy, Colombo, 25 September 2001, emphasis added.
56. 'The Attack on America Revisited', *The Island*, 24 September 2001.
57. 'The American Way – Part II', *The Island*, 24 September 2001.
58. 'Terrorists We Harbour', *Sunday Times*, 30 September 2001.
59. *Daily News*, 24 September 2001.
60. *Daily Mirror*, 24 September 2001.
61. Reprint from the *Times of India*, published in *The Daily Mirror*, 24 September 2001.
62. 'Sri Lanka Ready to Go to Any Length to Tie the Tamil Tigers with Al-Qaida', available from Tamil Eelam News Service, <http://www.tamileelamnews.com>. See also 'Attempts to Implicate LTTE in WTC Attack,' *SuderOli*, 27 September 2001; and Australasian Federation of Tamil Associations, 'Cashing in on the Carnage', available from <http://www.sangam.org>.
63. 'Religious Extremism Everywhere Knows No Compromise', *Tamil Guardian*, 26 September 2001.
64. Ibid.
65. D.B.S. Jeyaraj, 'USA policy towards LTTE', *Sunday Leader*, 30 September 2001.
66. 'Authorised Force: The UN Edict on Terrorism Ensures its Practice', *Tamil Guardian*, 3 October 2001; and 'Binary Logic: Efforts to Criminalize Non-state Violence will Fuel it', *Tamil Guardian*, 10 October 2001.
67. 'Distinction between Terrorism and National Liberation Struggle – WTCWA', available from the Tamil Canadian website, <http://www.tamilcanadian.com>.
68. 'Pirapaharan' is transliterated from Tamil into English in several different ways. 'Pirapaharan' is used by the LTTE and the Sri Lankan Tamil diaspora, most recently. 'Prabhakaran' is the spelling used by the Sri Lankan press in southern Sri Lanka and by the western press. Where Pirapaharan's name is quoted in a headline or article, I have used the author's spelling. In all other cases, I have used the LTTE's preferred transliteration.
69. 'LTTE wants Tamil Parties to Unite', *Daily News*, 15 October 2001; 'LTTE Funds UNP Horse Deal', *Daily News*, 16 October 2001; 'PA Challenges UNP and SB Group to Reveal Secret Pact', *Daily News*, 17 October 2001; 'Separatist Alliance with UNP to Fulfill Ulterior Motives – PM', *Daily News*, 22 October 2001; and 'Tamil Alliance Nominations: Tigers to have Final Say', *Daily News*, 27 October 2001.
70. The Associated Newspapers of Ceylon Ltd owns 86 per cent of the *Daily News*.
71. C. Weeraratne, 'Karu goes to Supreme Court on Lake House Reports' *The Island*, 25 October 2001; and C. Weeraratne, 'Rights Plea by UNP Deputy Leader', *Island*, 29 October 2001.
72. 'Suranimala', 'Cloak and Dagger Politics,' *Sunday Leader*, 11 November 2001.

73. '"BBC Breakfast with Frost" interview: President Kumaratunga, Sept. 11 – "Wake Up Call to World to Combat Terrorism', *The Island*, 30 October 2001.

74. '"Frosty" Breakfast and "Hard Talk" Trap on BBC', *The Island*, 10 November 2001.

75. 'UNP's Pregnant Silence as the Tamil Alliance Shows its Hand', *Sunday Observer*, 4 November 2001.

76. R. Ladduwahetty, 'If UNP wins, Prabhakaran will be President – President *Kumaratunga*,' *Daily News*, 04 November 2001.

77. '"Terrorist" Interpretations', from *ThinakKural*, available from Tamil Canadian, <http://www.tamilcanadian.com>.

78. N. Subramanian, 'Chrandrika Plays the LTTE Card to the Hilt', *The Hindu*, 5 November 2001. See also N. Wijedasa, 'The Things They Say! And What They Do and Don't Do', *The Island*, 11 November 2001; B. Jayasekara, 'Tigers have no Permanent Pact with Anybody: Champika', *Daily Mirror*, 22 November 2001.

79. 'LTTE Leader Makes Special Plea to the Sinhalese: Reject Racist Forces: Offer Justice to the Tamils', LTTE press release, 27 November 2001.

80. Ibid.

81. Ibid.

82. Ibid.

83. '"Maligawa Bombing Same as Bombing of Bamiyan Buddhas by Taliban" – *Lakshman Kadirgamar*', *Sunday Observer*, 2 December 2001.

84. Ibid.

Environmental Terrorism: A Critique

SHANNON O'LEAR

'Myopia and lack of imagination are diseases that afflict warriors and anti-warriors alike.'
Alvin Toffler and Heidi Toffler, *War and Anti-War*, p.124.

Introduction

As the dust settles in the aftermath of 11 September, academics in a broad range of disciplines have once again taken up an interest in research on terrorism. Researchers are asking questions about how they can contribute to a better understanding of terrorism from a multitude of perspectives: political, social, economic, psychological, infrastructural and legal, to name a few. Chronologically straddling the events of 11 September is a small body of literature on environmental terrorism that, given the current political climate and popular concern with environmental issues, appears to be well positioned to expand as a sub-field of research. The label, 'environmental terrorism' evokes a sense of seriousness or urgency, yet it is an inherently vague and unclear topic. Although scholarly work to this point has provided a few interpretations of environmental terrorism, a critical perspective has not been applied to this area.

To date, the literature on environmental terrorism includes contributions from different perspectives. An examination of legal definitions, government agencies and response options related to terrorism provides an overview of this theme within the context of the United States.[1] In another study, a schema was constructed for the purpose of discerning which types of environmental destruction can be labeled 'terrorism' and which types can be labeled 'environmental terrorism'.[2] Labeling a particular phenomenon would, by this view, depend upon whether or not the environmental destruction breaches national or international restrictions on peacetime activities, the type of destruction and the definition of terrorism employed. The resulting taxonomy allows the categorisation of environmental destruction by general type (e.g., deliberate or unintentional, peacetime or wartime, etc.) and recognises that ultimately the labeling will depend upon the chosen definition of terrorism. A more recent contribution to this literature focuses on identifying risks of environmental terrorism.[3] Pointing to heightened security at energy and water facilities across the United States as an indicator of increased awareness of environment-related vulnerability, that paper provides an overview of the concept of environmental terrorism as it may relate to vulnerable resource areas such as water bodies, agriculture and forest sites, mineral and petroleum sites and ecosystem sites. These pieces provide thoughtful groundwork on the concept of environmental terrorism, but they do not engage with the notion on a more critical level.

Previous critical work on terrorism notes that:

> A discourse such as the discourse on terrorism is usually neither elaborate nor nuanced, in part, because of the simple economy of use that such a discourse requires: repeated, common and continued use of undifferentiated words/language without any trace of subtlety by a socially-validated community of interpretation. Indeed through this practice of iteration the process of social transubstantiation – or perhaps an alchemy-like transmutation – produces ... the distilled, ready-to-abuse and value-laden concept of terrorism.[4]

The subset of environmental terrorism, much like the topic of environmental security, at first instance appears to label a specific category of activity. Yet from the substantial literature on environmental security have emerged critiques of that sub-field questioning its usefulness for advancing theory or supporting rigorous empirical research. What have we learned from concentrated work on environmental security that can help us understand more clearly the notion of environmental terrorism or the direction of research in such an area? Geographic contributions to scholarly work on terrorism are few,[5] yet as a discipline, geography can contribute both applied methodologies as well as critical perspectives to the complex subject of terrorism and the networks and interconnected scales of activity embedded within it. An objective of this essay is to initiate a conversation on terrorism from a geographic perspective which will no doubt require an ongoing discussion. The next section provides a brief overview of main themes in the environmental security literature and points to three main critiques of environmental security that provide insights into potential pitfalls and opportunities for the development of studies on environmental terrorism.

Environmental Security: Overview and Critiques

Since the end of the Cold War, and in the wake of growing public awareness of environmental problems associated with western-style capitalism, an interdisciplinary research focus on environmental security has garnered attention in academic circles. At this time when human-caused climate change is widely recognised, when the world's population continues to grow, consume, and produce waste in a geographically disproportionate manner, and as viable ecosystems are increasingly degraded by human activity, environmental aspects of political relationships have gained the attention of researchers and scholars. It is not a new realisation that environmental issues, related to ecosystems, natural resources, and wastes from human consumption, challenge the traditional rubric of territory and state power as a means to security.[6] State actions and accountability in relation to resource use and pollution extend beyond state boundaries, and it has been recognised that 'our accepted definition of the limits of national sovereignty as coinciding with national borders is obsolete'.[7]

Despite this early recognition in the literature that environmental problems are not contained within states, some of the work commonly cited as making up the core of environmental security literature examines how environmental and resource-related issues are connected to conflict in a state-centric sense.[8] For example, much work generated by a group at the University of Toronto has focused on how environmental scarcity can ignite market failure, social friction and/or lack of capital into conflict.[9] In that work, supply-induced scarcity, demand-induced scarcity and structural scarcity within the state are facets of environmental resource issues that have been examined in case studies of conflict.

Natural resources may play a role in inter-state relations as well, but that role is neither clear nor universal. It is a basic fact of geography that resources are unevenly distributed. Some researchers argue that increasing global competition for resources such as petroleum, water, gems and timber will lead to conflict in a predictable, geographic pattern.[10] Yet it may be that the increasing reach of global trade and economic networks overcome these imbalances at least for some groups of people. So long as a state has the wherewithal to control access to stocks and flows of resources, regardless of the source of the supply, a state does not need to be resource rich to be wealthy (e.g., Japan). In addition to the fact that natural resources have historically been involved in conflict as goals, tools and targets, other researchers argue, the more recently acknowledged threat of global climate change and the disruption of environmental services (e.g., benefits of clean air or the carbon sink of healthy forests) may play an increasing role in shaping inter-state relationships.[11]

As the literature on environmental security grows, so too do critiques of this body of work. One critique of environmental security as a field of research is that work to date is insufficiently rigorous to contribute to the development of theory.[12] The argument is that the causal linkages between scarcity and inter- and intra-state conflict have not been adequately theorised. If we are to progress in our understanding of how processes, connections, and disjunctures of real-world environmental stress are related to conflict, we must be able to apply or test a theory via empirical cases. Questions of data, scale, duration of study, and number of subjects or case studies and number of variables occupy scholars interested in advancing and testing models of environmental security.[13] Also questionable is the assumption that different forms of scarcity could occur to a degree significant enough to be a driving cause of conflict. Just as 'overpopulation' and 'ethnic differences' are generic labels that do not lead to a contextually informed understanding of conflict, environmental scarcity – of any kind – must be examined closely and analytically in order for us to understand and to theorise how environmental issues are connected to conflict.[14] What is more, some research has even investigated ways in which resource abundance, rather than resource scarcity, can contribute to tension and conflict.[15]

A second critique of environmental security research concerns the matter of labels, language and discourse. Merely joining the words 'environment' and 'security' together does not provide a sufficient basis from which to advance theory or to undertake empirical studies in the name of understanding and testing how environmental issues are related to conflict. The term, 'environmental security', is so commonly utilised as to become diluted in its explanatory power.[16] What is meant by 'environment'? 'Environment' can refer to renewable and nonrenewable resources and imply access to those resources. 'Environment' might include stationary resources (such as arable land), mobile resources (such as migratory species), and seasonal resources (such as water availability or crops). Environmental quality might vary in terms of air, water and soil quality, radiation levels and ecosystemic resilience. Natural resources might render the environment more or less valuable in terms of water, food supply, wood, fibre and other materials used by humans and in terms of energy resources for immediate use, for future use, or for export and economic use. In assessing the value of the environment, we weigh current use against future use and instrumental value against aesthetic value and inherent value. In short, the term 'environment' is less than immediately clear as a research guide.

A third critique has challenged the realist, state-centred underpinnings of environmental security research. More detailed discussions are available elsewhere,[17] but I will note a few of the main points here. This critique views military solutions as not only inappropriate for environmental threats,[18] but mobilising environmental awareness or activism based on national sentiments (reacting to an environmental threat to the state or nation) may have unintended, negative consequences.[19] The term 'environmental security' suggests that we are interested in traditional security issues (boundary skirmishes, territorial control, military preparation and engagement, etc.) but with some kind of environmental twist. 'Security' concerns generally relate to state-centred, 'us versus them' thinking, whereas environmentalist concerns generally focus on stewardship and on the interconnectedness, not the division, of systems.[20] The term 'security' itself is further problematic in that it is not clear which aspect or collection of aspects of the environment are being secured.[21] Additionally, if one actor or group of people is rendered environmentally secure, the corollary is that another actor or group of people is rendered insecure.[22] What is being secured: power, wealth and stability? Who is benefiting from this security? As the status quo of power relations is maintained (or secured), someone or some group is rendered secure, but at the same time another group is rendered insecure. Environmental threats, furthermore, are perceived subjectively and are best understood within their particular contexts.[23] An important point that emerges from these discussions is that utilising the word 'security' implies a state-centric, militaristic focus that, although useful for some purposes, is less than useful for examining human well-being at sub-state levels or for understanding complex networks that enable the transfer of natural resource benefits or environmental degradation costs across and within state boundaries.

In sum, three critiques of environmental security literature argue that there is insufficient clarity on how natural resources are linked to conflict, that the term 'environment' is not sufficiently clear as a guide to or boundary of a research area, and that the term 'security' prioritises a realist, state-centric perspective that may not be the most useful or appropriate scale for understanding relationships between resources and conflict. By the same token, the theme of environmental terrorism may be subjected to parallel critiques as a way to understand more clearly what environmental terrorism is or if this label is appropriate or useful for framing an area of research. The following sections interpret each of the above critiques of environmental security as they relate to the theme of environmental terrorism.

Defining Terrorism: Problems and Prospects

The first critique of environmental security points to an unclear understanding of the relationship between environment and security or conflict. At a basic level, that critique asks how resource scarcity (or abundance) is related to security without questioning either of the terms 'environment' or 'security' in and of themselves. In a similar fashion, an initial approach to environmental terrorism might question if current understanding of terrorism could include an environmental component.

Defining terrorism is like aiming at a moving target since the meaning of the word changes over time. During the French Revolution, when the term emerged into common usage, the term 'terrorism' had a positive connotation. Its strongest proponent, Maximiline Robespierre argued that 'terror is nothing but justice, prompt, severe and inflexible; it is therefore an emanation of virtue'.[24] The notion of terrorism has clearly shifted from being perceived as a virtue to being perceived as a threat in the current context. It has been suggested that Colin Powell's declaration that America is 'at war' against terrorism, a struggle which by its nature should involve patient secrecy and covert intelligence, positions terrorists in a win–win situation if they succeed in provoking an armed response while positioning the United States in the unenviable role of 'trying to eradicate cancer cells with a blowtorch'.[25] Additionally, whether or not the term 'terrorism' identifies a clear category or direction of research is also a question. Comparing research on terrorism to research on witchcraft, Zulaika notes:

> We should learn a lesson from the anthropologists who devoted themselves to producing dozens of theories on animism, totemism, witchcraft, and so on, only to realise that the category in question should be dropped as semantic nonsense. This does not mean, of course, that totems, dreams, witches, evil eyes and the like are not real, or that once they are analytically dissolved they disappear from the face of the earth ... We are thus confronted with the dilemma of whether we shall advance in understanding terrorism by adding new definitions and typologies and by trying to grasp the essence of the phenomenon in its most general context of international and cross-cultural comparison, or whether our theoretical task is to rethink critically the very category of terrorism and possibly dissolve it within a wider politico-military space into the types of behavior and person that are constitutive of the phenomenon.[26]

Similar to the critique that environmental security does not inherently clarify how natural resources and conflict are related, so the label 'terrorism' may not aid an advancement of research on certain types of political activism. Indeed, as Edward Said has noted:

> The use of the word terrorism is usually unfocused, it usually has all kinds of implicit validations of one's own brand of violence, it's highly selective. If you accept this norm, then it becomes so universally applicable that it loses any force whatsoever. I think it is better to drop it.[27]

This statement may also be true for the label of 'environmental terrorism'. Defining terrorism runs the risk of subjective, negative evaluation of certain political acts just by labeling them 'terrorism', but a watertight definition of terrorism is not necessarily a prerequisite to examining certain types of political activity.[28]

Legalistic definitions of terrorism shape state-level and international community response to terrorism and therefore provide an important baseline for operational understandings of terrorism. Below are some widely recognised and official definitions of terrorism which are commonly cited in related literature. These definitions are included here as a starting point for examining what role the environment may have in current understandings of terrorism.

The US Department of Defense (DOD) defines terrorism following Title 22 of the US Code, Section 2656(d):

- The term 'terrorism' means premeditated, politically motivated violence perpetrated against noncombatant targets by subnational groups or clandestine agents, usually intended to influence an audience.
- The term 'international terrorism' means terrorism involving the territory or the citizens of more than one country.
- The term 'terrorist group' means any group that practices, or has significant subgroups that practice, international terrorism.[29]

Targets of terrorism, by this definition, consist of noncombatant targets. Considering the role the environment might have in this definition of terrorism, environmental areas or resources such as forests, water supplies, national parks, etc. would fall under the category of 'noncombatant targets' and could be involved in terrorist activity in ways that would 'influence an audience'. Such influence could entail, for example, incurring economic loss, imposing health risks or intentional imbalance within an ecosystem. The DOD definition is general enough that we could conceive of terrorist actors focusing on environmental targets as a way to exert an impact on a particular audience. Also by this definition, political motivation of terrorism implies that terrorism is a response to a power imbalance. States, from the DOD perspective, cannot be terrorists but would instead be viewed as waging war unless a state is acting as a 'clandestine agent' rather than openly acting on official state interests.

In contrast to the DOD, the United Nations has not agreed upon a single, comprehensive definition of terrorism. In 1999, the UN General Assembly established a Terrorism Prevention Branch, and has over recent decades adopted several case-specific conventions and treaties (See Table 1). Current UN resolution language, established in 1999, is as follows:

1. *Strongly condemns* all acts, methods and practices of terrorism as criminal and unjustifiable, wherever and by whomsoever committed;
2. *Reiterates* that criminal acts intended or calculated to provoke a state of terror in the general public, a group of persons or particular persons for

political purposes are in any circumstance unjustifiable, whatever the considerations of a political, philosophical, ideological, racial, ethnic, religious or other nature that may be invoked to justify them.[30]

FIGURE 1
INTERNATIONAL, ACT-SPECIFIC CONVENTIONS OF THE UNITED NATIONS

Name of Convention	Year adopted
Geneva Convention on the High Seas	1958
UN Convention on the Law of the Sea	1982
Tokyo Convention on Offenses and Certain Acts Committed on Board of Aircraft	1963
Hague Convention of the Suppression of Unlawful Seizure of Aircraft	1970
Montreal Convention for the Suppression of Unlawful Acts Against the Safety of Civil Aviation	1971
Convention on the Prevention and Punishment of Crimes against Internationally Protected Persons, including Diplomatic Agents	1973
International Convention against the Taking of Hostages	1979
Convention on the Physical Protection of Nuclear Material ('Nuclear Materials Convention')	1980
Protocol for the Suppression of Unlawful Acts of Violence at Airports Serving International Civil Aviation, supplementary to the Convention for the Suppression of Unlawful Acts against the Safety of Civil Aviation (Extends and supplement the Montreal Convention on Air Safety)	1988
Convention for the Suppression of Unlawful Acts Against the Safety of Maritime Navigation	1988
Protocol for the Suppression of Unlawful Acts Against the Safety of Fixed Platforms Located on the Continental Shelf (applies to terrorist activities on fixed offshore platforms)	1988
Convention on the Marking of Plastic Explosives for the Purpose of Detection	1991
International Convention for the Suppression of Terrorist Bombings	1997
International Convention for the Suppression of the Financing of Terrorism	1999

Source: The UN web site <http://www.odccp.org/terrorism_definitions.html>, accessed 17 December 2001).

This wording distinguishes among different target audiences (e.g., the general public, a group of persons, etc.) but does not distinguish between types of targets. By this definition it seems that if an attack on an environmental or natural resource entity could incite terror in a given audience, these types of targets could be included as a form of terrorism. This wording, however, does not clarify whether or not states can act as terrorists, but it does suggest an array of motivating factors of terrorism (e.g., political, philosophical, etc.).

In addition to the above resolution, the UN distributes the following academic consensus definition of terrorism short of officially adopting this definition:

Terrorism is an anxiety-inspiring method of repeated violent action, employed by (semi-) clandestine individual, group or state actors, for idiosyncratic, criminal or political reasons, whereby – in contrast to assassination – the direct targets of violence are not the main targets. The immediate human victims of violence are generally chosen randomly (targets of opportunity) or selectively (representative or symbolic targets) from a target population, and serve as message generators. Threat- and violence-based communication processes between terrorist (organization), (imperiled) victims, and main targets are used to manipulate the main target (audience(s)), turning it into a target of terror, a target of demands, or a target of attention, depending on whether intimidation, coercion, or propaganda is primarily sought'.[31]

By this consensus, environmental targets, so long as they are in some capacity symbolic of the targeted group, network or concept, could be considered viable targets of terrorism. This definition provides a more fine-tuned perspective on terrorism as a form of communication with the message dependent on the objectives of the terrorist group and with the targets playing a symbolic role. From this perspective, states may act as terrorists distinct from waging war. That suggests that target audiences may not be states but networks and other tangible and non-tangible entities not 'contained' within fixed boundaries. Additionally, the UN recognises several region-specific conventions on terrorism (See Table 2).

FIGURE 2

REGIONAL CONVENTIONS ON TERRORISM

Name of regional convention	Year adopted
Organisation of American States (OAS) Convention to Prevent and Punish Acts of Terrorism Taking the Form of Crimes against Persons and Related Extortion that are of International Significance	1971
European Convention on the Suppression of Terrorism	1977
South Asian Association for Regional Cooperation (SAARC) Regional Convention on Suppression of Terrorism	1987
Arab Convention on the Suppression of Terrorism	1998
Convention of the Organisation of the Islamic Conference on Combating International Terrorism	1999
Organisation of African Unity (OAU) Convention on the Prevention and Combating of Terrorism	1999
Treaty on Cooperation among States Members of the Commonwealth of Independent States in Combating Terrorism	1999

Source: <http://untreaty.un.org/English/Terrorism.asp>, accessed 17 December 2001.

From a strategic perspective, it is more important to identify the terrorist rather than the technique. If we understand terrorism as a form of communication (as suggested in the UN's academic consensus on terrorism noted above), then one approach to studying terrorism is to analyse what a terrorist or terrorist organisation intends to communicate. As premeditated acts, terrorist acts are designed to communicate a message that reflects the terrorist group's political position or objective through the selection of an appropriate target, symbolic target and/or target audience.[32] In an effort to gain power, terrorists will use tactics, targets and weapons suitable for communicating their message within their resource, logistical and financial constraints.[33] Yet in the case of terrorism, it seems, the medium is not necessarily the message,[34] and it is likely that the role of the environment in terrorist acts would not hold a universal meaning, either.

From the above definitions and interpretations of terrorism, we can see that environmental resources and other entities beyond the built environment could feasibly be targets of terrorist acts if these targets in some way symbolise or convey a meaning intended by the terrorist agenda. Although the above definitions provide an apparent and implicit consensus that the environment may have some kind of role in terrorism, it remains unclear what kinds of acts or messages would fall into a category known as environmental terrorism. Furthermore, even a cursory consideration of legalistic definitions introduces a new issue. Namely, can a state act as a terrorist? This issue is addressed in the third critique section. Another shortcoming with the legalistic definitions of terrorism is that they may be too vague or too inflexible to be usefully applied in the current, dynamic context. Despite these shortcomings, we might use these legalistic definitions to arrive at a working definition of environmental terrorism. Based on these widely accepted definitions of terrorism, environmental terrorism might be conceived as a form of terrorism which selects environmental or natural resource targets either for their symbolic impact, as a means to inflict collateral damage, or to provoke fear and disruption in an intended audience. For example, destruction of forests for economic consumption or illegal dumping of toxic wastes to avoid the expense of proper disposal would not be considered environmental terrorism by such a definition because these acts are not carried out with the intention of communicating a message to a particular audience. Purposefully destroying or contaminating agricultural areas or water sources, as a way to attract attention to a particular, political cause, however, could be understood as an act of environmental terrorism, by this definition, if the destruction is intended as a message to a particular audience.

Indeed, a significant challenge to understanding terrorism at this time is the growing recognition that the very nature of terrorism has changed. Since the end of the Cold War, several factors have contributed to the growing incidence of terrorist acts perpetrated by groups and individuals. Ethno-religious, nationalistic, and extremist religious groups (such as militant Islamic, Zionist or Christian groups, millenarian cults, and radical Sikh and Hindu groups) have increasingly relied on terrorist tactics as have other groups promoting 'amateur' forms of political violence.[35] The lethality of these groups is compounded both by extreme ideological rationale and by instrumental variables such as the range of weapons available to terrorist groups.[36] Other factors contributing to this 'new breed of terrorists' include the diffusion of technological know-how resulting from out-migration of expertise following the collapse of the Soviet Union and technological advances and opportunities such as recruitment via the Internet.[37] Although terrorist acts have, historically, evoked only limited if not unintended responses, the range of aims and approaches demonstrated by 'postmodern' terrorist groups today suggests that the success of even a few, small groups could equate to significant impacts (e.g., successful hacking into critical computer systems in an act of 'cyberwar').[38] Indeed, the literature suggests that current forms of terrorism appear to be transitioning from hierarchical to networked organisational structures across international boundaries and through use of the Internet, thus posing new challenges for counterterrorism.[39]

An examination of this profusion of terrorist types, objectives and strategies is partially enabled by databases on international terrorist incidences. One of these, International Terrorism: Attributes of Terrorist Events,[40] is available online but includes data only from 1968–1977. A more up-to-date database for terrorism is the Political Terrorism Database,[41] which includes a database on International Terrorism and Political Violence Incidents. Although these databases remain a unique source of international-scale, state-based data, they are, however, not particularly useful in the pursuit of more theoretically informed questions related to possible life-cycles, consequences, public perception, heterogeneity and appropriate scales of analysis of terrorism.[42] If the objective is to understand complexities of new forms of terrorism, research on terrorism is likely to make greater advances through more refined, place-specific empirical studies than through complex models of terrorism at the international scale.[43]

According to the UN, terrorism is generally understood to be a peacetime equivalent of a war crime,[44] but the role of the environment within terrorism is unclear. Widely recognised definitions and descriptions of terrorism do not address this point specifically, and the changing nature of terrorism further complicates the issue. Just as the 'environment' in environmental security has been scrutinised for failing to designate a particular focus for meaningful research in that field, so we must also question what is meant by 'environment' in a discussion on environmental terrorism.

Terrorism and the Environment

A second critique of the environmental security literature argues that the 'environment' is such a general term that it loses usefulness as a means of delimiting or identifying a particular research area. As the above discussion notes, by most official definitions environmental targets could possibly be considered to fall within the category of terrorism. Yet adding 'environment' to an already unclear term would appear to muddy the waters even further rather than honing in on an identifiable subset of terrorism. How are we to define the 'environment' in 'environmental terrorism'? Does the environment include only natural ecosystems, or does it include manipulated, industrial areas such as agricultural sites, hydroelectric dams and pipelines transporting oil or gas? Environmental targets, if they are part of a pre-meditated act to communicate a particular message, would most likely be selected, in part, according to their economic or aesthetic value. If a bomb goes off in a forest and there is no one there to lose a view or to suffer collateral damage, is it terrorism? This raises questions of how and by whom the environment is valued, on what time scale these values are identified, and to what use the environment or elements of the environment are put. Such questions are beyond the scope of this essay. Here, a main question concerns the role of the environment in environmental terrorism. Does environmental terrorism imply that environmental entities are tools, objectives or targets of terrorist acts?

Environment as Tool: Harnessing the Environment and Bio-Warfare

A multi-disciplinary branch of research has been devoted to the investigation of how elements of the physical environment might be harnessed for military purposes. Practice and speculation on the 'hostile manipulation of celestial bodies' has focused on the atmosphere (altering weather patterns, ozone concentration and electrical properties for communication purposes), the lithosphere (releasing stored energy in the earth's crust to induce rock slides or avalanches or instigating earthquakes, destroying dams or altering permafrost stability), the hydrosphere (physical or chemical disruption of electromagnetic properties and the generation of tsunamis) and the biosphere (applying poisons or introducing exotic species, incendiary or mechanical means of destruction).[45] The harnessing and utilisation of materials derived from meteors for military purposes have also been explored.[46]

Biological warfare is another example of harnessing elements of the environment for hostile purposes. Although literature on biological terrorism, which is usually lumped together thematically with nuclear and chemical terrorism, recognises that attacks could come from state or non-state actors;[47] it has also been noted that traditional approaches to biological terrorism – 'military defense, hazardous-material defense teams, and high-technology sensors' – are inadequate for dealing with the actual threat of hostile biological attack.[48] Current knowledge of which countries possess biological weapons (see Table 3) is probably imperfect and does not address sub-state groups or networks that might have access to these kinds of weapons. Experts have urged the strengthening of local and national responsibilities under the Biological and Toxin Weapons Convention, originally established in 1972, as a critical step toward reducing the risk of hostile biological attack.[49] The fact that the US government has stifled progress towards ensuring compliance with the convention[50] is an important feature since it returns our inquiry to the issue of the role of the state, its relationship to terrorist activity and its relationship to international networks that transcend state borders.

TABLE 3
SUSPECTED POSSESSION OF BIOLOGICAL WEAPONS BY STATE

Suspected possessors	Suspected of attempting acquisition	Abandoned or reversed programmes
China, Egypt, Iran, Iraq, Israel, North Korea, Syria, Taiwan, Vietnam	Libya	Canada, France, Japan, South Africa, United Kingdom, United States

Source: R.A. Falkenrath, R.D. Newman and B.A. Thayer, *America's Achille's Heel: Nuclear, Biological and Chemical Terrorism and Cover Attack* (Cambridge, MA: The MIT Press 1998) p.64.

Environment as Objective: Ecoterrorism

Rather than inflicting damage to natural systems or natural resource entities as symbols of a political agenda, proponents of direct, violent action in defense of the environment target the built environment as it encroaches on natural environments. Similar to labeling anyone a 'terrorist', labeling groups as 'eco-terrorist' organisations is an explicit judgement of their illegitimacy. Organisations such as the Environmental Liberation Front (ELF) act in defence of ecosystems and animals they believe to be endangered from human activity. One of this group's most famous actions took place in the Vail, Colorado ski resort area in the fall of 1998 when they torched four new buildings in protest of the ski area's expansion into a wildlife area that provided habitat to an endangered species of lynx. Colorado's Governor Roy Romer called the action, which incurred approximately $12 million in damages, an 'act of terrorism'.[51] ELF, an underground operation that works through anonymous cells, has been named by the FBI as one of the most active domestic terrorist groups in the United States.[52]

Other pro-environment groups, such as EarthFirst!, take a similarly radical approach to activism in defence of the environment as a last resort when all other measures have failed. According to the EarthFirst! web site, all forms of 'monkeywrenching', a term made famous by Edward Abbey's, *The Monkey Wrench Gang*, including 'ecotage, ecodefense, billboard bandits, desurveying, road reclamation' and tree spiking, are neither advocated nor condemned by EarthFirst!.[53] This type of activism is aimed at inanimate objects with the objective of inflicting economic damage on industrial developers and other despoilers of ecosystems. Environmental systems and resources, themselves, are not the targets of this form of direct, violent action. Rather, these entities are exactly what 'eco-terrorism' aims to protect. This type of activity in the United States has fluctuated in recent years and seems closely connected to local and national environmental policy decisions.[54] As a form of political activism, 'eco-terrorism' merits further study and deeper analysis.

Environment as Target

Throughout history, the environment and human-altered environmental features have been targeted in times of war. For example, Romans salted the fields of Carthage, the Soviet scorched-earth policy during the Second World War denied food to invading Nazi troops, the United States used defoliants in Vietnam,[55] and in an often-cited example retreating Iraqi soldiers set fire to Kuwaiti oil fields in 1991.[56] A point of consensus in the literature on terrorism, however, is that terrorism is distinct from interstate or civil war, so intentional environmental destruction during wartime would not fall within a category of terrorism.

During times of peace, aspects of the environment, including human-manipulated landscapes, could be targets of intentional acts of destruction intended to communicate a particular message. As noted previously, agricultural, forest, mineral, petroleum and ecosystem sites and water resources have been identified as being particularly vulnerable targets for environmental terrorism.[57] Biological organisms, such as those that cause the highly infectious foot-and-mouth disease in farm animals, could feasibly be employed to damage or kill crops or animals. It may also be possible one day to engineer an insect to eat a particular crop.[58] Such 'biological agroterrorism' could have multiplier effects across economic sectors and in the realm of consumer confidence.[59] Analysis of agriculture in the United States concludes that steroid use and animal husbandry practices increase susceptibility of crops and farm animals to diseases, and the industrial scale and monocrop approaches to agriculture could translate into significant economic and social destabilisation should these sites be attacked.[60]

Attacks on energy systems might also be construed as environmental terrorism based on the working definition introduced in a previous section of this essay. Targets in this category might include energy generation sources such as power plants, pipeline networks or power grids, supplies of coal, uranium, nuclear or other fuels.[61] A problem with traditional approaches to defending these kinds of large scale and extensively networked energy systems is that defending them is not the same as protecting territory. For example, oil-loading terminals in the Persian Gulf region are a critical link in the oil delivery system. They are essentially fixed docks or offshore terminals connecting oil storage units to tankers via pipelines. The offshore pump stations, housed on floating platforms, must be located sufficiently offshore to accommodate supertankers. These stations are vulnerable to aerial attack, but anti-aircraft weaponry is not always standing by for their protection.[62] Other large-scale energy systems such as hydroelectric energy-producing dams and extensive power grids may particularly stand out as vulnerable targets due to their size, concentration, and the scale of service for which they were originally designed. Decentralising these systems, to the dismay of capitalistic conglomerates, would allow smaller-scale service delivery of alternative energy and greatly decreased levels of vulnerability.[63] Another example of concentrated vulnerability of environment-related features is the aesthetic, symbolic or intergenerational value of national parks, wildlife preserves and localised, rare landscape phenomena.

Similar to official definitions of terrorism presented earlier in this essay, an official convention on the use of the environment for hostile purposes also exists. International agreement on the appropriateness of biological warfare and other environmentally damaging practices is reflected in the United Nations Convention on The Prohibition of Military or Any Other Hostile Use of Environmental Modification Techniques, which was enacted in 1976. This convention essentially restricts the legality of the manipulation of the environment for hostile purposes, as summarised in three core articles:

> Article I. 1. Each State Party to this Convention undertakes not to engage in military or any other hostile use of environmental modification techniques having widespread, long-lasting or severe effects as the means of destruction, damage or injury to any other State Party.

Article II. As used in article I, the term 'environmental modification techniques' refers to any technique for changing – through the deliberate manipulation of natural processes – the dynamics, composition or structure of the earth, including its biota, lithosphere, hydrosphere and atmosphere, or of outer space.'

Article III. 1. The provisions of this Convention shall not hinder the use of environmental modification techniques for peaceful purposes and shall be without prejudice to the generally recognized principles and applicable rules of international law concerning such use.[64]

Although it does not provide a process by which trespassers would be prosecuted, this convention provides legal grounds for establishing the illegality of peacetime aggression targeted at environmental or natural systems of another state. The fact that states are the actors pursuant to this agreement indicates that this convention is limited to state sovereignty including state-controlled military forces. In that sense, this convention is somewhat inflexible in addressing issues of sub-state terrorist activity or activity stemming from a network of participants spanning different states. Just as national laws generally apply to individuals living within a particular state, the UN convention should perhaps be updated to apply to non-state groups, as was done for air and marine policy.[65]

Part of the challenge of devising theories of environmental terrorism toward improving defence policies is that peacetime acts of environmental destruction are context-specific. If we accept the premise that terrorism is an act of communication with carefully selected targets or tools, then it would be most useful to examine instances of terrorism within a particular temporal and spatial context. For example, in July 2001, 153 workers laid off from their jobs at the Cellatex plant in the French town of Givet dumped 790 gallons of sulfuric acid into a tributary of the Meuse River as a negotiating tactic in their labour struggle.[66] This peacetime attack on an environmental element was intended to illustrate worker dissatisfaction with the condition of their severance. Although this example may well be labeled as 'environmental terrorism', it is clear that it also raises many questions about how environmental terrorism is defined. Stating that a condition of terrorism is occurrence during peacetime focuses attention on peace between or among states but says nothing of conflict within a state. In the case of the French workers, France may have been at peace but clearly the workers and their employer were not. Similarly, although previous work on environmental terrorism may suggest ways of reducing the vulnerability of particular types of ecosystems or landscapes, how could the dumping of toxins into a river by disgruntled workers have been prevented? Tighter military security is unlikely to have prevented this act of environmental destruction. The means to understanding and possibly avoiding such a destructive act would appear to lie in the hands of corporate and union management and secure handling of toxins rather than a perspective called environmental terrorism. This close examination of one instance that might be understood as an act of environmental terrorism suggests that a general theory of environmental terrorism writ large may be less useful than a much more explicit and context-based approach to understanding the conflict between the French workers and their employer, economic conditions of northern France and connections at other scales of economic activity, corporate decline, and the workers' decision to act destructively as they did. Again, because the 'environment' can refer to an impressive range of features, referring to a sub field of environmental terrorism seems unlikely to identify a clear path of research.

Terrorism, the State and the Environment

A third critique of environmental security questions the realist, state-centric thinking embedded in the label of and in much of the early work, in particular, on environmental security. A parallel question of environmental terrorism might ask what the role of the state might be in such an area of work. Is the purpose of pursuing a study of environmental terrorism to understand better how to extend military control over environmental entities to protect them from attack? This kind of approach to environmental terrorism reverberates with implications that environmental degradation looms as a threat to state stability.[67] Yet such an approach to environmental terrorism might be criticised for equating unexpected environmental damage or degradation directly to diminished national security without establishing clear, causal linkages.[68] Additionally, militaristic approaches to controlling terrorist attacks against environmental entities might only promote further reliance on industrial weaponry and state-level acceptance of environmental damage incurred by military operations.[69] Interpreting relationships between the state and environmental terrorism is, as these points suggest, an exercise in interpreting the construction and promotion of discourse.

If we return to the above legalistic definitions to clarify the role of the state vis-à-vis terrorism, we soon see that there is no clear consensus as to the role of the state within those most frequently cited definitions of terrorism. Indeed, history indicates that state governments have systematically used or sponsored terror to manipulate populations and in an attempt to influence other states:

But what sets these (and indeed many other historical) cases apart from the type of state-sponsored terrorism that has emerged since the early 1980s is the way in which some governments have now come to embrace terrorism as a deliberate instrument of foreign policy: a cost-effective means of waging war covertly, through the use of surrogate warriors or 'guns for hire' – terrorists.[70]

As of 1998, the United States designated seven countries as sponsors of terrorism: Cuba, Iran, Iraq, Libya, North Korea, Sudan and Syria,[71] and since then Afghanistan would probably have made the list as well. These are states that, according the US government, have not responded to economic sanctions or military reprisals to relinquish their support of terrorism as defined by US leaders.

How states create and promote discourses of terrorism is an important matter. Neil Smith has commented on how the events of 11 September 11 have been naturalised to suit a national agenda:

The need to nationalize September 11 arose from the need to justify war. Nationalism *is* the discourse of war under modern capitalism, in which the national state has cornered a monopoly on violence. Part of the affront of September 11 is that it challenges this state monopoly on violence, indeed that is precisely the traditional definition of terrorism – non-state-organized violence. The fraud of the 'war against terrorism' is that the US government has arrogated to itself the right to decide who does not count as a terrorist … The definition of terrorism is passed off in universalist terms while its operative demarcation is 'enemy of the United States'.[72]

Other geographers have also commented on the events of 11 September, raising questions regarding how the United States might react both to recent events and to its own past foreign policy choices[73] and questions regarding positive, negative and lasting consequences of 11 September 11.[74] Others have suggested that the events of 11 September could serve to motivate geographers, particularly, to challenge 'geopolitical abstractions' underpinning dangerous generalities used to fuel violence in many forms.[75] Also, scholars could pay closer attention to global injustices which have contributed, directly or indirectly, to the events of 11 September 11 with a recognition that the United States has played a role in many of these injustices through both intervention (e.g., bombing Iraq, positioning troops to fight in Colombia, trade embargoes on Iraq and Cuba) and non-intervention (e.g. in Bosnia-Herzegovina and Rwanda and Burundi).[76] Clearly, how a state defines and pursues terrorism provides a richly textured discourse that merits close inspection and analysis.

Reflections on discourses of terrorism and the state lead us to apply similar questions to relationships between the state and environmental terrorism. Are there cases where, during peacetime, states have supported the intentional damage or destruction of environmental systems in an effort to ·instil fear in elements of the population in that state or elsewhere? Perhaps the case of the Soviet Union and its legacy of environmental mismanagement could provide one example of vast and irreparable destruction of natural systems.[77] In the case of the Aral Sea, for example, state-sponsored manipulation of natural systems, in the name of economic advancement, altered ecosystems so drastically as to merit recognition from the United Nations as a World Heritage Site – an example of outstanding environmental destruction. Although coercion and fear were integral to Soviet style totalitarianism,[78] environmentally destructive practices were most likely not conducted with the primary intent of terrorising the population. Furthermore, disrupting one's own state would not likely be of interest to a state's government unless it had power to gain through destabilisation. The Aral Sea provides an illustration of how the promotion of state-centric priorities and a nationalist discourse can, in effect, contribute to irreparable destruction of environmental systems. Asking whether or not such activity should be defined as 'terrorism' highlights limitations of the commonly cited definitions of terrorism discussed earlier in this essay.

The state may not be the only actor promoting or justifying actions that result in the side effect of environmental degradation. Given the changing nature of terrorism discussed above, it is also important to recognise that 'to a far greater extent than in the past, both terrorists and their victims may have little to do with states and much more to do with nonstate – even private or criminal – concerns'.[79]

This point introduces another side to the relationship of the state to environmental terrorism, namely, a weak or hidden role in policy implementation and enforcement as well as the regulation of responsible and transparent business practices. Instances such as the *Exxon Valdez* oil spill in Alaska or the incidence at Love Canal, New York, for example, suggest that corporate influence on state regulation and oversight can have negative consequences for natural system viability and ecosystem stability. A legalistic interpretation of these and other corporate actions might not suggest that these acts were done with an interest of instilling fear in or directing a message to a particular target audience. However, we could examine officially promoted discourses surrounding these activities as a way to apply a critical perspective to the notion of environmental terrorism and the role of the state.

Entire branches of academia and government administration have long focused on effects of ongoing industrial mis-use of the environment. Illicit industrial dumping in the air, soil or water, insufficiently monitored nuclear waste transport and storage, and even inadequate environmental policies or a lack of sound implementation of environmental policies, to cite a few examples, would seem to be beyond studies of terrorism since they occur outside of war or since they are not done with an explicit political message aimed at a particular audience. If anything, these and other instances of environmental mismanagement or neglect are executed with a desire for little or no public awareness. No target audience is sought or, indeed, identified, and the source of problems related to contamination, misuse and mismanagement remains anonymous. Although labeling industrial abuses of natural systems as cases of 'environmental terrorism' is unlikely to be persuasive, it is difficult to overlook the impacts of a lack of accountability and policy coordination and enforcement in cases such as the Valdez oil spill, the Union Carbide gas leak in Bhopal, and the enduring legacy of Superfund sites in the United States. How these and similar, ongoing incidents are interpreted and described by whom and to whom are relevant for building a more informed understanding of relationships between the state and environmental features. It is also useful to note that disparities between powerful, corporate decision makers and communities negatively affected by corporate activity have garnered attention in the field of environmental security where, again, discourses promoted by one group may not reflect the lived reality of less powerful groups.[80] The notion of environmental terrorism may not be particularly useful in cases of corporate or industrial environmental damage since these types of incidents do not have the immediacy we might associate with terrorism. However, as the previously noted geographers have commented in regards to the events of 11 September, critical interpretations of terrorism must by their nature explore complexities, roots and consequences of events over time and space. Likewise, we must continue to examine incremental decision-making and creeping environmental problems[81] as important indicators the health of ecosystems and their relationship to the state.

Conclusion

This essay has examined the concept of environmental terrorism by subjecting it to critiques emerging from a somewhat similar research area, namely, environmental security. The literature cited here demonstrates a vast body of work on terrorism in general and a smaller, but possibly growing body of work on environmental terrorism. Terrorism is a term that changes meaning over time and by context, so it deserves careful attention to avoid becoming overused and under thought. This essay has highlighted some drawbacks of relying on legalistic definitions of terrorism to frame further research since the definitions most widely cited in the terrorism literature constrain how we might conceive of terrorism and its proponents. Adding an environmental element does not add clarity. Environmental terrorism has been used to refer to cases wherein features of the physical environment have been objects, tools and targets of activism, and clearly these activities are motivated from very different agendas. The term 'environmental terrorism' would seem to suggest that phenomena under discussion are peacetime events not initiated by states, but this interpretation misses important scales and types of hostile, unexpected activity that might be eclipsed by an unnecessarily narrow approach.

Perhaps more useful than pursuing a one-size-fits-all definition of terrorism – or environmental terrorism – a more practical and promising approach to research would examine case-specific events for theoretical insights. Rather than be constrained by assumptions inherent in current interpretations of terrorism, geographers are well-positioned to make applied and critical contributions to specific segments relating to terrorism, including infrastructural, physical, ecosystemic, health, medical, political, social and economic. Geographers, by the nature of our discipline which aims to understand and theorise connections among overlapping or networked scales of interaction, are well suited to examine unexpected, hostile acts by examining them as forms of communication, as involving resources and targets specific to an agenda, and by considering an array of involved actors. Just as critiques of environmental security literature have questioned deep and multi-directional implications of that label, so must geographers continue to examine the meanings and consequences of discourses surrounding terrorism and environmental terrorism.

ACKNOWLEDGEMENTS

The author thanks Cliff Singer, Julian Palmore and Col. Dave LaRivee at the Arms Control Disarmament and International Security Program at the University of Illinois at Urbana-Champaign, Richard Jaehne at the University of Illinois, and Stan Brunn at the University of Kentucky for their helpful comments during the planning stages of this essay. The author also wishes to thank three anonymous reviewers for their thoughtful comments on an earlier version of the essay.

NOTES

1. J.A. Walter, *Environmental Terrorism* (Carlisle Barracks, PA: United States Army War College 1992).
2. D.M. Schwartz, 'Environmental Terrorism: Analyzing the Concept', *Journal of Peace Research* 35/4 (1998) pp.483–96.
3. E.L. Chalecki, 'A New Vigilance: Identifying and Reducing the Risks of Environmental Terrorism', *Global Environmental Politics*, 2/1 (2002) pp.46–64.
4. M. Gold-Biss, *The Discourse on Terrorism: Political Violence and the Subcommittee on Security and Terrorism 1981–1986* (New York: Peter Lang 1994) p.7.

5. See J.D. Sidway, 'Geopolitics, Geography and "Terrorism" in the Middle East', *Environment and Planning D: Society and Space* 12/3 (1994) pp.357–72.
6. R. Falk, *This Endangered Planet* (New York: Random House 1971); R. Ullman, 'Redefining Security', *International Security* 8/1 (1983) pp.129–53.
7. J.T. Mathews, 'Redefining Security', *Foreign Affairs* 68/2 (1989) p.174
8. M. Soroos, 'Global Change, Environmental Security, and the Prisoner's Dilemma', *Journal of Peace Research* 31/3 (1994) pp.317–32.; S.M. Lynn-Jones and S.E. Miller, *Global Dangers: Changing Dimensions of International Security* (Cambridge, MA: The MIT Press 1995).
9. T. Homer-Dixon, 'On the Threshold: Environmental Changes as Causes of Acute Conflict', *International Security* 16/2 (1991) pp.76–117; idem, 'Environmental Scarcities and Violent Conflict: Evidence From Cases', *International Security* 19/1 (1994) pp.5–40; idem, *Environment, Security and Violence* (Princeton, NJ: Princeton University Press 1999); T. Homer-Dixon and J. Blitt, *Ecoviolence: Links Among Environment, Population, and Security* (Lanham, MD: Rowman & Littleman 1998).
10. See, for example M.T. Klare, *Resource Wars: The New Landscape of Conflict* (New York: Metropolitan Books 2000).
11. P.H. Gleick, 'Environment and Security: The Clear Connections', *Bulletin of the Atomic Scientists* 47/3 (1991) pp.16–21.
12. P.H. Diehl and N.P. Gleditsch (eds), *Environmental Conflict* (Boulder, CO: Westview Press 2001).
13. N.P. Gleditsch, 'Armed Conflict and the Environment', in Diehl and Gleditsch (note 12) pp.251–72.
14. N. Hildyard. 'Blood, Babies and the Social Roots of Conflict', in M. Suliman (ed.), *Ecology, Politics and Violent Conflict* (New York: Zed Books 1999) pp.3–24.
15. See for example T.L. Karl, *The Paradox of Plenty: Oil Booms and Petro-States* (Berkeley, CA: University of California Press 1997); R.M. Auty. 'Reforming Resource-Abundant Transition Economies: Kazakstan and Uzbekistsan', in R.M. Auty (ed.), *Resource Abundance and Economic Development* (New York: Oxford University Press 2001); P. Le Billon, 'The Political Ecology of War: Natural Resources and Armed Conflicts', *Political Geography* 20/5 (2001) pp.561–84.
16. J. Barnett. *The Meaning of Environmental Security: Ecological Politics and Policy in the New Security Era* (New York: Zed Books 2001).
17. See R.D. Lipschutz and K. Conca (eds), *The State and Social Power in Global Environmental Politics* (New York: Columbia University Press 1993); D.H. Deudney and R.A. Matthew, *Contested Grounds: Security and Conflict in the New Environmental Politics* (Albany, NY: State University of New York Press 1999); Suliman (note 14), Barnett (note 16).
18. M.A. Levy, 'Is the Environment a National Security Issue?', *International Security* 20/2 (1995) pp.35–62.
19. D. Deudney, 'The Case Against Linking Environmental Degradation and National Security', *Millennium: Journal of International Studies* 19/3 (1990) pp.461–76.
20. D. Deudney, 'Environment and Security: Muddled Thinking', *Bulletin of the Atomic Scientists* 47/3 (1991) pp.22–9.
21. S. Dalby, 'Security, Modernity, Ecology: The Dilemmas of Post-Cold War "Security Discourse"', *Alternatives* 17/1 (1992) pp.95–134.
22. S. Dalby. 'Environmental Security: Geopolitics, Ecology and the New World Order', in J.B. Braden, H. Folmer and T. Ulen (eds), *Environmental Policy With Political and Economic Integration: The European Union and the United States* (Cheltenham: Edward Elgar 1996) pp.452–75.
23. M. Tennberg, 'Risky Business: Defining the Concept of Environmental Security', *Cooperation and Conflict* 30/3 (1995) pp.239–58.
24. As quoted in B. Hoffman, *Inside Terrorism* (New York: Columbia University Press 1998) p.16.
25. Howard, M., 'Stumbling Into Battle', *Harper's*, January (2002) pp.13–18.
26. J. Zulaika. 'Terror, Totem, and Taboo: Reporting on a Report', in C. McCauley (ed.), *Terrorism Research and Public Policy* (London: Frank Cass 1991) p.43.
27. As quoted in Gold-Biss (note 4) p.11.

28. C. McCauley. 'Terrorism, Research and Public Policy: An Overview', in idem, *Terrorism Research* (note 26) pp.126–44.
29. Department of Defense web site <http://www.odci.gov/terrorism/faqs.html>, accessed 17 December 2001.
30. The United Nations web site <http://www.odccp.org/terrorism_definitions.html>, accessed 17 December 2001.
31. Ibid.
32. Hoffman (note 24).
33. Ibid.
34. J.B. Tucker. 'Lessons from the Case Studies', in idem (ed.), *Toxic Terror: Assessing Terrorist Use of Chemical and Biological Weapons* (Cambridge: MIT Press, 2000) pp.249–69.
35. P. Chalk, *Non-Military Security and Global Order: The Impact of Extremism, Violence and Chaos on National and International Security* (London: MacMillan Press 2000).
36. Chalk (note 35), chapter one, 'Terrorism'; Hoffman (note 24).
37. J. Stern, *The Ultimate Terrorists* (Cambridge, MA: Harvard University Press 1999).
38. W. Laqueur, 'Postmodern Terrorism', *Foreign Affairs* 75/5 (1996) pp.24–36.
39. J. Arquilla, D. Ronfeldt and M. Zanini, 'Networks, Netwar, and Information-Age Terrorism', in I.O. Lesser, B. Hoffman, J. Arquilla, D. Ronfeldt and M. Zanini, *Countering the New Terrorism* (Santa Monica: RAND 1999) pp39–84.
40. International Terrorism: Attributes of Terrorist Events database is available online at <http://www.sscnet.ucla.edu/issr/da/index/techinfo/i79471.htm>, accessed 21 December 2001.
41. Political Terrorism Database is available online at <http://polisci.home.mindspring.com/ptd/>, accessed 21 December 2001.
42. M. Crenshaw, 'Current Research on Terrorism: The Academic Perspective', *Studies in Conflict and Terrorism* 15 (1992) pp.1–11.
43. Ibid.
44. United Nations website, <http://www.odccp.org/terrorism_definitions.html>, accessed 17 December 2001.
45. A.H. Westing (ed.), *Environmental Warfare: A Technical, Legal and Policy Appraisal* (Stockholm: Stockholm International Peace Research Institute 1984).
46. C.E. Singer, 'Collisional Orbital Change of Asteroidal Materials', in J. Grey and C. Krop (eds), *Space Manufacturing III, Proceedings of the 4th Princeton/AIAA Conference* (New York: American Institute of Aeronautics and Astronautics 1979) pp.556–60.
47. R.A. Falkenrath, R.D. Newman and B.A. Thayer, *America's Achille's Heel: Nuclear, Biological and Chemical Terrorism and Covert Attack* (Cambridge, MA: The MIT Press 1998); C.C. Combs, *Terrorism in the Twenty-First Century* (Upper Saddle River, NJ: Prentice Hall 1997).
48. L. Garrett, 'The Nightmare of Bioterrorism', *Foreign Affairs* 80/1 (2001) pp.76–89.
49. T. O'Toole and D.A. Henderson, 'A Clearly Present Danger: Confronting the Threat of Bioterrorism', *Harvard International Review* 23/3 (2001) pp.49–53.
50. See J.B. Tucker and R.A. Zilinskas, 'Assessing U.S. Proposals to Strengthen the Biological Weapons Convention', *Arms Control Today* 32/3 (2002) pp.10–14, available online at <http://www.armscontrol.org/act/2002_04/tuczilapril02.asp>; 20/20 Vision web site <http://capwiz.com/vision/issues/alert/?alertid=68913&type=AN&azip>, accessed 29 January 2002.
51. Rocky Mountain News Archives, <http://nl12.newsbank.com/nl-search/we/Archives>, accessed 17 December 2001.
52. 'Fighting Eco-terrorism: The Green Threat?', *The Economist*, 1 December 2001, pp.31–2.
53. Earth First! web site, <http://www.earthfirstjournal.org/primer/Monkeywrench.html>, accessed 18 December 2001.
54. S.P. Eagan, 'From Spikes to Bombs: The Rise of Eco-Terrorism', *Studies in Conflict & Terrorism* 19/1 (1996) pp.1–18.
55. A. Toffler and H. Toffler, *War and Anti-War: Survival at the Dawn of the 21st Century* (Boston, MA: Little, Brown and Company 1993).
56. T.M. Hawley, *Against the Fires of Hell: The Environmental Disaster of the Gulf War* (New York: Harcourt Brace Jovanovich Publishers 1992); E. Badolato, 'Pollution as Ammunition', *U.S. Naval Institute Proceedings* 117/10 (1991) pp.68–70.

57. Chalecki (note 3).
58. Toffler and Toffler (note 55) p.123
59. P. Chalk, 'The U.S. Agricultural Sector: A New Target for Terrorism?', *Jane's Intelligence Review*13/2 (2001) pp.12–15.
60. P. Chalk, *Terrorism, Infrastructure Protection, and the U.S. Food and Agricultural Sector* (Santa Monica, CA: RAND 2001).
61. See Y. Alexander and C.K. Ebinger (eds), *Political Terrorism and Energy: The Threat and Response* (New York: Praeger 1982).
62. L. Maechling and Y. Alexander, 'Risks to Energy Production and Trade', in Alexander and Ebinger (note 61) pp.107–40.
63. O. Morton, 'Divided We Stand', *Wired* 9/12 (2001) pp.152–5.
64. The United Nations website <http://untreaty.un.org/ENGLISH/bible/englishinternetbible/partI/chapterXXVI/treaty1.asp>, accessed 17 December 2001.
65. I thank an anonymous reviewer for drawing this point to my attention.
66. E. Cué, 'Ecoterrorism as Negotiating Tactic', *The Christian Science Monitor*, 21 July 2000.
67. For a parallel argument in the environmental security literature, see R.D. Kaplan, 'The Coming Anarchy', *The Atlantic Monthly* 273/2 (1994) pp.44–76, available online at <http://www.theatlantic.com/politics/foreign/anarchy.htm>.
68. S. Dalby. 'Reading Robert Kaplan's 'Coming Anarchy'', in G. O Tuathail, S. Dalby and P. Routledge (eds), *The Geopolitics Reader* (New York: Routledge 1998) pp.197–203.
69. M. Finger. 'The Military, the Nation State and the Environment', in O Tuathail, Dalby and Routledge (note 68) pp. 78–91.
70. Hoffman (note 23) p.186.
71. Ibid. p.191.
72. N. Smith, 'Scales of Terror and the Resort to Geography: September 11, October 7', *Environment and Planning D: Society and Space*, 19/6 (2001) pp.631–7.
73. M. Abu-Nimer, 'Another Voice Against the War', *The Arab World Geographer*, 4/2 (2001), available online at <http://www.frw.uva.nl/ggct/awg/forum2/abu-nimer.html>.
74. R. McColl, 'The Law of Unintended Consequences: Reflections on Some Global and National Changes Following the Events of 11 September 2001, *The Arab World Geographer* 4/2 (2001), available online at <http://www.frw.uva.nl/ggct/awg/forum2/mccoll.html>.
75. J. Agnew, 'Not the Wretched of the Earth: Osama Bin Laden And the "Clash of Civilizations"', *The Arab World Geographer* 4/2 (2001), available online at <http://www.frw.uva.nl/ggct/awg/forum2/agnew.html>.
76. N. Smith, 'Ashes and Aftermath', *The Arab World Geographer* 4/2 (2001) available online at <http://www.frw.uva.nl/ggct/awg/forum2/smith.html>.
77. See, for example, T. Saiko, *Environmental Crises: Geographical Case Studies in Post-socialist Eurasia* (Harlow: Pearson Education 2001); J. DeBardeleben and J. Hannigan (eds), *Environmental Security and Quality after Communism: Eastern Europe and the Soviet Successor States* (Boulder, CO: Westview Press 1995); D. J. Peterson, Troubled Lands: The Legacy of Soviet Environmental Destruction (Boulder, CO: Westview Press 1993).
78. G. Smith, *The Post-Soviet States: Mapping the Politics of Transition* (London: Arnold 1999) pp.16–17.
79. I.O. Lesser. 'Countering the New Terrorism: Implications for Strategy', in I.O. Lesser, B. Hoffman, J. Arquilla, D. Ronfeldt and M. Zanini, *Countering the New Terrorism* (Santa Monica, CA: RAND 1999) p.110.
80. V. Shiva. 'The Greening of Global Reach', in O Tuathail, Dalby and Routledge (note 68) pp.231–6.
81. M. Glantz, 'Creeping Environmental Problems in the Aral Sea Basin', paper presented at the United Nations University Public Forum, Tokyo, 27 March 1995; idem (ed.), *Creeping Environmental Problems and Sustainable Development in the Aral Sea Basin* (New York: Cambridge University Press 1999).

Tabloid Realism and the Revival of American Security Culture

FRANÇOIS DEBRIX

We are entering a bifurcated world. Part of the globe is inhabited by Hegel's and Fukuyama's Last Man, healthy, well fed, and pampered by technology. The other, larger, part is inhabited by Hobbes's First Man, condemned to a life that is 'poor, nasty, brutish, and short'. Although both parts will be threatened by environmental stress, the Last Man will be able to master it; the First Man will not. The Last Man will adjust to the loss of underground water tables in the western United States. He will build dikes to save Cape Hatteras and the Chesapeake beaches from rising sea levels, even as the Maldive Islands, off the coast of India, sink into oblivion, and the shorelines of Egypt, Bangladesh, and South-east Asia recede, driving tens of millions of people inland where there is no room for them, and thus sharpening ethnic divisions.[1]

Tabloid Culture

Pointing to the inescapable conditioning power of tabloid press and tabloid talk shows (and their hosts) in late twentieth-century America, culture critic Joshua Gamson once wrote: 'You know you're in trouble when Sally Jessy Raphael seems like your best bet for being heard, understood, respected and protected.'[2] Paraphrasing Gamson, I would like to suggest that you are equally in trouble when Robert D. Kaplan seems like your best bet to redefine geopolitical realities, diagnose foreign policy threats, and prescribe new ways of thinking about national security in the twenty-first century. In the case of Sally Jessy Raphael's talk show and of Kaplan's endless succession of doomsday prophecies, we are witnessing a similar popular socio-cultural phenomenon: tabloid realism at its best (or worst).

The notion of tabloid literature is not novel.[3] In the United States, it dates back to the 1920s–1930s when 'true confession' magazines and 'yellow journalism' started to grab the American public's attention with news stories, photographs and public testimonies which mostly catered to a working-class audience.[4] The popular impact of tabloid publications found its point of departure in the need, created by the print media mostly, to sensationalise reality at all cost. Tabloid realism's premise was and still is that the public does not want to be told about their everyday life. Americans do not want to read or hear that they are underpaid, overworked, bullied at work, in the home, when serving their country in foreign lands. They want glamorous stories, scandals, exceptional events, news they can build dreams on or develop a sense of anger from. In short, they want to be entertained.

And yet, consumers of tabloid literature do not want total fiction either. They do not want the newspapers they read or the shows they watch to be about someone else's reality. They still insist on reading stories that somehow are about them, are related to their own life, work environment or cultural practices. Tabloid literature must be based on a reality-like context, something that the public has had a chance to experience, if only in small doses, because they know or have heard of somebody else (a neighbour, a colleague at work, a cousin) whose situation is exactly what the tabloid story reveals. Jane Shattuc summarises the intention of tabloid reporting by noting that tabloid texts must have a 'populist emphasis on the injustices done to the "average" American' and, at the same time, they must display 'the allure of the extremes of vividly told stories'.[5] In the tabloid medium, reality must be described and truth must be revealed in a flashy, surprising, gripping, shocking, often moralising, and sometimes anxiety-spreading manner. The reality of tabloid realism is a sensational one.[6] But the tabloid narrative must also be made accessible to a large amount of people. It must use images and languages that can be readily understood and easily recognised by the vast majority of 'Americans'.

Tabloid realism today is not confined to yellow journalism, daytime talk shows, a few publications that one quickly glances at while waiting in a checkout lane at the grocery store, or *Entertainment Tonight*. Tabloid realism is not only about 'low culture' (middle-class popular papers and shows) anymore. Elizabeth Bird notes that, traditionally, the tabloids almost never covered politics.[7] More and more so today, however, tabloids delve into the so-called 'high culture' of politics, policy making and foreign policy decision making. Should anyone have any doubt about the forceful penetration of tabloid literature into the culture of 'high politics', the Clinton–Lewinsky sex scandal could serve as a blatant reminder of today's inevitable fusion between tabloid sensationalism and policy making.[8]

If the tabloid genre of reporting and 'truth telling' has retained many of its initial aspects today, even when it dwells in the previously 'sacred' domain of high politics, tabloid culture has also undergone crucial modifications over the past 10 to 20 years. The tabloid genre has gone postmodern in order to, as Kevin Glynn notes, adapt to a media 'environment that is marked by such an odd yet increasingly characteristic mélange of images and discourses [which provokes for the public] a strange admixture of exhaustion and desire for the next media event long before the present one has even reached its culmination'.[9] Clearly, a passion for the sleaze, the graphic, and the provoking event was always part of tabloid literature. But postmodern culture provides the tabloid genre with additional tools and techniques that allow the proponents and consumers of this media/literary discourse to enhance their experience. Postmodernity, in a sense, is the crowning stage of tabloid culture. As Glynn suggests, postmodernity comes equipped with four main modalities of analysis and experimentation that serve tabloid realism's purposes.[10]

First, in the condition of postmodernity, increased media coverage and image saturation embellish the always graphic and spectacular mode of tabloid reporting by attaching visual signs to the story. Nor is tabloid reporting to be confined to newspapers and periodicals; television too can become tabloid. In fact, some television shows (talk shows in particular, but also investigative reports) become prototypical cases of tabloid 'truth telling' in postmodern times.

Second, postmodern analysis (allegedly a reflection on postmodern times) offers the possibility to challenge and unsettle modern categories of thinking and representation. The very notion of 'reality' is problematised as media culture provides daily material proof of the existence of multiple levels of 'reality' and 'representation'. The world 'out there' (a naturalist assumption) and the world perceived from the perspective of the rational subject (rationalism) are no longer the only existing alternatives for human cognition. Instead, and increasingly so, the world of the media and their reality-constructing effects must be considered too in order to adjudicate between different domains of experience or between different 'truths'. Tabloid literatures and shows in a postmodern era benefit from this ability of the media (and culture in general) to make multiple truths possible.

The third modality of postmodernity/postmodernism affecting tabloid reporting is directly derived from the previous point. As claims to unique, clearly identifiable truths are being challenged, the tendency of social, political and cultural thinkers to provide 'grand narratives' to make sense of society, politics and culture is abandoned. Rather, all sorts of stories, events, questions and choices can be objects of worthwhile knowledge and of information production. As 'grand narratives' disappear and more relativistic debates set in, knowledge can also be more fragmented, dispersed and plural. To some extent, anything can become a 'subject of knowledge', a motto which of course tabloid culture had already made its own well before the advent of postmodernity.

This relativist attack against meta-narratives also opens up the way one goes about collecting information and disseminating it. This is Glynn's fourth main point about postmodernity. As the 'truth' is no longer held inside a sacred sphere which must remain unsoiled by popular activities (not even in 'high politics'), multiple 'cultural products marked by stylistic eclecticism and bricolage' can be valid tools of knowledge too.[11] An aesthetic apprehension of the world can become the main determinant for investigation and analysis. And aesthetics can be found to be a sufficient justification for politics and/or ethics (and their representation).

The result of this encounter between postmodernity and tabloid culture is a general uncertainty as to the 'nature' of the product that is being consumed by the readers/viewers of the tabloid spectacle. Yet, far from feeling discomfort about this 'uncertainty' (Is this true or not? Is it credible? Is that what I want to see or not?), the consumers of the genre embrace the spectacle, its message, and perhaps more importantly its image. The tabloid story in a postmodern age remains popular, not only because of the contents of the stories (they by and large still cater to a working/lower middle class audience), but also because of the entertaining style/form on which this cultural medium is based. As Glynn already mentioned, in postmodern tabloid culture, the next image must be consumed even when the previous one has not had a chance to reach its completion. Yet, the entertaining presentation of the tabloid genre does not limit this mode of reporting to typically 'trash cultural' topics.[12] Rather, so-called serious topics can be treated as well. But when these topics are covered, they are still treated as entertainment. As entertainment, these 'serious' issues are introduced as events whose image lingers long enough for certain social/cultural effects to be produced, but never long enough for such events to be thoroughly analysed and adjudicated by methods other than postmodern modalities of investigation.

Popular Geopolitics and the American Media

In an age dominated by tabloid culture and in which politics is increasingly experienced by the public as 'trash' entertainment, international politics also becomes a prime target for sensationalism, scandal news, injustice reporting and crude moralising. American foreign policy and those who hope to influence its formulation are not immune from the spread of tabloid culture. Moreover, those who write about the foreign affairs of the United States today, consciously or not, often find themselves adopting a style of writing and presentation that is characteristically tabloid. They seek to shock their audience, take them by surprise, announce impending dangers for the American nation, develop stereotypes about the world outside US borders, and desperately seek to construct new international relations villains. While the intervention of tabloid culture into the domain of international politics can be seen to be a postmodern phenomenon, the conceptualisation of international politics in the United States has gone through historical stages when relatively similar discourses of popular and populist geopolitics took place. The point I wish to make about tabloid culture's use in certain foreign policy and security studies circles today is not that it is a unique trend or that it is not based on any prior discursive tradition. On the contrary, the tabloid realist genre of writing American foreign policy draws on a rich legacy of pop cultural and 'middle-brow' media fabrications. And yet, as I suggested above, the tabloid realist genre also possesses particular (postmodern) traits that explain its contemporary appeal and suggest that it is not just any reproduction of popular geopolitics.

The desire to condition the public to certain beliefs and attitudes through the dissemination of a popular but often paranoid political discourse is not novel. As Tom Engelhardt has shown in his study of American popular culture during the Cold War, the creation and reconstitution of America's ideas of 'triumphalism' and Manifest Destiny have often been achieved with the assistance of various national media, literary genres and art forms which, particularly in times of crisis, have tried to shape America's imaginary of the political world.[13] Throughout American history, media and literary outlets as varied as puritan sermons, best-selling novels, television programmes, Hollywood blockbuster films and news magazines have been in charge of periodically rekindling basic American values and dominant political doctrines to (re)define America. Of particular interest is the relationship between these popular media outlets and the construction of American identity both within the borders (who the American citizen is, what the nation is made of) and outside them (who America's enemies are, who we are at war with).

In recent years, critical geographers and international relations scholars have treated popular geopolitics as a genre/discourse in its own right. Focusing on what Joanne Sharp has called the 'relationship of state elite geopolitics to popular conceptualizations of the working of the world',[14] scholars and students of popular geopolitics have refused to distinguish between 'elite' texts and so-called 'low-brow' entertainment. Clearly, as David Campbell has shown, 'elite' foreign policy texts 'have been important in establishing the discursive boundaries of United States foreign policy'.[15] But foreign policy texts are rarely intended to be directly accessed by the vast majority of the population. Rather, the cultural forms and media upon which popular geopolitical constructs rely present 'elite literatures' as materials that can and should be consumed by the general public. As Sharp puts it, 'members of a distinctively elite institutional locale contribute to and consume popular media'.[16] Additionally, since popular geopolitics also turns to non-political texts to produce its desired effects, 'the political encoding

of such texts is more subtle and more easily reproduced'.[17] Popular media
such as those described above offer a mode of presentation of political
realities that generally remains free of jargon, is caricaturally simplistic, and
often juxtaposes more personal issues to current political problems. As
global political events are fused with more mundane stories in these media,
the reader/viewer is more directly interpellated as a direct participant of/in
the geopolitical scene. To quote Sharpe again, these media provide
'individuals with a particular understanding of the political system and their
position within it'.[18] I mentioned above that the tabloid genre of reporting
has traditionally refrained from using politics as a starting point for its
stories. But I also indicated that, particularly in postmodern times, the
tabloid medium has found a way of encoding political issues in what appear
to be matters of popular entertainment. On this account, tabloid media
partially fit the definition of popular geopolitics.

Sharp looks at *Reader's Digest*, a popular 'middle-brow' American
magazine, and performs a critical analysis of the production of popular
geopolitical imaginaries. She notes that during the Cold War the *Digest's*
condensed stories helped to shape American mentalities and attitudes vis-à-
vis communism and the Soviet Union through the use of narratives,
metaphors, graphic details, caricatures and paranoid images. *Reader's
Digest's* clear style of presentation of political realities, its use of selected
experts explaining the threat in vivid but accessible terms, and the mode of
dissemination of the magazine (it comes in the mail and directly reaches
millions of Americans) brought 'knowledge' to the vast majority of the
American public. The *Digest's* subscribers were made an integral part of the
construction of America's Cold War geopolitical structure. From reading
the magazine, they were given specific tasks to accomplish and specific
roles to play in America's new 'war'. The number one task was of course to
understand the structure of the world as the *Digest* meant to present it. And
the *Digest's* geopolitical representation of the Cold War was very much in
line with the view of the US government and most conservative US policymakers at the time. The world of the 1950s–1960s, the *Digest* told its
readers, was divided into two main ideological camps: the US-led world;
and the Soviet communist 'empire'. This geopolitical delineation intimated
by the *Digest* would have remained incomplete though if it had not been
accompanied by specific lessons to be learned from such a geographical
design. The main lesson was that the *Digest's* readers had to be able to
recognise Soviet communism as the United States' mortal enemy. To
embellish this exercise in cartographical pedagogy, the *Digest* was also full
of stories describing the basic traits of the Soviet Union and communism.
Often, in these stories, generalised features of Soviet communism veered
into individualised characteristics, meant to stigmatise the communist

individual as an 'enemy'. The American reader of the *Digest* could thus easily identify the physical, moral and ideological appearances of any communist, anywhere, and anytime. As Sharp remarks, '*Reader's Digest* had established America as the space opposite to that of communism, so the United States would always be on the receiving end of communist threats'.[19] But the *Digest*'s deployment of popular geopolitics did not stop here. The *Digest* also had 'to bring the threat of communism directly home to all individual Americans'.[20] Sharp adds that, during the Cold War, the *Digest* truly believed that 'at some "deep" level, the political identity of an individual [was] either "democrat" or "communist"'.[21]

While the many stories in the *Digest* gave (and perhaps still give) the American citizen a place in the world and a sense of who s/he was (is) fighting, the magazine also brought panic and uncertainty to the American home during the Cold War. The popularity of *Reader's Digest*'s Cold War geopolitical mappings in the 1950s–1960s coincided with the deployment of what Richard Hofstadter has called 'the paranoid style' among American politicians. Since, after all, the communist enemy could allegedly infiltrate the nation anywhere and anytime, conservative politicians found it necessary to 'stigmatise' America's feeling of danger and 'persecution' in 'grandiose theories of conspiracy'.[22] Of course, Senator Joseph McCarthy and those who supported him did not need to manipulate popular reads like the *Digest* to condition the nation to the idea of the 'enemy within'. Clearly, the *Digest*'s geopolitics had already prepared the American public for the onslaught of Cold War conservatism. To use Louis Althusser's language, Americans had already been interpellated to this ideological reality.[23]

The *Digest*'s contribution to popular geopolitics is obvious. Sharp offers the following summary of it: 'The magazine has produced for its readers a set of "imagined geographies" to show how politics works at a global level, what America's role is in these political geographies, and where the readers themselves are actually positioned relative to the events being described. This results in the construction of a model of an active subject through these geographical imaginations'.[24] As mentioned above, this 'active American subject' of popular geopolitics may have to be made fearful in order to become more vigilant. The infiltration of tabloid culture in the domain of 'high politics' today may be seen as a new instance of popular geopolitics. Fear and vigilantism achieved through geopolitical constructs are often the outcome of contemporary tabloid realist literatures too. But tabloid realism's use of geopolitics also displays several traits that differentiate it from Sharp's analysis of 'middle-brow' magazines during the Cold War.

First, it appears that the conditioning message of the *Digest* was partly determined by the historical and ideological context within which this American medium operated. As Sharp demonstrates, as times changed and the Cold War evolved, the *Digest* felt it had to modify the tone and rhetoric of its stories. What was asked of the American public varied according to larger political demands. In the period of détente, for example, the *Digest*'s coverage of the Cold War changed a bit to reflect what the magazine perceived as different political realities.[25] This point suggests that the institution of the *Digest* was still in part conditioned by larger ideological structures. By contrast, the tabloid genre of geopolitical reporting is much more affected by the form of the medium than by its message or content. As will be seen, the particular form of this medium is a primary reason why producers of geopolitical discourses, foreign policy analyses and American security today find the tabloid genre attractive. The tabloid medium allows scholars and journalists to deploy relatively ahistorical discourses in 'contexts' that do not have to abide by rules of temporal and spatial contingency (the realities they describe are at once past, present or future).

Second, Sharp indicates that the *Digest*'s production of 'clearheaded facts' was crucial to the magazine's mission of educating the public.[26] The American citizen had to learn about the Cold War (from the United States' perspective of course) in order to become more knowledgeable about the threats and dangers, but also in order to understand what her/his place in the overall system was. This was mostly achieved through the *Digest*'s decision to stay away from jargon-laden stories but also through the mobilisation of common sense as a rhetorical strategy. Common-sense language is a tool of generalised knowledge that 'appeals through the obviousness of its claims' and presents itself as naturally democratic.[27] A form of conditioning by knowledge was necessary to American Cold War objectives and the *Digest*'s 'experts' claimed to be willing to generously share their knowledge with the public. As will be shown later, the tabloid discourse of contemporary international politics does not claim to provide knowledge and its geopolitical imageries are not meant to be instructive. Instead, tabloid geopolitics intends to spread a sense of panic by providing spectacular scenarios and doomsday prophecies about 'realities' that are generally not tangible or even directly meaningful to the reader/viewer's experience. The 'dumbing down' of the tabloid genre gives priority to entertainment value and conditions the public through a lack of knowledge (which often is also an excess of information). Tabloid realism's 'experts' can thus remain uncontested 'authority figures' as the last thing they want is for their audience to know (what they are up to).

Finally, contrary to Sharp's argument, I do not believe that all forms of popular geopolitics create the kind of 'active subject' she describes. Indeed, one of the main discrepancies between the *Digest*'s Cold War mappings and contemporary tabloid realist renditions of world politics is the fact that the reading/viewing subject in the tabloid genre is generally asked to occupy a very passive position. The postmodern version of popular geopolitics adopts a tabloid approach so that the main task asked of the reader/viewer is to sit down, enjoy the show, and be fearful. Other subjects/agents, the tabloid reader/viewer is told, are doing the acting and are being vigilant. The consumer of tabloid realist literatures and shows does not have to constantly 'spy on his/her neighbours' since the producers of the spectacle are already doing this. In the tabloid version of popular geopolitics, vigilantism is a passive (but still reactive) activity carried out by individuals only by proxy. Adherence to the tabloid narrative is the only thing that is demanded of the 'subject' in this genre. Certainly, an absence of critical awareness was part of the *Digest*'s ideological mission too. Still, the *Digest* did not totally deprive its readers of their critical faculties, as it expected them to be overtly critical of anything and anyone that looked non-American. The tabloid narrative, by contrast, erases any critical ability since the discourse it provides is to be taken at face value. The facts, events, issues and more importantly images displayed in the tabloid medium are what they are, so-called 'pure objective realities' which, on the surface of things, are not supposed to be contested or accepted.

Tabloid International Politics

Much has been made of late in international relations circles of the multiple transformations that have apparently affected traditional visions of state sovereignty. Notions like globalisation, de-territorialisation, cultural fragmentation, and the proliferation of information have been advanced to suggest that the 'condition of postmodernity' has finally reached the domain of international politics. Postmodern times in international relations are marked by changes that appear to affect the traditionally fixed markers and concepts of international political analysis.[28] The nation state, sovereignty and the state's territorial claims (behind clearly identifiable borders) are no longer sacrosanct 'truths' as a sense of political relativism combined with an absence of structural fixity are witnessed by practitioners and scholars. It is precisely this sense of political relativism supplemented by an apparent lack of structural certainty after the Cold War which gives rise to the construction of new concepts (globalisation, de-territorialisation, and so on) allegedly better able to make sense of contemporary political realities. But these new concepts often remain vague, imprecise, fleeting and changeable. They are in fact as vague, imprecise, fleeting and changeable as the postmodern realities they purport to represent.

Among so many disparate and confusing notions, conceptual clarity is lacking. And once again, as in previous times of political doubt, a rhetoric of danger, security and national identity can be seen to resurface in intellectual circles as a reaction to these alleged postmodern phenomena. Similar to previous historical periods marked by a sense of geopolitical uncertainty, a coherent, populist and, at the same time, panic-inducing discourse returns and combines elements of 'expert' knowledge with popular media representations. Emerging in the mid 1990s, this new discourse of popular geopolitics claims to make better sense of the diverse phenomena and processes identified above by returning to some of political realism's basic tenets. This rekindled realist spirit is a way of stabilising geopolitical discourse in postmodern times. It allows its proponents to argue that today's international politics still reveals the basic greed and desire for power in human beings. The revival of political realism serves as a confirmation to these newly populist intellectuals that human nature in parts of the world, and sometimes not so far from the US shores, has turned for the worst. Realism reveals to them that, even though states seem at times to be relinquishing their central place in international affairs, they are still to be taken into account, if only because they are about to fall prey to new power groupings such as ethnic organisations, new nations, civilisations, multinational economic conglomerates, drug cartels or terrorist groups. In fact, because these new salient groupings are taking over the state, selfish interest defined in terms of power and often expressed in violent forms is once again becoming a political reality. Finally, the revival of this sort of panic realist discourse allows these intellectuals to announce that anarchy is taking over the fragile order that the Cold War brought and the semblance of a new order that the post-Cold War period ushered. Thanks to this re-invented discourse of (realist) geopolitical certainty, the doubts and dangers of postmodern international politics can be conquered and managed.

This return to an apparently crudely realist approach to world affairs is interested in identifying clear threats and spreading a sense of urgency in dealing with those dangers. For this contemporary mode of political analysis, it is American national security that mostly is at stake and, consequently, it is the American nation (perhaps the last bastion of sovereign power) that is the inevitable target. The 11 September 2001 attacks against the United States in New York and Washington are obvious confirmations to the advocates of this discourse that what they have forecast since the mid 1990s is about to take place: the United States is losing its traditional sense of sovereignty because globalisation, de-territorialisation, displacements, porous borders and the spread of transnational crime are penetrating US territory and altering the American way of life. The condition of postmodernity is slowly but surely dismantling American sovereignty and security. Thus, it is essential for the American population to develop a sense of urgency. According to this re-energised approach to popular geopolitics, the recognition that borders are no longer inviolable, that populations are increasingly mixed and culturally plural, and that political power often has to be shared with (and sometimes taken away from) subnational groups must give rise to a rather persistent discourse of danger, security and popular vigilantism.

At the same time though, this persistent discourse is more than a return to traditional realist postulates. It is also more than a return to the Cold War geopolitics of fear that could be found throughout the pages of *Reader's Digest*. This discourse is more importantly a tabloid discourse. It is what can be called 'tabloid realism' in contemporary international politics. Found in texts authored by scholars like Benjamin Barber, Zbigniew Brzezinski, Samuel Huntington, Robert D. Kaplan, Michael Klare, John Mearsheimer, and many others, tabloid realism is not to be interpreted as a uniform theoretical model.[29] Tabloid realism is not a new theory of international politics. If anything, it is composed of fragments of realist geopolitics, American nationalist ideology and cultural reactionism that are loosely put together to propagate shock effects in the public.

As these texts and authors do not form a coherent theoretical paradigm, they may be best understood as what Michel Foucault has called a discursive formation. A discursive formation is, as Foucault suggests, a 'system of dispersion'. Far from demanding adherence to a unity of content, to a theoretical matrix and to a proper methodology, a discursive formation operates at the level of statements (*énoncés*) that are often diffuse, disparate and dispersed. The point is not to arbitrarily regroup such statements but instead to emphasise their 'rules of formation' (their correlations, positions, transformations over time) and see how such rules sometimes come to form (or be taken as) epistemological regularities, particularly by those who produce such statements.[30]

Tabloid realism's constant hammering of the difficulty for the United States of adapting to the new international environment where transnational phenomena often appear to matter more to international subjects/agents (people, nations, organisations, corporations, business interests, terrorist networks) than the state itself is the most common denominator between these varied texts. This is, in a sense, the common message of the tabloid realist discursive formation. But what makes this tabloid mode of reporting and explaining contemporary political realities interesting, and what at the same time makes it different from previous discourses of panic geopolitics, is tabloid realism's adoption and apparent embrace of the postmodern style of analysis. Tabloid realism is ideologically reminiscent of the popular cultural geopolitical analyses of the Cold War (in the United States at least) when classical realism and right-wing conservatism merged to exclude non-American ideals and people, protect the American nation behind a rhetoric of securitisation, and redraw the map of the world so that it would evidence an obvious West vs East dichotomy. But tabloid realism has chosen to adapt to postmodern times. It has chosen to deal with the postmodern realities of globalisation, cultural fragmentation, human displacements and so forth. It recognises post-industrial economic flows and post-realist geopolitical realities to better make sense of them and later cast them away through a discourse which, as previously indicated, returns to basic realist postulates. In short, tabloid realism understands the postmodern premises about social and political conditions in the aftermath of the Cold War. And, as will be shown later, tabloid realism is masterful at 'mimicking' a postmodern style of describing current political realities that will strike a cord with a younger generation of geopolitical students for whom the Cold War is mostly a lengthy chapter in World History textbooks.

To reproduce 'postmodern rhetorics', tabloid realism starts from the premise of culture. It talks about cultural signs and icons, which it admits are free flowing in contemporary world politics. Linked to culture, tabloid realist geopolitics also spends a great deal of time emphasising the power of identity constructs. Power struggles and rivalries are embedded in identity debates. Additionally, to fit neatly in the postmodern mood, tabloid realist texts are very visual. The writings are made up of short, lapidary sentences, riddled with metaphors that call for the audience to maintain a mostly visual, figurative and imaginary apprehension of the intellectual arguments. As will be seen, maps are the necessary technical supports for this genre. After all, what could be more visual and familiar than a map? As Denis Cosgrove remarks, 'in the contemporary world, with its seemingly limitless capacities for producing, reproducing and transmitting graphic images, the map is a ubiquitous feature of daily life: the route map at the bus stop or subway station, the weather map on television, the location map in the travel brochure, the iconic map of the commercial advertisement'.[31] But the tabloid realist maps are no longer the binary, simplistic, red versus blue cartographical representations of the Cold War era. They are now fluid, multi-dimensional, almost 'holographic' projections of this geopolitical discourse. This does not mean, though, that these different-looking maps are necessarily less artificial, delimiting and reality producing than the older maps. Despite their apparent graphic complexities, postmodern maps drawn in tabloid realist texts can still be constraining and self-defining. Finally, tabloid realism absorbs the postmodern genre of reporting to better capture audiences by replicating the televisual, graphic, spectacular, sensationalistic pop cultural model of 'trash' talk show/tabloid television 'truth telling'. To captivate the audience with 'extreme' stories which are most likely to stir up popular emotions, tabloid realism also describes and explains contemporary geopolitical realities in a manner which is meant to be thoroughly gripping and entertaining, even if, at the end, the reality the audience is left with (and cannot act upon) is quite dramatic and often terrifying. To put it bluntly, tabloid realist geopolitics revels in postmodern 'trash culture'.

In the end, though, this adoption of postmodern tools and tricks in contemporary tabloid realist discourse is nothing more than a facade. To use terms borrowed from postmodern pop cultural analysis, it is tabloid realism's 'hook' and 'buffer'. While a postmodern apprehension of political realities is set up, and a semblance of appreciation for the postmodern genre is established, tabloid realism's eminently realist, conservative and reactionary discourse cannot hold on to the claims of political relativism, the lack of objective knowledge, the disdain for historical certainties and the epistemological doubt with regard to 'truth telling' which necessarily accompany postmodern analyses. And so, far from maintaining the postmodern/'trash' cultural course, tabloid realists eventually wish to steer their geopolitical writings (about the postmodern) away from postmodern uncertainities. Instead, they set up a spectre of postmodernity, of postmodern geopolitical realities, and of postmodern literary/cultural genres to better conjure it up, exorcise it, and cast it away. As will be shown, behind the veil of their postmodern/tabloid/'trash' cultural mode of presentation, tabloid realists nostalgically and often desperately long for the return of modern political certainties, Cold War geographical structures and schemes, national security programmes, and culturally protectionist foreign policies.

Any popular tabloid storyteller or TV 'trash' talk show host knows that the problems, crises, injustices, abnormalities and other villainies must be blatantly displayed for their story to be read or their show to be watched. To be blunt, the symptoms must take centre-stage. To examine the relation between tabloid realism, the securitisation of today's American culture, and the rebirth of cultural conservatism in certain circles of geopolitical analysis, I spend the rest of this essay featuring some tabloid realist authors and stories. By placing the spotlight on the tabloid realists, I wish to make visible some of the basic political, cultural, and ideological rules of formation that constitute this mode of writing/thinking/projecting international and domestic politics. In the following pages, three popular tabloid realists and their respective texts are highlighted. I look at Robert Kaplan and his paranoid vision of a 'coming anarchy'. I then turn to Samuel Huntington and examine his belief that a fundamental 'clash' of the world's main 'civilisations' is about to occur. And I finish the presentation with former Cold War realist politician Zbigniew Brzezinski and his displayed anxieties about a post-Cold War world which, in his view, has gone 'out of control'.

Robert Kaplan: The Tabloid Realist Search for a Secure Space

In his *The Coming Anarchy: Shattering the Dreams of the Post-Cold War*,[32] Kaplan gathers many of the articles on foreign affairs he has written for *The Atlantic Monthly* since 1994 (starting with his 'Coming Anarchy' article). In this book (and the 1994 article for which the book is named), Kaplan declares that the map of the world has forever been altered. States and their borders are in constant flux. Flows have replaced scales. Dromography has replaced geography. Ethno-religious disturbances and ecological disasters have replaced geopolitical order and security. The map of the Cold War is totally obsolete. Mapping, the very need to draw maps, to chart lands and people, needs to be reconsidered altogether in order to reflect these global insecurities.

In lieu of traditional cartography, Kaplan calls for a 'holographic' representation of the multiple layers in motion that make up the fabric of the twenty-first century world. 'Imagine', he writes, 'cartography in three dimensions, as if in a hologram'.[33] Kaplan continues:

> In this hologram would be the overlapping sediments of group and other identities atop the merely two dimensional color markings of city states and the remaining nations, themselves confused in places by shadowy tentacles, hovering overhead, indicating the power of drug cartels, mafias and private security agencies. Instead of borders there would be moving 'centers' of power, as in the Middle-Ages.[34]

This is what Kaplan calls the 'last map'. Indeed, the aim of this map is to be final, fatal and apocalyptic. It will end modern civilisation as we know it. It will forever alter our lifestyles, even in the West that appears to be buffered from the growing chaos emanating from Africa, South-east Asia and Latin America (see Kaplan's opening quote above).

The problem for Kaplan is as much the map itself as what it supposedly represents. The map is doomed to remain fluid, porous, disorganised and disorderly. It is, as Kaplan affirms, a postmodern map. It cannot fix, nor can it stabilise. It cannot mark, identify and differentiate. At best it traces paths and records flows that may have already passed on. It does not capture, but instead releases. In a strange operation of cartographic cathexis, Kaplan dumps onto the new map all that he thinks and fears is wrong with today's international politics. His fears are not only shown *on* the map. They *are* the map!

While Kaplan tries to hide his anxiety about the new world with its disasters and plagues behind such a cartographic (or is it holographic?) screen, he still has a hard time containing his discomfort with what he just described. His discomfort has to do with what he feels will happen to the

United States in such a quickly mutating world. 'It is not clear that the United States will survive the next century in exactly its present form',[35] Kaplan reveals. In fact, one may never be able to identify the United States on such a holographic image anymore. One might find instead a few city-ethno states (the Tijuana to Los Angeles corridor; the Portland–Seattle–Vancouver Asian Pacific coastal zone), several regional links stretching across oceans, rivers, and landmasses (the two sides of the Rio Grande; the Miami–Caribbean link; the Arizona desert), some left-over urban wastelands no longer connected to any political or economic core (the inner cities of what formerly was the industrial belt for instance), and many self-contained, self-sufficient, cleansed and barricaded suburban communities which could be anywhere from Florida to North Dakota. Kaplan actually wrote an entire book describing this new American geography.[36]

But despite his intent to fold all that is apparently destabilising about the post-Cold War world into new maps, Kaplan does not succeed in fending off the threats and the panic attacks they appear to produce. The maps, holographic and postmodern as they may be, remain disturbing to the Western (tabloid) realpolitiker in search of comfort and stability. What for Kaplan is disturbing about the new maps is that they indicate that doomsday has finally hit home. The chaos of the post-Cold War world is not, cannot be contained to the 'wild zones' of the globe (Africa, the Middle-East, Central Asia, some parts of Latin America) that he describes at length in all his narratives. The contagion is spreading and the cure is not available. Containment is the only possibility, but not every American citizen, not every large city or small town in the good old United States of America will be prepared when global chaos hits. In fact, it may already be too late: 'The signs hardly need belaboring: racial polarity, educational dysfunction, social fragmentation of many and various kinds'.[37] America's 'domestic peace' is 'further eroding'.[38] The very fact that we need to think about designing new maps to orient ourselves in this new world is a clear sign that problems are looming on the horizon.

Kaplan's obvious discomfort with this impending geographical reality is interesting. What was first designed by Kaplan himself to buffer us from the 'coming anarchy' – the new holographic, three-dimensional map – is becoming the very symptom of disorder, the exact representational proof that hell is about to break loose. The cartographic cathexis is not working well. Instead of hiding and containing, it reveals, projects and proliferates even more fears. Instead of providing solace to the new tabloid geopolitikers, it is a constant reminder of how insecure we (in the West) are. Simon Dalby has criticised Kaplan's mapping strategy by pointing out that 'resurgent cultural fears about the Other' and 'political angst about the collapse of order' infuse his pre-apocalyptic vision.[39] While this map of the frightening new world is labeled 'holographic' or 'postmodern', it is in fact driven by very traditionalist considerations about the 'here' and the 'there', the 'us' and the 'them', sameness and otherness. Behind the plastic covers of a high-tech, three-dimensional, virtual representation of space, Kaplan is worried about the state, borders, order and national security. Kaplan draws new maps to better contain what he clearly perceives to be 'outside' threats and to try to redefine what he considers to be the core of order, power and stability in the postmodern world, namely, the American nation. Unfortunately (for him mostly), this does not work too well, as the spectre of doom lingers.

Such an approach to drawing maps, no matter how technically innovative they are made to appear, and more revealingly, the need to turn to maps to achieve geopolitical security, are classic political realist concerns. The attempt here is to defend what the scholar considers to be the national interest at all cost, starting with the United States' borders and the protection of the American lifestyle. The problem is not inside but outside. As Dalby mentions, Kaplan does note 'the dangers of the criminals from "there" compromising the safety of "here" but never countenances the possibility that the economic affluence of "here" is related to the poverty of "there"'.[40] To the extent that the 'inside' becomes compromised it is only because the 'outside' has managed to penetrate the insufficiently protected boundary-lines.[41] The trouble is not and cannot be with the inside, with the American nation and its changing culture. Rather, the American nation and its culture are in trouble because of what's coming at them.

Kaplan is an exemplary tabloid realist scholar who plays with postmodern terms, techniques and images but, in the end, is bedeviled by them. Kaplan recognises the fluidity of contemporary geopolitics and he presents it in a (geo)graphic postmodern manner: the virtual map, its flows, its absence of containment and finality. But, more importantly, Kaplan understands that in postmodernity fictions can be more 'real than reality itself'.[42] Images are their own reality. If done well, fictions without referents can nonetheless produce desirable effects in society and culture. This is precisely the point of Kaplan's tabloid realist mapping. A simulation of geopolitics at the turn of the century, Kaplan's geographical imagery relies upon bits and pieces of information data about the post-Cold War (dis)order, popular global news stories (environmental degradation, the growth of transnational crime, etc.), and snapshots of disasters and conflicts in the 1990s seen by everyone on CNN or on the covers of *Time* and *Newsweek* to 'substantiate' his vision of an inevitable political anarchy. To further establish the veracity (or 'reality effect') of his global dystopia, Kaplan tells his reader that these frightening scenes of impending chaos cannot be doubted (even if the reader/viewer has no direct experience of them). After all, he, Kaplan, reporter of the tabloid story, has seen them all in his many travels. But, even with Kaplan's dramatic narrative, a reporter's story can always be doubted. Kaplan's story, however, is not supposed to be doubted or believed, accepted or rejected. It stands beyond 'truth claims' and 'historical certainty'. As a postmodern story, it is a simulation of reality that cannot be assessed and accessed as either true or false. Even if one were to counter Kaplan's version of post-Cold War geopolitics by bringing different factoids, news events and stories into the picture,[43] Kaplan's tabloid realist narrative would still hold 'true' at some level because, according to his own visual and cartographical premises, no other conclusion can be derived but that of the recognition of a generalised sense of impending chaos. Ultimately, what this 'coming anarchy' is built on is a self-evident 'holographic' map that, beyond facts and data, can say it all. In an age when all sorts of narratives can be produced and supported by all sorts of information, the visual becomes the final refuge of what counts as 'true'. In an exceedingly mediatised universe, what's on screen stands in for what can be positively verified. Kaplan's postmodern map is this tabloid realist's final visual/virtual evidence. The map, only the map, confirms Kaplan's journalistic testimonies and grants them credibility. In this simulated universe where the map creates 'realities' which in turn justify the deployment of the map, 'reality effects' are self-referentially constructed and, again, are neither true nor false.

But the construction of this self-referential mapping is only half of Kaplan's tabloid discourse. Indeed, even though Kaplan offers his readers a postmodern simulation of geopolitical (dis)order, he still appears to be caught by surprise by what he created. The simulated object (Kaplan's map) obliterates any possible return to modern political order, security and the nation state. Caught in his own postmodern game, Kaplan makes an about-face and suddenly refuses to recognise the 'realities' that his 'holographic' map unleashes. Instead of drawing the logical conclusions one might be led to derive from such a chaotic, dizzying and fluid cartographical fiction, Kaplan's tabloid realist discourse turns reactive and protective. Instead of following his postmodern premises to what may be their fatal outcome, Kaplan chooses to extol the virtues of the 'inside', the nation, the state, us, in a word, America, which must be defended at all cost even if, earlier in his text, Kaplan showed his reader how futile and doomed national defence and security measures may be in a postmodern age.

Kaplan's deployment of a postmodern imagery of uncertainty and chaos and his subsequent rejection of it is a common case of tabloid realist self-induced paranoia. As will be shown later, both Huntington and Brzezinski display similar syndromes. Unable to 'have it both ways' (postmodern yet modern, fluid yet secure, relativistic yet believable), tabloid realists provide a spectacular, entertaining, gripping and sometimes chilling 'reality' that they later must totally discard. Interpreted as a symptom of this tabloid realist genre, Kaplan's map is not so original after all. Below the opaque, fluctuating and confusing layers of his postmodern map lies the stable, orderly and static map of twentieth-century America that is slowly but surely being obliterated. As Brian Jarvis notes, postmodern cartographies do not always 'constitute a decisive break from the dominant tradition of landscape representation'.[44] Instead, in American geopolitical culture in particular, some new maps simply 'represent a reworking of the raw materials that have always been central to the American geographical imagination'.[45] Kaplan's postmodern cartography exemplifies this tendency since his map betrays a profound anxiety about the integrity of the old map. After throwing away the new map, only one possible conclusion remains (no matter how illogical and incoherent this conclusion is in relation to Kaplan's original premises): the old map must be restored. And the old map shows us that it may be tolerable for the rest of the world (mostly the non-Western world) to live in a spatial universe made up of uncontrollable flows and uncertain identities. But this is not acceptable for the United States that must remain rooted in a space where sovereign power, national culture and fixed borders are still visible and meaningful. Consequently, and once again in contradiction with his initial postmodern cartographical designs, Kaplan affirms that a spatial delineation of an 'inside' and an 'outside' is more than ever required. This spatial distinction, drawn out of the fear caused by the new map rather than as its inherent condition, must take over the public imaginary so that the produced fears may be controlled and the identified dangerous flows coming from 'outside' may be stemmed.

Samuel Huntington: Tabloid Realist Cultural Conservatism

It may seem odd to classify Samuel Huntington as a tabloid realist since, after all, his work has influenced many generations of political scientists who would not necessarily consider themselves to be tabloid realists. Currently serving as director of the John Olin Institute for Strategic Studies at Harvard, Huntington's academic research has always revolved around the notions of security and political order. A founder of the journal *Foreign Policy* and the author of close to ten books, Huntington is a classical figure in American political science. Since the 1950s, students taking courses in Comparative Political Systems, US Foreign Policy, Security Studies, and Democracy and Politics have found his works to be part of the basic curriculum. Throughout his career, though, Huntington has shown a constant preoccupation for the issue of political order. In his classic

Political Order in Changing Societies,[46] Huntington demonstrated that attempts at democratisation in 'changing political systems' (what later he would rename 'transitional democracies') could not succeed and in fact could even become detrimental to the development of mature democratic regimes if they were not accompanied by institutions capable of establishing political order first. The imposition of institutional guarantees and political safeguards, even if these sometimes must take the form of authoritarian structures, is preferable to the immediate introduction of democratic values in formerly non-democratic social systems. Even though Huntington revises this formulation in a later work (written as the Cold War vanishes),[47] Huntington's approach has sometimes been labeled conservative and reactive to the extent that it places the achievement of social order before the enjoyment of democratic freedoms and rights.[48] Additionally, as an American academic writing during the Cold War, Huntington always kept an eye on the problem of order in American society. By extension, this concern with American order in an era of bipolar political and ideological struggles at times led him to consider the situation of some of America's allies and enemies too.[49]

The end of the Cold War has not abated Huntington's intellectual quest for political order, both at home and abroad. Of late, and because of the changing geopolitics of the post-Cold War era, Huntington has spent a great deal of time rethinking order in relation to space. Based on what he calls the 'cultural reconfiguation of world politics', Huntington presented another map of post-Cold War international politics in his 1996 bestseller *The Clash of Civilizations and the Remaking of World Order.*[50] In this book, Huntington claims that the structure of civilisations is starting to take over a world organised around the needs, interests and prerogatives of sovereign states. State-to-state politics is quickly disappearing, Huntington believes. With the Cold War over, bipolar geopolitics no longer makes sense. In fact, the vanishing of the Cold War has allowed new forces of integration and fragmentation to come to the forefront of international affairs. Religious preferences, ethnic identifications and cultural values can now be advanced as the geopolitical and ideological dialectic between East and West is gone.

Similar to Kaplan before, Huntington has adapted his old Cold War rhetoric of order to postmodern times. Equating the postmodern era of geopolitics with a 'cultural turn', Huntington affirms that cultural politics is the dominant reality of this new age.[51] With Huntington's vision of cultural politics come new divisions and new alliances, new fault lines and forms of co-operation. As culture becomes the determining factor in people's lives globally, Huntington claims, a clash of cultural civilisations is sure to follow. Geopoliticians and policy makers must find ways to deal with it. Huntington is eager to prepare political leaders and foreign policy makers in the West, and in the United States above all, for what is about to come. To be prepared to face the clash of civilisations, one can no longer rely on a conception of geopolitics that takes Cold War maps as a representational support. Modern international relations thinking was based on maps. These maps showed the clash between the West and the East, Western Liberalism and Communism. They told us who we were and where we stood. These old maps served their purpose. They averted global destruction during the Cold War. They saved us from a nuclear holocaust. They preserved the West and America. They brought stability and order. They kept us free.

But the new international relations are different, Huntington asserts. Post-Cold War international politics requires the creation of new maps, the development of what Kaplan would call a 'postmodern cartography' as a point of departure, so that we may know who *we* are again, and more importantly, who *they* are and where *they* stand. A map, Huntington adds, is here to 'best serve our purposes' and to provide a 'necessary simplification that allows us to see where we may be going'.[52] Huntington no doubt has the road map model in mind. For Huntington, maps serve to show the road ahead. They trace a path to the future and direct the scholar in his/her re-envisioning of the world out there. Down the line, maps help to protect the nation.

Even if the new map is representationally postmodern (as will momentarily be shown, the map partly reveals a post-statist international system), Huntington's intention is still very much modern. The temporal linearity and causal relations that Huntington hopes the new map will engender are traditional modern concerns. Similar to Kaplan, Huntington's new map is a bridge from postmodern geopolitics back to modernity and modern political order. At first glance, the map Huntington offers is much more orderly than Kaplan's. Chaos is not readily evident on Huntington's map. Rather, chaos or geopolitical instability is the threat Huntington's map brings if states (and mostly the United States of course) do not react and adopt a defensive posture. Huntington's map is multi-dimensional too: it has two main superimposed layers. The first layer is made up of nine civilisational clusters. These clusters represent the major cultural civilisations that Huntington perceives will be taking over international politics in the century to come. Latin American, Islamic, African, Sinic, Hindu, Orthodox, Buddhist, Japanese and Western are the labels given to the civilisations, to the nine main new geopolitical players. These civilisations are self-sufficient and self-fulfilling. They include and exclude on religious, ethnic and often linguistic bases. More importantly, they are antagonistic and sometimes mutually incompatible. These civilisations are destined to do battle with one another now that Cold War politics is out of the picture. States who fall within those large cultural clusters are stuck.

They follow the dominant cultural logic to which they have been ascribed. States' policies will have to be readjusted to exemplify civilisational claims and concerns. Continents and sub-continents are divided and reformed too in order to be in line with the major civilisational fault lines. Africa, for example, is divided in two at about the 15th parallel to mark the separation allegedly found there between the Islamic and African civilisations.

The second layer is more conventional. It takes sovereign nation states as its main marker and traces boundary-lines around them. As Huntington reminds us, the state is far from being absent from this global clash of civilisations. The sovereign state is the political unit which is most affected by the cultural redistributions exemplified by the first map. Thus, Huntington continues, it is necessary to have a secondary map that reflects the deep 'cultural' transformations at both the inter-state and intra-state levels. The second map is more classical to the extent that geopolitical divides take place between and within states. But it is still very different from the previous maps of the Cold War since the structure of the post-Cold War inter-state map is now made to depend upon a conditioning super-structural clash of civilisational clusters (as opposed to the superstructure of balance of power politics during the Cold War, for instance). Both internally and externally, 'state alignments' are being modified, and this is precisely what the second map intends to reveal.

This substructural cartographic layer is composed of four different categories of states. Every sovereign state on the planet falls into one of those four categories. The categories are defined by the degree of involvement, reception, inclusion, resistance or rejection of the state (any state) vis-à-vis the civilisational cluster within which it is found. In other words, culture is the determining variable of a state's identity. The four categories are the following ones: core states, lone countries, cleft countries and torn countries. Core states are 'places which are viewed by [a civilisation's] members as the principal source ... of the civilization's culture'.[53] They are often central to the civilisational cluster, and they define the cultural politics that all the members of the civilisation (states, subgroups, ethnic entities, and individuals) will adopt. China, for example, is the core-state of the Sinic civilisation, while India is the core of the Hindu cluster. The new cultural geopolitics of the post-Cold War era radiates from these different cores (more or less nine of them; one per civilisation). The core states have the power to culturally permeate other, more peripheral countries within the civilisational bloc. They also have the ability to draw the main battle-lines with other civilisations. In many ways, the 'road-map' of cultural clashes Huntington wants to imprint finds its point of origin in these civilisational cores.

A lone-country is, as its name indicates, a country that is left alone.[54] It does not have the desire, or rather capacity, to belong to any of the nine dominant civilisations. Ethiopia is given as an example of a lone-country. Haiti is supposedly another case in point. These lone-countries are potentially problematic for Huntington. Since they have no determining alignment, they can more easily sell themselves out to any civilisation that wants to incorporate them. But the potential problem posed by lone-countries is minimal compared to the danger that cleft-countries represent. Cleft-countries, Huntington indicates, 'territorially bestride the fault lines between civilizations'.[55] Cleft-states are multi-civilisational states, with generally two major civilisations wanting to take over that state. In short, cleft-countries are internally divided along cultural lines. For these states, the civilisational fault line is not outside but inside. Driven by repulsion, cleft-countries are a constant source of geopolitical instability. Their internal disputes may affect the geopolitics of civilisational blocs as these countries may exacerbate the already existing cultural tensions and widen the fault lines. Thus, it is feared that cleft-countries may affect the politics of non-cleft countries. They may drag non-cleft countries, including core-states, in an open civilisational war. For this reason, cleft-countries must be closely monitored, particularly by all the core-states, in all civilisations. Cleft-countries are the main source of division and conflict in a cultural world. What has happened to Yugoslavia over the past decade is for Huntington a blatant example of the global risk of insecurity cleft-countries represent.

Finally, a torn-country 'has a single predominant culture which places it in one civilization, but its [political] leaders want to shift it to another civilization'.[56] Risks are also apparent in these countries that often 'bestride' fault lines against the will of the populations. Political leaders want their countries to bridge East and West, Europe and Asia, Islam and Western Enlightenment, and so forth (Huntington points to Turkey as an example of a torn-country). But the populations, also influenced by their cultural leaders, sometimes resist the formation of the civilisational bridge recommended by the political leaders. Once again, for Huntington, this sort of forced positioning across cultures is a potential source of geopolitical instability.

For Huntington, this multi-layered map of a world dominated by post-statist cultural alliances and allegiances is a necessity. It is the basic visual representation of what is happening 'out there' in the early twenty-first century. All can be explained by referring oneself to the map. More importantly, while the first map evidences the new dominant geopolitical reality, the second map bears witness to how unstable the new world currently is and may remain if no action is taken to either smoothen the fault lines or protect oneself from them. On the second map, anything goes and, potentially, cultural conflicts abound. Huntington's civilisational map projects instability and uncertainty. It does so, not by presenting itself as a fluctuating map like Kaplan's, but rather by inscribing a new order, the order of civilisations. Because of their cultural natures, these civilisations are generally hostile to one another. And, because they are hostile to one another, the civilisations will lead the world into endless crises, conflicts and human dramas, dramas similar to those the United States faced on 11 September. In short, it is in the very nature of this new (cultural) order to be disorderly. Huntington's postmodern map is a harbinger of doom. And doom on this map is particularly manifest on the secondary level where states have no choice but to rearrange their strategic positioning in terms of core, cleft, torn or isolated cultural categorical imperatives.

The second map is concerned with states and attempts to redraw boundaries (some strong, others quite weak) around them. For Huntington as for Kaplan before, it is clearly the state that is being threatened by all those civilisational re-alignments. The map tells us as much. As Michael Shapiro suggests, despite all the appearance of novelty, transformation and re-mapping, Huntington is a cartographical 'recidivist' of sorts.[57] And despite his attempt at painting twenty-first century international relations as the inevitable outcome of a post-structural cartography, Huntington is also a structural recidivist who ascribes states to a specific place that has already been carved out by the preconditions of the larger superstructural order. Even when states are being (re)defined by cultural superstructural positions, state-to-state geopolitics remains the main issue. The new affiliations still conform to 'a state-oriented set of antagonisms',[58] except that today's antagonism is allegedly much more unpredictable (hence, more dangerous) than the previous one.

Huntington's mapping strategy and the geopolitical analysis it enables conform to tabloid realist tenets. Indeed, Huntington combines a stereotypical understanding of postmodern political analysis with a keen sense for the dramatic and the spectacular to produce a hoped-for reaction (or outrage perhaps) on the part of his audience/readership. This reaction, Huntington calculates, will bring a return to modern preoccupations with order that should focus on the always necessary and salutary presence of the sovereign state. To repeat, Huntington's arrangement of post-Cold War international space and his construction of impassable fault lines make chaos the only possible geopolitical outcome. This, of course, is done by design and with a clear sense of what is being produced. Again, the desired effect here is borrowed from the tabloid model of truth telling and reporting. Huntington must give his audience the image of a map that inevitably will lead to anarchy so that they may more effectively conjure up the prospect of such a global disorder.[59] In particular, foreign policy makers must react to this mapping, rebel against it, conservatively protect their possessions, and culturally regroup. Similar to Kaplan, by painting a potentially disastrous portrait of the civilisational structure of twenty-first century international politics, Huntington hopes to 'rally the troops' around the idea of a traditional geopolitical space, a space governed and controlled by fixed and stable sovereign states. Gearoid O Tuathail is on target when he diagnoses Huntington's work as a form of 'neoconservative cultural anxiety'.[60] Tabloid realism, despite its co-optation of postmodern cultural tools, remains an eminently nostalgic and melancholic discourse. Huntington is nostalgic for the good old past, the Cold War, its 'long peace', and the maps of yore that 'imposed closure upon events, situations and people'.[61]

Huntington's model is its own message too. It is a pointed warning sent to one of the identified civilisations, the West. Huntington writes: 'The Islamic resurgence and the economic dynamism of Asia demonstrate that *other* civilisations are alive and well and at least potentially threatening to the West. A major war involving the West and the core states of other civilisations is not inevitable, but it could happen'.[62] Here, Huntington taps into popular fears, thinking that mobilising these will yield a populist appeal to his prophecies. The security of the West is at stake. The West is a prime target of inter-civilisational disorder. Why worry so much about the West, and the West only? The answer is simple, and it is a blatant proof of tabloid realism's Western ethnocentrism. The West matters because it is 'our' civilisation, the one that invented modern political order, sovereignty, statehood, nationality, the rule of law and democracy. The West matters because it has invented modern international relations, power politics, the balance of power and the Cold War. The West matters because it is culturally solid and homogeneous. Finally, the West matters because that's where 'we' are and who 'we' are (on the map); it is the place from which Huntington is writing. It is the civilisation of the United States, the nation that feeds the West its core values.

For Huntington, this ethnocentric message is beyond questioning. It goes without saying. It must have mass appeal too. It explains that any cultural attack against the West is an attack against the United States, against America's culture, against America's lifestyle, against America's civilising mission. After all, 'without the United States the West becomes a minuscule and declining part of the world's population on a small and inconsequential peninsula at the extremity of the Eurasian landmass',[63] Huntington adds. To protect itself and its civilisation, the United States must solidify its cultural borders. It must pursue the inclusion of the Western cultural bloc. It must keep the Western bloc Western. Cultural renewal is the answer. Cultural renewal is the way for the United States to regain geostrategic control over international relations and recreate a sense of

Western alliance, complicity and common interest. Huntington's brand of tabloid realist analysis is highly nationalist and culturally protectionist. Cultural protectionism is Huntington's way of normalising twenty-first century international politics and, by the same token, of securitising domestic politics.

Cultural renewal must start at home, in the heartland of Western civilisation. Multiculturalism, allegedly promoted by American political leaders in the 1990s, Huntington claims, is dangerous and must be contained before it is too late. Multiculturalism is a political abnormality, one that runs the risk of turning the US into a cleft-country and of destroying the West and its geopolitical mission of order and security. American leaders in the 1990s were confused, Huntington intimates. They did not realise how deep the cultural fault lines were. They, more than anybody else, should have been able to heed the warnings visible on Huntington's map and, as a response, should have developed nationalist, territorialist and security-driven policies. As a result, today's politicians have no choice but to protect the 'homeland' so that, instead of wishing 'to create a country of many civilisations', they can finally promote the 'unity of the people they govern'.[64] In the wake of the 11 September terrorist attacks against the United States, Huntington's culturally protectionist incantations have found eager supporters both in the general public and in foreign policy/homeland security policy circles.[65]

Once again, America is the champion of the West. The West, infused with America's values, is a model of unity. Multiculturalism threatens this unity. Multiculturalism can cause civilisational warfare and internal divisions. The West and its people must remember that they are valuable, 'not because [the West] is universal, but because it *is* unique'.[66] If retaining Western uniqueness and preserving American cultural leadership mean that other civilisations have to be declared antagonistic, then be it. At least, the average American will know who s/he is, where s/he stands, and who the 'others' are.

Zbigniew Brzezinski: Tabloid Realism and Orientalist Melancholy

I now wish to turn to the case of Zbigniew Brzezinski. Two of Brzezinski's works, *Out of Control*[67] and *The Grand Chessboard*,[68] are prime examples of the tabloid genre of realist writing. More than Kaplan's or Huntington's texts, these two volumes show us the extent to which tabloid realists are (still) obsessed with power, its structural conditions and the geostrategic 'games' power used to allow foreign policy makers to play. Of the three tabloid realists examined in this study, Brzezinski is probably the one who is the least willing to adapt to postmodern times. Brzezinski was thrown into postmodern geopolitics against his wishes. He had no choice but to accept the end of the Cold War even if, as many other former cold warriors, he would have preferred to see the 'Long Peace' stretch its stabilising wings into the twenty-first century. Inevitably, the end of the Cold War has brought a sense of melancholy among the foreign policy makers that invented, lived under, and thrived during the Cold War. Nostalgic for the strategic games of an era that apparently no longer is, realist foreign policy makers turn tabloid realists partly to relive the old fantasies and partly to cope with the new realities.[69] As a postmodern cultural genre, tabloid realism is not burdened by claims of authenticity and historical accuracy. Accordingly, in the tabloid genre, any story can be replayed and thus potentially given a different outcome. This retelling or replaying of history and its stories is precisely what Brzezinski's brand of tabloid discourse does. Tabloid realism gives former cold warriors the opportunity to re-imagine Cold War scenarios in a post-Cold War era. It allows them to continue to fight the old struggles and, they hope, to postpone the end of the story and history.

Zbigniew Brzezinski, a professor of American Foreign Policy at Johns Hopkins University and a counselor at the Center for Strategic International Studies in Washington, DC, was Jimmy Carter's national security advisor (from 1977 to 1981). Subsequently, he served as co-chairman of George Bush's National Security Advisory Task Force in 1988 and oversaw most of US intelligence activities up to 1989 as part of the President's Foreign Intelligence Advisory Board. Brzezinski started to work for the Department of State in the 1960s. Born in Poland and educated in the United States (Harvard) after the Second World War, Brzezinski is an American cold warrior with a deep nostalgia for the cultural roots he left on the other side of the Atlantic. For Brzezinski, as for many other US foreign policy makers of the Cold War, personal history is not just an anecdote. It is part and parcel of their world outlook, their understanding of ideological differences and their passion for international politics.

While serving as National Security Advisor, Brzezinski adopted a blatantly anti-communist, mostly anti-Soviet, stance. He was credited in 1981 with normalising diplomatic relations between the US and China. At the same time, however, he positioned himself as one of the most ardent detractors of the Soviet regime, vehemently criticising the Soviet invasion of Afghanistan. Brzezinski responded to the Soviet occupation of Afghanistan by reviving John Foster Dulles' famous 'dominoes theory': if the US lets Afghanistan fall to Soviet communism, Pakistan and Iran would soon follow. Throughout his diplomatic career, Brzezinski chose to devise a foreign policy geared toward Eastern Europe, Central Asia and Soviet communism. Analysing Soviet moves and advances was his first preoccupation as national security advisor. An effective national security policy, he affirmed, required developing an anticipated sense of what the

Soviets would do next. After serving the US government, Brzezinski never ceased to remind scholars about this primary foreign policy objective. He wrote two books, *The Grand Chessboard* and *The Grand Failure* [70] (about the demise of Soviet communism), to emphasise the fact that the key to (American) geopolitical stability is Eastern Europe and Central Asia, or what he recently renamed Eurasia.

The post-Cold War era has presented a challenge to Brzezinski's foreign policy beliefs. The Soviet Union has collapsed. Measuring American security in relation to the Soviet threat is no longer possible. Russia is still around, but building up defence strategies at home and abroad to contain the spread of communism specifically is no longer a credible option. Or so it appears. Instead of going into pre-retirement, Brzezinski has found a new motivation in the post-Cold War world. The end of the Cold War is both a challenge and an opportunity. Since no clear order seems to have succeeded the Cold War and postmodern times authorise multiple geopolitical scenarios to be played out, why not pretend the Cold War (or something closely resembling it) is still a contemporary reality? Why not simply point to the same old threats (Russia, Eastern Europe) and write pamphlets about the panic and destruction that would certainly ensue if the US failed to contain the menace? This is exactly what Brzezinski's tabloid realism suggests. Brzezinski's tabloid realism anachronistically revives Cold War politics in an age when most (but not Brzezinski) believe that the Cold War is over.

Tabloid realism as a discursive genre gives Brzezinski something to do and hope for (other than teach a few foreign policy courses). It also offers him a semblance of public responsibility, gives him the impression that he is still useful to the American government. What's left to do now, even though Soviet communism is gone, is convince the American public that it is *still* a dangerous world out there. In fact, Brzezinski argues, it may be a more dangerous world now that communism has lost its grip on many third-world nations. What the collapse of communism has produced is the vision that multiple nations exist and that there is a plethora of leaders and disenfranchised groups of people who selfishly seek power, legitimacy and wealth. In the territories formerly controlled or influenced by the Soviet Union (including parts of the Middle East and Central Asia), one now finds groups of individuals bearing a grudge against the United States. This anti-US sentiment is perhaps the main common goal these groups have inherited from the old Soviet Union. Adding to the danger, many of these groups (what some today would prefer to call networks) have gained control over the weapons that were formerly owned by the Soviets, and they now have the capacity to hurt the United States. Furthermore, many of these post-Soviet organisations/groups are unwilling to partake of the West's prosperity. For them, being free from communism does not necessarily mean that they will unequivocally embrace Western liberalism. As Brzezinski notes, 'one billion Moslems will not be impressed by a West that is perceived as preaching to them the values of consumerism, the merits of amorality, and the blessings of atheism. To many Moslems, the West's message (and especially America's) is repulsive'.[71]

For Brzezinski, Soviet communism can still be blamed for leaving us (the United States) with a world that looks to be 'out of control'.[72] Communism did not die peacefully. It left its marks on the free world and still haunts America's security in the post- Cold War. There is no time for the United States to rejoice after the collapse of Eastern European and Central Asian communist regimes. Post-communism must still be contained. The old Cold War geopolitical strategies must be maintained. Balancing, deterring, containing, and building alliances (Brzezinski is one of the main proponents of NATO's enlargement[73]) should continue to be America's top geostrategic priorities.

Central to this re-invented Cold War realpolitik is the need for the US to control what Brzezinski calls the 'Eurasian Chessboard'. The 'Eurasian Chessboard' is a geostrategic zone that stretches from the shores of Brittany to the tundras of Siberia.[74] This 'oval-shaped' board is the 'setting for the game' of geopolitics in the next century.[75] What is crucial to the 'game' is the empty middle of the board. The two extremities are relatively stable (the EU on one side; Japan and China on the other) and densely populated. But 'stretching between the western and eastern extremities is a sparsely populated and currently politically fluid and organizationally fragmented vast middle space that was formerly occupied by a powerful rival to US preeminence, a rival that was once committed to the goal of pushing America out of Eurasia'.[76]

This vast middle space is the locus of the power vacuum left by the Soviet Union. This is where post-communism is at its worst. This is the space the United States must occupy and control. In drawing the rules of this board game, Brzezinski reaffirms Eastern Europe and Central Asia's primacy to American foreign policy: 'For America, the chief geopolitical prize is Eurasia'.[77] History has demonstrated, Brzezinski affirms, that a power vacuum in Eastern Europe often leads to major international crises. In the twentieth century, the United States had twice been dragged into European conflicts caused by similar types of power vacuums (in both the first and second world wars). After the Second World War, the United States rightly intervened to make sure that the Soviet Union would not take advantage of the Eurasian power vacuum. This led to the Cold War, but also to geopolitical stability for Europe (and the United States) for roughly forty years. Today, such an intervention is once again necessary so that stability may be maintained. If the United States does not intervene to occupy the centre of the board, the geostrategic game will be lost: enemies of the United States (from Southeast Asia to the Balkans) will surely take over Eurasia. Once Eurasia is lost, the United States is in direct danger. If the United States cannot control Eurasia's empty middle, it will not be able to remain safe within its own borders.

Revealingly, Brzezinski's Eurasian political strategy is premised upon yet another cartography of international politics. Tabloid realism starts with cartographical imageries, and Brzezinski's analysis is no exception to the rule. Brzezinski takes the old Cold War map and, starting with it, redraws Europe and Asia that now form one single geopolitical entity characterised by its structural weakness in the middle. Brzezinski's map of Europe and Asia as one, with heavy extremities but an empty core, yields the image of a disarticulated body, one that is about to break apart. The limbs of this geopolitical body are stretching in different directions, leaving the frame of the structure to be ripped to shreds by hostile political organisms that are about to invade this weakened body. This is what the Cold War map would look like today, in the early twenty-first century. And this is precisely why the United States must not lose sight of the Eurasian chessboard. The United States has an opportunity to strengthen the core of the structure. It must lend its vital strengths to this apparently diseased body politic.

This cartographical imagery is of course structurally constraining. For Brzezinski, it serves the purpose of legitimising America's continued control of the region while identifying the threats, pointing to the dangers, and mobilising the necessary energies. Brzezinski calls this new map the 'Grand Chessboard'. The point of the 'Grand Chessboard' is to visually represent the United States' (inter)national interests. Brzezinski reminds us that 'the exercise of American global primacy must be sensitive to the fact that political geography remains a critical consideration in international affairs'.[78] But, he adds, 'political geography, however, must adapt to the new realities of power'.[79] On this map, political geography is clearly adapted to America's desire for power in Eastern Europe and Central Asia. Without deploying this so-called 'new' map, the need to fill the Eurasian vacuum could not be easily visualised by foreign policy makers whom, like Huntington before, Brzezinski is also hoping to persuade. Without visualising the vacuum, US national security could be redirected toward other parts of the globe (the Middle East, Latin America, Southeast Asia) and away from Eastern Europe and Central Asia. Brzezinski needs this map so that his tabloid games can make sense and be played by America's foreign policy makers. No longer a foreign policy maker himself, Brzezinski can thus still 'make' foreign policy by proxy. All this scheming is quite self serving and, in a sense, self referential. Containing the attacks of the rogues, the outlaws, and the villains – from Eastern Europe to Central Asia – who still want to shatter America's hegemony requires Brzezinski to reinvent the spectre of a Eurasian anarchy. For Brzezinski, Eurasia is the objective today, as it was back then at the time when communism was predominant in that region. In Brzezinski's tabloid realist imaginary, the spectre to conjure up is not communism, then. Rather, the spectre that haunts Brzezinski is Eurasia itself, no matter whether Eurasia is seen as being taken over by communism or perceived as a structural void.

During the Cold War and afterwards, Eurasia plays a similar role for Brzezinski. Eurasia must be controlled by the United States because, when all is said and done, Eurasia is 'our' geographical buffer. Conceptually, Eurasia buffers the West from the East, the 'us' from the rest. Eurasia as a buffer allows the United States to remain unique and superior in its own sphere of influence (which, increasingly so after the Cold War, seems to span the entire surface of the globe). Of course, the Eurasian buffer serves to justify the involvement of the United States in the political affairs of another continent. But it also operates as a conceptual device that works to preserve America's difference with the rest of the world, a rest of the world that America ought to either control or contain. This buffering/distancing effect provided by the Eurasian Chessboard is what can be called Brzezinski's contribution to orientalist discourses. Orientalism is the main ideology behind Brzezinski's tabloid realist games. Orientalism was also the ideology that Brzezinski championed when he worked for the US government. What remains constant in Brzezinski's geopolitical analyses (during and after the Cold War) is a persistent attempt at redefining the West by deploying a strategic discourse about the Orient, the East, the Other, in other words, that very place which Brzezinski himself left at a young age (being born in Eastern Europe).[80]

As it turns out, the invention of a Eurasian strategy is not simply a geopolitical necessity for Brzezinski. It is a moral duty as well. And here comes the popular/populist punch line of his tabloid realist story. The moral symbol that *is* the United States has always stood behind a strong military arsenal and a clear geostrategy of power. This is why the West and the United States (as the flagship of morality) prevailed over the Soviet Union and, perhaps too prematurely, declared victory in the Cold War. The United States beat the Soviet Union on moral grounds by displacing communism from Eastern Europe and Central Asia. But the moral quest does not end with the disappearance of Soviet communism from Eurasia. It cannot. The permanent reconstruction of the United States, of its moral strength, requires that Eurasia be endlessly positioned as a subaltern, inferior, and in need of (Western) help geographical entity.

Because the moral battles of the Cold War have not completely been won, the West and the United States cannot let their guard down. The production of orientalist discourses about the West and the United States cannot end.[81] In Brzezinski's analysis, the way the West orients itself in relation to the East is a guarantee against moral decay. It perpetuates the moral crusade. For the United States to reduce its power capacities or ignore the geopolitical games in Eurasia would be a sure path toward amoral anarchy or, as Brzezinski calls it, 'permissive cornucopia'.[82] 'Permissive cornucopia' is the fateful moral consequence of the euphoria that followed the death of communism. The feeling that all threats are gone, that everything is possible, that money can lavishly be spent in global commercial ventures (globalisation) and in new modes of technological interactions (the Internet) is a dangerous mistake. 'Permissive cornucopia' is a syndrome of postmodern times, when values, truths and historical certainties all become questioned. 'Permissive cornucopia' makes possible the erroneous belief (according to Brzezinski) that America's Cold War values are obsolete. And so, 'permissive cornucopia' develops at the expanse of national security and political hegemony. If the careless spending (of money, rationality, morality and security) continues on the pace it followed in the 1990s, the late-twentieth-century Pax Americana is likely to fall prey to the same forces that once destroyed the Pax Romana. As Brzezinski concludes: 'Unless there is some deliberate effort to re-establish the centrality of some moral criteria for the exercise of self-control over gratification as an end in itself, the phase of American preponderance may not last long, despite the absence of any self-evident replacement'.[83] This is why America's preponderance requires the deployment of an orientalist discourse of geopolitics.

Of course, orientalism is too technical a word to be used in tabloid literatures such as Brzezinski's text. Again, tabloid realism's mass appeal demands that technical terms be excised from the text. Instead of orientalism, the image of a grand chessboard combined with the map of a Eurasian vacuum is mobilised to convey the same message. As with Kaplan's and Huntington's own versions, Brzezinski's tabloid realism is infused with a sense of moral conservatism and national exceptionalism. But this tabloid realism is further adorned with orientalist ideology that guarantees the continuity of the story and of the geopolitical imperative from the Cold War to its aftermath.

Conclusion: Tabloid Realism, or America's New Geopolitical Therapy

Geography – the 'writing of space' – is crucial to the formulation of politics. Through the ages, 'intellectuals of statecraft' (to borrow O Tuathail's terminology) have combined 'geographical knowledge with political imperatives ... to envision and script global space in an imperial manner'.[84] More recent scholarship has shown that 'elite texts' produced by these 'intellectuals' are not the only discursive domains where geopolitical conditioning/imperialism takes place. It has been argued that geopolitics 'is a constant process, operating throughout society in everyday political discussion, in media reports, and in education'.[85] Thus, the powerful representations and claims to 'knowledge' geopolitics engenders are also spread through the use of what Michel de Certeau has called 'the practice of everyday life'.[86] Since they are crucial sites of production of geopolitical knowledge, media and popular cultural forms must be critically investigated in order to 'problematize how global space is increasingly reimagined and rewritten by centres of power' today.[87] Unlike more traditional currents of geopolitical and/or international relations research, the study of popular geopolitics is not afraid to dive into the universe of 'low' and 'middle brow' culture in order to identify newly forming institutional locales where political discourses of identity, security, and often enmity are being created. In an age dominated by tabloid journalistic productions and 'trash' entertainment, popular cultural signs and artefacts become desirable channels of knowledge. Sometimes, popular cultural genres also serve as conceptual models that contemporary 'intellectuals of statecraft' employ to propagate narratives of danger, exclusion and securitisation.

Postmodern times are opportunistic times. But, as Sharp's study of *Reader's Digest* has shown, the geopolitical opportunities provided by popular media were discovered before the advent of postmodernity. Additionally, tabloid culture has been around for decades. What postmodernity has introduced though is the ability to use popular entertainment and the tabloid genre of reporting as generalised models of knowledge construction. Today, even 'high politics' experts can unabashedly make use of 'trash' culture and its tools to give substance to their ideologies. The apparent free flow of cultural signs and objects, the more readily accepted challenges to modernity's 'grand narratives' and the growing suspicion about historical certainties (all of which are characteristics generally attributed to postmodern culture) have spurred the belief among geopolitical scholars that form, style and medium are sufficient instruments with which new discourses of order can be constructed. I have labeled these geopolitical scholars who apparently embrace postmodern stylistics tabloid realists. Behind the veil of their postmodern imageries, tabloid realists wish to re-inject stable meanings to the nation, the modern state, Western civilisation, and what they consider to be the West's messianic leader, the United States. Tabloid realism is a postmodern discursive formation (in Foucault's sense), a loose collage of various ideological elements and rhetorical techniques, which also intends to bring back into contemporary geopolitical imaginaries a dose of political realism. As the analysis of Kaplan's text has revealed, the only way this collage can fit together and give the appearance of a coherent whole is by functioning as a simulation of postmodern geopolitics. Neither true nor false, the 'new' geopolitical representations established by tabloid realist scholars like Kaplan, Huntington and Brzezinski can only work because they are premised upon a cartographical model (these scholars' respective maps) which becomes the sole point of reference for the political situations and processes that supposedly exist in the world 'out there' and which allegedly make 'this' world a dangerous one to live in. A simulation, as Jean Baudrillard explains, 'is characterised by a *precession of the model*, of all models around the merest fact – the models come first, and their orbital circulation constitutes the genuine magnetic field of events'.[88] The tabloid realist simulation of postmodern/post-Cold War geopolitics can be all the more powerful since it does not have to be supported by facts and 'real' events. Tabloid realist geopolitics offers its own facts and realities, and derives cultural effects (danger, fear) and ideological lessons (passive acceptance of the model, rekindling of security measures) from them. But tabloid realist geopolitics does not stop here and, in a sense, goes past the postmodern simulation it tries to establish. Far from being comfortable with the postmodern models they construct, tabloid realists are wary of them too. Caught in their own spectacular games and ultimately frightened by the thought that no real referent may ever be recovered from their maps, tabloid realists abruptly turn their backs against their simulated exercises and hope to show their readers that the very map they offered must be cast away. Paranoid about the loss of meaning and certainty (that they too fostered), tabloid realists abandon their postmodern designs and desperately call for a return to good old modern (Cold War) politics, when America supposedly possessed a clear sense of its own identity and understood what and whom it needed to be protected from.

But perhaps it is not only this overtly spectacular and sensationalistic, but later reactive and conservative (in a word, tabloid), rendition of contemporary American geopolitics that attracts people to the tabloid realist genre (Kaplan's, Huntington's and Brzezinski's books have all been national best-sellers). Something akin to what sociologists and cultural studies specialists have witnessed with people who read tabloid newspapers or watch television 'trash' talk shows is happening too. Scholars who have examined tabloid culture have remarked that, while watching the *Oprah Winfrey Show*, for example, or reading the *National Enquirer* may have entertainment value, there is also something comforting for the (American) public about the stories these media present and, of course, about the way they are being presented. Simply put, tabloid stories have a therapeutic effect.[89] When social and political realities do not readily make sense, when political ideologies are not immediately present to provide a sense of rationality to the events (because perhaps there is no longer any major conflict between dominant ideologies), and when a previous social order is seemingly transformed through an acceleration of styles, processes and technologies, tabloid realism 'keeps things just as they were'.[90] Of course, this may seem contradictory, since the tabloid genre employs all sorts of postmodern visual and narrative devices that apparently destabilise. But precisely because the tabloid story is a simulation, a show which cannot be accepted or rejected but simply is meant to be absorbed/consumed as a whole, it gives the impression that everything, in the end, is back to normal. In the simulated (partly true and partly fabricated, at once real and fake) universe of tabloid reality and realism, and despite the oddities, monstrosities, injustices and disasters that are being displayed, things rediscover their ascribed place. Social/political meaning is (attempted to be) recovered. Order is restored or, if it is not yet completely restored (as in Huntington's and Brzezinski's texts), simple recipes for order and control are provided. And, exacerbating the sense of passivity which is part of tabloid entertainment, these recipes can be followed by the reader/viewer with relative ease and without much (re)action. The reader/viewer does not have to constantly be on the lookout, hunting for the 'enemy within', as was the case with the stories found in Cold War popular magazines. Simply, the consumers of these tabloid stories are asked to accept that the identity of the enemy that is presented to them, on television or in tabloid realist literatures, is meaningful to them, as citizens of the American nation of the twenty-first century.[91]

Tabloid realism's therapeutic remedy takes the form of an appeal to order and security. Order and security, tabloid realists tell us, must be reinserted into society. American politicians, tabloid realists tell their readers, must make the securitisation of the nation the number one foreign policy priority. Once again, this is a claim that has been forcefully voiced in the United States since 11 September. Cultural, racial, and ideological measures must be taken to protect and solidify American society, but also to homogenise it. And tabloid realists announce to their audience that this is what the public wants because, as Americans, it is what they need to fend off postmodern challenges and dangers coming mostly from abroad.[92] This conservative, protectionist, and possibly reassuring discourse is then presented as the best remedy against the world's current pathologies. Or so tabloid realists would like their readers to believe. Even when they mobilise the spectres of chaos and national insecurity, Kaplan, Huntington and Brzezinski also wish to rally the (national) troops, regroup, reorganise and reinscribe meaning where they fear it has been lost. Sometimes their attempt backfires, as was the case with Kaplan's model of a 'holographic and postmodern map' that, in the end, may breed more uncertainty than security. Most of the time, though, it succeeds. Huntington managed to retrieve a crucial role for the nation state (mostly the American nation) in a world replete with cultural fault lines. And, in the wake of the terrorist attacks against the United States in September 2001, Huntington has been hailed as this country's new 'prophet'.[93] Brzezinski also reinvented a stabilising function for post-Cold War American foreign policy by (re)introducing orientalist beliefs and premising a new geostrategic balancing system upon such an ideological vision.

The troubling part is that the pathologies identified by these tabloid realists are the direct product of their simulated scenarios. The pathologies are the result of the geopolitical models and their images from which tabloid realists hope to draw ideological lessons and conservatively remobilise their audience. In other words, it is these tabloid realists' self-constructed, self-referential and self-fulfilling pathologies that make possible the need for (their) therapeutic remedies. Thus, their desperate calls for a return to the 'modern' ideas of the American nation, American citizenship, America's 'war', and American national security are as fictitious as the conceptual model from which they are derived. Again, this is not to say that the therapies (like the pathologies to which they respond) are false, incorrect or unsubstantiated. Some members of the public may indeed find the tabloid therapy useful. The point is rather to recognise that the therapies are convenient ideological measures (with important political consequences for America if indeed they are implemented) that are merely the outcome of conceptual models with a capacity to fabricate reality, any reality. Placed in the hands of media theorists or cultural studies scholars, postmodern tools and techniques may be pleasing, entertaining and illuminating. Placed in the hands of early twenty-first century 'intellectuals of statecraft', these same instruments may become terrifying and terror producing as, for many people in the United States and beyond, the proposed therapy can easily be perceived as the pathology.

ACKNOWLEDGEMENTS

The author wishes to thank Clair Apodaca, Gail Hollander, Tim Luke, Rod Neumann, Nick Onuf, Patricia Price and Julie Webber for their comments and suggestions.

NOTES

1. Robert D. Kaplan, *The Coming Anarchy: Shattering the Dreams of the Post-Cold War* (New York: Random House 2000) p.24.
2. Joshua Gamson, *Freaks Talk Back: Tabloid Talk Shows and Sexual Nonconformity* (Chicago: University of Chicago Press 1998) p.224.
3. Initially, the term 'tabloid' referred to the half-broadsheet format of the paper on which the stories were printed. See S. Elizabeth Bird, *For Enquiring Minds: A Cultural Study of Supermarket Tabloids* (Knoxville: University of Tennessee Press 1992) p.8.
4. Ibid.
5. Jane Shattuc, *The Talking Cure: TV Talk Shows and Women* (New York: Routledge 1997) pp.17–18.
6. According to Stephen Hinerman, tabloid literature's goal is to sensationalise reality while keeping it at the level of people's experience. To provide a basic moralising discourse centred on everyday petty injustices, the tabloid text must maintain an appearance of authenticity. Even when it showcases the lives of popular stars, it must make sure that it does not fall into fiction. The Hollywood star scandals people read or hear about in the tabloids are about people whose lives have been publicly displayed in the media. These media icons are sport celebrities, sitcom or soap opera stars, game show hosts, or political figures. These individuals are part of everyday life for the average American. They are what American daily life on TV or in magazines is made of. See Stephen Hinerman, '(Don't) Leave Me Alone: Tabloid Narrative and the Michael Jackson Child-Abuse Scandal', in James Lull and Stephen Hinerman (eds), *Media Scandals: Morality and Desire in the Popular Culture Marketplace* (New York: Columbia University Press 1997) pp.143–63. On the moralising discourse of the tabloids, see also Matthew Ehrlich, 'Not Ready for Prime Time: Tabloid and Investigative TV journalism', in Marilyn Greenwald and Joseph Bernt (eds), *The Big Chill: Investigative Reporting in the Current Media Environment* (Ames: Iowa State University Press 2000) p.113.
7. Except for personality portraits. See Bird (note 3) p.8.
8. On the treatment of the Clinton–Lewinsky affair by the tabloids, see John Judis, 'Irresponsible News Elites', *The American Prospect* 9/38 (1998) pp.14–17; Andrew Phillips, 'The Clinton Paradox: The Lewinsky Scandal Shines a New Light on Morality and the Sexes', *Maclean's* 111/7 (1998) p.30; Linda Feldmann, 'Press and Politics in the Age of "Flynting"', *The Christian Science Monitor*, 11 Jan.1999, p.1. On the effects of the Clinton–Lewinsky scandal on American political culture see Diana Owen, 'Popular Politics and the Clinton/Lewinsky Affair: The Implication for Leadership', *Political Psychology* 21/1 (2000) pp.161–77.
9. See Kevin Glynn, *Tabloid Culture: Trash Taste, Popular Power, and the Transformation of American Television* (Durham: Duke University Press 2000) pp.18–19.
10. Ibid. pp.17–18.
11. Ibid. p.18.
12. The term 'trash culture' is today often used as a synonym for tabloid culture. While tabloid culture makes reference to a larger tradition of tabloid journalism and reporting, trash culture more specifically denotes the commodified objects and signs of contemporary (tele)visual entertainment. Additionally, trash culture is often defined in opposition to the so-called 'great tradition' of literary works. See Richard Keller Simon, *Trash Culture: Popular Culture and the Great Tradition* (Berkeley: University of California Press 1999).
13. See Tom Engelhardt, *The End of Victory Culture: Cold War America and the Disillusioning of a Generation* (New York: Basic Books 1995).
14. Joanne P. Sharp, *Condensing the Cold War: Reader's Digest and American Identity* (Minneapolis: University of Minnesota Press 2000) p.35.
15. See David Campbell, *Writing Security: United States Foreign Policy and the Politics of Identity*, rev. ed. (Minneapolis: University of Minnesota Press 1998) p.23.
16. Sharp (note 14) p.35.
17. Ibid. p.36.
18. Ibid.

19. Ibid. p.89.
20. Ibid. p.93.
21. Ibid. p.88.
22. These are the exact words that Hofstadter used to describe the 'paranoid style of politics'. See Richard Hofstadter, *The Paranoid Style in American Politics, and Other Essays* (New York: Vintage Books 1967) p.4. For an insightful analysis of Hofstadter's thought on paranoia and popular politics, see Mark Fenster, *Conspiracy Theories: Secrecy and Power in American Culture* (Minneapolis: University of Minnesota Press 1999).
23. See Louis Althusser, 'Ideology and Ideological State Apparatuses', in idem, *Lenin and Philosophy, and Other Essays*, trans. Ben Brewster (New York: Monthly Review Press 1971) pp.127–86.
24. Sharp (note 14) p.164.
25. Ibid. pp.107–21.
26. Ibid., pp.13–14.
27. Ibid., pp.41–2.
28. For a reflection on the effects of postmodernity and postmodern phenomena on international relations and geopolitics, see Paul Virilio, *Speed and Politics: An Essay on Dromology* (New York: Semiotext(e) 1986); Edward Soja, *Postmodern Geographies: The Reassertion of Space in Critical Social Theory* (New York: Verso 1989); James Der Derian, *Antidiplomacy: Spies, Terror, Speed and War* (Cambridge, MA: Blackwell 1992); Timothy W. Luke, 'Discourses of Disintegration, Texts of Transformation: Re-reading Realism in the New World Order,' *Alternatives* 18/2 (1993) pp.229–58; John Agnew and Stuart Corbridge, *Mastering Space: Hegemony, Territory and International Political Economy* (New York: Routledge 1995).
29. See, for example, Benjamin Barber, *Jihad versus McWorld: How Globalism and Tribalism Are Reshaping the World* (New York: Ballantine Books 1995); Zbigniew Brzezinski, *Out of Control: Global Turmoil on the Eve of the Twenty-First Century* (New York: Maxwell Macmillan 1993); idem, *The Grand Chessboard: American Primacy and Its Geostrategic Imperatives* (New York: Basic Books 1997); Samuel Huntington, *The Clash of Civilizations and the Remaking of World Order* (New York: Touchstone 1996); Kaplan, *The Coming Anarchy* (note 1); Michael Klare, *Rogue States and Nuclear Outlaws: America's Search for a New Foreign Policy* (New York: Hill and Wang 1995); idem, *Resource Wars: The New Landscape of Global Conflict* (New York: Metropolitan Books 2001); John Mearsheimer, 'Why We Will Soon Miss the Cold War', *The Atlantic*, 266/2 (1990) pp.35–50; Max Singer and Aaron Wildavsky, *The Real World Order: Zones of Peace/Zones of Turmoil* (Chatham: Chatham House 1996). But even some traditionally non-realist scholars have attempted to partake of this literary genre. See, in particular, Francis Fukuyama, *The Great Disruption: Human Nature and the Reconstitution of Social Order* (New York: Touchstone 1999); Stanley Hoffmann, *World Disorders: Troubled Peace in the Post-Cold War Era* (Lanham: Rowman and Littlefield 1998); and James Rosenau, *Turbulence in World Politics: A Theory of Change and Continuity* (Princeton: Princeton University Press 1990).
30. Michel Foucault, *The Archeology of Knowledge* (New York: Pantheon Books 1972) pp.31–9.
31. Denis Cosgrove, 'Introduction: Mapping Meaning', in idem (ed.), *Mappings* (London: Reaktion Books 1999) p.2.
32. Kaplan, *The Coming Anarchy* (note 1).
33. Ibid. p.50.
34. Ibid.
35. Ibid. p.54.
36. In this book, *An Empire Wilderness*, Kaplan laments: 'But now we face the loss of the protection that geography once provided. Because the United States has been so overwhelmingly a creature of geography, in the twenty-first century shrinking distances will affect us more than they will our competitors, whose economic development never depended on continental isolation [unlike the United States' path of development].' See Robert D. Kaplan, *An Empire Wilderness: Travels into America's Future* (New York: Vintage Books 1998) p.15; my inserts.

37. Kaplan, *The Coming Anarchy* (note 1) p.54.
38. Ibid. p.55.
39. Simon Dalby, 'Reading Robert Kaplan's "Coming Anarchy"', in Gearoid O Tuathail, Simon Dalby and Paul Routledge (eds), *The Geopolitics Reader* (London and New York: Routledge 1998) p.199.
40. Ibid. p.199.
41. See, for example, Kaplan's panic about what he understands to be the fragility of the US–Mexican border. For Kaplan, the border is merely a vanishing metaphor. In reality, what was once the border has become a site of passage for drugs and criminality. Through this passage, dangerous flows only move in a northward trajectory, from Mexico to the US. See Kaplan, *An Empire Wilderness* (note 36) pp.142–5.
42. To quote one of Baudrillard's famous mottos about postmodernity, an age of simulated reality. See Jean Baudrillard, *Simulations* (New York: Semiotext(e) 1983).
43. As some of his detractors are often tempted to do. See, for example, Christopher Hitchens, 'Africa Adrift', *The Nation*, Minority Report, 27 May 1996, online version available at <http://past.thenation.com/issue/960527/0527hitc.htm>; or Goran Hyden, 'Livelihood and Security in Africa: Contending Perspectives in the New World Order', *African Studies Quarterly* 1/1 (1997), available at <www.africa.ufl.edu/asq/>.
44. Brian Jarvis, *Postmodern Cartographies: The Geographical Imagination in Contemporary American Culture* (New York: St Martin's Press 1998) p.188.
45. Ibid., p.188.
46. Samuel Huntington, *Political Order in Changing Societies* (New Haven: Yale University Press 1968).
47. See Samuel Huntington, *The Third Wave: Democratization in the Late Twentieth Century* (Norman, OK: University of Oklahoma Press 1991).
48. A recent article by Robert Kaplan on the meaning of Huntington's work in the aftermath of the 11 September attacks seeks to explain (and at times champions) Huntington's conservative perspective on politics and social order. Kaplan believes that Huntington's vision of conservatism 'recognizes the primacy of power in international affairs; it accepts existing institutions; and its goals are limited. It eschews grand designs, because it has no universal value system that it seeks to impose on others'. See Robert D. Kaplan, 'Looking the World in the Eye', *The Atlantic Monthly* 288/5 (2001) pp.68–82. Huntington's conservatism has also been noted by David Campbell, who reminds us that, in the 1960s, Huntington warned against the danger of social justice programmes. Huntington believed that such programmes 'could not be met by a fiscally constrained state' but that rising expectations would create a 'disjunction between the extent of governmental activity and its authority'. This 'excess of democratic measures' (Huntington's terms) would thus be American democracy's greatest threat, Huntington claimed. See Campbell (note 15) p.163.
49. See, for example, Samuel Huntington, *The Common Defense: Strategic Programs in National Politics* (New York: Columbia University Press 1961); and Zbigniew Brzezinski and Samuel Huntington, *Political Power: USA/USSR* (New York: Viking Press 1964).
50. Huntington, *The Clash of Civilizations* (note 29). Similar to Kaplan's book, Huntington's book is an extension of the essay 'The Clash of Civilizations' that he published in the journal *Foreign Affairs* several years previously.
51. See also Lawrence Harrison and Samuel Huntington (eds), *Culture Matters: How Values Shape Human Progress* (New York: Basic Books 2000).
52. Huntington, *The Clash of Civilizations* (note 29) pp.30–31.
53. Ibid. p.135.
54. Ibid. p.136.
55. Ibid. p.137.
56. Ibid. p.138.
57. Michael J. Shapiro, *Violent Cartographies: Mapping Cultures of War* (Minneapolis: University of Minnesota Press 1997) p.30.
58. Ibid. p.30.
59. Of course, Huntington's readers are not asked to actively cast away this picture of disorder. What they are mostly asked to do is follow Huntington's own lessons and conclusions to

their bitter end since, after all, he has the answer to the problem too. Again, typical of the tabloid genre, adherence to the model offered (without a possibility to reflect upon it) is simply what is demanded of the reading subject.

60. Gearoid O Tuathail, *Critical Geopolitics: The Politics of Writing Global Space* (Minneapolis, MN: University of Minnesota Press 1996) p.246.

61. Ibid. p.244.

62. Huntington, *The Clash of Civilizations* (note 29) p.302; my emphasis.

63. Ibid. p.307.

64. Ibid. p.306.

65. *Boston Globe* journalist Patrick Healy recently noted that, in the aftermath of the terrorist attacks in the United States, Simon and Schuster, the publishers of Huntington's *Clash*, had rushed 20,000 new copies into print. Asked by the journalist how he felt knowing that his predictions had apparently come true on 11 September, Huntington replied: 'Events are showing it [his book] to have a certain amount of validity. I wish it were otherwise'. Still, it is hard to believe that Huntington may really have wished for his predictions about civilisational clashes to be wrong. In fact, he concludes this interview by adding: 'I fear that while Sept. 11 united the West, the response to Sept. 11 will unite the Muslim world'. Far from reconsidering his earlier prophesies in the wake of the attacks, Huntington is actually hammering them in further. See Patrick Healy, 'Harvard Scholar's 96 Book Becomes the Word on War,' *The Boston Globe*, 6 November 2001.

66. Huntington, *The Clash of Civilizations* (note 29) p.311; author's emphasis.

67. Brzezinski, *Out of Control* (note 29).

68. Brzezinski, *The Grand Chessboard* (note 29).

69. It is in this sense that Huntington writes that Brzezinski's *The Grand Chessboard* 'is the book we have been waiting for'. See Huntington, jacket quotation for *The Grand Chessboard* (note 29).

70. Zbigniew Brzezinski, *The Grand Failure: The Birth and Death of Communism in the 20th Century* (New York: Scribner 1989).

71. Brzezinski, *Out of Control* (note 29) p.210. Note in passing that Brzezinski panders to popular sentiments by identifying the new threats as Moslem.

72. After all, Soviet communism is 'the most costly human failure in all of history', Brzezinski asserts. Ibid. p.17.

73. Zbigniew Brzezinski, 'A Post-Divided Europe: Principles and Precepts for American Foreign Policy', lecture given at the Woodrow Wilson Center for Scholars, 19 July 2000, available at <http://wwics.si.edu/organiza/affil/wwics/news/speeches/brzezinski.htm>.

74. It is the core of what he has recently renamed (in one of his many pamphlets) the 'Geostrategic Triad'. The Geostrategic Triad – Europe, Russia and China – are the three main pieces of this geopolitical puzzle. See Zbigniew Brzezinski, *The Geostrategic Triad: Living with China, Europe, and Russia* (Washington, DC: Center for Strategic and International Studies 2001).

75. Brzezinski, *The Grand Chessboard* (note 29) pp.34–5.

76. Ibid. p.34.

77. Ibid. p.30.

78. Ibid. p.37.

79. Ibid.

80. My understanding of orientalism is derived from Edward Said's seminal work on the subject. For Said, orientalism is not only 'a Western style for dominating, restructuring, and having authority over the Orient'. It is also a way according to which 'European culture gained in strength and identity by setting itself off against the Orient as a sort of surrogate and even underground self'. Edward Said, *Orientalism* (New York: Vintage Books 1979) p.3.

81. For another recent tabloid and orientalist vision of global politics, see Barber (note 29). Although for Barber the term Jihad is supposed to refer to more than a Moslim holy war (against the West mostly), the very choice of the term denoted a stereotypical orientalist posture on the part of this author.

82. Brzezinski, *Out of Control* (note 29) p.xii.

83. Ibid. p.xiii.
84. See O Tuathail (note 60) p.249.
85. Sharp (note 14) p.30.
86. Michel de Certeau, *The Practice of Everyday Life* (Berkeley, CA: University of California Press 1984).
87. O Tuathail (note 60) p.249.
88. Baudrillard, (note 42) p.32; author's emphasis.
89. Gamson (note 2) p.96.
90. Ibid. p.168.
91. Osama Bin Laden, America's new mortal enemy, is a 'real' threat to America's lifestyle today, mostly because his image (and his alleged videotaped confession of the 11 September attacks) has been broadcast by news networks into the American home.
92. In the aftermath of 11 September in the United States, many political chroniclers, pundits and intellectuals did not hesitate to equate the terrorist attacks with postmodernism. See, for example, Edward Rothstein, 'Attacks on US Challenge the Perspective of Postmodern True Believers', *The New York Times*, 22 September 2001, available at <www.nytimes.com/2001/09/22/arts/22conn.html>.
93. 'The Prophet' was the December 2001 *Atlantic Monthly*'s headline advertising Robert Kaplan's (note 48) piece on the life and work of Samuel Huntington.

11 September and Popular Geopolitics: A Study of Websites Run for and by Dutch Moroccans

VIRGINIE MAMADOUH

Introduction

In the Netherlands, the events of 11 September 2001 have fuelled the ongoing public debate about Islam in Dutch society and the integration of Muslim immigrants and their descendants.[1] A main protagonist in this discussion was sociologist and columnist Pim Fortuyn, who stood in the 2002 municipal and general elections.[2] For Fortuyn and his supporters, Islam is not compatible with Dutch society.[3] In the eyes of many, the events of 11 September validated Huntington's prediction that there would be a clash of civilisations between Islam and the West.[4] In their view, Muslim communities in the West are vanguards of a hostile civilisation (while being regarded by those on the other side as vanguards of Islam in a hostile society). This essay examines the position of these communities from the perspective of popular geopolitics.

A preliminary discussion in the first section provides an introduction to popular geopolitics and geopolitical scripts. Huntington's thesis of a clash of civilisations is discussed as a relevant script for the framing of the position of Muslim migrants in western Europe. Instead of dealing with mass popular geopolitics, the essay focuses on a 'significant minority' (Muslims in the West) and its own media. 11 September is seen as a 'peak experience'. News coverage and debates about that peak experience are used to investigate the relevance of the 'civilisational script'. The aim of the study is to answer two questions. First, does the civilisational script inform the representation of 11 September in the media of this significant minority? Second, does self-representation on this occasion provide further evidence about the strength of that script?

The second section focuses on Dutch Moroccans. It provides background information about Moroccan migration to the Netherlands and the integration of these migrants, as well as contextual information about the geopolitical context and the mass media coverage of 11 September. The third section deals with the media of Dutch Moroccans, the selection of the two websites under scrutiny, and methodological issues. It then presents the results of the analyses of two websites run for and by young Moroccans in the Netherlands. The first part of the analysis scrutinises the news section, while the second deals with the forums where visitors debate topical issues. The conclusion summarises the findings regarding the relevance of the civilisational script found on these websites, and discusses the significance of the findings for Dutch Moroccans, the Dutch context and Muslims in the West.

Popular Geopolitics: Huntington's Clash of Civilisations as Possible Script

Popular Geopolitics

In the past decade, political geographers have put popular geopolitics on their research agenda. They have broadened the field of geopolitical inquiry from the circle of statesmen to that of society at large. In their introduction to a large collection of such essays, Gearóid Ó Tuathail and Simon Dalby present a threefold typology of geopolitical reasoning.[5] Next to formal geopolitics (the reasoning produced by strategic institutes, think tanks and academia) and practical geopolitics (the reasoning of state leaders, foreign policy bureaucrats and political institutions), they acknowledge popular geopolitics of the mass media, movies, novels and other expressions of popular culture. All three contribute to the representation of the global political space and the spatialisation of boundaries and dangers. For popular geopolitics, the media are essential, because they are the main channels through which most people obtain information about foreign affairs.

Political geographers have studied the importance of geopolitical assumptions and representations of world politics in popular culture. Using different types of media, various authors have addressed the relation between practical and popular geopolitics; for example, Dijkink[6] examines the relation between geopolitical visions and national identity in several countries, and Paasi[7] focuses on the Finnish–Russian border, Finnish national identity and geopolitical codes. By contrast, other studies concentrate on specific media. Sharp has scrutinised the Cold War through the lens of *The Reader's Digest*.[8] Other examples include Dodds' analysis of the British cartoonist Steve Bell,[9] Sharp's analysis of movies,[10] diverse studies of websites,[11] and the comparison of the news coverage of the conflicts in Rwanda and Bosnia in the mid-1990s in American quality newspapers.[12] In the last case, Myers and co-authors reveal how different scripts and the corresponding 'frames' (in the language of communication studies) structure the selection and the presentation of events in these two crises. Scripts give meanings to events and ultimately justify foreign policy actions[13] or other collective actions. The assumption of a civilisational clash between the West and the Muslim world is such a geopolitical script.

Huntington's Clash of Civilisations: Poor Analysis, Powerful Script?

Samuel Huntington's 'clash of civilisations' is a much quoted and debated thesis. The debate erupted after the publication of an article in *Foreign Affairs*[14] under the title 'The Clash of Civilizations?' Although the discussion was very animated,[15] the criticism did not have much effect on Huntington,[16] who three years later elaborated his thesis in a full volume – from the title of which the question mark had been removed: *The Clash of Civilizations and the Remaking of World Order.*[17]

Huntington's analysis was a contribution to the debate about the nature of global politics after the Cold War, offering an alternative to the blatant positivism of Francis Fukuyama.[18] Huntington's thesis is that civilisational identity will be increasingly important in the future and that conflicts between civilisations will be the 'latest phase of conflict in the modern world'.[19] Six assumptions are offered in the original article[20] to explain why civilisations will clash. First, differences between civilisations are not only real: they are basic. Second, the interactions between peoples of different civilisations are increasing, and therefore civilisation consciousness is intensifying. Third, economic modernisation has weakened the nation state as a source of identity and world religion is filling this gap. Fourth, the West is at a peak of power and there is a return-to-the-roots movement in non-Western civilisations. Fifth, cultural characteristics are 'less mutable and less easily compromised' than political and economic ones. Sixth, economic regionalism reinforces civilisation consciousness. The conflicts of the future will occur along the cultural fault lines separating civilisations, because these conflicts escalate through civilisation-rallying (e.g. the support of members of their own civilisation, what Huntington calls the kin-country syndrome). The author predicts that the main civilisational conflict will pit 'the West against the rest' and that the Islamic and the Confucian civilisations are, both separately and combined, the West's main challengers. The original article also deals with the situation of countries torn between two civilisations (e.g. Turkey, Mexico, Russia), where the elite is trying to become part of the West, while the masses remain loyal to another civilisation.

In his 1996 book, Huntington elaborates his thesis, assessing the world of civilisations, the relation between Westernisation and modernisation, and the shifting balance of civilisations, before addressing the emerging order of civilisations (the core states and the delimitation of the key civilisations) and the clashes. Despite the fundamental nature of civilisations, Huntington has difficulties deciding how many there actually are: in the article there are seven or eight and in the book there are nine. The first seven are Western, Confucian or Sinic, Japanese, Islamic, Hindu, Orthodox or Slavic-Orthodox, and Latin American; the eighth is African, and the ninth Buddhism. In the book he introduces another civilisation-rallying mechanism next to kin countries: diaspora.[21] He also introduces the concepts of lone countries (e.g. Haiti, Ethiopia, Japan) – which do not form part of any civilisation – cleft countries (e.g. India, Sudan) – which are divided by a fault line between civilisations – and torn countries, in which the leaders choose a direction different from that chosen by the masses. Immigration is considered a major problem for the West, because immigrants are increasingly of non-Western origin. Huntington discusses the fear-provoking Muslim immigrants and the rise of anti-Muslim parties in several European countries, especially in France, speaking of 'a Muslim community that cuts across European lines, a sort of thirteenth nation of the European Community' (quoting a phrase by Jean Marie Domenach from 1991).[22]

The critiques of Huntington's article and book are abundant. They range from fundamental critiques of the basic assumptions (both the state-centric approach to global politics and the predominance of civilisational identity), to more specific critiques of the development of the thesis, such as the number and the delimitation of the civilisations, their relevant borders, and – last but not least – the empirical accuracy of the claim that conflicts between civilisations escalate more, and are more harmful than others. His assessment of the Islamic threat and the predicted coalition between Islamic and Confucian civilisations against the West are also much-disputed matters.

For political geographers, it is fascinating that the thesis attracted so much attention. Nierop argues that among the factors that explain the appeal of Huntington's theory are the rising importance of culture when ideologies fade, the fear of religious fundamentalism, the presence and growth of Muslim diasporas in Western countries, the globalisation paradox (i.e. the rising interest in national regional and local cultures as a reaction to the gradual Americanisation of global popular culture) and the significance of ethnic conflicts in Europe and Africa.[23]

The clash of civilisations is a script that emerged for formal geopolitics (Huntington is a professor at Harvard University) to serve practical geopolitics (he aims at informing geopolitical practices of US foreign policy makers), and which became widely echoed in popular geopolitics. As a catchy expression, it is widely used in news media to account for conflicts between protagonists from the Western world and protagonists with a Muslim background. Such geopolitical scripts are self-fulfilling prophecies:[24] what is framed as an essential conflict is likely to become one, even if it was not prior to that framing. Representations are always real in their consequences – especially when similar worldviews are voiced and discussed on both sides. It is no coincidence that Huntington explicitly refers to statements by Safar Al-Hawali of Umm al-Qura University in Mecca interpreting the Gulf War as 'the West against Islam' in his article.[25] In his book, he also deals at length with Islamic movements against Westernisation. More generally, there is a broad reassessment of religion as a powerful factor of identification, and these analyses often focus on Islam as the most powerful challenge to Westernisation and globalisation.[26] For example, Barber's study of the impact of globalisation and tribalism on democracy was publicised under the catchy title *Jihad vs. McWorld*[27] because, while many of his examples of tribalism were foreign to the Muslim world, he saw Islamic fundamentalism as exemplary.

Dar al Islam/Dar al Harb as a Mirror Geopolitical Script

Osama bin Laden – who is waging a holy war against the West (or, more specifically, against the United States) – was the most emblematic of these anti-Western activists long before 11 September.[28] He was suspected of being the instigator of the first bombing of the World Trade Center in 1993, and of the attacks on the US embassies in Nairobi and Dar-es-Salaam in 1998, and on the American destroyer USS Cole in Aden in 2000. In August 1996, in an interview with the London daily newspaper *The Independent*, bin Laden called the June 1995 truck bomb in Dhahran, Saudi Arabia, 'the beginning of war between Muslims and the United States'. He has since made several similar statements.

> Muslim scholars have issued a fatwa against any American who pays taxes to his government. He [sic] is our target because he is helping the American war machine against the Muslim nation.[29]

Bin Laden may well be 'the modern Arab geopolitician par excellence',[30] but he is a practical geopolitician, without the academic legitimacy that Huntington earned at Yale University, the University of Chicago and Harvard University – where he is a professor of the Science of Government, director of the John M. Olin Institute for Strategic Studies and chairman of the Harvard Academy for International and Area Studies in the Center for International Affairs. Bin Laden's renewed version of the traditional distinction between *Dar al Islam* (the Realm of Islam) and *Dar al Harb* (the Realm of Conflict) is as disputed as Huntington's thesis, but also as attractive to frame news about global politics in both practical and popular geopolitics. Both can be characterised as versions of the same civilisational script that postulates a fundamental incompatibility between Islam and the West.

Muslims in the West as 'Significant Minorities'

While geographers generally try to grasp mass popular geopolitics – for example the predominant geopolitical visions in a society – I want to argue that it is also necessary to examine geopolitical visions of 'significant minorities'. Regarding the civilisational script, Muslims in North America and in Western Europe are such significant minorities. Muslim communities in the West can be seen as vanguards of a hostile civilisation in the West or, alternatively, as the vanguard of Islam in a hostile society. It is crucial to understand their geopolitical views because they have a critical role to play. If the civilisational script informs their views, they will be more prone to act as such a vanguard in potential conflicts than they would were this script irrelevant to them.

Although some European regions are traditionally populated by Muslims (i.e. parts of the former Ottoman Empire – Albania, Kosovo, Bosnia, Bulgaria, Turkey), most Muslims in Europe are immigrants or direct descendants of immigrants. They are involved in transnational networks[31] in which they interact with relatives, friends and groups in countries of the Muslim world. As such, they might be influenced by mass popular geopolitics in the country where they live but also by mass popular geopolitics in their country of origin. To grasp the geopolitical views of a significant minority, one needs to concentrate on its own media (e.g. newspapers, magazines and web sites produced for that specific audience), rather than on the mass media.

11 September as a Peak Experience

Peak experiences have been acknowledged as major events in the formation of geopolitical visions and their representation.[32] 11 September was such a peak experience, and one with a global reach. It was one of those events that affect collective memories world-wide. It has provided an opportunity to study whether and, if so, how the civilisational script informs media and collective memories. Outside the United States, those involved in transnational networks across civilisational boundaries, especially between the Muslim world and the West, are likely to be the most affected, because the motives of the perpetrators were justified in religious terms. Studying the way such a peak experience is discussed in a specific community provides us with more general insights into the worldviews of that community. Analysing how this peak event is framed as well as the way the own position is assessed and reassessed on that occasion, discloses the importance of 'the clash' as a geopolitical script.

The relevance of the civilisational script will be assessed in two ways. First, I focus on the framing of 11 September as the outcome of a civilisational clash between Islam and the West. Alternative explanations based on alternative frames include the 'exploitation script' – which focuses on uneven economic development and the concentration of economic power in American hands and especially on Wall Street – and the 'foreign policy script' which focuses on the role of the United States as a global superpower and its foreign policy, especially in the Middle East. Second, I analyse whether their self-assessment informs or confirms the civilisational script. Do they see themselves as an Islamic vanguard in a hostile Western society? The script presupposes that they see themselves primarily as Muslims, that they feel united with Muslims in the rest of the world, and that they see Islamic and Western values as antagonistic. Therefore three indicators will be used: the role of religion as identity marker (alternatives include ethnic, national, gender, sexual, race or class identities), the expression of solidarity with fellow believers in the rest of the world (alternatives include solidarity based on nationality, language or race, or a lack of interest for what happens elsewhere in the world) and the notion that Islamic and Western values and norms are incompatible and therefore are bound to clash (alternatively they can be seen as complementary, or at least reconcilable).

It would be unwise to study 'Muslims in the West' as a single community. As communication media are highly fragmented (as a result of different national and linguistic backgrounds, in terms of both their countries of origin and the countries in which they have settled), Muslims in Western Europe cannot be expected to share a unique public space, nor similar geopolitical visions. Therefore it is necessary to focus on one nationally defined group in one country. This essay deals with the Netherlands, a country in which the position of Muslims has been hotly debated since 11 September, and more specifically with Dutch Moroccans, the group most targeted in the public debate.

Dutch Moroccans and 11 September

Context 1: The Position of Moroccan Immigrants and their Descendants in the Netherlands

Moroccan immigrants started arriving in the Netherlands in the 1960s. They were first recruited as unskilled guest workers, mostly from the deprived Rif in the north of Morocco, a region with a distinct colonial history, as it had been a Spanish protectorate while the rest of Morocco had been ruled by the French. After the 1973 oil crisis, guest worker recruitment was stopped, labour migrants settled, and family reunification and family formation became the main causes of immigration. Today there are about 250,000 ethnic Moroccans[33] in the Netherlands, of whom 40 per cent were born in the Netherlands. One-fifth of these ethnic Moroccans live in Amsterdam.

The socio-economic position of Moroccan immigrants and their descendants is not good, and generally is even worse than that of other groups of migrants: they have a low level of education, a high level of unemployment, low incomes and poor housing.[34] This applies to the second generation as well, with high numbers of school dropouts and delinquents, although some observers underline the educational and socio-economic success of a minority of social climbers.[35] For this essay, the ethno-cultural position of Moroccans, and especially religious issues, are crucial matters.

Morocco is a traditional Muslim state in which religion and state are not separated. Under pressure from the rise of Islamic fundamentalism in Iran and the Arab world in the preceding two decades, Hassan II (the father of the present king Mohammed VI) re-emphasised his descent from the Prophet and his role as the Commander of the Faithful. Although about 98 per cent of the Moroccan population is Muslim (Sunni), it is divided linguistically and culturally, as a significant minority consists of Imazighen (Berbers) who have resisted Arabisation.[36] Imazighen are largely over-represented among the Moroccan migrants in the Netherlands.

The Netherlands is traditionally a multi-religious nation-state, one in which relations between Protestants and Catholics have been settled through arrangements known as pillarisation.[37] Immigrants of various origins have brought new religions to the Netherlands in the past decades. The largest among the 'new' religions is Islam. The largest national groups among Muslims are Turks and Moroccans. Islam is a minority religion among the Surinamese; smaller groups include Palestinians, Iranians, Iraqis, Azeris and Afghans (mostly asylum seekers).

Since the beginning of the 1980s, the institutionalisation of Islam in the Netherlands has been facilitated by Dutch pillarisation traditions and Dutch minority policies.[38] These integration policies are based on a multicultural society model,[39] although in recent years this has been increasingly criticised and the call for assimilation has become louder. Immigrants have established their own associations and facilities, benefiting from national and municipal subventions. There are numerous Islamic institutions (e.g. mosques, Islamic schools, a small Dutch Islamic broadcast association with weekly programmes on public television). With a few exceptions, associations are generally organised nationally or even ethnically. Among Moroccan organisations, religious organisations are predominant.[40]

Context 2: The Geopolitical Context

Regarding international politics, both the Netherlands and Morocco are loyal allies of the United States and are participating in the 'coalition against terrorism'. The Netherlands is a member state of the European Union. Its military and foreign policy is based on the Atlantic partnership between Western Europe and the United States in NATO, which was seen as the only possible protection against invasions from the east (first by the Germans, then by the Soviets) after the traditional neutrality policy failed in 1940. At the same time, the Dutch public has been quite critical of US policies, demonstrating against the US intervention in Vietnam in the 1960s and the stationing of US nuclear cruise missiles in the Netherlands and elsewhere in Western Europe in the early 1980s, a critical attitude labelled 'Hollanditis' during the second Cold War, as a disease that could spread to other NATO members.[41]

Morocco is a long-standing ally of the United States. It was the first state to recognise the government of the United States, in 1777. Formal US relations with Morocco date from 1787, when the two nations negotiated a 'treaty of peace and friendship', which was renegotiated in 1836 and is the longest unbroken treaty relationship in US history. In short, both Dutch and Moroccan practical geopolitics (to the extent that the latter also influences Dutch Moroccans) are clearly pro-American by tradition, and this has been reaffirmed since 11 September.

Context 3: Mass Media Coverage of 11 September
In a country where foreign news coverage is usually extensive, 11 September and its aftermath dominated the news media for months. Like other Western European countries, the Netherlands discovered the reach of transnational terrorist networks. Intelligence information published in the media showed that fundamentalist organisations supporting the recruitment of young Muslims for wars in Muslim countries (e.g. Afghanistan and Chechnya) and for a religious war against the West were active also in the Netherlands. Various bomb alerts and letters containing anthrax nurtured the fear that the country was a potential target. On 27 September a bomb alert that announced an attack on road tunnels during the morning rush hour, paralysing the conurbation in the western part of the Netherlands (including Rotterdam and Amsterdam). Foreign news was dominated by the continuing developments in the United States, the formation of a world-wide coalition against terrorism, and the war in Afghanistan.

Domestic news was also largely influenced by 11 September, due to its alleged impact on the position of Muslims in the Netherlands and on the relations between Muslims and non-Muslims. Although the media spoke of 'Muslims', their attention was focused on the Moroccans, as the main Arab group present in the country. 11 September fueled the ongoing debate about the position of Muslims in the Netherlands. It had started in 2000 with a public discussion about the failure of the multicultural model and the marginalisation of the descendants of migrants from Muslim countries,[42] and had gained further momentum just before the attacks on the United States with the candidacy of the populist columnist Pim Fortuyn on an anti-immigrant platform for the 2002 municipal elections in Rotterdam and the 2002 national elections.

In the weeks following 11 September, the loyalty of Muslim immigrants (especially Moroccans) and their descendants became a disputed matter. Surveys investigating Muslims' support for Islamic fundamentalism and the Dutch population's fear of Islam were used by the media to assess the gap between the two population groups, a gap that elected politicians, religious organisations, migrant associations and groups fighting racism actively tried to bridge by means of statements, open letters, public debates, reciprocal visits and manifestations. An opinion poll carried out on behalf of the main news radio channel (public channel Radio 1) in mid-September showed that 87 per cent of the Dutch population feared clashes between Muslims and Christians. A week later, an opinion poll carried out for *Contrast* (a weekly magazine for the multicultural society) revealed that five per cent of Dutch Muslims approved of the attacks and that about half of them understood the motivation behind them – an alarming result that was later imputed to the formulation of the question. A few days later a poll held by the main poll organisation NIPO for the daily newspaper *De Volkskrant* showed that 60 per cent of the Dutch population thought that Muslims who support the terrorist attacks should be expelled from the country. A third wanted to reintroduce border controls (which have been abolished as part of the Schengen Agreement), half were afraid of a third world war (although only six per cent considered the Netherlands to be a country at war) and two-thirds expected an economic recession.[43] In short, the mass media echoed serious problems with the position of Muslims in the Netherlands in the aftermath of 11 September.[44] But what was the other side of the story – the view of the minority?

Dealing with 11 September on Dutch Moroccan Web Sites

Dutch Moroccan Media: Web Sites Run For and By Young Moroccans in the Netherlands

The Dutch Moroccan community has no newspaper or magazine, but it is targeted by several web sites. Most visitors to these sites are young and were born in the Netherlands (the working language is Dutch and the first generation of immigrants consists largely of uneducated guest workers and their wives who thus do not have access to written Dutch or to the new media). This limitation is not a problem, however. The opinions of the second generation of Muslims are highly significant. They often hold Dutch citizenship and, as such, are part of the Dutch electorate. In addition, their views provide a better insight into the future evolution of a Muslim community in Western Europe than do those of the migrant generation. Also, the interactive character of the web sites is an asset: next to the information provided by gatekeepers in a way comparable to what happens in periodicals, web sites make interactions between visitors possible in forums and chat rooms. This tends to bring about more diverse opinions than would be represented in printed publications.

Dutch Moroccans are particularly active on the Internet. This fact has been acknowledged by the mass media[45] and has been documented in an anthology[46] and in several recent studies of Dutch Moroccan web sites.[47] Of the most popular web sites, the two largest and most active were selected for the present study of the geopolitical visions of Dutch Moroccans:

- Maroc.nl (<http://www.maroc.nl>), which claims to be 'the largest Moroccan community online', was created in 1999 by a non-profit organisation based in Amsterdam and reports about 90,000 visitors each month.
- Maghreb.nl (<http://www.maghreb.nl>), which proclaims itself 'the virtual home of Morocco in the Netherlands' was created in 2000 by a marketing company based in Rotterdam; and reports also about 90,000 visitors each month.

These web sites offer a new kind of public space. First, they fulfil the function of group news media targeting a specific group – in this case an ethnically defined group. Second, they offer a platform for exchanges between group members, and also to anyone who wants to interact with group members. Forums on such web sites contribute to the formation of opinions in the interaction between participants, and additionally to the formation of opinions among a broader public, because the forum contributions remain available to outsiders long after the interaction took place. This makes the exchanges on web site forums more influential than face-to-face interactions in coffee shops and mosques. In addition, web sites increase the general public's awareness of the existence and the position of the minority group. While few outsiders would purchase a group-specific magazine, the threshold to visit a web site is rather low.

Internet qualitative research is a rapidly developing field of study.[48] The methodology applied is a combination of content analysis and online ethnographic fieldwork. The two web sites were intensively monitored in September and October 2001, and regularly examined in the succeeding months. The study of the web sites comprised two examinations. The first looked at the way the owners of the sites dealt with the event and its aftermath in their news section in the period 11 September–31 October 2001. The analysis focused on the topic and the content of the news items, as well as on their sources. The aim was to assess how 11 September and the position of Dutch Moroccans in the Netherlands were represented in the news section. Was much attention paid to 11 September and its aftermath? Was 11 September presented as the outcome of a clash of civilisations? Did the selection of the news and the way it was presented reflect a key role of religion as identity marker for Dutch Moroccans, solidarity with fellow Muslims across the world, and an interpretation of Western and Islamic values as antagonistic?

The second part of the study looked at the forum section of the web sites, where the discussions between visitors take place.[49] The forums are numerous and are constantly evolving. The number of threads (several hundred) and exchanges (thousands of printed pages) on the forums makes it impossible to provide an exhaustive and systematic account of the discussions. This analysis selected forums and threads dealing with the news. Both web sites have a forum called 'Nieuws van de dag' (news of the day), while the forum 'Wie schrijft die blijft' (Who writes, remains) on Maroc.nl also deals with topical issues. The forums during the period 11 September–31 October 2001 were scrutinised. The analysis of the selected threads focused on the topic and the content of the messages as well as on their authors. It should be underlined that these visitors, whether members or unregistered guests, were not necessarily young Dutch Moroccans; anyone can access the forum and contribute to the discussion – unless the IP address of their computer has been blacklisted because of previous misbehaviour on the forums.[50] Contributors are able to conceal their ethnic identity (gender, age and any other identity markers) in their self-presentation by choosing an assumed name.[51] This analysis aimed at assessing how 11 September and the position of Dutch Moroccans in the Netherlands were represented in these discussions. Was there much discussion on the forums about 11 September and its aftermath? Was 11 September presented as the outcome of a clash of civilisations? Did contributions (including self-presentation) to the forums reveal a key role of religion as identity marker for Dutch Moroccans, solidarity with fellow Muslims across the world, and/or an interpretation of Western and Islamic values as mainly antagonistic?

News Provision: 11 September on the News Sections of the Web Sites

11 September was a very important event on the news sections of both web sites. Special temporary features on the sites underline the exceptional character of the events.[52] For about a week, a separate window with a

webcam view of lower Manhattan would pop up at Maroc.nl. At Maghreb.nl, an extra page condemning the attacks appeared before one reached the homepage. The screen of Maghreb.nl went black for three minutes at noon on 14 September (the day the victims of the 11 September attack were commemorated throughout the EU), to commemorate the 'victims of terror war and intolerance in the north, the east, the south and the west of the world'. Later on, a separate window would pop up with a photograph of the American boxer Muhammed Ali and two quotes in English (Figure 1).

FIGURE 1
MOHAMMED ALI: 'ISLAM IS A RELIGION OF PEACE', 14 SEPTEMBER 2001

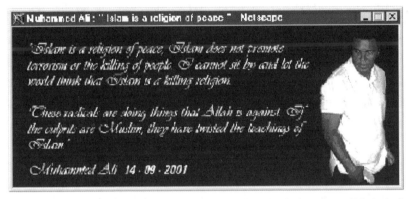

Source: Pop-up window 'Islam is a religion of peace' activated at the homepage of Maghreb.nl
in the second half of September 2001.

Most of the news items on both web sites were copied from news providers, with mention of the original source. These sources included the major Dutch newspapers (*De Volkskrant, NRC, Trouw, De Telegraaf*), the Amsterdam daily *Het Parool* (only on Maroc.nl), the Rotterdam daily *Algemeen Dagblad* (only on Maghreb.nl), occasionally one of the regional dailies and the free daily *Metro*, the Dutch news agency ANP, online news providers such as Nu.nl and the web sites of newspapers, the teletext pages and web sites of Dutch (NOS) and international (especially CNN, but also Al Jazeera, CBS2TV and MTV) television channels, and last but not least, the web sites of and press releases from independent organisations. What is striking is the total absence of Moroccan sources.

Both web sites posted news items on the attacks early on 11 September: Maghreb.nl did so at 16:00 local time (10:00 Eastern Time) and Maroc.nl followed suit 93 minutes later. The posting and selection of news items is mainly dependent on the availability of a web editor; sometimes there were no new postings for several days in a row, at other times five or six new items appeared within a few minutes. There were slightly more news items on Maghreb.nl than on Maroc.nl, but the two often selected the same items and posted exactly the same documents obtained from the same sources. 11 September and its aftermath dominated the news sections for weeks.

The news items during the six weeks following the attacks can be grouped into three main categories. The first includes coverage of the attacks and reports about the hijackers, the investigation, possible effects, arrests in Germany, bin Laden's denial, etc. There was also some coverage of reactions in the rest of world, including the interpretation of the Hamas leader, the empathy of Hezbollah, attacks on Muslims in the US, attacks on Christians in Pakistan, the withdrawal of Saudi support for the Taliban, the statement made by the European Commissioner Bolkenstein (a Dutch politician) about Islam and the subsequent angry reaction of the European Parliament, and violent clashes between Muslims and Christians in Kano, Nigeria. Thereafter came the preparation of the campaigns against Afghanistan, reports about the American attacks in Afghanistan, about envelopes containing anthrax, statements from Bush, bin Laden, Al Qaeda, Carlos, etc.

The second category of items that was quantitatively dominant deals with the consequences in the Netherlands. It all started on 12 September with a message about Moroccan youngsters celebrating in the streets of Ede (a small town in the middle of the Netherlands) and continued with statements about what really happened that evening, as well as the condemnation of this incident by Moroccan and Muslim organisations in the Netherlands. Many news items reported on the relations between Muslims and others in the Netherlands, including schools' fear that they would be unable to enforce three minutes of silence for the EU-wide tribute to the victims on 14 September, and later the case of a police officer who was fired because she refused to participate in that commemoration. Moreover, postings included the coverage of arson attacks on mosques and Islamic schools; several opinion polls showing Muslims' understanding for the motivations of the hijackers (whether it meant comprehension or empathy remained unclear), native resentment/fear of Muslims, fear of clashes between the two population groups, and agitation about the illustrations on a calendar distributed by an Islamic school. Additional items dealt with attempts to prevent such clashes, the support of Jewish organisations (voiced by Rabin Soetendorp in an open letter on the occasion of Yom Kippur), statements made by various migrant organisations, the visit of Prime Minister Wim Kok and Secretary of State for Integration Rogier van Boxtel to an Amsterdam mosque on 20 September; and also an attack on a petrol station run by a Dutch Turk and an attack on a Dutch Turk by a Dutch soldier.

The third large category includes some coverage of the Dutch debate about terrorism, including the bomb alert of 27 September, calls for the introduction of the obligation to carry an identification card, the peace demonstration in Amsterdam on Sunday 30 September organised by the *Platform tegen de 'nieuwe oorlog'* (platform against the 'new war') (Figure 2) and the support or condemnation of the attack on Afghanistan voiced by Dutch Muslim organisations. Finally at the end of October, the protest by a Moluccan youth organisation *Vrije Molukse Jongeren* was publicised. The Moluccans complained about the double standards of the Dutch government, which condemned bin Laden and the Taliban after the attacks of 11 September on Americans, but did not do so earlier, when bin Laden and the Taliban were supporting the attacks of Laskar Jihad on Moluccans in Indonesia in the past years. These double standards were also deeply resented by Dutch Moroccans.

FIGURE 2

POSTER ANNOUNCING THE *MANIFESTATION AGAINST THE 'NEW WAR'* ON SUNDAY 30 SEPTEMBER IN AMSTERDAM (WITH TEXT IN DUTCH, ENGLISH AND ARABIC)

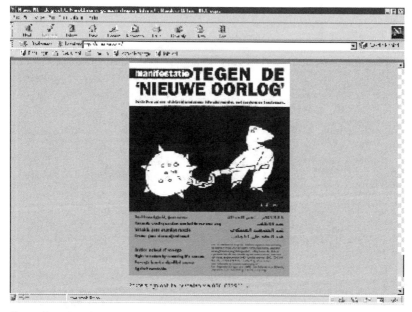

Source: Posted on the news section of Maroc.nl on Friday 28 September 2001.

Between 12 September and the end of October, only a few items were not related to the attacks. Dutch items included the closing of the Internet café Easy Everything in Rotterdam (only on the Rotterdam based Maghreb.nl), the introduction of a sport headscarf, the addition of Al Jazeera to the local offer of the cable provider Casema, the publication of a PhD thesis about the 'Dutchification' of Turkish Islam in the Netherlands, an internal conflict at Rotterdam Islamic University, a statement by Imam Haselhoef (an imam of Surinamese descent, and as such one of the few to preach in Dutch) about the death penalty for homosexuals, and the setback of the Moroccan-born MP Ousama Cherribi who was denied the chance of re-election by the right-wing liberal party VVD for the next general election. Foreign items included lawsuits against homosexuals in Egypt, Israeli attacks in Gaza, the Israeli occupation of Palestinian cities, the recognition of the Berber language in Algeria, the creation of a new nationalist party in Belgium, and the withdrawal of the Moroccan ambassador from Spain.

Clearly, the webmasters, who acted as gatekeepers for the Moroccan community they aimed to serve, selected news about and from the Moroccan group in the Netherlands, including news about religious affairs, and the international news that pertained to the Arab world: the Palestinian–Israeli conflict, Algeria, Morocco and the 11 September attacks on New York and Washington, DC. 11 September and its aftermath were deemed highly relevant to their audience. The content of the news coverage was pretty similar to that of the general media, for the basic reason that the messages were generally copied and pasted from the conventional media. The only Arabic source was Al Jazeera, which at the time was often also quoted by the Western mass media, including the American channel CNN.

All in all, the analysis of the news pages of the two websites shows that Islam is a key marker of the identity of Dutch Moroccans and that there is a feeling of solidarity with – or at least great interest in – fellow Muslims in the Middle East, especially Palestinians and Afghans. Regarding Islamic values, the news messages emphasised the condemnation of the attacks (and of those who approve of them) by imams, Muslim celebrities and Muslim organisations, thereby underlining commonalities of Islam and West. In addition to Mohammed Ali, the British singer Yusuf Islam (formerly known as Cat Stevens) was quoted on Maghreb.nl as condemning the attacks and underlining the peacefulness of Islam.[53] Both famous Western converts were quoted in English and both articles were borrowed on 20 September from MTV.com to be included in the site's news section. Both source and role models seem to imply an appreciated mix of Islamic and Western values.

As for the coverage of 11 September and its aftermath, the selection of news reveals both a foreign policy script in news items dealing with the policies of different states and a civilisational script in news items dealing with confrontations between Muslims and non-Muslims in general and specifically in the Netherlands. However, rather than propagating the civilisational script, the web site highlighted initiatives aimed at preventing escalation and clashes between Muslims and non-Muslims, especially regarding the situation in the Netherlands.

Debates: 11 September on the Forum Pages of the Web Sites

Both Maroc.nl and Magheb.nl hosted very lively forums, and the activity was important after 11 September, especially on the forums dealing with the news of the day. Threads addressing 11 September and related events were scrutinised with four main questions in mind. Who were the contributors (as far as one could rely on their self-proclaimed identities)? Which issues were addressed? Which opinions were voiced? And how was 11 September explained?

Based on self-presentation in the content of the message combined with nicknames and signatures,[54] it is safe to conclude that contributors to the forum had very diverse backgrounds: there were men and women, Muslims and non-Muslims, Moroccans and non-Moroccans. Religion was often mentioned as an identifier, by both Muslims and non-Muslims.

The discussions on the forums dealt with various topics related to the attacks and the consequences for relations between Muslims and non-Muslims in the Netherlands and in other parts of the world. A major topic was the identity and the motives of the perpetrators. Many postings expressed their distrust of the rapid accusation of Osama bin Laden. Discontent was expressed about the suspicion thrown upon all Muslims because of the acts committed by a few Muslims. But many Moroccan contributors doubted that the perpetrators were Muslims: they denied the involvement of Muslims either by pointing to American extremists (e.g. Timothy McVeigh) or to Israel (sometimes even in the variant of Osama bin Laden being manipulated by the Mossad), or by stating that people committing such a crime could not remain Muslims. In other words, the hijackers may have been Muslims, but Islam cannot be blamed for the attacks. There was clearly a strong need to dissociate their religion from the attacks. On the other hand, many non-Moroccan contributors expressed their outrage about the continuing denial of the involvement of Muslims in the attacks. Occasionally, contributions were sympathetic to bin Laden and Al Qaeda, including some quotes from bin Laden's videotaped speeches.

At the same time, solidarity with Muslims around the world was repeatedly displayed, particularly on Maroc.nl, and especially when criticising the reactions in the West, the non-stop media attention to the events in New York and the organisation of a EU-wide commemoration with three minutes of silence on 14 September. Without denying the horror of the 11 September attacks, many contributors felt disgusted by the special treatment of American victims, compared to the indifference to victims of violence in the South, and more specifically to Palestinian victims. Were American deaths more tragic than those of people in other parts of the world? Morocco and Arafat were also criticised: both had been quick to send a letter of condolence.[55] Contributors who tried to explain the impact of the attacks by pointing to their novelty and scale were not found convincing.

The role of the mass media was extensively discussed; they were accused of being uncritical of the allegations made by the Bush administration (which pointed the finger at Osama bin Laden and the Taliban without solid evidence), blaming all Muslims for the attacks, and last but not least giving a lot of publicity to the images of small groups of Muslims celebrating the attack (images of cheering Palestinians and of Dutch Moroccans celebrating in Ede were broadcast around the world, via CNN International). Many contributors heavily criticised each other's sources when discussing arguments and biases. Western media were accused of being biased against Muslims and especially against Arabs, and of being dominated by a Zionist or Jewish lobby.[56] One of the arguments for the Israeli involvement in the attack was a rumour that all Jews working at the WTC had been absent that day, a rumour publicised by several newspapers in the Arab world and by Manar TV, a Lebanese television channel which, according to another contributor to the thread, is affiliated to Hezbollah.[57]

Fears were also expressed that Israel would take advantage of the situation (the media covering the American events, the American administration looking inwards and being expected to be more supportive of Israel than ever) to repress the ongoing intifada. Likewise the fate of fellow Muslims in Afghanistan, which was likely to be attacked by the United States, was a matter for concern.

There were heated discussions about explanations for the attacks, generally pointing at the foreign policy of the United States in the Middle East, especially regarding Israel and Palestine, but also at the support for authoritarian regimes in the Muslim world. Interestingly, 'Muslim' and 'Arab' were used as synonyms. While most often 'Muslim' was used to refer mainly or exclusively to Arabs and the Arab world, the reverse also occurred: 'You can't provoke 1 billion Arabs [sic] anymore by supporting Israel (the occupying force) and after that pull an implausible face when this kind of thing happens.'[58]

However, the most important and recurrent theme was that of the position of Muslims in the Netherlands and relations between Muslims and non-Muslims. Here too 'Muslim' was used while a more specific group –

the Moroccan community – was meant. Discussions concerned the alleged tolerance of Dutch society, its hostility towards Muslims since 11 September, threats to Muslims and Muslim institutions, attacks on Islamic schools and mosques, insults hurled at Muslims in public places, and aggression on the forums themselves. This consisted of verbal violence against individual contributors and of general statements against certain groups, including statements against Muslims, such as contributors who posted messages stating that they hate Muslims and that Muslims should leave the West if they do not like it.

In conclusion, the analysis of the discussions on the news forums of Maroc.nl and Maghreb.nl shows that Islam was a key identity marker for young Moroccans in the Netherlands. It also shows that solidarity with fellow Muslims, especially with Palestinians, was widely shared. Western values and Muslim values were seen as antagonistic by only a small group of extremists, both Muslim and non-Muslim.

However, there was not much evidence of a civilisational script when 11 September was discussed. For most contributors – even those convinced most strongly that the Americans were to blame for the attacks – the root cause of the bitterness or even animosity against the US was US foreign policy, especially its policies in the Middle East and more specifically those concerning the Palestinian–Israeli conflict. The foreign policy script was much stronger than the civilisational one.

Discussion and Conclusions

The analysis of the two main web sites created for and run by Dutch Moroccans shows the importance of religious identity for these young Muslims. This is in line with earlier findings of more general studies of these web sites[59] and with more general assessments of the second and the third generation of Muslims in Western Europe, especially in France, Britain and Germany, with North Africans, Pakistanis and Turks, respectively.[60]

The analysis also shows that solidarity with fellow Muslims in the Netherlands and in the rest of the world is strong, but that the Islamic world is mainly defined as the Arab world and the main objects of solidarity are without doubt a specific group, that is, the Palestinians. Again, this is in line with earlier findings in general studies of these web sites in which the Palestinian–Israeli conflict has been observed as a major issue. Solidarity with the Palestinians has been demonstrated during the first and the second intifada among Arab communities in the United States and in Western Europe, through information campaigns, demonstrations and lobby campaigns against Israeli policies. In 2001 and 2002, this solidarity was seen as the main cause of the increasing occurrence of attacks by youngsters of Arab origin on Jews and Jewish institutions in Western Europe, especially in France.[61]

The fact that religious identity was a key marker and that solidarity with fellow members of the same religion was widely professed seems to provide evidence for the relevance of the civilisational script among young Dutch Moroccans groups, but these two indicators are not sufficient. The last indicator shows different results. The alleged antagonism between Western and Islamic values was voiced only marginally on the web sites. The gap between Muslims and non-Muslims was discussed extensively, but most voices concerned the need and the ways to bridge that gap. This gap was not seen as civilisational, essential and unbridgeable. Nevertheless, the predominance of Islam and Islamic arguments (verses from the Koran and statements by religious leaders) to justify acts and opinions in many debates can be seen as alarming, particularly in a secular European context. It is important to note that contributions often showed a combination of Western arguments (criticising the discrimination against Arabs and Muslims, the restricted freedom of speech for Muslims, the biased information provision by corporate news media, etc.) and moralistic arguments based on Moroccan traditions, Islamic rules and – on occasion – on traditionalist, fundamentalist or even Islamist interpretations of the Koran. The uneasy cohabitation of the norms and values of different cultures led to heated discussions on these forums. Such confrontation between Islam and the West better fits Barber's assumptions of the mishmash of tribalism and globalism than Huntington's clash of civilisations does. It belongs to the uneasy individual process of coming to terms with sweeping social changes induced by migration and globalisation.

As for the other aspect – the framing of the 11 September attacks as the exponent of a civilisational conflict – the civilisational script was hardly present. The conflict behind the attacks was repeatedly explained in terms of power politics, where the Arab street (i.e. the public opinion in the Arab world) or more broadly the Muslim community stood against the United States because of its policies in the Middle East. The foreign policy script was the strongest script on the forums. Nevertheless, on the news sections, most attention was paid to clashes between Muslims and non-Muslims all over the world, therefore reinforcing the civilisational script even if initiatives to bridge the gap between communities were highlighted.

Although proponents of the clash were rare, the most distressing finding is that the clash of civilisations is a powerful script that is strengthened by its denial. If the events are framed as the clash again and again, it reproduces the script, even if it is done to explicitly reject it as the right interpretation. This creates a vicious circle: denying the reality of the clash paradoxically strengthens it as a frame of reference. American politicians (including the American president) have emphasised, for example, that Muslim and Arab Americans are full citizens and 'good Americans', but inevitably suggesting that there were numerous reasons to questions their loyalty (after all, they did not state that Catholic or Chinese Americans are good Americans too).[62] A similar mechanism is at work in this study: the civilisational script is necessarily given some relevance when assuming Muslim communities in the West are a significant minority. This is also true of the many items concerning conflicts between Muslims and non-Muslims in the news sections of the web sites. Conversely, the forums, because they are interactive, disclosed a much more dynamic situation in which Islamic and Western values were disputed, socially reconstructed and made compatible. That is where bridges are built and where the civilisational script is most effectively undermined, even if it is, at the same time, the place where proponents of the civilisational clash can voice their ideas most radically.

These findings need to be considered in the light of the overall relevance of the web sites, both for the Dutch Moroccan community and for mass popular geopolitics. How representative are these web sites? How much impact do opinions voiced on these forums have on political action? And how do they affect the position of Muslims in the West? Let me comment on these three questions in turn. First, contributors to the forums are not representative of the Dutch Moroccan community: they are younger, they have access to the Internet, they are better educated and more articulate than those who do not have Internet access or do not express their opinions. However, they do not need to be representative to be interesting. They are relevant because they act as opinion makers. As such, the opinions voiced and published on the web sites are both significant and influential.

Second, there could be a large gap between words on anonymous virtual forums and opinions and acts in real life. We know that radical youngsters sometimes actualise what they preach. For example, on 13 January 2002 two young Dutchmen were shot dead by an Indian border patrol in Kashmir.[63] The police claimed they were terrorists trying to attack the soldiers. However, because other versions of the story were circulating, the Home Minister of the Indian state of Kashmir and Jammu ordered an enquiry. These two young men were Dutch Moroccans from Eindhoven, an industrial city in the south of the Netherlands. Both had been visitors to Maroc.nl, and one of them had been very active on the forums under the pseudonym 'lucky_luke' and was renowned for his radical opinions. With hindsight, his contributions to the forums can be read as explanations for their journey to Kashmir; for example, he once asked on a Maroc.nl forum: 'What are we gonna tell Allah if he asks us what we were doing when the

Koeffaar [the unbelievers] were slaughtering our Muslim brothers in Afghanistan, in Iraq, in Palestine, in Chechnya?'[54]

Third, the role of the web sites is not limited to the community. Discussions on the web sites have been reported in the mass media, therefore influencing the representation of the Dutch Moroccan community in the Dutch public, while reports and quotes in the conventional media are in turn discussed on the web sites. This occurred both after 11 September when the mass media used the forums to sound out Dutch Moroccan opinions and again after the Kashmir incident when they used the forum to browse through lucky_luke's contributions.[65] These exchanges between Dutch Moroccan media and mass media suggest that the findings are relevant to the geopolitical reasoning of both the Dutch Moroccan community and the rest of Dutch society. Unfortunately, those expecting a civilisational clash acknowledge the importance of religious identity and solidarity with fellow Muslims and see them as confirming their fears, without paying much attention to the ongoing process of social construction of a Dutch Islam.

Last but not least, it is difficult to generalise the findings for Dutch Moroccans to other Muslim communities in the Netherlands and in other Western countries. Similar processes are probably at work, as shown by the existence of Muslim organisations and networks, the strength of mobilisations against Muslims, and the participation of Western combatants (converts included) in Islamic campaigns.[66] On the other hand, the public debate is possibly more animated in the Netherlands than in other Western European countries. Both empirical studies of other significant minorities and comparative studies are necessary to assess commonalities and differences, and to explain them.

NOTES

1. For an account see M. Fennema, 'Persstemmingen na 11 september', *De Gids* 165/3 (2001) pp.229–44.
2. He was murdered on 6 May 2002. The animal activist arrested on the spot has not yet explained his act. On 15 May, Fortuyn's party won 26 of the 150 seats in parliament (the largest share ever obtained by a new party at a general election). His party became the second largest one and participated in the new coalition cabinet led by the Christian-Democrat Balkenende.
3. See e.g. his earlier book, P. Fortuyn, *Tegen de islamisering van onze cultuur, Nederlandse identiteit als fundament* (Utrecht: Bruna 1997).
4. S. Huntington, 'The Clash of Civilizations?', *Foreign Affairs* 72/3 (1993) pp.22–49; idem, *The Clash of Civilizations and the Remaking of World Order* (New York: Simon and Schuster 1996).
5. G. Ó Tuathail and S. Dalby (eds), *Rethinking Geopolitics* (London: Routledge 1998).
6. G. Dijkink, *National Identity and Geopolitical Visions, Maps of Pride and Pain* (London: Routledge 1996). See also idem, 'Geopolitical Codes and Popular Representations',

GeoJournal 46/4 (1998) pp.397–403 (wrongly numbered 293–9).

7. Paasi notably examines schoolbooks, but his research methodology is broader as it also includes fieldwork and interviews. A. Paasi, *Territories, Boundaries and Consciousness; The Changing Geographies of the Finnish-Russian Border* (Chichester: John Wiley 1996).

8. J.P. Sharp, 'Publishing American Identity: Popular Geopolitics, Myth and *The Reader's Digest*', *Political Geography* 12 (1993); idem, 'Hegemony, Popular Culture and Geopolitics: *The Reader's Digest* and the Construction of Danger', *Political Geography* 15/6–7 (1996) pp.557–70; idem, *Condensing the Cold War, Reader's Digest and American Identity* (Minneapolis, MN: University of Minnesota Press 2000).

9. K. Dodds, 'The 1982 Falklands War and a Critical Geopolitical Eye: Steve Bell and the If... Cartoons', *Political Geography* 15/6–7 (1996) pp.571–92; idem, 'Enframing Bosnia: The Geopolitical Iconography of Steve Bell', in Ó Tuathail and Dalby (note 5) pp.170–97. See also his general introduction to popular geopolitics in K. Dodds, *Geopolitics in a Changing World* (Harlow: Prentice Hall/Pearson Education 2000) ch.4, pp.71–91.

10. J.P. Sharp, 'Reel Geographies of the New World Order: Patriotism, Masculinity, and Geopolitics in Post-Cold War American Movies', in Ó Tuathail and Dalby (note 5) pp.152–69.

11. P. Routledge 'Going Globile: Spatiality, Embodiment, and Media-tion in the Zapatista Insurgency', in Ó Tuathail and Dalby (note 5) pp.240–60; several contributions from the special issue of *The Geographical Review*: Michael H. Jackson and Darren Purcell, 'Politics and Media Richness in World Wide Web Representations of the Former Yugoslavia', *The Geographical Review* 87/2 (1997) pp.219–40; Stanley D. Brunn and Charles D. Cottle, 'Small States and Cyberboosterism', *The Geographical Review* 87/2 (1997) pp.240–58; Barney Warf and John Grimes, 'Counterhegemonic Discourses and the Internet', *The Geographical Review* 87/2 (1997) pp.259–74; Shannon O'Lear, 'Electronic Communication and Environmental Policy in Russia and Estonia', *The Geographical Review* 87/2 (1997) pp.275–90; Oliver Froehling, 'The Cyberspace "War of Ink and Internet" in Chiapas, Mexico', *The Geographical Review* 87/2 (1997) pp.291–307.

12. G. Myers, T. Klak and T. Koehl, 'The Inscription of Difference: News Coverage of the Conflicts in Rwanda and Bosnia', *Political Geography* 15/1 (1996) pp.21–46.

13. E.g. G. Ó Tuathail, 'Foreign Policy and the Hyperreal: The Reagan Administration and the Framing of South Africa', in T. Barnes and J. Duncan (eds), *Writing Worlds; Discourse, Text and Metaphors in the Representation of Landscape* (New York: Routledge 1992) pp.155–75.

14. Huntington, 'Clash' (note 4).

15. For two accounts of the debate from a geographical perspective, see H. Kreutzmann, 'From Modernization Theory Towards the "Clash of Civilizations": Directions and Paradigm Shifts in Samuel Huntington's Analysis and Prognosis of Global Development', *GeoJournal* 46/4 (1998) pp.255–65; T. Nierop, 'The Clash of Civilizations: Cultural Conflict, the State and Geographical Scale', in G. Dijkink and H. Knippenberg (eds), *The Territorial Factor* (Amsterdam: Vossiuspers UvA 2001) pp.51–76.

16. See his reply in *Foreign Affairs*: S.P. Huntington, 'If not Civilizations, What?', *Foreign Affairs* 72/5 (1993) p.186.

17. Huntington, *Clash* (note 4).

18. Fukuyama, F., 1989, 'The End of History', *The National Interest* 16/2 (1989) pp.3–18 and idem, *The End of History and the Last Man* (New York: The Free Press 1992). Other significant proposals for alternative interpretations were Kaplan's and Lutwak's contributions. R. Kaplan, 'The Coming Anarchy', *The Atlantic Monthly* 273/2 (1994) pp.44–76 and idem, *The Ends of the Earth, A Journey to the Frontiers of Anarchy* (New York: Vintage Books 1996); E.N. Lutwak, *The Endangered American Dream: How to Stop the United States from Becoming a Third World Country and how to win the Geo-economic Struggle for Industrial Supremacy* (New York: Simon & Schuster 1993).

19. Huntington, 'Clash' (note 4) p.22.

20. Ibid. pp.25–7.

21. Huntington, *Clash* (note 4) pp.272–91.

22. Ibid. p.200.

23. See Nierop (note 15).
24. The danger of thinking in terms of civilisational clashes has not gone unnoticed. It is worth acknowledging that 2001 was proclaimed the United Nations Year of Dialogue among Civilisations. The General Assembly of the United Nations adopted in November 1998 a proposal of the president of the Islamic Republic of Iran, Seyed Mohammad Khatami, for that purpose. The report of a group of eminent persons featuring among others the French politician Jacques Delors (president of the European Commission 1985–1995), the South African novelist Nadine Gordimer (Nobel Prize 1991) and the Indian economist Amartya Sen (Nobel Prize 1998), was completed just after the 11 September attacks. The first sentence is therefore a memorable one: 'History has not ended and civilizations have not clashed, even after September 11, 2001', referring both to Huntington and Fukuyama. G. Picco (ed.), *Crossing the Divide, Dialogue among Civilizations* (South Orange, NJ: School of Diplomacy and International Relations 2001).
25. Huntington, 'Clash' (note 4) p.35.
26. B. Beeley, 'Global Options: Islamic Alternatives', in J. Anderson, C. Brook and A. Cochrane (eds), *A Global World?* (Oxford: Oxford University Press 1995) pp.167–207.
27. B.R. Barber, *Jihad vs. McWorld* (New York: Ballantine Books 1995).
28. Although it is worth mentioning that there is no trace of his name or Al Qaeda in the index of Huntington's book.
29. 'Bin Laden Speaks', *Newsweek*, 133/2 (11 January 1999) pp.36–7.
30. J. Agnew, 'Not the Wretched of the Earth: Osama bin Laden and the 'Clash of Civilizations', *The Arab World Geographer* 4/2 (2001) pp.85–8.
31. On transnational networks see e.g. S. Vertovec and R. Cohen (eds), *Migration, Diasporas and Transnationalism* (Cheltenham: Edward Elgar 1999); T. Faist, 'Transnationalization in International Migration: Implications for the Study of Citizenship and Culture', *Ethnic and Racial Studies* 23/2 (2000) pp.189–222.
32. See e.g. Dijkink, *National Identity* (note 6) and Paasi (note 7).
33. Ethnic Moroccans are defined in official statistics as inhabitants of the Netherlands born in Morocco or born in the Netherlands but with at least one parent born in Morocco.
34. R. Penninx, J. Schoorl and C.v. Praag, *The Impact of International Migration on Receiving Countries: The Case of The Netherlands*, Vol.37 (Den Haag: NIDI 1994); J. Lucassen and R. Penninx, *Newcomers, Immigrants and their Descendants in the Netherlands, 1550–1995* (Amsterdam: Het Spinhuis 1997); R. Penninx, H. Münstermann and H. Entzinger (eds), *Etnische minderheden en de multiculturele samenleving* (Groningen: Wolters-Noordhoff 1998).
35. H. Obdeijn and P. De Mas, *De Marokkaanse uitdaging, De tweede generatie in een veranderend Nederland* (Utrecht: FORUM 2001).
36. About 20–30 per cent of the population speaks Berber.
37. A. Lijphart, *The Politics of Accommodation: Pluralism and Democracy in the Netherlands* (Berkeley, CA: University of California Press 1968).
38. N. Landman, *Van mat tot minaret. De institutionalisering van de Islam in Nederland* (Amsterdam: VU Uitgeverij 1992); J. Rath et al., *Nederland en zijn Islam, een ontzuilende samenleving reageert op het ontstaan van een geloofsgemeenschap* (Amsterdam: Het Spinhuis 1996); W.A.R. Shadid and P.S. van Koningsveld, *Moslims in Nederland, Minderheden en religie in een multiculturele samenleving* (Alphen aan den Rijn: Samsom 1990).
39. For a comparative assessment of immigration and integration policies of the Netherlands with other European countries, see G. Brochmann and T. Hammar (eds), *Mechanisms of Immigration Control: A Comparative Analysis of European Regulation Policies* (Oxford: Berg 1999).
40. F. Alink, M. Berger, M. Fennema and J. Tillie, *Marokkaanse organisaties in Amsterdam* (Amsterdam: Het Spinhuis 1998); A. Van Heelsum, *Marokkaanse organisaties in Nederland, een netwerk analyse* (Amsterdam: Het Spinhuis 2001); K. Kraal and A. Van Heelsum, *Dynamisch mozaïek, Nieuwe trends bij Marokkaanse organisaties* (Utrecht: Samenwerkingsverband van Marokkanen en Tunesiërs (SMT) 2002).
41. W. Laqueur, 'Hollanditis: A New Stage in European Neutralism', *Commentary* 72/2 (1981)

pp.19–26.

42. The article that launched the debate was Paul Scheffer, 'Het multiculurele drama', *NRC Handelsblad*, 29 January 2000.

43. 'Radicale moslims moeten het land uit', *De Volkskrant*, 26 September 2001; on Maghreb.nl, 28 September 2001; on Maroc.nl, 27 September 2001.

44. Fennema, 'Persstemmingen' (note 1)..

45. Toine Heijmans, 'Zit het maagdenvlies tussen de oren?' *De Volkskrant*, 22 February 2001; Rachida Azough, 'Even kankeren op Hema-worsten', *De Volkskrant*, 2 March 2001; Rachida Azough and Maud Effting,'Vluchten naar het net', *De Volkskrant*, 27 July 2002.

46. Stichting Maroc.nl, *MAROC.NL: Digitaal lief en leed van Marokkaanse jongeren* (Amsterdam/Antwerp: Contact 2001). The book was reviewed in the two major daily newspapers: Aleid Truijens, 'De dilemma's van Dadeltje en Maagd', *De Volkskrant*, 5 October 2001; Titia Ketelaar, 'Masker on onder kazen', *NRC Handelsblad*, 16 November 2001.

47. L. Brouwer, 'Virtuele identiteiten van Marokkaanse jongeren', in F. Lindo and M. van Niekerk (eds), *Dedication & Detachment, Essays in Honour of Hans Vermeulen* (Amsterdam: Het Spinhuis 2001) pp.71–85; V. Mamadouh, 'Constructing a Dutch Moroccan Identity through the World Wide Web', *The Arab World Geographer* 4/4 (2001) pp.258–74; Kraal and Van Heelsum (note 40).

48. Inspiring literature on the matter includes D. Gauntlett (ed.), *Web.studies: Rewiring Media Studies for the Digital Age* (London: Arnold 2000); C. Hine, *Virtual Ethnography* (London: Sage 2000); S. Jones (ed.), *Doing Internet Research; Critical Issues and Methods for Examining the Net* (Thousand Oaks, CA: Sage 1999); C. Mann and F. Stewart, *Internet Communication and Qualitative Research; A Handbook for Research Online* (London: Sage 2000); K.A. Hill and J.E. Hughes, *Cyberpolitics; Citizen Activism in the Age of the Internet* (Lanham, MD: Rowman & Littlefield 1998); D. Miller and D. Slater, *The Internet: An Ethnographic Approach* (Oxford: Berg 2000).

49. The chatrooms with exchanges in real time have been left out of the research.

50. Misbehaviour is basically defined in terms of statements of abuse, racism, anti-Semitism and sexism.

51. In this report, nicknames used by contributors are used in quotes, as the original material is accessible to the public.

52. Other occasions in the past months were Ramadan (on Maroc.nl), special events such as the election of a Miss Maghreb.nl, and the wedding of the crown prince of the Netherlands (on Maghreb.nl).

53. The message also discusses his controversial past, as he is reported to have supported Ayatollah Khomeini's fatwa against novelist Salman Rushdie in the 1980s, and more recently, he had been accused by the Israeli government of financially supporting the Islamic terrorist group Hamas.

54. Nicknames are chosen at registration and they often refer to a geographical or a cultural identity. Signatures are automatic additions at the end of the messages that are also used to make a statement online and for personal expression.

55. Abdelkarim on 12 September, on thread 'Aanslagen in VS!' (Attacks in the US!) on the forum Wie schrijft die blijft on Maroc.nl.

56. One contributor, Hasni, posted on 1 October an impressive lists of Jewish persons holding influential positions in American state institutions, in the business world or in the press (in English, obviously copied from an American forum) in an attempt to demonstrate the size of the Jewish lobby. He met rather lukewarm reactions ('What about it?') and a heated discussion on the Jewish lobby in American politics referring to Norman Finkelstein and Noam Chomsky (thread 'Nederland in doodangst voor Islam' (The Netherlands deadly scared of Islam) on Maghreb.nl).

57. Thread 'Israel heeft het gedaan: bewijs' (Israel did it: evidence) on the forum Wie schrijft die blijft and 'Did Israelis evacuate the towers?' on the forum Het nieuws van de dag on Maroc.nl.

58. Oualily on 12 September, on the thread 'Amerika getroffen door zware aanslagen' (America hit by heavy attacks) on Maroc.nl.

59. See note 46.
60. N. Le Quesne, 'Islam in Europe: A Changing Faith', *Time Europe,* 18 January 2002. See also the special issue of *Manière de voir/Le Monde diplomatique* entitled *Islam contre Islam* (July–August 2002).
61. P. Van den Blink, '"Vandalisme" verontrust Parijse joden', *Trouw,* 5 februari 2002; M. Sommer, 'Algerijnen in Franse voorsteden identificeren zich met Palestijnen', *De Volkskrant,* 2 April 2002; P. Kottman, 'De dubbele angst van Franse joden', *NRC,* 25 April 2002.
62. See the discussion in N. Smith, 'Ashes and Aftermath', *The Arab World Geographer* 4/2 (2001) pp.81–4.
63. Widely covered in the Dutch dailies (e.g. *De Volkskrant,* 14, 15, 17, 23 January, 4 March 2002, *NRC Handelsblad,* 15, 23 January, 29 May 2002, *Trouw,* 14, 16, 17, 18, 19 January, 18, 29 May 2002) and abroad (e.g. *KashmirLive* 15 January 2002 and *The Guardian* 16 January 2002).
64. Quoted in 'De jongens wilden mujahedin steunen' (The boys wanted to support the Mujahedins), an article published on the front page of *De Volkskrant* on 15 January 2002, copied and pasted on 16 January in the thread 'Nederlandse paparazzi op prikbord' (Dutch paparazzi on forum) on the forum Het nieuws van de dag on Maroc.nl. See also the thread 'Ahahaha ik sta in de krant!' (Ahahaha I'm in the paper!) on the same forum.
65. This has dramatic consequences for the web site Maroc.nl: it was paralysed by a huge number of new visitors, many forums were removed to avoid misuse by the mass media of lucky_luke's contributions, lively discussions focused on the media and journalists as lurkers.
66. E.g. the Belgian Tunisian murders of the leader of the Northern Alliance, Ahmed Shah Massoud, on 9 September 2001.

Editorials and Geopolitical Explanations for 11 September

JONATHAN TAYLOR AND CHRIS JASPARO

The shift in public consciousness in the United States which occurred after the 11 September attacks has affected public interest in terrorism and security, contemporary global geopolitics, Middle Eastern studies, and Islam. Within a short time, suddenly large segments of the American public were aware of such issues as the United States' prior involvement in Afghanistan and its funding of the mujahideen, and had begun, to some extent, to debate whether in retrospect this has been a particularly good idea. The nitty-gritty of geopolitics and security studies, however briefly, had been violently reinserted into American political discourse.

Leading the debate initially were the pundits and editorialists. As would be expected, columnists from the mainstream press as well as a number of left- and right-affiliated magazines and web journals began to issue a steady stream of commentaries as soon as the day of the attack. With a lot of repetition, explanations for why the United States was attacked and 'why they hate us' were the main subjects of many of these pieces.

These op-ed pieces and commentaries came from many of the best-know political columnists of the left and the right. They came as well from academicians, essayists, novelists and retired government officials. They appeared in publications around the world, in the United States, United Kingdom, Europe, the Middle East, East Asia and Latin America at least.

This essay surveys the public debates about the roots of the mass-casualty terrorism of the 11 September attacks found in editorials published in their wake. Public opinion is informed, sometimes indirectly, by policy analysis and academic discourse, yet is more beholden to the media for explanation. Thus we seek to understand the explanations offered by public intellectuals and op-ed writers in order to assess the saliency of these explanations and their interpretation of the academic and policy debates that inform them. In this essay we review a number of editorial pieces from newspapers, magazines and news web sites to find the most popular categories of explanation offered after the attacks. In our conclusion we evaluate the saliency of each of these categories of explanation and offer some suggestions for future geographical research into the causes of terrorism.

We analyse newspaper and magazine editorials for a number of reasons. First, we find that editorials provide a good cross-section of the explanatory frameworks being used to understand the attacks. They reflect most of the main themes highlighted in other types of media coverage, and they both reflect and influence policy debates. They demonstrate the perspectives of individuals whose views have influence upon policymakers and the general public. While we realise their limitations, we feel they are a good entry point for a larger and more complex debate about terrorism's root causes that we hope the geographical community will join in the future.

Finally, we find an analysis of editorials germane to political geography because most of the categories of explanation we find are inherently *geopolitical*. It is notable that President George Bush, in his first lengthy public statements after the attack, presented geopolitical explanations for the attack. Most subsequent commentaries followed the same path. It is now widely held by commentators from all sides of the political spectrum that geopolitics is the key to understanding the attacks of 11 September. Thus describing and analysing editorials and the saliency of their geopolitical explanations in the wake of the attacks is the goal of this essay.

Editorials and Explanations

In this article we analyse some sixty editorial pieces to find explanations offered for the attacks. We chose pieces from a wide spectrum of political opinion, with a focus on both well-established 'mainstream' newspapers

TABLE 1
NEWSPAPERS SELECTED FOR ANALYSIS, BY CATEGORY

Left/liberal	Centre	Right/conservative	**Foreign/unclassified**
The Nation (5)	*Boston Globe* (2)	*Front Page Magazine*	*Sunday Times* (2)
Counterpunch.org (6)	*New York Times* (7)	*Washington Times*	*Jerusalem Post* (2)
New Statesmen	*Slate*	*Wall Street Journal*	*Egypt Today*
	LA Times (10)		*Yomiuri Shimbun*
	Washington Post (4)		*The Guardian* (3)
	Int. Herald Tribune (2)		*Foreign Affairs* (3)
	USA Today		*Weekly Standard*
	Salon.com (2)		*Pakistan Today*
	Inter Press Service		*Asia Week*
	New Republic (3)		
	The Atlantic (2)		
	Christian Science Monitor		
12	36	3	15

Total = 66.

(*New York Times*, *LA Times*, *Washington Post*) as well as news sources more clearly identified with 'left' or 'right' positions.

In addition, we selected a number of editorials from publications outside of the United States, from the UK, Pakistan, Egypt, Israel, and Japan. Overall, as Table 1 indicates, we tried to represent 'left' and 'right' although no categorisation of news sources into a triparate political framework is truly accurate (articles may be initially written by a columnist for *The Nation* for example, yet also run in the *LA Times*). Thus we do not claim to have achieved a representative sample either geographically or politically. Our choice of columns was largely based on our systematic attempt to classify the modes of explanation utilised by the editorials, as discussed below. Of course our choice of which pieces to include was based on our news-reading habits, geographical location, and to a lesser extent our political inclinations; nonetheless we feel we have identified a reasonably broad spectrum of opinion. While some op-ed pieces were difficult to categorise, many exhibited a few main themes which helped us form categories of geopolitical explanation for the 11 September attacks. These theoretical categories, in order of our discussion of them, though not necessarily their importance, are imperialism, 'blowback', state decline, Islamism, and 'the clash of civilizations'.

The following summation of these categories of explanation is necessarily brief; however, a far more detailed theoretical analysis of each perspective follows in the body of the essay. By imperialism, we refer to a category of thought in which the actions of the West, and the United States specifically, have caused deep divisions between the developed and developing world, with the developing world relegated to a politically and economically marginalised position. Terrorism and the 11 September attacks stem from this inequality and the resentment this produces. Within this category we can also differentiate between geopolitical and geoeconomic variants. In geopolitical imperialism, states allied with the United States, particularly Israel, have been aided at the expense of Arab states, and corrupt or authoritarian Arab rulers have been propped up because it suits US foreign policy goals to do so. Geoeconomic imperialism conjectures that the United States has pursued imperialist policies for economic goals such as maintaining a steady supply of oil imports from the Middle East. Of course geopolitical and geoeconomic concerns may frequently merge. In either case, states are supported, ignored, or opposed based on their usefulness to US interests. The policies of the United States towards many Muslim countries and in particular in the Middle East have negatively impacted these nations' citizens, and terrorism against the United States, no matter how horrifying, is an understandable response of the weak and disenfranchised against the strong.

'Blowback' refers to the unintended consequences of US foreign policy and intelligence operations. Proponents of this explanation feel that specific US actions have led to terrorist responses. While they may not necessarily share the worldview of those who espouse imperialist explanations, proponents of blowback may simply view US foreign policy and intelligence actions and terrorist attacks as having a cause-and-effect relationship.

State-decline incorporates demographic, environmental, economic and other factors into a theory of how states collapse or weaken, spurring increasing lawlessness, violence, conflict and societal breakdown. From this perspective failed or failing states are the main breeding grounds as well as training and operational sites for a variety of terrorist actors. These states generally fail for a number of reasons, both internal to the state and external. In addition, in the context of globalisation, states overall are losing their power and relevance as non-state actors and transnational forces proliferate and gain power.

Islamism is described as a radical variant of Islamic thought which underlies Al Qaeda and a large number of affiliated groups' ideologies. Not all Islamists are terrorists, however, and vice versa. Those who consider Islamism the chief explanation for the 11 September attacks nonetheless find the links between terrorism and Islamism incontrovertible and argue that Islamism is an inherently threatening and destabilising ideology which has set itself up against modernity, secularism, the West or democracy. Additionally, Islamism is viewed as an expansionist force which promotes global disorder.

Finally, the 'clash of civilisations' thesis depicts Western and Islamic civilisational realms in an epic and to some extent unavoidable clash based on major differences in culture and belief systems. Because the nature of the relationship between the West and Islam is bound to be conflictual, the 11 September attacks are quite likely a prelude to a longer and wider battle.

In what follows, we discuss each of these categories of explanation, highlighting both their theoretical basis and their use by editorialists in response to 11 September.

Imperialism

One of the more popular explanations for 11 September globally are ideas associated with the term 'imperialism'. Imperialism is a complicated word, referring to among other things, the disproportionate economic influence of the countries of the North, the influence and 'neo-colonialism' of transnational corporations, the recent interventionist military policies of the United States, the role of the United States and other major powers in dominating international institutions, and 'the fashioning and management of the Third World as subordinate to the West'.[1] Thus the anti-globalisation movement, those distrustful of US foreign policy in the Middle East and elsewhere, Third World Nationalist movements, Marxists and many others view imperialism as an ongoing project which continues the colonial and imperial traditions of European powers, Japan, and the United States in the nineteenth and early twentieth centuries. Others argue that the imperialism of nation states has been superseded by a new domain of power and authority, in which power lies in the system itself, which some term 'Empire'.[2] Regardless, for many imperialism is the final stage of capitalism, the clearly expressed policy of the United States and other major Northern powers as well as their transnational corporations, and the ideology behind the subjugation of the Third World. Present-day imperialism is conjectured to have many manifestations and components; one notable one being continuing efforts to denigrate Third World nationalist movements as being essentially anti-modern[3] and even 'terrorist'.[4] Ultimately, imperialism is continually locked into a state of conflict against an array of anti-colonial forces, emanating largely from the Third World. This is because there is 'recognition that the social, economic, and political problems of the Third World, from repression to hunger, were integrally connected to Western domination'.[5]

The origin of this perspective is most firmly rooted historically in the work of J.A. Hobson, and later V.I. Lenin. For Hobson, imperialism involved a dangerous and aggressive struggle between nations in a fight over markets.[6] Lenin viewed imperialism as being a final stage of capitalism in which monopolism would combine with the annexation of the world by the major capitalist nations.[7] Subsequent variations on these themes have been proposed by numerous other theorists of underdevelopment (Baran), dependency (Frank), world-system theory (Wallerstein) etc. Nonetheless, we can see from the definition above that at present there are many imperialisms, some of which are far more relevant to explaining 11 September than others. While stressing different events and processes, the various opinions we categorise as proposing imperialism as the primary explanation for 11 September would probably agree with the following: legitimate Muslim grievances with the West (and specifically with the United States as the West's foremost capitalist hegemon) form at least the undercurrent if not the actual motivation for those participating in the 11 September attacks. These grievances in turn stem from imperialism – from the largely economic (though also strategic geopolitical) motivations which have influenced Western expansionist policies from at least the fifteenth century onwards.[8]

In the Middle East, US imperialism is thought to have been centred on one main object, the acquisition of stable and inexpensive sources of oil.[9]

Generally speaking, 'the cycles of imperialist incursions into the region have turned this historic corner of the world into a zone of bloodshed and death, destruction and despair'.[10] More specifically, accusations of imperialism have been levied not only against the United States and Britain but against Israel, which has historically been viewed by large segments of the left as a 'colonial-settler state' which oppresses the Palestinians.[11] As Robinson explains, for the Arabs 'Israel is an imperialist base set up in the Middle East by British imperialism in collusion with others; it is part of a worldwide imperialist system; and therefore the activity it carries on throughout the world, whether on its own behalf or on behalf of American and European imperialism is of an imperialist nature'.[12] For Berberoglu, 'the creation of the State of Israel became a convenient geopolitical strategy for the imperialist states to dominate the entire Middle East region in the postcolonial period following the Second World War'.[12]

Mirroring these academic discourses, but differing in their concreteness, specificity and policy orientation, editorialists influenced by the thesis of imperialism generally stress one or more of the following dimensions in explaining the attacks:

- September 11 was an act of revenge for the victims of prior military actions pursued by the imperialistic policies of the United States (i.e. the Gulf War, US air strikes on Sudan, Libya and Afghanistan, military aid to Israel).
- The attacks were driven by general resentment by Muslims and Arabs over the United States' imperialist policies in the Middle East, especially its policies toward Israel/Palestine and Iraq.
- The attacks were driven by resentment over US support of repressive, undemocratic governments in the Middle East and elsewhere. These governments are supported because imperialist goals favour status quo governments who will co-operate politically and economically with the imperial powers, and shun nationalist or other movements which might challenge their authority. Prominent examples of undemocratic Middle Eastern states supported by the United States might include Saudi Arabia and Egypt.
- The attacks were driven by resentment over economic inequality between North and South, the developed and Third World, or were general responses by the disenfranchised to globalisation and global capitalism.
- The attacks were symbolic expressions of anger against US hegemony: the United States as Pax Americana, and arrogant superpower.
- The attacks were caused by the root of US imperialism in the Middle East, the United States' single-minded pursuit of Mideast oil.

A number of editorials published soon after the attacks reflected these perspectives. Editorials by Jackson and Kamiya blamed the attacks primarily on US support for Israel.[13] Kamiya writes 'we must remember that there is one specific grievance that rankles in the breasts of millions of Arab and Islamic people in the world', namely US support of Israel and the lack of resolution to the Palestinian–Israeli conflict.[14] This has fueled increasing Palestinian rage which has exploded into a violent conflict which increases hatred of Israel and the United States. He concludes that 'as long as millions of Islamic and Arab people hate America because of its Mideast policies, we will be in danger'[15] and supports this by discussing poll results showing that the Palestinian–Israeli situation is the most important issue to many people in Arab and Muslim nations. Thus, for some critics, failing to solve the Israel–Palestinian crisis will create unrelenting terrorism against the United States and ultimately lead to wider war.

Other editorialists stress the fact that the United States promotes the ideas of democracy but does not actively seek to have those ideals realised within the Middle East; instead it actively supports dictatorships. According to Fuller, Muslims are upset at US policies because they do not reflect the values the United States claims as its own.[16] The United States is seen as hypocritical, especially since it singles out dictators in the Arab world as worthy of support if they co-operate with US foreign policy, while promoting democracy in Africa, Latin America and elsewhere. When we support unpopular governments, 'it is the extremists who reap the discontent'.[17] Said echoes these comments, writing that in the Muslim world anti-Americanism is largely a reaction to the United States' hypocritical behaviour.[18]

Other columns insisted that the attacks were due to resentment not just against US Middle East policies but to the overall pattern of US global military violence. For some, American military hubris has led to a 'cycle of violence' between the West and the Arab world similar to the one currently existing between Palestinians and Israelis. Zinn decries 'our overbearing posture astride the globe, with military bases in nineteen countries, with our warships on every sea'.[19] Inevitably, he argues, driven by desperation at confronting a seemingly invulnerable foe such as the United States, 'some of those people will go beyond fear and anger to acts of terrorism'.[20]

For others, explanations for 11 September can be found largely in the global disparity of wealth between North and South and the resentment this engenders among the world's poor. Nahid finds the problems lie in 'our unsustainable medley of privileges'. 'our material and ideological gluttony in the West', and 'the arrogance of our super-affluence, the injustice and extreme disparity to which we expect the rest of the world to get accustomed'.[21] Similarly, Wade describes the United States' domination of global financial systems and global economic governance as having created a situation in which 'slow economic growth and vast income disparities, when seen as such, breed cohorts of partly educated young people who grow up in anger and despair'.[22] These people then may eventually fall prey to the rhetoric of terrorism. Although the economic structure which the United States has designed to its own benefit does not directly lead to terrorism, Wade insists that the structures which create inequality have to be redesigned to put an end to the economic conditions which play a role in creating religious/political terrorists.

Another variant on these themes of economic imperialism are commentaries on the role of US pursuit of oil as a foreign policy goal. This theme is expressed by both left and right. Editorials in such conservative sources as <www.frontpagemag.com> lambasted the United States for its support of Saudi Arabia, whom it castigated as a totalitarian regime exporting terrorism.[23] Wall[24] and Charen[25] argue that we have befriended and supported Saudi Arabia with military forces stationed in that country, now the increased focus of bin Laden's wrath, only because of our desire for Saudi oil. This perspective was largely shared by commentators on the left and centre. For Klare our pursuit of oil has been the key to our foreign policy since the end of the Second World War and we are now waging a geopolitical war against bin Laden and associated forces over Middle Eastern and Central Asian oil[26] (a position agreed on by Devraj[27]). This position was also argued by Taliban spokesmen during the fighting. Nixon argues that 'for 70 years, oil has been responsible for more of America's international entanglements and anxieties than any other industry. Oil continues to be a major source both of America's strategic vulnerability and of its reputation as a bully, in the Islamic world and beyond.'[28] For others, oil money transferred through Saudi Arabia makes up the chief funding source for terrorist attacks such as those of 11 September.[29] A number of commentators focused on the role oil giant Unocal and its proposed oil pipeline project played in Pakistan's support of and the United States' initial tolerance for the Taliban regime in Afghanistan.[30]

Finally, many of those in the imperialist camp viewed the attacks as being due to the convergence of the above-named factors. For example, Mahajan and Jensen write that

> the United States should do what is most obviously within its power to do to lower the risk of further terrorist attacks: Begin to change US foreign policy in a way that could win over the people of the Islamic world by acknowledging that many of their grievances – such as the sanctions on Iraq, the presence of US troops in Saudi Arabia, Israel's

occupation of and aggression against Palestine – are legitimate and must be addressed.[31]

The Nation magazine argued that we must consider Israel and the Palestinians, the lack of support for democracy, and economic reasons, reminding readers that 'there are a billion Muslims, most of them desperately poor'.[32] Cockburn blamed the west (especially the United States) for supporting Israel's occupation of Palestine, keeping corrupt rulers in power (largely because of oil) and intervening in the region militarily for its own purposes (Afghanistan in the 1970s, Iraq, etc.).[33] Pilger writes that bin Laden's videotaped words themselves indicated that imperialism was the motivation, not an irrational hatred of Western culture such as that suggested by commentators on the right.[34] In addition, the response of 'the war on terrorism' is further imperialism:

> The ultimate goal (of the war) is not the capture of a fanatic, which would be no more than a media circus, but the acceleration of western imperial power ... The economic and political crises in the developing world, largely the result of imperialism, such as the blood-letting in the Middle East and the destruction of commodity markets in Africa, now serve as retrospective justification for imperialism.[35]

In an interview, Noam Chomsky says that to understand 11 September we must think in terms of both the people who actually committed the crime and the reservoir of support and sympathy these individuals drew from.[36] For Chomsky, the people themselves are Islamists, but Islamism draws from general anti-imperialist feelings throughout the Middle East, and indeed, much of the world. Chomsky's distinction between the perpetrators' motivations and the motivations of those who support them allows for an accommodation of the imperialism perspective with the Islamism explanation. Rhetoric about US imperialism is unquestionably used as a recruiting tool by bin Laden and other similar groups. Making the recruits feel they are fighting in self-defence of Muslims against an overwhelming enemy like the United States corroborates the 'self-defence' perspective which terrorism experts claim forms the main rhetorical hook for recruiting young men into jihad organisations. As terrorism expert Magnus Ranstorp wrote in 1998:

> In an effort to mobilise the masses to support this "self-defensive" struggle, bin-Laden taps into the collective Muslim psyche by skillfully exploiting massacres of Muslims in Iraq, Bosnia, Chechnia, and even Qana (Lebanon), linking these to historical battles between Muslims and their enemies by remolding them into a contemporary context.[37]

This is a hallmark of the Islamist movement in general, which conjectures a Western conspiracy with designs to destroy Islam.[38] Along with general self-defence is a geopolitical defence of the Muslim community from

> a phased plan by the Christian-Judeo conspiracy (spearheaded by the US) to gradually de-Islamize and occupy the Muslim holy places in the Arabian peninsula, as occurred when the Palestinians lost the al-Aqsa mosque and al-Quds (Jerusalem) in 1967. Indeed, it is through this prism that Bin-Laden views the Saudi–US relationship and the presence of American troops in the region, the 'nefarious' dimensions of internal Saudi politics, and the development of broader regional issues.[39]

Thus, few would dispute that whether imperialism is real or not, the idea of its existence inflames the passions of Al Qaeda and aids its recruitment.

Against Imperialism

The counterargument presented by some editorialists is that the motivations ascribed to Al Qaeda by those arguing for imperialist explanations are not the correct or primary ones. Furthermore, the grievances of the Muslim world are less real than perceived. The specific arguments offered against the Imperialist explanations are as follows.

- Bin Laden and Al Qaeda do not actually care about the Palestinians and Israelis, or if they do, they hate Israel for its secularism and the presence of Jews in a position of power over Muslims in an Islamic region.
- They are not upset with the United States because the regimes it supports are not democratic, but because the regimes are either not Islamic states or are not strict enough Islamic states. They are not bothered by the United States being *anti-democratic*, since they themselves are as well. Rather they are disturbed by US support for governments which are *anti-Islamist*.
- There is little or no talk of economic motivation in bin Laden and associates' rhetoric, thus the global inequality and poverty thesis is largely invalid. This is bolstered by the argument that other regions of the world with higher rates of poverty have not turned to anti-American terrorism, and that al Qaeda seems able to recruit easily from the wealthier classes.

Thus while these commentators would largely agree that many Muslims do have grievances with US policies, this has little to do with the attackers' own motivations.

Primary in establishing this case is a debate about to what degree the problems faced by the average citizen of the Middle East are in any way attributable to Israel or US support for Israel. The argument here is that although the Israeli–Palestinian conflict is important for Israelis and Palestinians, it has only symbolic value in affecting other economic and political realities in the region, and that in point of fact, Arab governments use the Israeli–Palestinian conflict to divert attention from their own problematic governance. This is argued by Freedland, for whom the Israeli–Palestinian conflict 'does not begin to explain the dire state of today's Arab and Muslim world, nor why it has spent decades languishing in economic stagnation and political suffocation'.[40] In point of fact, the Palestinian–Israeli conflict is used as a means of distracting the populace from government's own failures: 'Of course, the governments of those countries would like their peoples to think precisely that – that Israel is the satanic force responsible for all their woes. "Don't look at us, with all our corruption and incompetence; it's Israel's fault!" has been the cry of rotting dictatorships from Algeria to Iran.'[41]

Other editorials support this argument by offering further evidence that even during periods of relative quiescence, during administrations which favoured the Palestinians more or were more critical of Israel, or during the negotiations after the Oslo accords the United States was still being attacked by Islamic terrorists (Ajami makes this point, among others).[42] Bin Laden's own statements illustrate that other reasons are certainly more important than Israel, writes Levin, who concludes that 'the antagonism of a bin Laden and his myriad followers toward America, by the terrorist's own testimony, would be little different if there were no Israel'.[43] This point is reiterated by Hitchens, who in a widely discussed column, asks rhetorically whether 'an Israeli withdrawal from Gaza would have forestalled the slaughter in Manhattan?' and insists that the Islamists 'quarrel is with Judaism and secularism on principle, not with (or not just with) Zionism'.[44] Furthermore, Hitchens insists, what the bombers 'abominate about "the West", to put it in a phrase, is not what Western liberals don't like and can't defend about their own system, but what they *do* like about it and must defend: its emancipated women, its scientific inquiry, its separation of religion from the state'.[45] Thus, for some editorialists, the attacks were not an attack against imperialism, but an attack against secularism and modernism.

From this perspective, the anti-Americanism of either the terrorists or their supporters is not based so much on *legitimate* grievances as it is on anti-secularism, anti-Christian and anti-Semitic sentiments, conspiracy theories, and scapegoating. Applyard writes that America is hated not because of imperialism, but because of anti-Americanism which itself is composed of both anti-Semitism and hatred of America because 'it's on top'.[46] Rieff comments that we should not pretend that the terrorists are 'somehow people who are putting forward the message of the world's oppressed'.[47] He states that bin Laden himself has clearly said that 'he is not fighting for the oppressed. He is fighting for Islam, or, rather – and the point cannot be emphasised enough – for his primitive, barbarous version of Islam'.[48] Even Said, who supports part of the imperialist argument, has trouble with the concept of oppression and desperation driving young Middle Eastern men to participate in terrorist attacks:

> I know it is often argued that suicide bombings are either the result of frustration and desperation, or that they emerge from the criminal pathology of deranged religious fanatics. But these are inadequate explanations. The New York and Washington suicide terrorists were middle-class, far from illiterate men, perfectly capable of modern planning, audacious as well as terrifyingly deliberate destruction ... The real culprit is a system of primary education that is woefully piecemeal, cobbled together out of the Qur'an, rote exercises based on outdated 50-year-old textbooks, hopelessly large classes, woefully ill-equipped teachers, and a nearly total inability to think critically.[49]

Alongside of these educational failings is a reliance on conspiracy theory to explain world events. After the 11 September attacks, stories that no Jews were killed in the attacks and that 4,000 Jews were warned not to go to work in the World Trade Center that day were transmitted by major Middle Eastern media sources around the world. These conspiracy theories are not free floating, but are themselves promoted by the political and religious establishments of Muslim countries. As Ajami comments, although the United States gives Egypt large amounts of aid, Egyptian state-run dailies print wild stories of American–Jewish conspiracies directed against Egypt. This helps channel frustration with the nation's economic and military failures and 'a pain born of the gap between Egypt's exalted idea of itself and the poverty and foreign dependence that have marked its modern history' into the 'safety valve' of anti-Americanism and anti-Semitism.[50]

Some commentators voice the opinion that anti-Americanism, rather than being a sign of America's hegemonic presence, is based on perceptions of American weakness. Gerecht insists that the fuel for anti-Americanism has been 'the impression, more or less justified, that the United States has been on the run ... What actually propels men to take airplanes and drive them into skyscrapers, and to blow themselves up on buses, is the sense that they're actually winning. They're not killing themselves out of desperation – they are killing themselves eagerly and with euphoria. They think they can win.'[51]

Blowback

Following the 11 September attacks a hitherto fairly uncommon term, 'blowback', began showing up in op-ed pieces and news accounts.[52] The term has its origins in the CIA, where it was used to describe the unintended consequences of intelligence operations. The term's more recent popularisation comes largely from Chalmers Johnson, an East Asia specialist and leading theorist of Japan's political economy, whose book of the same name does exhibit an eerie prescience of the attacks.[53] For Johnson and others, blowback's meaning has expanded beyond the consequences of intelligence operations to now mean 'the unintended consequences of American policies abroad, including polices that are kept secret from the American public'.[54] To separate this definition from imperialism, a good working notion of blowback is the following statement by Beinart whom describes the perspective of blowback as follows: 'Our foreign policy doesn't just create enemies in a general sense, it creates them in a very specific sense: *We fund and train the people who later attack us*' (emphasis added).[55] Thus Scheer claims explicitly that the CIA 'helped train Osama bin Laden and many of the other terrorists who have turned against us'.[56]

Johnson claims the term 'blowback' originated in Operation Ajax, the CIA's operation to remove Mohammed Mossadegh's government from power in Iran in 1953.[57] This ostensibly successful operation brought with it the Shah's rule and the repression of his regime. The unintended consequence of this covert action was the Iranian revolution and a rise in legitimacy of Islamic fundamentalism. In an editorial Bouzid traces the influence this action had upon contemporary events in the Middle East.[58] Had there been no CIA operation, there would have been no coup; no repressive regime; popular Iranian support for the government; an understanding that Islam and democracy could coexist; far less religious fervour for the ayatollahs; no war between Iraq and Iran; thus no Gulf War; no stationing of troops in Saudi Arabia; and ultimately, no 11 September attacks. Moreover, by not taking these actions, the United States 'would not have rendered talk about human rights and international law totally meaningless and hypocritical to Arab and Muslim ears'.[59]

Johnson has also argued that the term 'blowback' originated in US support for the mujahideen in Afghanistan during the Cold War and the later discovery that the first World Trade Center bombers were associated with the mujahideen. As Johnson describes it, 'to CIA officials and an increasing number of American pundits, blowback has become a term of art acknowledging that the unconstrained, often illegal, secret acts of the United States in other countries can result in retaliation against innocent American citizens'.[60] Thus the funding of the Afghan Arabs in efforts to help the mujahideen fight the Soviet Union resulted in the creation of organisations such as Al Qaeda, the spread of the Afghan jihad veterans around the world, and ultimately the attacks of 11 September.

We must, however, differentiate between three levels of blowback. The first posits a direct causal relationship between the CIA and the emergence of bin Laden and Al Qaeda by claiming that the CIA funded and trained Bin Laden.[61] The second view states that while we do not have hard evidence of this, the fact that we trained and armed other mujahideen means that we *may as well* have trained bin Laden (alleged by a number of columnists on the left after 11 September). The third and more nuanced view is that we accidentally created Al Qaeda and their umbrella terror network by creating the circumstances in Afghanistan (and neighboring Peshwar) in which various jihad and Islamic terrorist groups could meet and form allegiances.[62]

None of these points of view is actually new. Questions of this nature began to arise at least as early as 1994 following the investigation into the first attack on the World Trade Center, perhaps best framed by Rubin: 'Did the CIA, in its all-out effort to oust the Soviets from Afghanistan, secretly train fanatical Muslim Arab terrorists who had now turned their US-supplied weapons and skills on their former masters?'[63] Such was the case alleged in some quarters of the US press as well as by President Mubarak of Egypt.[64] What was undoubtedly true was that most of the suspects as well as Afghan Arab combatants found in numerous other jihads could be traced back to having worked with Gulbuddin Hikmatyar's Hizbi-I Islami (Islamic Party), and that this organisation was the principal beneficiary of aid from the United States and Saudi Arabia administered through Pakistan's ISI.[65] Rubin elsewhere suggests that bin Laden's presence in Afghanistan was at the behest of Pakistan, who wanted him there to help train the Pakistani Harakat-ul-mujahidin group fighting in Kashmir[66] and that a large portion of blame must go to the former Soviet Union for destroying the institutions of Afghanistan.[67]

The claim that the funding of jihad brought together numerous Islamist groups from around the region to Afghanistan is true, although Islamist groups had long previously cemented ties with, among others, the Egyptian Muslim Brotherhood. These ties, however, were facilitated and bolstered by the actions of the United States, Saudi Arabia and Pakistan.[68] The participants in the Afghan jihad against the Soviet Union brought prisoners from the Middle East, young disaffected jihadis and others who eventually became part of the international jihad movement. Thus the US policies did help inadvertently to create the circumstances that led to the eventual birth of Al Qaeda.

Johnson's broader thesis, however, is that the United States' continued large overseas military presence in so many countries, despite the end of the

Cold War, is evidence that as a nation we have embarked upon an imperial strategy. This strategy has and will continue to backfire, and the unexpected and unintended consequences of our policies are blowback. For Johnson, blowback effects are tied to two aspects of US foreign policy: a global military presence and an insistence on other nations' economic globalisation. Mirroring the imperialism explanation previously discussed, Johnson writes that

> the continuous trail of military 'accidents' and of terrorist attacks on American installations and embassies, are all portents of a twenty-first century crisis in America's informal empire, an empire based on the projection of military power to every corner of the world and on the use of American capital and markets to force global economic integration on our terms, at whatever costs to others.[69]

Before 11 September Johnson wrote:

> In the world today, any number of Americans can wander into an imperial scenario they know nothing about, but which could have truly lethal consequences for them. Like the blowing up of an airplane with American citizens on board. Or sitting in the World Trade Center when some former mujahideen from Afghanistan decided to bomb it; or the Americans killed in Karachi; or the whole Bin Laden affair. All of these had their origin in US policies abroad.[70]

Johnson specifically calls the bin Laden organised attacks on US embassies in Africa in 1998 blowback, 'rather than unprovoked terrorism', since bin Laden viewed 'the stationing of American troops in his native Saudi Arabia during and after the Persian Gulf War as a violation of his religious beliefs'.[71]

The blowback thesis seems incontrovertible. By relating specific US prior involvements to their supposed effects, the argument that we have erred in ways that harms our own interests is difficult to negate. The only effective counterargument is to challenge the accuracy of the model of causality being suggested. In an editorial piece Beinart does exactly this, insisting that bin Laden and the Arabs' increasing role in Afghanistan came not because of US actions, but because the United States was too *uninvolved* in Afghanistan, leaving much of the groundwork to Pakistan and then abandoning the country after the Soviet withdrawal.[72] Beinart concludes:

> There was no blowback. America's involvement in Afghanistan in the 1980s didn't help create Osama bin Laden; Saudi Arabia's involvement in Afghanistan in the 1980s helped create Osama bin Laden, in large part because the United States was too timid to direct

the war itself. Similarly, it wasn't America's intervention in Afghanistan in the 1990s that created the Taliban; it was Pakistan's intervention and America's non-intervention. Doves might consider this as they counsel the US to respond to September 11 by leaving the rest of the world to its own devices.[73]

State Decline

State decline is both discussed as an independent factor and in combination with the other explanations in some editorial pieces. Falling under the rubric of state decline are two primary themes. First, weak and failing states plagued by corruption and a lack of strong legal institutions are unable to adequately provide economic opportunity and services for their citizens, thus creating environments suitable for terrorists to operate in. What results is a pool of discontent that breeds support for terrorism, if not actual terrorists themselves. This theory portrays the contemporary Arab world as being plagued by despotic states with under-performing economies and burgeoning populations. The consequent disaffection produces a market for alternative religious and political ideologies such as Islamism and aids in the recruitment of disaffected youths. According to Bergen, political distortions in the Middle East are mirrored by economic distortions, resulting in limited economic opportunities and disenfranchisement that 'propels many towards Islamism because it proposes a simple fix to all of society's problems'.[74]

The phenomenon of state failure is argued to result from a combination of economic problems, poor governance, demographic trends and in some cases environmental pressures. Foremost among the purveyors of this theory is Robert Kaplan, who argues that demographic change, urbanisation, environmental degradation, access to arms and corruption are the driving forces behind state failures, increased migration and violent conflicts in many parts of the third world.[75] Kaplan draws inspiration from the 'environmental security' literature, and in particular the work of Thomas Homer-Dixon, who proposes that environmental degradation helps undermine economic production and political stability through the diminution of eco-system services, renewable resource scarcities, and 'push-factor' migration.[76] Homer-Dixon's critics, however, argue that while this thesis is plausible (in the case of intrastate violence and disintegration) though not yet proven, the international ramifications of state collapse and internal disarray are not particularly significant and generally speaking pose a minimal threat to outside states.[77]

A second theme in the category of state decline is that relative to the power of non-state actors, the power of all states are declining. This argument rests on theories highlighting the impacts of globalisation on the structure of the international system. States are losing their ability to monopolise violence, and the threat of terrorism suggests a trend by which war based upon the 'division between government, army, and people seems to be on the way out'.[78] As the primacy of the state is attacked, conflict and tension will increase, resulting in contradictory reliance on super-smart weaponry and terrorism as the primary forms of violence in the international system.[79] Furthermore, states and groups that perceive themselves as at a disadvantage in the international system may see violating the rules as the only effective means of competing in the era of globalisation. Actors who do not want to play by the rules (such as terrorists groups and drug cartels) know it is 'extremely difficult for major powers to exert effective pressure on them' and that their status in large part results from their ability to flagrantly disregard the norms and values of major states.[80]

For example, Al Qaeda has been described as being similar to an NGO or a transnational corporation, as a rather sinister example of the changes unleashed in the international system by globalisation. The group can be seen as a product and beneficiary of globalisation that has been able to exploit such weaknesses of modern Western states as porous borders and inadequate immigration controls.[81] Bin Laden (who studied public administration and economics) is said to have run and organised Al Qaeda along the lines of a CEO managing a multinational corporation. Bergen argues that bin Laden is a product of the transnational world that emerged in the1990s. Without the Internet, satellite phones and cheap and easy travel bin Laden could not have existed: 'Bin Ladenism is created by globalisation and is also a response to globalisation.'[82]

Countering this version of 'state decline' are scholars who insist that states are still the ultimate units of power in the international system and do not face significant threats from non-state actors. Many governments and analysts 'continue to view them not so much as serious security threats but as nuisances'.[83] Others disagree outright with the idea that non-state actors and globalisation are undermining the power and sovereignty of states. For example, Krasner admits that globalisation has increased state control in some areas and reduced it in others. However, he argues that state control has always been challenged by technological changes and global processes and that globalisation has in fact made it easier for states to manage such issues.[84] The net result is stronger states.

Both strands of 'state decline' thinking made their way into the post-11 September editorial commentary. As Thomas Friedman writes:

> While the 22 Arab states currently have 280 million people, soaring birthrates indicate that by 2020 they will have 410 to 459 million. If

this new generation is not to grow up angry and impoverished, in already overcrowded cities, the Arab world will have to overcome its poverty – which is not a poverty of resources but a 'poverty of capabilities and poverty of opportunities,' the report argues[Arab Human Development Report].[85]

Similarly, Raspberry comments that 'it is important to understand that while the seeds of terrorism may have any number of sources (Osama Bin Laden is hardly reacting out of grinding poverty), they find their nurture in the fertile fields of despair'.[86]

The fact that 12 of the 19 hijackers on 11 September were from the southwestern provinces of Saudi Arabia, which are among the most economically depressed and conservative regions of the country, has been used to bolster this position in the press. While most of the 12 were from middle-class backgrounds there are strong indications that they were socially, economically and politically disaffected. For instance, Hani Hanjour was the 29-year-old scion of a prominent family who wanted desperately to become a pilot for the Saudi national airline, but even after completing flight training and FAA certification he failed to obtain his childhood goal. According to friends he increasingly turned his attention to the study of militant Islamic texts, tapes and preachers.[87] Other commentators uphold the idea that failed states (e.g. Somalia, Afghanistan) provide political vacuums where terrorist organisations can set up headquarters and training areas, and launch operations with impunity. Rice opines that

> Africa is the world's soft underbelly for terrorism ... Terrorist organizations take advantage of Africa's porous borders and weak law enforcement, judicial institutions and security services to move men, money, and weapons around the world. They manipulate poor, disillusioned populations often with religious or ethnic grievances, to recruit for jihad.[88]

In a 6 March 2002 speech UN Secretary-General Kofi Annan expostulated that terrorism resulted from a mix of problems caused by bad government, opportunistic politicians and militant leaders who exploit grievances as well as poverty: 'Where massive and systematic political, economic and social inequalities are found, and where no legitimate means of addressing them exists', Mr. Annan said, 'an environment is created in which peaceful solutions all too often lose out against extreme and violent alternatives'.[89]

Meanwhile, terrorist organisations fill service vacuums in these states through the establishment of charities, NGOs and schools. The role of madrasahs in providing schooling and propagating jihad has received particular attention. For example, Fritsch writes that in Pakistan 'public schools starved for resources barely function. The nation's hermetic madrasahs fill most of this enormous gap ... in Pakistan madrasahs receive much of their money from hard-line Islamic groups ... officials say some schools have received funds from alleged terrorist master-mind Osama bin Laden.'[90] Critics contend, however, that rather than providing evidence that state power is weakening, the events of 11 September will in the long run bolster state power. Thayer, for example, comments that while terrorism incubates in failed states, major state actors will come together in a contemporary version of the Concert of Powers to defeat groups like Al Qaeda, thus reasserting their dominant role in the international system.[91]

Islamism

Perhaps the most widely discussed explanation offered overall for the 11 September attacks was that they were the direct result of rising militancy within Islam. Indeed, the planners and agents of the attacks seem to have three things in common – they were male, young and Muslim. According to Al Qaeda's own training manual the first necessary qualification for membership in the organisation is

> Islam: The member of the organization must be a Muslim. How can an unbeliever, someone from a revealed religion (Christian, Jew), a secular person, a communist, etc. protect Islam and Muslims and defend their goals and secrets when he does not believe in that religion.[92]

Al Qaeda and other groups have been variously referred to – not always precisely or accurately – as particularly virulent manifestation of Islamic extremism, Islamism, Wahabism, primitive Islam, militant Islam, and Salafiyya. Regardless of the label, many commentators would agree that this strain is

> a hybrid and simplistic blend of Islamic fundamentalism that seeks to eradicate all other forms of Islam other than its own strict literal interpretation of the Koran. It comes packaged with a set of now well-known political grievances, often directed at US foreign policy, and justifies violence as a means of purging nations of corruption, moral degradation, and spiritual torpor.[93]

For purposes of this essay we will use the term 'Islamism' in reference to the phenomenon described in the preceding definition because this is how the term has been generally used in the context of the pieces we reviewed (not as an endorsement or criticism of the descriptive accuracy of the term itself).

Recent years have seen copious writings on the phenomenon of Islamism. While the depth and breadth of these works cannot be adequately addressed here, a number of key themes and debates emerge. First, most academic work on Islamism strongly contests the idea that Islamism is a natural outgrowth of Islam. Instead, many argue that Islamism is essentially a political ideology, cynically linked to a religion, in this case Islam, which in actuality is just a manifestation of a larger phenomena of political ideologies posing as religious fundamentalisms.[94] Thus whatever tendencies towards violence or terrorism are inherent in Islamism, these are problems of Islamism as a political ideology, not problems inherent to the religious teachings of Islam itself.

Another important theme is the context in which Islamism as a political–religious ideology has developed. Islamism is part of an 'Islamic resurgence', which is itself part of a long and rich Islamic tradition of revival and reform which has spawned innumerable individual reformers as well as broader-based movements, both non-violent and militant. According to Esposito, the recent Islamist resurgence is largely a successor to failed secular nationalist states in the Middle East. Given the failure of pan-Arabism and nationalism, the Islamists in particular have offered an alternative ideology to western political and developmental models.[95] Tibi similarly argues that failure of nation states to develop in the Muslim world has resulted in the development of Islamism as an alternative political model.[96] While revivalism has varied in different geographical contexts, it does have a number of common themes:

> A sense that existing political, economic, and social systems had failed; a disenchantment with, and at times a rejection of, the West; a quest for identity and greater authenticity; and the conviction that Islam provides a self-sufficient ideology for state and society, a valid alternative to secular nationalism, socialism, and capitalism.[97]

Unlike the view of those who find capitalism responsible for the malaise of the Arab world, however, Islamists also reject Marxist socialism as 'a godless alternative which struck at the heart of religion'[98] Ultimately, some have concluded, Islamism's enemy is secular democracy, which it would replace with a totalitarian rule based on a radical interpretation of Islamic law.[99]

A related theme is the debate about whether and to what extent Islamism is compatible with democracy and secular government. Esposito and Fuller[100] regard Islamism and democracy as at least potentially compatible, while Tibi insists that they are utterly irreconcilable. He argues that the Islamists promote Islamism not as an alternative to nationalism or the Western nation state they saw imposed upon Islamic lands, but as a universalist claim for a dominant Islamist world order, a 'pax islamica' to compete with the 'pax Americana' of Western civilisation.[101] This expansionist vision seeks to establish a global Islamic world order, and thus views the battle in 'civilisational' terms. The conflict between civilisations is necessary since the modern system of nation states dominated by the West is at odds with the Islamic universalism 'which recognizes no boundaries and claims to be a *da'wa*/universal mission for all of humanity'.[102] Establishing a Muslim caliphate in the Middle East, which appears to have been the long-term plan which 11 September was intended to begin, is itself a step on the way to world domination.

These themes are echoed in analysis of Al Qaeda and bin Laden's motivations. Bernard Lewis has written that over the course of the twentieth century it became clear throughout the Islamic world and Middle East that 'things had gone badly wrong' while the military, political, and economic efforts of modernisers have resulted in disappointment.[103] Consequently, three questions have arisen: 'Who did this to us?' 'What did we do wrong?' 'And how do we put it right?'[104] From the ideological vantage point of bin Laden and Al Qaeda the answer is clear. Apostate regimes backed by the imperial power of the United States (whom is largely perceived by Islamists as being run by Zionists) have deviated from the true path of Islam and must return through the imposition of Sharia and by following the example of the Prophet. Bin Laden's own words, as well as various analyses, support the position that Al Qaeda has both a religious and political ideology with specific (though evolving) objectives. When asked in August of 2001 of his opinion of Saudi policy towards the rest of the Islamic world and what the Saudi regime should do in the face of the 'Muslim uprising' [i.e. jihad], bin Laden replied:

> The external policy of the Saudi regime toward Islamic issues is a policy which is tied to the British outlook ... then it became attached to the American outlook ... There are several choices for the regime ... the most important is to bring back Islamic law and practice real Shura ... As for the other option ... this involves an escalation in the confrontation between the Muslim people and the American occupiers and to confront the economic hemorrhage. Its most important goal would be to change the regime.[105]

Thus bin Laden's war with the United States can be viewed as a political struggle justified by his personal understanding of Islam[106] as well as by the political ideology of Islamism.

Al Qaeda's ideology reflects the educational, political and religious background of bin Laden and other Al Qaeda leaders such as Ayman Zawahiri. Bin Laden's political views and understanding of Islam draw heavily from the tenets of Wahabism, Deobandism and Salafyism. Of particular importance are the teachings of Sayid Qutb and Abdullah Azzam. Organisationally and philosophically, Al Qaeda has been heavily influenced by the Muslim Brotherhood and Algerian and Egyptian Salafyist groups such as the GIA (Armed Islamic Group), SIA (Salvation Islamic Group), Egyptian Islamic Jihad, and others. These groups have effectively been absorbed into Al Qaeda and their leaders make up an important part of bin Laden's inner circle. Bin Laden's mentor Abdullah Azzam and his second-in-command Ayman Zawahiri gave Al Qaeda an internationalist ideology and were able to extend a war against apostate governments in the Muslim world to the United States, who supplied the power behind the throne and whose political and cultural hegemony could be perceived as a threat to Islamic society itself.

The Egyptian influence on Al Qaeda is probably the most important factor behind the expansion of its war to the United States[107] and ultimately to the 11 September attacks. Sayyid Qutb is widely regarded as the founder of the modern jihadi movement and his writings as well as the personnel influence of his brother Mohammed were important influences on bin Laden as an undergraduate. Qutb challenged the commonly held precept of jihad as defensive and advocated offensive action against Muslim governments not following the letter of the Koran, as well as infidels. For Qutb, jihad was in fact 'Islamic world revolution' against the forces of the West, which he viewed as representing a pre-Islamic civilisation engaged in a new crusade against Islam. According to Hourani, Qutb represented the extreme end of the spectrum of those trying to address the question of 'What went wrong?',[108] while Tibi argues that Qutb's work has been as influential as the early spread of the Communist Manifesto. The attacks on apostate governments and their non-Muslim backers advocated by bin Laden today spring directly from the pen of Qutb, who 'proclaimed that the days of the West's dominance over the world are numbered, and that the time has come for Islam to claim its world leadership'.[109]

The other important influence on Al Qaeda appears to be Zawahiri, who is credited with making bin Laden and the network more radical and bent on unrestricted violence. In 1998 Zawahiri and bin Laden formally joined forces, merging Al Qaeda with the Egyptian Islamic Jihad. America became the prime target of both groups, instead of the Muslim regimes that had been their traditional first priority. Zawahiri explained that replacing Egypt's government remained the goal but was 'not an easy objective that is close at hand'. America, he said, propped up 'infidel' Arab governments and would let them fall 'only if the shrapnel from the battle reaches their own homes and bodies'.[110] Some believe Zawahiri shifted focus to America because of desperation and the effectiveness of the Egyptian government's crackdown on Islamist groups. Zawahiri's career has been marked by the advocacy of increasing levels and indiscriminateness of violence, an influence he seems to have imprinted on bin Laden and Al Qaeda, which had previously stuck to military and government targets outside the United States. Ironically, former associates credit much of Zawahiri's violent bent to three years he spent in an Egyptian prison as part of a round-up of Islamists after the 1981 assassination of Anwar Sadat (of which he was not a part).[111] In 1994 Esposito warned that Islamists imprisoned and tortured by such regimes 'will become convinced that force is their only recourse'.[112]

The particular choice of targets for the 11 September attacks not surprisingly appears to have had political, symbolic and personal motivations consistent with the ideological bent of Al Qaeda's leadership. The Pentagon and World Trade Center are symbols of American military and economic power while the choice of Saudis as the main nationality of the hijackers may have been in part an attempt by bin Laden to drive a wedge between the United States and Saudi Arabia.[113] Some analysts have suggested that personal motives may have also played a part, namely that an air attack against the World Trade Center was a tribute to Ramzi Yousef, the Al Qaeda associate who attempted the 1993 World Trade Center bombing as well as the failed Project Bojinka (which intended to blow up 11 US airliners and crash a plane into CIA headquarters).[114]

There has been some, albeit little, criticism of the Islamism perspective as an explanatory framework for understanding 11 September based on differences in perceptions of the extent to which Islamism poses a threat to the West. Three main arguments have been employed against the Islamist explanation. First, the attacks are not only not condoned by most Islamic scholars but in fact are considered un-Islamic or deviant. This has led many, especially in the Arab world, to deny Islam (and sometimes even bin Laden) had anything to do with 11 September. Lewis's claim that something has 'gone wrong' in the Islamic world is poignantly and ironically illustrated by the dismissal of claims that Arab Muslims could have perpetuated the attacks. For example according to one Egyptian woman, 'this is not an Arab mentality! We're not that intelligent. Bin Laden does not have the financial resources or the brilliance to execute such an attack. Those are foreign terrorists.'[115]

There are others who suggest that America was targeted on 11 September because it had stumbled into a war within Islam (being fought between moderates and Islamist extremists). This is not so much a counterargument against the Islamism explanation as a suggestion that the struggle is largely within Islam, as opposed to between Islamists and the United States. Another counterargument is that 11 September was primarily a political phenomenon (either a political reaction against the United States

– i.e. imperialism or blowback, or an internal political struggle with the Islamic world). Roy states that 'bin Laden is not a theologian ... he's a political activist ... he has Islamized the traditional discourse of Western Imperialism'.[116] The last counter to the Islamist argument is that the attacks represent an *actual clash between the West and Islam in general* as opposed to a contest between the West and an extreme element within Islam (or the West having become embroiled in an intra-Islamic contest). We will address this notion in the following section.

Many of the themes discussed above have made their way onto the editorial pages. There are those who dismiss the 11 September attackers as merely irrational fanatics, arguing that 'radical religio-political zealotry' [abetted by poverty and poor governance] are the primary motivations of Islamist extremists; 'nut[s]' who engage in 'sick pursuits of lethal zealotry'.[117] This line is a particular favourite of ultra-conservative American commentators, who demand that Muslims 'either restore the proper Allah or get ready for a holy war'[118] and characterise Islamists as 'nihilistic terrorists who despise mere health, comfort, and life' and 'worship death – not just our death, but their own apocalyptic, civilisation-destroying suicide'.[119]

In contrast, commentators further to the left tend to stress Islamism's opposition to secularism and secular government and their opposition to moderate Moslems.[120] Hitchens writes that 'the tolerant, the open-minded, the apostate or the followers of different branches of The Faith are fit only for slaughter and contempt'.[121]

Others inquire as to what role Islamism plays in the unleashing of mass casualty terror. Rushdie states that Islam itself must face up to why it breeds violent fanaticism: 'There needs to be a thorough examination by Muslims everywhere, of why it is that the faith they love breeds so many violent mutant strains.'[122] Other commentators suggest that the Islamist dimensions of 11 September need to be examined within a complex cultural, religious, historical, political and psychological context. For as one Pakistani editorialist writes, 'Never in its 1,422 year history has Islam reached such a crossroads as it did on September 11. It put itself under a microscope on that fateful day for the entire world to examine it meticulously.'[123] Still others argue that that a critical reexamination of the interaction between US foreign policy arrogance and Islamic religious fanaticism is essential in order to fully understand Islamist terrorism. Hoodbhoy suggests that historic question must be answered in order to understand how Islam could be used to justify such actions:

> First, Islam – like Christianity, Judaism, or Hinduism, or any other religion – is not about peace. Nor is it about war. Every religion is

about absolute belief in its own superiority and the divine right to impose itself upon others ... Even if Islam had, in some metaphorical sense, been hijacked, that event did not occur on 11 September 2001. It happened in the 13th century.[124]

According to an interview that Ramzi Bin al-Shibh (one of the key planners of the 11 September attacks) gave to Al Jazeera:

Violence is a 'tax' that all Muslims 'must pay'. 'This is the tax for gaining authority on earth. It is imperative to pay a price for Heaven, for the commodity of Allah is dear, very dear. It is not acquired through rest, but [rather] blood and torn-off limbs must be the price ... the obligation of jihad, is just like the other religious obligations. In terms of prayer and zakat [charity] and the like; this obligation has been forsaken, thus it must be established, and the punishment awaiting those who neglect it is painful and harsh.' He goes on to state, 'He [the Muslim] who does not grasp this understanding, he does not perceive the nature of this religion.'[125]

In other words Qutb's offensive-oriented jihad has been elevated to equal footing with the 'Five Pillars of Islam' – a proposition that most Muslims would probably find offensive and an indication of how the Islamist movement is attempting to supplant traditional teachings with a more radical and violent interpretation.

Some commentators contextualise Islamism by suggesting that the rise of Islamist terrorism culminating in the 11 September attacks results as much from the policies of the US and Arab governments as it does from the political goals of the terrorists. Friedman contends that in addition to anger at US Middle Eastern policy, the brutal crackdown on Islamic militant movements in countries such as Algeria, Egypt, Syria and Saudi Arabia contributed to the dispersal of these groups abroad. Islamists sought refuge in failed states or open western societies, while some Arab regimes allowed the Islamists to continue fundraising 'on the condition that the Islamic extremists not attack these regimes', while in order to deflect internal criticism other Arab governments encouraged their press to attack America and Israel.[126]

The thesis that the 11 September attacks represent a religio-political fusion of bin Laden's and other Al Qaeda leaders' personal ideologies with Salafyism and other strains of Islamist thought has also been a prominent feature of press commentary.

In bin Laden's imagery, the leaders of the Arab and Islamic worlds today are hypocrites, idol worshippers cowering behind America, the Hubal of the age. Salafis regard the Islam that most Muslims practice

> today as polluted by idolatry; they seek to reform the religion by emulating the first generation of Muslims.[127]

While another piece concludes:

> Osama bin Laden – the attack's suspected mastermind – has laid out political goals that extend well beyond a primal rage at America. Indeed those who have studied him most carefully agree that bin Laden seems as intent on toppling Arab regimes as on weakening the United States – though he clearly sees the two goals as interconnected.[128]

Others have suggested that symbolic familial and religious motivations may have also played a role in the choice of targets.[129]

Overall, many commentaries stressed the role of Islamism in the attacks, despite some of the differing analyses of Islamism's origins and implications discussed above. Some, however, viewed the conflict as a darker battle between the forces of the West and Islam.

Clash of Civilisations

The first weeks following the 11 September attacks saw a burst of renewed interest in and support of Samuel Huntington's controversial 'clash of civilisation' thesis. The explanations we have analysed so far have pointed to a complex and not entirely clear-cut convergence of factors leading up to the attacks. The concept of civilisation clash promotes a much simpler explanation. Huntington's thesis does not downplay other factors but gives primacy to culture as opposed to the previous frameworks which generally see culture as one of a number of variables, or would perceive divisions along cultural lines as the end result of a convergence of particular circumstances. To some of Huntington's proponents, 11 September and Al Qaeda represent evidence of a larger and ultimately inevitable struggle between the West and the entire Islamic world. 'The underlying problem for the West is not Islamic fundamentalism. It is Islam.'[130]

'Clash' proponents elicited vigorous responses. Said, for instance, blasted Huntington as

> an ideologist, someone who wants to make civilizations and identities into what they are not: shut-down, sealed off entities that have been purged of the myriad currents and counter-currents that animated human history, and that over the centuries have made it possible for that history not only to contain wars of religion and imperial conquest but also to be one of exchange, cultural cross-fertilization and sharing.[131]

In the immediate aftermath of 11 September the relative lack of street protests in the Islamic world, the co-operation extended by Islamic countries to the 'war on terror', and the repeated insistences by Western leaders that their actions are directed at terrorism and not Islam appeared to give lie to claims that 11 September and the wider phenomena of terrorism (especially as pursued by Al Qaeda) heralds the arrival of Huntington's clash of civilisations. Acharya comments that

> the response of governments and peoples around the world proved this was no clash of civilizations ... From Saudi Arabia to Pakistan, from Iran to Indonesia, Islamic Nations denounced bin Laden ... Each of these nations put national interests and modern principals of international conduct above primordial sentiment and transnational religious or cultural identity.[132]

While Singer poses the following:

> Does this mean the West is now at war with Islam? Not yet, exactly ... in some ways, Islamists such as Bin Ladin understand the situation much better than we do. They realize the struggle is whether Islamism – a militant, politicized form of Islam – or western liberal democracy will define the political structure of the Islamic world.[133]

An Egyptian commentary insisted: 'The war between civilizations does not exist. What exists is a war for interests and power. America should not play on the religious front, because its war could turn into a war of Christianity against Islam.'[134]

Even Huntington himself claims the 11 September attacks were not a clash of civilisation but rather 'an attack by an extremist terrorist group on civilised society in the United States, but also on civilized society everywhere',[135] a position closer to the Islamist explanations already discussed. Huntington also cites undemocratic governments and resentment of the United States (blowback and imperialism) as part of the cause of 11 September.[136] In the months since 11 September, 'clash' rhetoric has largely disappeared from the serious western press.

Of course, if bin Laden and his ilk can ultimately polarise the struggle into Islam versus the rest, it could drive a wedge between the West, regimes allied with the West, and secular democracies in the Islamic world, thus making it easier to achieve their religo-political goals in the Islamic world. Benjamin Barber, author of *Jihad vs McWorld*, comments: 'bin Ladin is the primary publicist for Huntington's Theory.'[137] Indeed, Islamist leaders use clash of civilisation rhetoric to bolster their cause, painting attacks against America as jihad waged in defence of Islam. According to Mullah Omar, 'America has taken Islam hostage ... America controls the governments of

Islam ... if someone follows the path of Islam the government arrests him, tortures him, or kills him. This is the doing of America ... America has created the evil that is attacking it.'[138]

Because Islam is under threat defensive jihad is 'absolutely obligatory on all Muslims.'[139] In his 1998 fatwa bin Laden declared, 'All of these crimes and sins committed by the Americans are a clear declaration of war on God, his messenger, and Muslims. And the Ulema have throughout Islamic history unanimously agreed that jihad is an individual duty if the Enemy destroys the Muslim countries.'[140] The 'crimes' referred to in bin Laden's fatwa, however, are not merely religious but are economic, geopolitical and cultural as well. Thus in this sense interests and power are important in this conflict, not just religion. The danger is that the use of absolutist rhetoric in the pursuit of these broader interests could lead to the degeneration of what are actually complex phenomena into simplistic lines. Such rhetoric pervades bin Laden's fatwa and his statements that to 'kill the *Americans* and *their allies – civilian and military –* is the duty of *every* Muslim' (emphasis added).[141]

In an October 2001 response to 'clash of civilisation' proponents, Said quotes the late Eqbal Ahmad, who warned in 1999 that Islamic absolutists and fanatics were promoting an absolutist, stripped down view of Islam and the world. This sentiment is echoed by Rieff, who comments that the Islamic extremists believe that they 'are only defending themselves against what they call Westernisation and we call modernisation, which they believe will lead to the end of human stability and belief'.[142] Thus Muslims are being warned against the West in a fashion similar to Huntington's warning to the West about Islam. For the radical Islamists, this *is* a clash of civilisation, a battle of Islam against the West in its entirety (rather than just against its injustices real and perceived). The *New York Times* quotes Sheik Muqbel bin Hadi-al Wadie (a Yemeni Salafyist): 'In this sheik's view, the most dangerous enemies of Islam, before the United States and Israel, are *western life* and *culture*'.[143] Michael Doran in a recent *Foreign Affairs* article writes that:

> Sayyid Qutb, Osama bin Laden, and the entire extremist Salafiyya see Western civilization, in all periods and in all guises, as innately hostile to Muslims and to Islam itself. The West and Islam are locked in a prolonged conflict. Islam will eventually triumph, of course, but only after enduring great hardship. Contemporary history, defined as it is by Western domination, constitutes the darkest era in the entire history of Islam.[144]

This line of argument turns Huntington's warning about Islam on its head. Islamists are more likely to attempt to turn this into a war between

Islam and the West than the United States is to turn its 'war on terrorism' into a crusade against Islam. The results of a Gallup poll taken in December 2001 and January 2002 suggest that there is in fact significant anti-western sentiment in much of the Islamic world. According to Frank Newport, Gallup editor-in-chief, 'The people of Islamic countries have significant grievances with the West in general and the United States in particular.'[145] Some commentators have suggested that misinterpretations of Huntington's thesis may in fact have contributed to the Islamic world's perceptions of western bias. According to Ahmed, after the publication of Huntington's thesis, this was a common point of conversation in Morocco and Pakistan. 'They were saying the West wants a war with Islam. I would say how do you come to this conclusion? And they would say the leading Harvard professor wants a war with Islam.'[146]

The poll results suggest that many Muslims feel the West lacks respect for Arab and Islamic values, and treat Arabs unfairly. On closer inspection, however, Gallup respondents seem to make a distinction between the United States and other Western countries. While interviewees found the United States to be arrogant, aggressive and biased, majorities did not feel this way about France, Russia or Britain. Furthermore, most saw the 11 September attacks as unjustifiable, indicating that despite their dislike of the West they do not support Islamist terrorism (although the poll also revealed that the majority claimed the attacks were not the work of Muslims). These results suggest that people in Islamic countries are not taking a strictly civilisational stance but are making distinctions between Western countries and policies, and that their dissatisfaction with the West has not necessarily evolved into support for anti-Western terrorism.

Huntington provides us less with an explanation than a warning. If civilisational discourses dominate the discussion of the issues which frame 11 September, than there is a very real risk that affairs will polarise along civilisation lines. Therefore the question should not be whether 11 September is a clash of civilisation but rather whether it will be allowed to create one.

Conclusion

Taken singly, each of the explanatory categories we have examined shed light on some aspect of the situation leading up to the 11 September attacks. For instance, the explanation of imperialism demonstrates that certain US geopolitical and geoeconomic policies (and perceptions of them) have created a sense of grievance towards America in much of the Muslim world, and some US policies continue to provide rhetorical grist for Islamist movements. The reality and perceptions of US and more generally Western imperialism are also important in contextualising the growth of Islamism, Arab rage and ultimately terrorism. More narrowly, blowback demonstrates how certain actions designed for short-term geopolitical expediency may have helped foster conditions favourable for the development and global spread of organisations such as Al Qaeda. However, in counter to these explanations are a number of other arguments. While many throughout the world resent American policies, and while the United States has intervened in numerous regions, few in other regions of the world have advocated or engaged in anti-American terrorism. Moreover, many states pursue policies that produce the risk of blowback without it ever occurring. Though state interventions may be more likely to lead to blowback than isolationism, the primary question about blowback is whether a higher degree of involvement with the Middle East and a commitment to following through on US interventions in the region might conversely make blowback less likely to occur.

While imperialist explanations are important, their weakness is that in assigning such a large proportion of culpability to the United States and the West, they miss a host of other factors more properly laid at the feet of the governments of the Middle East and their policies. Additionally, explanations based on imperialism and blowback display some of the same arrogance the United States is accused of in its dealings with the world since, in these characterisations, without the United States the motive and ability to conceive of and plan an 11 September-type operation would not exist. These perspectives downplay agency outside of the United States and ignore the internal motivations and political calculations of the attackers, who are viewed as only 'reacting', not acting towards their own interests.

However, uncritical acceptance of these critiques and rejection of the merits of the imperialist and blowback theses may lead to the assumption amongst policymakers that blowback has occurred because US intervention has been half-hearted and that terrorism is fueled by perceptions of American weakness more than from a desperation born of imperialism. Ultimately this line of reasoning leads to the view that terrorism is being fueled less by imperialism and blowback than by Islamism and the Islamists' ambition to achieve concrete political goals. This could encourage a policy of strong interventions which may lead to both the short-term deterrence of terrorism while also possibly adding to the grievances in the Muslim world. These propositions, however, are only testable via the pursuit of actual policies whose results are unpredictable. In either case, there is a profound implication that policymakers acting in a globalised world must be aware of the strong reactions their policies will produce, thus requiring a well-reasoned consideration of exactly where policies will lead.

State decline suggests failed or autocratic and non-performing states create both disaffection and power vacuums that provide both incubation and opportunities for terrorist organisations. This theory is somewhat belied by the numerous examples of state decline which have not produced global terrorism, as well as by the existence of Al Qaeda cells and support activities in non-failed states such as France, Britain and the United States. Nonetheless, state decline does have some policy implications; broadly, failed states are breeding grounds for local problems which may become global ones and the United States should be involved in helping prevent states from failing.

Islamism suggests that in addition to disaffection within the Islamic world and anger at the United States there are other factors and contexts to be consider, such as the historic development of Islam and struggles over its meaning, internal political conflicts within the Islamic world, and the personal beliefs of both perpetrators and supporters. Of course, Islam has a rich history of revivalism and fundamentalism and not all Islamists are terrorists or seek global jihad. Nonetheless, the global threat posed by Islamist groups and ideology can no longer be discounted. At its worst, Islamism is an expansionist ideology seeking to overthrow not only moderate regimes, but eventually secularism, democracy and the West. This suggests that the worst of its supporters should be recognised as an entity that should not be appeased or bargained with, and that US policy changes alone may not be sufficient to deal with the problem.

The 'clash of civilisation' thesis holds the least water but does raise two useful points. First, it points to the importance of history and culture in understanding Islamic antipathy to the West. More importantly, however, in a complex world of instant global communications, it shows that simplified theories pose the danger of being appropriated by ideologues and used to polarise opinions in ways that create additional conflict. Future events such as Western intervention in the Middle East or further mass casualty terrorist attacks could very well help polarise the Western and Islamic worlds, setting the stage for a real clash of civilisations.

Ultimately the 11 September attacks and Al Qaeda cannot be explained easily by any of the single theories discussed here. Rather, they represent a unique convergence of factors at a particular point in time and space. Various combinations of these explanations form a more satisfying and complete picture than any one by itself. While we find the Islamist explanation the most powerful in explaining the mindsets of the actual perpetrators, elements of the other theories have validity and should be incorporated into any detailed analysis of the cause of the 11 September attacks and the wider phenomenon of Islamist terrorism. Islamism itself must be viewed not in a vacuum but in relation to historical and contemporary manifestations of imperialism. Legitimate grievances intermingle with Islamist rhetoric to create public sentiment against the West and the United States in particular in much of the Arab and Islamic world, and contribute to perceptions of a clash of civilisations. Blowback can strengthen particular Islamist groups when intelligence operations and foreign policy goes awry, and this cannot be discounted in any analysis of the 11 September attacks. Furthermore failing/declining states can provide conditions in which terrorists groups such as Al Qaeda can coalesce, train and organise, while states with repressive and corrupt government contribute to the disaffection that helps spawn terrorism.

While editorial and op-ed pieces are generally ill-designed to provide comprehensive analysis, they are important in shaping opinion and policy. Yet rather than relying on single explanations, some convergence of theories is more suited to answering the questions raised by the 11 September attacks. Given the necessity of considering the convergence and intersection of multiple variables including economics, politics, demographics, religion, culture and history across space at specific times, analysis of the causes of terrorism should be a task suitable for geographers. In particular, geographic analysis could include the effects of globalisation, the role and changing place of the state in the international system, the complex phenomenon of state decline, and the powerful discourses of Islamism along with political geographers' more usual analysis of geopolitics and imperialism.

We believe there is a need for geographers to contribute their skill, training and talents to explaining and understanding the roots and causes of contemporary mass casualty terrorism. In doing so, however, it is vital to step beyond paradigmatic boundaries and to seek to combine some of the many explanatory frameworks suggested above. In this way, geographers can help shape the public debate on the causes of the 11 September attacks. If editorials reflect academic discourse, and academic discourse suggests a multifaceted view as opposed to monocausal explanatory frameworks, perhaps editorialists will also begin to provide a more nuanced blueprint for policy makers charged with preventing the emergence of future 11 Septembers.

NOTES

1. R.J. Johnston et al., *The Dictionary of Human Geography*, 4th ed. (Malden, MA: Blackwell 2000) p.375
2. M. Hardt and A. Negri, *Empire* (Cambridge, MA: Harvard University Press 2000).
3. F. Furedi, *The New Ideology of Imperialism* (Boulder, CO: Pluto Press 1994).
4. E. Hermann, *The Real Terror Network* (Boston: South End Press 1982).
5. Furedi (note 3) p.98
6. J.A. Hobson, *Imperialism* (Ann Arbor, MI: University of Michigan Press 1971).
7. V.I. Lenin, Imperialism: The Highest Stage of Capitalism (New York: International

Publishers 1939).

8. A. Brewer, *Marxist Theories of Imperialism: A Critical Survey* (London: Routledge and Kegan Paul 1980).

9. B. Berberoglu, *Turmoil in the Middle East: Imperialism, War, and Political Instability* (Albany, NY: State University of New York Press 1999).

10. Ibid p.1

11. M. Rodinson. Israel: A Colonial-Settler State (New York: Monad Press 1973).

12. Berberoglu, (note 9) p.95

13. D. Jackson, 'A Call for Us to be Fair to Palestinians', *Boston Globe*, 21 September 2001; G. Kamiya, 'The Bloody Jordan River now Flows through America', *Salon*, <http://salon.com>, 17 September 2001.

14. Kamiya, (note 13)

15. Ibid.

16. G.E. Fuller, 'Muslims Abhor the Double Standard', *Los Angeles Times*, 5 October 2001.

17. Ibid.

18. E. Said, 'A Vision to Lift the Spirit', *Counterpunch*, <http://counterpunch.org>, 26 October 2001

19. H. Zinn, 'America's Course', Los Angeles Times, 23 September 2001.

20. Ibid.

21. B. Nahid, 'A Suspect's Perspective', *Counterpunch*, <http://counterpunch.org>, 4 October 2001.

22. R.H. Wade, 'America's Empire Rules an Unbalanced World', *International Herald Tribune*, 3 January 2002.

23. A. Wall, 'Really Re-examining Middle East Policy', *FrontPage*, <http://www.frontpagemag.com>, 2 November 2001.

24. Ibid.

25. M. Charen, 'Who will Redraw the Map?', *Washington Times*, 29 October 2001.

26. M.T. Klare, 'The Geopolitics of War', *The Nation*, 5 November 2001.

27. R. Devraj, 'Energy a Major Factor in Looming Afghan Conflict', Inter Press Service, 5 October 2001.

28. R. Nixon, 'A Dangerous Appetite for Oil', *New York Times*, 29 October 2001.

29. G. Easterbrook, 'Why this War is also about Oil', *New Republic*, 8 October 2001.

30. G. Monbiot, 'War and Oil: America's Pipe Dream', *Counterpunch*, <http://counterpunch.org>, 23 October 2001; T. Rall, 'The New Great Game: Oil Politics in Central Asia', <http://www.alternet.org>, 11 October 2001; B. Soskis, 'When America Liked the Taliban', *New Republic*, 22 October 2001.

31. R. Mahajan and R. Jensen, 'Hearts and Minds: Avoiding a New Cold War', *Counterpunch*, <http://counterpunch.org>, 18 October 2001.

32. 'Hitting Terrorism's Roots', *The Nation*, 22 October 2001.

33. A. Cockburn, 'Their Evilness wasn't Outside History', *Los Angeles Times*, 30 September 2001

34. J. Pilger, 'The Great Power Game: War American Style', *The New Statesman,* 15 October 2001

35 Ibid.

36. N. Chomsky, 'The New War Against Terror', *Counterpunch*, <http://counterpunch.org>, 24 October 2001.

37. M. Ranstorp, 'Interpreting the Broader Context and Meaning of Bin-Laden's Fatwa', *Studies in Conflict and Terrorism* 21/4 (1998) p.325.

38. H. Khashan, *Arabs at the Crossroads: Political Identity and Nationalism* (Gainesville, FL: University Press of Florida 2000).

39. Ranstorp (note 37) p.325.

40. J. Freedland, 'A Socialism of Fools', *The Guardian*, 17 October 2001

41. Ibid.

42. F. Ajami, 'The Sentry's Solitude', *Foreign Affairs* 80/6 (2001) p.2.

43. A. Levin,' Is American Support for Israel to Blame?', *The Jerusalem Post*, 26 September 2001.

44. C. Hitchens, 'Against Rationalization', *The Nation*, 8 October 2001.
45. Ibid.
46. B. Appleyard, 'Why do they Hate America?', *The Sunday Times*, 23 September 2001.
47. D. Rieff, 'There is No Alternative to War', *Salon*, <http://salon.com>, 25 September 2001.
48. Ibid.
49. Said, 'A Vision' (note 18).
50. Ajami (note 42).
51. Katie Bacon, 'The Necessity of Fear' (interview, Reuel Marc Gerecht), *Atlantic Unbound*, 28 December 2001, <http://www.theatlantic.com/unbound/interviews/int2001-12-28.htm>.
52. For example, G. Foden, 'Blowback Chronicles', The Guardian, 15 September 2001.
53. C. Johnson, *Blowback: The Costs and Consequences of American Empire* (New York: Henry Holt 2000).
54. Idem, 'Q&A: A Conversation with Chalmers Johnson', *California Monthly* 111/1 (2000).
55. P. Beinart,'Back to Front', *The New Republic*, 26 September 2001.
56. R. Scheer, 'CIA's Tracks Lead in Disastrous Circle', *Los Angeles Times*, 17 September 2001.
57. C. Johnson, 'Blowback'. *The Nation* , 15 October 2001.
58. A. Bouzid, 'If the CIA Had Butted Out', *Los Angeles Times*, 21 October 2001.
59. Ibid.
60. C. Johnson, 'Americans Feeling the Effects of Blowback', *Los Angeles Times*, 4 May 2000.
61. Scheer, 'CIA's Tracks' (note 56).
62. M.A. Weaver, 'Blowback', *The Atlantic Magazine*, May 1996
63. B.R. Rubin, 'Arab Islamists in Afghanistan', in John Esposito (ed.), *Political Islam: Revolution, Radicalism, or Reform?* (Boulder, CO: Lynne Rienner 1997).
64. Ibid.
65. Ibid.
66. 'COLD WAR Chat: Barnett Rubin', CNN, 8 March 1999, <http://www.cnn.com/SPECIALS/cold.war/guides/debate/chats/rubin/>.
67. Rubin (note 63).
68. Ibid.
69. Johnson, 'Blowback' (note 57) p.7.
70. Johnson, 'Q&A' (note 54).
71. Johnson, 'Blowback' (note 57) p.11.
72. Beinart (note 55).
73. Ibid.
74. P. Bergen, *Holy War Inc.* (New York: Touchstone 2002) p.235.
75. R. Kaplan, 'The Coming Anarchy', *Atlantic Monthly*, February 1994
76. T. Homer-Dixon, 'On the Threshold; Environmental Changes as Causes of Acute Conflict', *International Security* 16/2 (1991) pp.76–116.
77. D. Deudney, 'Environmental Security A Critique' in D. Deudney and R. Matthews, *Contested Grounds: Security and Conflict in the New Environmental Politics* (Albany, NY: SUNY Press 1999) p. 212.
78. M. Van Creveld, *The Transformation of War* (New York: Free Press 1991).
79. R. Falk, 'World Prisms', *Harvard International Review*, Summer 1999, p.30.
80. R. Mandel, 'Deadly Transfers, National Hypocrasy, and Global Chaos', *Armed Forces and Society* 25/2 (1999) pp.307–27.
81. P. Smith, 'Transnational Terrorism and the al Qaeda Model: Confronting New Realities', *Parameters* 32/2 (2002) p.34.
82. B. Hoffman, 'Terrorism's CEO' (interview with Peter Bergen), *Atlantic Unbound*, <http://www.theatlantic.com/unbound/interviews/int2002-01-09.htm>, 9 January 2002.
83. Rohan Gunaratna, 'Transnational Threats in the Post-Cold War Era', *Jane's Intelligence Review*, 1 January 2001.
84. S. Krasner, 'Sovereignty', *Foreign Policy*, January–February 2001, pp.20–29.
85. T. Friedman, 'Arabs at the Crossroads', *New York Times*, 3 July 2002.
86. W. Raspberry, 'Terrorism's Fertile Fields', *Washington Post*, 21 October 2001, p.21.
87. C. Sennot, 'Driving a Wedge/Bin Laden, The US and Saudi Arabia', *Boston Globe*, 2 March

2002, p.1.
88. S. Rice, 'The Africa Battle', *Washington Post*, 11 December 2001, p.33.
89. B. Crosstte, 'Annan Says Terrorism's Roots Broader than Poverty', *New York Times*, 7 March 2002.
90. P. Fritsch, 'With Pakistan's Schools in Tatters, Madrasahs Spawn Young Warriors', *The Wall Street Journal,* 2 October 2001, p.1.
91. C. Thayer, 'Unity in Adversity', *Asia Week*, 9 November 2001, p.20.
92. *Al Qaeda Training Manual*, <http://www.usdoj.gov/ag/trainingmanual.htm>.
93. R. Marquand, 'The Tenets of Terror', *Christian Science Monitor*, 18 October 2001, p.10.
94. B. Tibi, *The Challenge of Fundamentalism: Political Islam and the New World Disorder* (Berkeley, CA: University of California Press 1998).
95. J. Esposito, 'Political Islam: Beyond the Green Menace', *Current History*, January 1994, p.19.
96. Tibi (note 94)
97. J. Esposito, *The Islamic Threat: Myth or Reality?*, 3rd ed. (New York: Oxford University Press 1999).
98. Ibid. p.13.
99. Tibi (note 94).
100. G.E. Fuller, 'The Future of Political Islam', *Foreign Affairs* 81/2 (2002) pp.48–60.
101. Tibi (note 94) p.43.
102. Ibid p.38.
103. B. Lewis, *What Went Wrong? Western Impact and Middle Eastern Response* (New York: Oxford University Press 2002).
104. Ibid.
105. 'Interview with Mujahid Usamah Bin Ladin', 18 August 2001, <http://www.Fear-Allah.com>.
106. P. Bergen (note 74) p.227.
107. Smith, 'Transnational Terrorism' (note 81) p.36.
108. A. Hourani, *A History of the Arab Peoples* (Cambridge, MA: Belknap Press 1991).
109. Tibi (note 94) p.60
110. A. Higgins, 'Saga Of Dr Zawahri Sheds Light On The Roots Of Al Qaeda Terror', *Wall Street Journal*, 2 July 2002.
111. Ibid.
112. Esposito, 'Political Islam' (note 95).
113. Sennot (note 87).
114. P. Smith, personal communication, June 2002.
115. H. Afifi, letter to the editor, *Egypt Today,* 22 October 2001, <http://www.egypttoday.com/main/fea_caged.htm>.
116. O. Roy, interviewed in J. Burns, 'One Sheik's Mission: Teach Hatred of the West', *New York Times*, 17 December 2001.
117. C. Nwangwu, 'What's Africa Have to do with the Events of September 11', *Counterpunch*, <http://www.counterpunch.com>, 30 September 2001.
118. W. Buckley, Jr, 'Renounce this Modern Islam or Face War', *Los Angeles Times*, 4 October 2001.
119. E. Cohen and W. Kristol, 'Dr West and Mr Bin Laden', *The Weekly Standard*, 17 December 2001, pp.12–13.
120. R. Scheer, 'Falwell should have Listened to the Feminists', *Los Angeles Times*, 25 September 2001.
121. C. Hitchens, 'Of Sin, the Left, and Islamic Fascism', *The Nation*, 24 September 2001.
122. S. Rushdie, 'Yes This Is about Islam', *New York Times*, 2 November 2001.
123. M. Riaz Hassan, 'Islam at the Crossroads', *Pakistan Today*, 14 December 2001, <http://paktoday.com>.
124. P. Hoodbhoy, 'Policy Forum Online: Muslims and the West After September 11', <http://www.nautilus.org/fora/Special-Policy-Forum/43_Hoodbhoy.html>, 18 December 2002.
125. J. Mowbray, 'How They Did It', *National Review*, 23 December 2002.

126. T. Friedman, 'Arab States Must Tell it Straight', *The Guardian*, 22 September 2001, p.11.
127. M. Doran, 'Somebody Else's Civil War', *Foreign Affairs* 81/1 (2002), p.22.
128. R. Brownstein and Robin Wright, 'Toppling of Arab Regimes Called Wider Goal of Terror', *Los Angeles Times*, 5 October 2001.
129 L. Kerr, 'The Mosque to Commerce: Bin Ladin's Special Complaint with the World Trade Center', *Slate*, <http://slate.msn.com>, 28 December 2001.
130. S. Huntington, *The Clash of Civilizations* (New York: Touchstone 1997).
131. E. Said, 'The Clash of Ignorance', *The Nation,* <http://www.thenation.com>, 22 October 2001.
132. A. Acharya, 'Clash of Civilizations? No, of National Interests and Principles', *International Herald Tribune*, 10 January 2002, p.8.
133. S. Singer, 'The Return of History', *Jerusalem Post*, 21 September 2001, p.9A.
134. M.A. el Alem 'New World Order', *Egypt Today*, <http://www.egypttoday.com>, 22 October 2001.
135. 'Terrorism Seeks to Foment 'Clash of Civilizations', *Yomiuri Shinbun*, 30 September 2001, p.1.
136. Ibid.
137. J. Achenbach, 'The Clash', *The Washington Post*, 16 December 2001, p.W17.
138. 'Mullah Omar in His Own Words', *The Guardian*, 26 September 2001.
139. Interview with bin Laden (note 105).
140. Osama bin Laden, 'World Islamic Front's Statement Urging Jihad Against Jews and Crusaders', *al-Quds al Arabi*, 23 February 1998.
141. Ibid.
142. Rieff (note 47).
143. Burns (note 116).
144. Doran (note 127).
145. A. Stone, 'In Poll Islamic World Says Arabs Not Involved in 9/11', *USA Today*, 27 February 2002, p.1.
146. Achenbach (note 137).

Reading Geopolitics Beyond the State: Organisational Discourse in Response to 11 September

CARL T. DAHLMAN and STANLEY D. BRUNN

Introduction

Among the important contributions of critical perspectives on geopolitics is the consideration of actors, social relations and discursive acts that both reflect upon and move well beyond conventional state-centred accounts.[1] Though not new, these perspectives on the discursive and material territorialisation of power help us to better situate conventional state-centric scholarship and practice within its larger social context while including alternative epistemological approaches to understanding geopolitical events. The breadth and depth of this larger social context was apparent in the myriad responses to the terrorist attacks of 11 September 2001 by organisations seeking to mediate and meditate on a geopolitical crisis that threatened international peace. The intent of this essay is to explore the geopolitical content of discourse produced by organisations in response to the events of 11 September, events that include both the horrible terrorist acts themselves and the policy responses of the US government. The purpose of this inquiry should be understood at the outset as an attempt to contemplate the rapidly unfolding events of the days and weeks immediately following the attacks as a period during which diverse and creative responses emerged, however quickly they faded into the current 'war on terrorism'.

Examining the sources of these alternative geopolitical visions leads this essay to its first task, which is to investigate non-governmental organisations (NGOs) as non-state actors in international affairs. In doing so, this essay seeks to contribute to a greater appreciation of non-governmental organisations as sources and vehicles of diverse and possibly alternative geopolitical visions in contrast to the state's more narrow application of security calculus and militarism. The second task of this essay is to identify and apply a methodological approach appropriate to the study of organisations that permits a greater appreciation of their potential for producing geopolitical alternatives to state policies as well as their potential for reproducing statist geopolitics. This essay's third task is to examine the events of 11 September through organisational responses in an effort to illuminate alternative voices and visions of international politics that may yet be more compatible with a world in need of greater imagination, tolerance and justice than offered by state-actors in resolving geopolitical crises.

Organisations, Civil Society and Geopolitics Beyond the State

The attacks of 11 September on the World Trade Center, the Pentagon and United Airlines Flight 93 tragically illustrated the force of political violence in altering the geopolitical priorities of states as well as the geopolitical self-awareness of people with no direct connection to the victims. Beyond those with ties to family or friends lost on that day, millions more in the United States and elsewhere experienced a vertiginous and panicked lifeworld where their understanding of world affairs and their position in it were radically and rapidly remapped. In the United States, the shifting geographical imaginations of the world following the events of 11 September emerged in expressions of rage against Muslims and persons of Middle Eastern descent, patriotic expressions through symbols of national unity, a surge in military volunteerism, continuous media coverage and speculation, mobilisations of material and financial support for victims and families, historical reflections on analogous events in US history, new public interest in the Middle East, Islam and US foreign policy, new opinions and criticisms of US foreign policy, speeches and protests, new legislation altering immigration rules and US foreign activities, changes in mundane activities like air travel, border crossings and bridge traffic, and expanded government surveillance. Each of these acts, however small or personal, engaged geopolitical categories such as security, patriotism, nationalism, militarism, pacifism, humanitarianism and others besides. While the United States soon thereafter executed a military operation in Afghanistan, such conventional understandings of 'geopolitics' should not displace the vast scale of the billions of everyday practices that are equally concerned with and influenced by geopolitical events.

In adopting a broader appreciation of what might constitute the geopolitical, we also gain access to imaginations of politics beyond the state. As the examples above illustrate, geopolitical issues are engaged in many practices besides decisions by the commander in chief. Furthermore, these practices have varied and unexpected geographical dimensions, in both their spatial extent and in their spatial understanding of the world. As Ó Tuathail and Dalby argue, 'each of these different forms of geopolitics has different sites of production, distribution and consumption', each requiring exploration as geopolitical spaces and as spaces of meaning, hemmed in and contextualised by social lifeworlds and with differing relations to state power.[2] Agnew has similarly argued that mainstream geographic thought on international affairs has long been trapped by frames of reference limited to the nation state. This 'territorial trap' is one that containerises social and political life in the mutually exclusive spaces of territorial domesticity, perpetuating a logic of territorial identity and a symmetry in institutional territoriality that undermine a better understanding of the contemporary world and its many unruly, transnational and unbounded phenomena.[3]

Captured perhaps most succinctly under the sign 'critical geopolitics', stepping outside the imposing, conceptual hegemony of state-centric analysis may yield a clearer perspective on the problematic of the state by recognising its constructed and contingent modes in reproducing very particular forms of social power via geopolitical representations and practices. In analysing these modes, Ó Tuathail divides geopolitics into formal, practical, popular and structural modes, each comprising particular versions of politicised geographical knowledge with different relations to the state. Briefly put, formal geopolitics are those representations and practices of the territorial state as explained by the theorist or grand strategist; practical geopolitics, those of everyday statecraft; popular geopolitics, those of mass media or local culture; and structural geopolitics relating to the context of broad trends shaping human thought, economies or cultures.[4]

Searching beyond the state for geopolitics, then, requires the examination of social practices or representations that map power onto space. We would like to expand the field of geopolitical actors and spaces by examining the representations and practices of non-governmental organisations as increasingly important entities in the modern political world. Our particular interest is in those organisations that lie outside the control of the state and the market and which are formed by networks or associations of individuals in society, forming spaces of civil discourse and interaction beyond the state itself. Understood generally as civil society, this sphere of social action is an important social and political space that bears increasing weight on the decisions and even the worldview held by decision makers in government.[5] As non-governmental organisations and social movements, both components of civil society, bring political questions to the public, lobby policy makers or promote new ideas and practices, there is a shift in the structural context of geopolitics. While civil society may not constitute a structural geopolitics itself, as it is far too diverse and incoherent, NGOs are increasingly taking part in sharing the task of governance with conventional government institutions. This 'hollowing out' of the state is a key part of the governance argument, which recognises that centralised and vertically integrated structures are no longer valid operating assumptions of Western democratic states.[6] Some of the organisations that comprise civil society may, therefore, be understood as contributing to a changing structural geopolitics that conditions or influences the terms of statecraft. Indeed, where NGOs execute functions once the provenance of states, the line between state and civil society becomes increasingly blurred.[7]

Non-governmental organisations are not unrelated to the other geopolitical modes identified above. To the extent that certain NGOs have access to or influence over political decision makers and where their agendas may be considered as part of the foreign-policy-making process, they may well be understood as expressing practical geopolitics, that is, contributing to the everyday process of foreign policy making, by providing representations and reflections of the meaning of world events of interest to government. In the United States, but less so in other Western democracies, NGOs have much greater access and ability to influence government either directly, through contact with executive or legislative officers, or indirectly, by access to the news media, disseminating information or via their membership or clientele.[8] For example, Amnesty International has frequently brought attention to geopolitical problems by popularising the stories and perspectives of individuals opposing oppressive regimes, including some regimes allied with the United States, thereby casting far-flung conflicts in terms that contrast sharply with official government representations. In the process of promoting their views and opinions of foreign affairs, NGOs may conversely participate in the production and popularisation of geopolitical visions more or less in line with government intent. Both of these representations and practices promote a type of popular geopolitics, including images, narratives and maps, which are also increasingly independent of mainstream media via the medium of the Internet.[9] In sum, the metaphorical and material spaces of organisations give lie to the idea that they are without politics and affirm that they are important agents in the production of ideational content and the circulation of contemporary global visions and political (re)orderings.[10]

Within the international relations literature, the origins and force-lines of these global visions and ideas also remain contested terrain – whether understood as policy pressures or, more complexly, as intersubjective meanings that underlie communicative and, therefore, practical action.[11] To the extent that organisations may be seen to influence world politics, their recognition as a site worthy of political study is an important development in contemporary political theory. For the purposes of this essay, we follow developments in international relations and geography in taking seriously NGOs in their social and political affectivity.[12] Rather than ignoring interstate relations, this literature calls for a complementary consideration of politics that more fully appreciates the activities of NGOs and associational networks in relation to state actors: 'Organizations are not simply transnational pressure groups, but rather are political actors in their own right.'[13]

A further understanding of organisations as a potential locus of social action emerges from the tremendous literature on civil society. Cast in simple terms, civil society may be understood as a space of associational life beyond the state and market; a sphere of social concern or political action involving networks of individuals, organised to promote particular visions or practices among its members, society or the world. Indeed, discussion over the role of organisations in society and politics today often implicitly assumes the concept of civil society, despite the debate over its conceptual parameters and its explanatory significance.[14] This is due in part to the fact that civil society gives a singular label to the complex web of voluntary associations outside the state and its attendant partisan associations, providing a useful, if not wholly precise, analytical category. In some renditions of the 'civil society argument', as Michael Walzer calls it, civil society comprises associational networks, NGOs, social-movements and grass-roots organisations that may variously promote positions and principles, provide unique services, increase social inclusivity and, importantly, reach across political cleavages in the polity.[15] In this sense, civil society is productive of stronger social ties, ameliorating the danger of political rancour and thereby ultimately strengthening the state. In other conceptualisations of civil society, the horizontal networks and associations provide an effective 'counterweight' to the state by mobilising oppositional politics against the intrusions and abuses of weakly democratic or authoritarian regimes. This understanding of civil society is most closely identified with the late-Soviet social movements in Eastern Europe and the oppositional politics of groups protesting against the practices of the military dictatorships in Latin America.

These competing visions of the relationship between civil society and the state are described by Michael Foley and Bob Edwards as constituting a paradox in which responsive democracies must be strong enough to weather the political process of debate, negotiation and accommodation that evidences strong civil society.[16] On the other hand, unresponsive and weak or undemocratic states are uncompromising in dealing with the positions of associational groupings, which are thereby mobilised towards increasingly anti-governmental, possibly militant, actions. Foley and Edwards argue that the resolution to this paradox is in recognising the relationship of civil society to the political process within the state, thereby putting into relation the political ideas of interests beyond the state with the sovereign functions and organisation of the state itself. In fact, the self-referential nature of sovereignty, the unique equivalences that a state draws between itself and its geopolitical interests, is markedly different from other aspects of governmental authority. On the one hand, in a strong democracy such as the United States, citizens always have the option of voting in the next election against administrations whose foreign policies are considered unjust or unwarranted. On the other hand, there is another option for productively and pre-emptively engaging the state when civil society is strong, as evidenced in NGOs and social movements that promote alternative geopolitical visions.

However, this model of political action, in which elements of civil society influence the state, presents several conceptual problems. First, in examining geopolitical orders, it is necessary to maintain a certain degree of state-centrism, if only because the state remains the primary geopolitical actor in its capacity to enact policy, diplomacy and war. This fact does not run contrary to civil society in particular, but it does suggest that in some areas of political action, sovereignty remains a jealously guarded prerogative of governments. We can find persuasive accounts of this 'selective sovereignty' in work by authors such as Saskia Sassen, who recognise the duality of the globalisation argument in its treatment of state power.[17] To that end, 'a new geography of power', as Sassen terms it, must consider the state's unique role in the geopolitical order as well as its service as a socio-spatial fix for some interests in civil society that seek to access and engage the polity via the state. This latter point is in keeping with the understanding of the paradox of civil society identified by Foley and Edwards, outlined previously, and serves to momentarily stabilise a complex and shifting field of institutional arrangements in the intersection between the goals of civil society and those of states.[18]

Second, and related to the first problem, civil society is hardly unified in its approach to the state or state power. Indeed, large segments of civil society, especially grassroots organisations, local community associations and transitory or informal social movements, may never seek state accommodation of their interests but rather wish to pursue their activities fully beyond the reach of the state. Some religious institutions in the United States offer a clear example of this independence, but the practice is not limited to them. In addition, civil society is ultimately a contested space, in which associational entities like NGOs, religious bodies and social movements often work at cross-purposes.[19] While civil society remains a useful category for describing the sphere of associational and political life outside the state proper, its dimensions and constituent elements remain too diverse to describe in any meaningfully singular way except as a broad theorisation of intra-societal relations beyond the state. This essay, therefore, maintains that NGOs, while elements of civil society and subject to our concepts of it, are not coterminous with civil society. Focusing on

NGOs instead of civil society permits a closer investigation of what Foley and Edwards call the 'nagging empirical questions about the ways in which social power is constituted, distributed and managed in contemporary societies'.[20] In this case, we are interested in how geopolitical alternatives emanating from beyond the state relate to the state in one of its least democratic functions, foreign affairs.

As made clear in the literature on dissident international relations and critical geopolitics, research must continue to examine the construction and maintenance of, as well as resistance to, geopolitical power through alternative sites and actors. On this latter point we wish to further narrow our interest to organisations as producers of discursive formations that seek to limit, extend, qualify or recast geopolitics. As such, the nature of this study is conceptually, methodologically and empirically exploratory – we seek to bring to bear on organisations a critical examination of their explicit and implicit visions of power relations related to territoriality and geopolitics. Rather than examining the state's response to 11 September in isolation, this essay instead investigates organisational responses to this particular geopolitical crisis. These visions, however conventional or radical, provide evidence of the multiple and socially contingent processes that operate beyond the state, seeking to influence its geopolitical goals.[21] In this way, we intend to capture the partiality, particularity and contested nature of space and power, one that resonates well with critical theories of geopolitics and civil society and is well served by the study of organisations. This study further develops methodological applications from critical geopolitics by indexing organisational politics to state geopolitics through discourse that maps ethical, moral and principled positions of the former onto the territorial exercises of the latter. We address the methodological issues associated with the study of organisations and geopolitics in the next section, before examining the responses of select organisations to the attacks of 11 September.

Reading Organisational Geopolitics

Informed by dissident international relations of the late 1980s, critical geopolitics has sought to move beyond the presuppositions of conventional state-centric theory in search of alternative and more satisfactory modes of explanation. These efforts have dwelt largely on the discursive formations of political actors embedded within state institutions and traditions of power contingent on geographical knowledge as well as the study of alternative sites and actors intersecting or opposing state practices.[22] Recent contributions in human geography offer further opportunities for the exploration of social life and geopolitics beyond the state by studying organisations as sites of action that reflect, produce and represent spatiality.[23]

> What is more, organizations are productive of certain meanings rather than others, and in this sense one can select them as candidates through which to view the operation of social power that limits what is thought, as well as what is thought to be possible.[24]

Organisations, therefore, are important, yet often neglected, sites of social power concerned with, attendant upon or in opposition to state practices. As conduits of relevant social interest in world affairs, organisations are also productive discursive sites in the interlocution between the adherents of principled worldviews and the messy political world itself. Organisations present visions of the world as they refract their understanding of and interest in world politics through the lens of their immediate concerns. Among other methodological frames, therefore, it is possible to study organisational discourse as part of 'a methodological program that takes seriously the role of organizations in … the production and reproduction of socio-spatial relations, and the construction of socio-spatial texts and identities'.[25] With relevance to this study, such an approach allows us to ask if geopolitical visions are evident in organisational responses to geopolitical events, specifically, 11 September. Furthermore, we seek to investigate what spatial epistemologies underlie these discursive formations, that is, how geopolitics are represented by NGOs.

To answer these questions we have gathered the press releases and public statements from major NGOs and international NGOs (INGOs) containing their immediate responses to 11 September. Our interest in the responses of organisations during the first days and weeks after 11 September reflects our contention that although such statements were made in the context of overwhelming tragedy and confusion, organisations nevertheless produced geopolitically informed visions and prescriptions designed to produce meaning where none seemed to exist. Organisations were not chosen randomly but were selected by the authors to provide an exploration of a broad spectrum of organisational types and issue orientations found at both the national (US) and international level. It must be recognised, moreover, that any systematic study of the thousands of NGOs in the United States and abroad would require a sampling frame and typological schema that are beyond the purposes of this study. In selecting organisations, the authors chose to include a broad array of organisations reflecting recent geopolitical studies on environmental, humanitarian and development NGOs while adding religious, human rights and economic organisations.[26] While these categories provide a broad range of organisational interests, they do not, and cannot be expected to, reflect the wider range of organisations nor the less formal social movements that are also part of civil society. Instead, they provide an established set of common organisational interest types that are useful for an exploratory study of organisational geopolitics. The selection of organisations for study is discussed in the next section.

Another methodological issue for this study is the use of press releases as objects of textual analysis. Such texts have been usefully analysed in political science, organisational studies and management science as disciplines in which the study of organisations has long formed the basis for social inquiry.[27] We also contend that such public statements are carefully constructed and intentional social acts – organisations use such channels to broadcast their position in an attempt to change the terms and material outcomes of issues of contemporary import. While there is considerable uncertainty regarding the representational process, i.e., the degree to which press releases are measured according to and consensually agreed upon by an organisation's formal or informal membership, we nonetheless recognise the social and political importance of such statements.[28] Put another way, public statements by organisations may or may not accurately represent the segment of society for which the organisation claims to speak, but the statements nevertheless carry social and political affectivity in the public sphere.[29] Furthermore, while it would be useful to study the effect of organisational discourse on government action, this study wishes to first investigate the discourse on its own merits – as geopolitical content – before reducing it to an analysis of cause and effect.

Social research has adopted content analysis for a wide variety of tasks, often focusing on detailed accounts of meaning and action in speech acts. Our scale of analysis, however, is geared toward appreciating the meaning of texts within a wider social – read geopolitical – frame. It is in this mode, what one might call the 'organisational speech act', that we seek to better understand the explicit and implicit political content of organisationally produced discourse relating to geopolitics. More precisely, we are interested in how organisations deploy various representations of geographically articulated power. In conducting this exploratory study of the spatial epistemologies of terrorism and the state among various NGOs, we have thus adopted discourse analysis as a methodological approach that is both systematic and interpretive.[30] Discourse analysis generally seeks to systematically describe a text to elicit the signs, semiotics or pragmatics that give it meaning. However, we eschew a determinist behavioural conceptualisation of content analysis that presumes texts to have direct social or policy effects and argue instead that texts have discursive effects, both social and political, but only in and with the context of their dissemination and reception. For this reason we adopt a critical discourse analysis, which 'is not concerned with language or language use per se, but with the linguistic character of social and cultural processes and structures' and which recognises that discourse is a social practice related to power-relations that cannot be removed from its historical, social and cultural context.[31] So while acknowledging the transmutive and multiple conditions that receptive context, or the condition of readership, gives to discourse, we nevertheless maintain that certain epistemological constructions may be appreciated through systematic interpretations of the text without measuring 'impact' of that discourse. These discursive constructions, then, may be more fully appreciated for their geopolitical content. Critical discourse analysis, or the investigation of language use 'as a form of social practice', is especially well suited for the study of underlying spatial epistemologies in organisations and institutional forms.[32] This is due, in part, to the emphasis of organisational and institutional research undertaken by its proponents.[33]

For our purposes, we employ Barthes' simple distinction between a text's denotative and connotative codes, the former marking a text's explicit meanings and the latter more fully relating a text to its socially contexualised and implied meanings.[34] Beyond the surface or denotative content of organisational statements made in response to 11 September, it is necessary to recognise their connotative meanings, i.e., to read them as texts embedded within and related to larger social and political contexts. In explaining the significance of Barthes' use of the term, Stuart Hall explains:

> Connotative codes are the configuration of meaning which permit a sign to signify, in addition to its denotative reference, other, additional implied meanings. These configurations of meaning are forms of social knowledge, derived from the social practices, the knowledge of institutions, the beliefs and the legitimations that exist in a diffused form within a society, and which order the society's apprehension of the world in terms of dominant meaning-patterns.[35]

By first reading the literal or surface meaning of the texts for their denotative content, a critical or connotative analysis further relates a text to meanings, themes and discursive norms present in the wider social conditions of its production and dissemination, i.e., its context. As such, nearly all the organisational responses to 11 September studied were, on a denotative level, public messages of sympathy and concern with many texts sharing common elements or phrases. For example, CARE released a statement titled 'CARE's Response to America's Tragedy' on 14 September:

> On behalf of our 12,000 staff and the people we serve, CARE expresses its deepest sorrow following the tragic events that took place Tuesday, 11 September, 2001, in New York City and Washington, D.C.

On a connotative level, many statements related the crisis to larger issues and concerns that reflected not only an organisation's primary concerns but tapped into broader issues concerning what the appropriate government response should be or how Americans should personally respond to the events. The Feminist Majority Foundation, for example, found its interests to be very much related to US goals in Afghanistan in their press release dated 18 September 2001 and entitled 'Special Message from the Feminist Majority on the Taliban, Osama bin Laden, and Afghan Women':

> As steps are taken to eliminate terrorists and those who support them in Afghanistan, we must make sure that the lives of women and girls are saved and that the restoration of the rights of women and girls is not marginalized as a side issue. As our government deliberates on the appropriate measures to respond to the heinous acts committed on Sept. 11, we must urge that the plight of Afghan women and girls not be forgotten.

In the next section, we briefly outline the organisations included in our study and discuss their relative positions within civil society and vis-à-vis the state. We then analyse the denotative content of press releases – textual objects put forward as the voice of the organisation – for their representations of the geographical arrangement of power, especially in relation to states, society, individual rights, ethnicity, race, gender, the environment etc. We then turn to an analysis of the geopolitical themes connotatively represented in organisational responses, themes that may be recognised by examining the contextual and embedded particularities of their discursive constructions in relation to states, conflict and society.

Organisational Reponses to 11 September

Many organisations issued formal statements concerning the 11 September attacks and this study cannot capture or represent the diversity of all such discourse. Instead, this study seeks to explore organisations and their discursive productions in relation to geopolitics. The 23 organisations selected for the study reflect a wide variety of organisations and interests and engage in both national and international activities (Figure 1). These organisations, though part of civil society, cannot be considered representative of all of civil society for reasons discussed in the previous section. Instead, we selected rather narrowly from among the wide range of social entities commonly identified as constitutive of civil society in order to explore substantive responses of non-governmental organisations to the 11 September attacks and how critical geopolitics might more fully appreciate their role in the formation of geopolitical visions beyond the

FIGURE 1
ORGANISATION TYPES AND THEIR RESPONSES TO 11 SEPTEMBER 2001

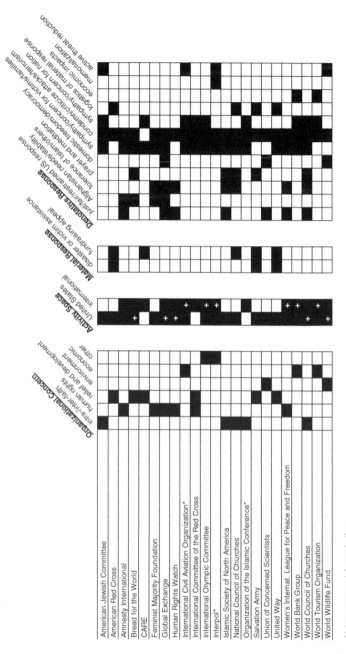

* inter-governmental organizations

+ locational emphasis of activity

state. Likewise, we have selected organisations with highly visible and well-established programmes because of the increased likelihood for public recognition of their message. Such large 'discursive producers', whose authority and influence are substantial, include the American Red Cross, Human Rights Watch and the World Council of Churches. Several other large or well-known organisations, such as the World Wildlife Fund, CARE and the Union of Concerned Scientists, reflecting environmental, humanitarian and professional interests that might not seem relevant to the events of 11 September, nevertheless made substantive comment worth investigating. We have included organisations concerned with commerce and trade activities, such as the World Bank and the International Civil Aviation Organisation, which not only commented on the attacks but also were concerned with the economic effects of the events.

Based on their mission statements or goals, the organisations under study may be classified according to six categories (see Figure 1): intra- and inter-faith associations; human rights advocates; relief and development work; environmental advocacy; trade and commerce; and other. The first category comprises organisations pursuing faith-based interests, ecumenical co-operation or inter-faith dialogue. Human rights advocacy organisations constitute the second category and are generally concerned with the improvement of the human condition, especially related to basic human freedoms and security and equal rights, as well as peace, social justice and tolerance. It should be noted that some religious organisations included in the first category, like the National Council of Churches and the World Council of Churches, also advocate for human rights as part of their work. The third category includes organisations whose primary goal is to provide relief for those in need or to promote the social and economic improvement of life in developing regions. The scope and range of relief and development organisations ranges from short-term domestic disaster response assistance, such as provided by the American Red Cross, to international hunger relief and food aid, e.g., CARE. A fourth group includes environmental advocacy groups: for some organisations, such as the Union of Concerned Scientists, environmental issues also include issues of national security. Economic organisations, such as the World Bank and the World Tourism Organisation, form the fifth category of organisations and are generally interested in promoting trade and commerce, especially on a global level. While some organisations, such as Global Exchange, are concerned with the effects of globalisation and trade, they address these issues as human rights issues and are therefore included in the second category. The sixth category includes organisations that do not easily fit into the five main areas of organisational concern, such as the International Olympic Committee and Interpol (the inter-governmental organisation of policing).

The organisations under study have also been classified according to their activity space (Figure 1), defined as either the 'United States' or 'international', where the former focus primarily on domestic agendas and the latter operate more transnationally. The organisations included maintain either a primary (national agenda) or secondary (membership or donor support) operational relationship to the United States. While it would be very useful to examine the responses of organisations with non-US national agendas, we have chosen a more narrow focus for conceptual reasons, i.e., we are especially interested in organisations related to the United States, either through their membership and support base, their relations with policy-makers or as their activity area. Finally, the texts of the press releases and statements were analysed for their semantic (word-level), thematic (phrase or sentence level) and discursive (textual and inter-textual level) content.[36] Semantic and thematic content were documented through the construction of word and theme lists, produced inductively through word searches in the texts themselves and which were used to analyse the denotative content of organisational responses. The connotative content was determined through discursive or inter-textual interpretation, i.e., comparing the concerns and issues raised in the text with contemporaneous discourse circulated by the media and public officials.

Produced during a period of enormous confusion and upset, the organisational responses to the events of 11 September reflected common elements within the dominant discourse of government statements and media speculation. Nevertheless, the days immediately following the attacks were ones in which the connections to bin Laden and Al Qaeda were either unknown or were yet to be confirmed and the 'war on terrorism' was yet to be formed. During this period, there were, however, many organisations seeking to mobilise material assistance to the sites in New York, Washington, DC and rural western Pennsylvania while others focused on calming the public and promoting their goals in the policies and actions that the government would surely take in the weeks that followed. In reading their responses, then, we can see something of the uncertainty and divergence present during a geopolitical crisis. The themes emerging from these 'surface' readings are examined below, in order of their prevalence or 'textual weight' among the texts studied. The rest of this section, therefore, describes the denotative content of the organisational responses to 11 September and is then followed by a section analysing the connotative or discursive content of the organisational texts.

Sympathy and Condemnation

As mentioned above, the denotative reading of the texts yielded remarkable similarities in the content and tone of organisational responses. Most organisations expressed sympathy for the victims, their families or the nation and used sharply critical language in describing or condemning the attacks. These concerns were uniformly scripted at the beginning of the responses and worded in sympathetic tones that also employed emotive terms to denote 'shock', 'horror', 'tragedy', 'anger', 'sad[ness]' or 'sorrow'. The attacks themselves were described in superlative criticism: 'heinous crimes', 'brutal attacks', 'crimes against all humanity', 'horrific', 'cruel', 'appall[ing]', 'horrendous', 'deliberate', 'catastroph[ic]' or 'terrible'. Together, the expressions of sympathy and condemnation generally denoted an organisational sense of injustice, thus eliciting from the organisations common thematic concerns of criminality: justice, culpability and punishment. Amnesty International's response was indicative of many organisations in stating its 'grief and solidarity with the victims of the 11 September atrocities and their families. The perpetrators of those heinous crimes must be brought justice'. CARE, however, was unique in its reserved description of the attacks as 'tragic events', but appeared to reflect more an organisational concentration on sympathy for victims and families of victims of the attacks than on justice. While most organisations criticised the attacks, not all expressly denoted sympathy for victims and families but rather focused on logistical issues of assistance (American Red Cross and Salvation Army); calling for restraint and justice in the US response (Feminist Majority Foundation, Global Exchange, Human Rights Watch, Union of Concerned Scientists); or relating other issues to the attacks (World Tourism Organisation and World Wildlife Fund). Common expressions of sympathy for survivors and condemnation of the attacks gave way, however, to divergent visions of the most appropriate response.

National Action and Restraint

Perhaps the most pronounced distinction among the organisational responses was the contrasting themes of what the reaction ought to be, especially in terms of the US government's reaction. As the second most pronounced denotative theme, organisations generally favoured either a restrained and non-violent response or a punitive and militarised response to the attacks of 11 September. Furthermore, organisational responses on this theme were generally consistent with their organisation's primary goals. Thus, organisations concerned with social justice – especially inter-faith dialogue, human rights and relief and development – were also vocal in seeking a US response that would promote 'justice', 'fairness', 'restraint' or 'non-violence' (Amnesty International, Global Exchange, Human Rights Watch, Islamic Society of North America, Union of Concerned Scientists, Women's International League for Peace and

Freedom and the World Council of Churches). These organisations also called for domestic 'tolerance', especially toward Muslims (joined by Feminist Majority Foundation and the National Council of Churches) and some were, within days of the attacks, focusing on the needs of innocent Afghanis who would suffer in a US war on the Taliban (Amnesty International, Bread for the World, Feminist Majority Foundation and Global Exchange). Faith-based organisations (except the American Jewish Congress and the Organisation of the Islamic Conference) called for reflection, meditation and prayer in seeking a just and peaceful response. Three organisations further identified the need to maintain US domestic freedoms, civil rights and democratic institutions over and against any government response to the attack that might be seen to limit these freedoms (Global Exchange, Union of Concerned Scientists and World Wildlife Fund).

In contrast to organisations espousing social justice in the reaction to the attacks, several organisations supported an active US or international response to 'eradicate' or 'punish' those responsible for the attacks. Each of these organisational responses was semantically and thematically unique yet they shared a common concern for state security in response to terrorism. In perhaps the most belligerent response among the organisations studied, the American Jewish Council called the events 'an act of war' and a 'day of infamy' necessitating that 'all Americans must unite behind our government and fully support any action taken to respond to the destruction'. The AJC further stated that they 'will support fully the United States government in using any and all measures at its disposal to punish those individuals, groups and any countries responsible'. Interpol was less forceful in its response, which called for international police co-operation to 'bring the perpetrators to justice'. Likewise, the International Civil Aviation Organisation, which was particularly concerned with the use of civilian aircraft as weapons, called for 'all nations to join forces in eradicating this new threat to our global society'. Finally, the World Wildlife Fund made clear its support for 'the effort of President Bush and the Congress to mobilise our national response' to the 'national security situation' while objecting to oil exploration in the Arctic National Wildlife Refuge as a means of promoting national security.

Neutrality and Neutralisation

Several other themes were identified in the organisational responses that indicated more geopolitically neutral concerns than the immediate US or international reactions. Especially prominent were the organisations expressing only sympathy and/or condemnation, such as CARE, International Committee of the Red Cross, International Olympic

Committee and Organisation of the Islamic Conference. It might be possible to interpret such neutrality as an indication of an organisation's desire to avoid statements that might politicise their mission (International Committee of the Red Cross and CARE) or alienate their membership/clientele (International Olympic Committee and Organisation of the Islamic Conference). It might be necessary for the International Committee of the Red Cross, whose mission includes monitoring and publicising violations of international humanitarian law, to reserve any comment beyond sympathy in order to maintain an unbiased and thus valuable position in international politics. Organisations such as the American Red Cross and United Way that sought to neutralise the immediate trauma and suffering of the attacks also maintained relative neutrality in their formal statements. These groups – including the National Council of Churches and the Salvation Army – focused on themes directly associated with the logistics of the material responses such as fund-raising or relief efforts to benefit the victims and their families. The American Red Cross also sought to counsel the public on dealing with emotional and psychological trauma, while other organisations additionally promoted prayer or meditation in response to the attacks.

In summary, organisational responses to the events of 11 September most clearly reflected the widely held concern for victims and their families as well as shock or outrage over the attacks, but were rarely limited to expressions of sympathy and condemnation. Instead, many organisations expressed the need for national action in either humanitarian or militaristic terms, therein reflecting the core interests or goals of the organisation. Other organisations expressed the need for governmental restraint in seeking justice that was appropriate either to domestic expectations of freedoms and protections or to international legal norms in seeking military solutions. Still other organisations encouraged peaceful or multilateral responses to the attacks, while others withheld any statements beyond condolence and sympathy. The divergent content found in a denotative reading of organisational responses to 11 September is giving further significance in a connotative reading of the texts as described next.

Organisations and Geopolitical Visions

In compiling semantic and thematic evidence presented in the organisational responses to 11 September, the previous section outlined the denotative or explicit content of those texts. In this section, the emphasis is on the inter-textual interpretation of the press releases, i.e., drawing from their semantic and thematic content to further relate each organisational response to larger discursive framings. The significance of this exercise is not to describe NGOs or civil society per se but to explore the manner in which organisations participate in the circulation of geopolitical narratives and categories. In fact, the identification of multiple and competing geopolitical visions among organisations establishes this 'space beyond the state' as a social and political realm complementary to the state yet at same time one that cannot be collapsed into the state or satisfactorily explained by state-centred political theory. We identify three significant discursive themes within the organisational responses to 11 September that relate to our larger research question concerning how organisations relate to geopolitical events: security–terrorism, nationalisation–universalisation and historicisation. Among these themes, organisations espoused varying positions and reformulations of important geopolitical categories which we discuss further in the last section.

Security and Terrorism

Many of the organisations in the study used the term 'security' in its conventional geopolitical connotation to describe the events of 11 September, i.e., the attacks constituted a threat to the nation state. The significant consequence of conventional accounts of security is that they view threats to a state's internal sovereign power as sufficient justification for exercising self-interested foreign policy, namely military action. However, not all organisations employing the term discuss its implicit meaning and significance while other organisations discussed national security in other terms. For example, the World Wildlife Fund referred to the 'gravity of the national security situation' in making relevant its agenda on national energy policy at a time of 'national need'. The American Jewish Committee, on the other hand, also invoked national security when it wrote: 'This act of war today is a rallying call for Americans to unite, to come together as never before to confront the scourge of international terrorism that challenges our nation and the democratic way of life.'[37]

The International Civil Aviation Organisation employed the term narrowly in relation to aviation security, part of its expressed agenda, and more generally in calling for 'all nations to join forces in eradicating this new threat to global society'. More overtly, the Feminist Majority Foundation drew a connection between the Taliban's 'gender apartheid' and 'global security and our national security': 'The link between the liberation of Afghan women and girls from the terrorist Taliban militia and preservation of democracy and freedom in America and worldwide has never been clearer.'[38]

Several organisations chose to redefine, but not reject, security in attempting to prompt government action. As mentioned before, the World

Wildlife Fund used the term as part of their objection to congressional haste in opening up the Arctic Wildlife Refuge for oil exploration – they redefined security as environmental and ecological rather than narrowly related to US dependence on foreign oil supplies. The Union of Concerned Scientists also expanded the definition of security as one that could not sustain narrow, unilateral, US military action but rather required continued multilateral institution building. Put another way, the organisation sought to limit the exceptionalism of US security rhetoric by describing a vision for a larger, international response to terrorism that provided security for civilian life globally.

More prevalent among organisations, however, was the use of the term 'terrorism' to connote the absence of security, i.e., as a both global and national threat. This was semantically conveyed in the denotative content of the responses by which some organisations used the more cautious term 'attacks' while others deployed the term 'terrorism'. While the dominant US media quickly labeled the attacks as terrorism, there remains conceptual debate as to what constitutes terrorism and whether the term maintains any stable or meaningful significance except as a connotation for threats to national security that also carry racist or ethnocentric bias.[39] Two organisations, Global Exchange and Human Rights Watch, addressed the meaning of the term 'terrorism' directly in their statements immediately following the attacks. Though Global Exchange described the events of 11 September as 'terrorist attacks' they criticised the administration's use of those attacks 'as pretext for curtailing civil liberties', stating further that 'if we surrender our freedoms, we have fallen into the attackers' trap'. In this case, the text of Global Exchange, which calls for peace and reconciliation rather than retaliation, would appear to employ the term 'terrorist' to forestall backlash against their larger critique of US foreign policy. Human Rights Watch described the 'cruel attacks' as 'an assault not merely on one nation or one people, but on principles of respect for civilian life cherished by all people'. Moreover, the organisation directly rejected the geopolitical response that the term 'terrorism' portends:

> There are people and governments in the world who believe that in the struggle against terrorism, ends always justify means. But that is also the logic of terrorism. Whatever the response to this outrage, it must not validate that logic. Rather it must uphold the principles that came under attack yesterday, respecting innocent life and international law. That is the way to deny the perpetrators of this crime their ultimate victory.[40]

This response, which rejects the categorisation of terrorism as a consummate threat to national security but rather as a crime to be brought before justice, denies the justification for military response that 'security threats' discursively imply. Human Rights Watch, in fact, draws a moral equivalence between US military action against 'states that harbor terrorists' and terrorism itself: 'People committed to justice and law and human rights must never descend to the level of the perpetrators of such acts.' This vision of a global civil life 'beyond the state' is distinctly opposed to 'national security interests' which pursue unilateral action in narrow self-defense, yet it is also a vision that demands that acts of terror be met with justice. The question of justice, however, requires both a definition of crime and of the body injured, issues more easily identifiable in the discursive formation of national as opposed to universal rights, which we turn to next.

Nationalisation and Universalisation

Written within hours or days of the attacks, organisations responded in markedly different fashion in terms of defining the injured party. While the actual immediate victims were individuals and their families or friends, the events of 11 September were discursively constructed as a distinctly national attack as opposed to a crime against individuals or the state. The nationalisation of harm connotatively incorporates national security and the narrative structure of sovereign rights and self-defense, i.e., the justification of militarised response within the inter-state system according to the doctrine *salus populi suprema lex* or 'the supreme law in the health and security of the people'.[41] This principle is an intrinsic component in *raison d'état* yet its unlimited scope is at times checked by international law, which attempts to limit the expansive pursuit of state self-interest in the larger interest of international society. Thus, appeals to universal rights or morals are frequently used to challenge state action by bringing the notion of individual harm back in; by citing, for example, military and police exercises that infringe on the civil liberties of individuals without just cause. Human rights, therefore, comprise an important dimension of universalist or internationalist precepts that seek not to remove the state but to redefine state action in keeping with universal individual rights. Within their responses to 11 September, organisations discursively constructed the attacks in either nationalised or universalised terms. The importance of this discursive difference, therefore, lies in the potential for organisations to act either as a green light to state action on behalf of a 'national interest' or as a source of alternative geopolitical principles that affirm geopolitical visions beyond the state.

Organisational responses to the attacks frequently made reference to the 'national tragedy' or crisis that had befallen the United States (Figure 1). Others described the need to unify as 'Americans' or to support 'our government' in responding to the attacks – as was present in the responses from organisations like the American Jewish Committee and the Islamic Society of North America with the former labeling the attacks an act of war and the latter calling for swift apprehension and punishment of the perpetrators. The World Council of Churches and the Organisation of the Islamic Conference both described the events as attacks on national sites and expressed sympathy to the US president and people, thereby nationalising the victim as government, citizens and places. The manner in which organisations incorporated nationalising or universalising themes in their statements was not consistent with their positions on security and terrorism, however, nor even with their expressed preferences for a US reaction. For example, Global Exchange and the World Council of Churches expressed nationalising themes in their responses, the former as national freedoms and the latter as national sympathy, yet both explicitly questioned the value or morality of a military response.

Discursive constructions that nationalise the victim are significant as mechanisms that situate the crisis at a particular scale and thus imply that the appropriate response must come from the complementary authority, i.e., the state. This 'national order of things' would appear to invalidate responses emerging from outside the state and its institutions.[42] Moreover, as an expression of territorial identity, nationalisation cannot be removed from the emotive and binding ties that emanated so forcefully in the days and weeks following the attacks. The highly visible and public response to the attacks incorporated nationalistic and patriotic themes, especially the iconic ubiquity of the flag, which discursively constructed the attacks as one against the national body, thus underwriting the perpetuation of events as a security crisis requiring a military response. The implicit and explicit nationalisation of the attacks also furthered the exceptionalist rendering of the attacks as a responsibility of the US alone. Although the attacks incurred high death tolls for non-US citizens and prompted strong international signs of support, the United States proceeded in its war on terrorism without the coalition building first promised by President Bush.

Some organisations, however, embraced a decidedly internationalist position, encouraging the United States to show restraint in its response and to pursue the attackers through international law (Figure 1). Most calls for a restrained US response came from organisations normally engaged in human rights or in humanitarian relief—organisations whose basic philosophies incorporate concepts of universal human rights or needs. The Women's International League for Peace and Freedom expressed in ways similar to Amnesty International, Global Exchange and Human Rights Watch an alternative definition of security by calling for 'restraint and non-violence': 'Our deepest beliefs hold that true security can only be rooted in social justice and strengthening the domestic and international rule of law.'[43]

The International Committee of the Red Cross, although issuing a relatively neutral statement in response to the attacks, incorporated a universalising discourse of events stating that 'such attacks negate the most basic principles of humanity'.[44] Likewise, in redefining the concept of security, the Union of Concerned Scientists also rejected the exceptionalism that marks nationalised responses to the attacks:

> American unilateralism must give way. As former President George H.W. Bush put it in a September 13 speech in Boston, the terrorist attacks should 'erase the concept that America can somehow go it alone in the fight against terrorism, or in anything else for that matter'.[45]

One year later, the G.W. Bush administration has proven its interest in pursuing a very weak form of international or multilateral support, one widely seen as simple unilateralism, in its war on terrorism.

Historicisation

In addition to the dominant discursive elements of security, terrorism, nationalisation and universalisation, several minor thematic issues were identified in the texts of organisational responses to 11 September. These are here remarked upon briefly, although their significance and interest is much larger. First, the historicisation of the events of 11 September marked an important distinction between organisational responses. While most organisations discussed the attacks with little historicisation, i.e., in terms bound very closely to the present and the near future, a few organisations situated the attacks in more explicitly historicised narrative. The Feminist Majority Foundation, which had long opposed the Taliban's treatment of women and girls, historicised the attacks as the outcome of Afghanistan's oppression left unchecked by the international community. The textual effect of linking the Taliban's gender policies to bin Laden's terrorism was greater than equating gender oppression with terrorism, it also equated gender oppression in Afghanistan with 'democracy and freedom in America'.

Although different than historicising the causes of the attacks, several organisations portrayed the attacks through a putative equivalence in US history, namely the attacks on Pearl Harbor. The discursive effect of the Pearl Harbor narrative was simple – it drew upon a long-standing notion that attacks on the American 'way of life' give unique exception to the popularity of isolationism. The American Jewish Committee made the equation clear when it described 11 September as 'this century's day of infamy'. The National Council of Churches issued a similar representation of the events as the 'worst attack on US territory since Pearl Harbor, [for which] we must turn our eyes to the God of us all'. The balance of the NCC's response, however, was more deeply meditative and reflective, in which it cautioned against the kind of rush to judgement that took place after the Oklahoma City bombing and encouraging prayer and practical assistance for the victims.

Perhaps more significant is the general lack of any historical context to the attacks in most organisational responses. Given the almost immediate and fast-moving public suspicion of bin Laden on the basis of extant geopolitical narratives circulated by the government and mainstream media, it is perhaps not surprising that organisations were unable or unwilling to provide further context to the events. This may be due, in part, to the shock at both the enormity of the attacks but also the method and targets, which seemed impossible given the US sense of security. The statement from Bread for the World contained a letter from a Rwandan clergyman that captured this sense of invulnerability: 'It is hard to understand why terrorists decided to kill innocent children and adults instead of trying to find a peaceful solution to their wants! It is hard to understand why it happened in important places where security is high'. In similar ways, most organisations represented the attacks as events out of place and out of time, events for which few domestic narratives could provide adequate explanation and thus why appeals to historical analogy were especially prevalent in the media. In general, however, organisations maintained their operational worldview, i.e., those promoting humanitarianism and human rights were concerned to limit additional loss of innocent or civilian life while those with narrowly economic agendas were more concerned with the impacts on commercial activity, including global trade and tourism (as voiced by the World Bank and World Tourism Organisation, respectively). In this way, organisations represented the attacks as contemporaneous with their interests, as well as those of society. The effect is nevertheless powerful in that organisations partially dissolved the confusion surrounding the attacks by placing the events within existing narrative frameworks and organisational concerns.

In summary, connotative readings of the organisational responses to the events of 11 September elicit a complex picture both of world politics and of organisations in relation to geopolitical events. Indeed, the divergent ends to which concepts like security and terrorism were employed in these texts illustrate this point. Not only did organisations seek to alter the meanings of the terms, but they sought to pursue and promote policy alternatives based, at least in part, on their interpretation of these concepts. Similarly, the manner in which some organisations nationalised the attacks of 11 September was at odds with those organisations that favoured internationalist or universalist understandings of the attacks and the actions the US should take in response, including concern over such issues as human rights, international law or multilateral coalition building. Finally, the use of historical analogy provided yet another dimension to organisational responses in their attempt to bring the significance of the events into focus. Most clear, however, is the diversity of meanings and geopolitical visions expressed by organisational responses to the events of 11 September. These visions of geopolitics vary widely: ranging from hawkish to dovish and unilateralist to universalist. Some organisations largely reflect goals in terms perhaps no different than the State Department, especially those focusing on security and military engagement. Others reflect more idealist positions, emphasising the need to promote diplomatic solutions while protecting human rights. Between these position are many variations, including those concerned primarily with inter-cultural tolerance on the domestic scene to those seeking justice within the terms of human rights and international law. Put another way, there are no obvious trends that emerge from this exploratory study of organisational geopolitics. Rather, there are common themes or dimensions that can be identified from the many unique and particular geopolitical visions expressed by organisations. This diversity of geopolitical visions confirm our contention that organisations in civil society are productive non-state actors in producing alternative, as well as reproducing dominant, geopolitical visions.

Conclusion

In this study, we have endeavoured to explore the geopolitical visions between various organisations in civil society. The results point to the potential for a greater appreciation of organisations as contentious sites through which circulate multiple and competing geopolitical discourses on the right role of both society and state. Reading organisations in this way makes clear the significance of geopolitical codes for organisations working in myriad areas of national and transnational public life. Likewise, the trenchant and particular worldviews expressed by these organisations serve to both reproduce and challenge state-centric geopolitical narratives that otherwise present an apparently logical world order through concepts such as nation and security as well as historicised frames of reference.[46] While we did not measure the discursive effect of organisations on state policy or popular discourse, we can begin to better appreciate the potential significance of organisations in world politics. That is, studying narrow cause and effect relationships between organisations and state-actors is possible, but would require a much more limited conceptualisation of how organisational discourse frames geopolitical events than is present in our findings.[47] Through a broader appreciation of organisational and geopolitical discourse, it is possible to recognise how frames of reference become important heuristic devices through which policy makers and the public may recast events and potential responses in pursuit of practical agendas and world-ordering epistemologies.

In reading the events of 11 September, organisations clearly responded through an examination of their organisational interests but necessarily represented those interests in relation to extant and emergent geopolitical narratives of the crisis. In the hours and days during which these responses were written – a time when many felt confused or unable to express a reaction – these organisations made clear and articulate statements that quickly went beyond mere condolence to pursue relevant issues according to their worldview, principled outlook or institutional context. Despite the distillation of common themes identified above, the different valences and inflections in organisational response invoked both explicit and implicit geopolitical codes. In recognising the varied and even contradictory worldviews expressed by the organisations studied, we find that they occupy, indeed create, a contentious site of political difference beyond the state.[48] Moreover, it is a potential site of geopolitical difference that is complementary to both civilian life and state-interests yet irreducible to either.

Indeed, if organisations have a geopolitical role then it must include the mediation of events – to create windows on the world through which events are seen from the particular concerns of non-state actors.[49] Furthermore, as there is no necessary or automatic relationship between organisations and the state, non-statist worldviews may variously support or critique, enlarge or narrow and adopt or refuse statist discourse and action. That organisations occupy a contested political space complementary to statist geopolitical space also marks a society's openness to alternative geopolitical visions. In recognising civil society as such, further research might productively consider its capacity to provide anti-geopolitical positions that disturb and disrupt statist narratives.[50] In doing so, we may begin to more fully appreciate organisations in civil society as producing, critiquing and consuming geopolitics thereby forming a significant space 'beyond the state' in which to situate retrenched, reformist or revolutionary movements.

Furthermore, organisations are not merely discursive agents, but may also mobilise material efforts to mediate the situation on the ground.[51] The contribution of money, time, material aid and even blood mark significant forms of redistribution in society that do not conform to state or market institutions. Organisational 'interventions' may even be understood as alternative geopolitical actions that involve complex relations between organisations, states and society. This is especially true of humanitarian relief organisations and other non-governmental organisations (NGOs) for which an extensive literature has emerged gauging the political and geopolitical significance of their material actions.[52] As was evident following the attacks, the material responses of organisations in dealing with the needs of survivors not only confirmed the importance of some segments of civil society in neutralising geopolitical crises but these efforts also gave rise to a national and international space between contributors and individuals-in-need, but one only partially mediated by the state. While such activities importantly address very real human needs, we must not lose sight of the geopolitical meaning that concepts such as 'pulling together' and 'uniting' convey, indexed as they are to nationalistic, patriotic or humanitarian socio-spatial narratives. It is in such times and spaces, as much as in daily life, that political identity is defined or redefined.

In its function as both a complementary and alternative space of political action, geographers might more usefully employ organisations and their discourse as phenomena that incorporate contextuality and contingency in the analysis of geopolitics. This article has investigated how organisations respond textually to specific geopolitical events – further research could examine more closely the material or textual responses of organisations to other geopolitical events. Future research could also include in-depth studies of specific organisations to examine the spatial epistemologies underlying their activities and their scalar mobility in responding to different geopolitical events, providing some sense of how organisations must flex and adapt to the particularities of different events. As organisations are increasingly used by states in responding to crises, the boundary between them will become increasingly blurred, begging the question of how principled political agendas are altered by such arrangements. Finally, the intersection of state security-interests and organisational activities – especially transnational activist networks – might yield valuable conclusions about how such organisations are viewed by different states. Perhaps most importantly, a geographical focus on organisations in civil society permits the development of critical inquiry into alternative spaces of geopolitical action as well as an expansion of what might be termed geopolitical society.

NOTES

1. See, for example, the collection edited by G. Ó Tuathail and S. Dalby, *Rethinking Geopolitics* (New York: Routledge 1998).
2. Ibid. pp.4–5.
3. John Agnew, *Geopolitics: Re-visioning World Politics* (New York: Routledge 1998) pp.49–52.
4. G. Ó Tuathail, 'Understanding Critical Geopolitics: Geopolitics and Risk Security' in C.S. Gray and G. Sloan (eds), *Geopolitics, Geography and Strategy* (London: Frank Cass 1999) pp.107–24.

5. W.F. Fisher, 'Doing Good? The Politics and Antipolitics of NGO Practices', *Annual Review of Anthropology* 26 (1997) pp.439–64.
6. R.A.W. Rhodes, *Understanding Governance: Policy Networks, Governance, Reflexivity and Accountability* (Buckingham: Open University Press 1997); O. Young, *Governance in World Affairs* (Ithaca, NY: Cornell University Press 1999); P. Wapner, 'Politics Beyond the State: Environmental Activism and World Civic Politics', *World Politics* 47/3 (1995) pp.311–41.
7. Fisher (note 5).
8. T. Risse-Kappen, 'Public Opinion, Domestic Structure and Foreign Policy in Liberal Democracies', *World Politics* 43/4 (1991) pp.479–512.
9. C. Warkentin and K. Mingst, 'International Institutions, the State, and Global Civil Society in the Age of the World Wide Web', *Global Governance* 6/2 (2000) pp.237–57; S. Sassen, 'A New Geogaphy of Power?', <http://www.globalpolicy.org/nations/sassen.htm>.
10. Miklós Marschall, 'From States to People: Civil Society and Its Role in Governance', *Civil Society at the Millenium* (West Hartford: Kumarian 1999).
11. This includes an enormous area of scholarship in International Relations of which some interesting examples include Risse-Kappen (note 8); D. Campbell, *Writing Security: United States Foreign Policy and the Politics of Identity* (Manchester: Manchester University Press 1992) p.12; A. Bieler, 'Questioning Cognitivism and Constructivism in IR Theory: Reflections on the Material Structure of Ideas', *Politics* 21/2 (2001) pp.93–101.
12. Wapner (note 6); L. Gordenker and T.G. Weiss, 'Devolving Responsibilities: A framework for analyzing NGOs and services', *Third World Quarterly* 18/3 (1997) pp.443–56; M. Price, 'Nongovernmental Organizations on the Geopolitical Front Line', in G.J. Demko and W.B. Wood (eds), *Reordering the World: Geopolitical Perspectives on the 21st Century*, 2nd ed. (Boulder, CO: Westview Press 1999) pp.260–78; V.J.Del Casino, A.J. Grimes, S.P. Hanna, and J.P. Jones III, 'Methodological Frameworks for the Geography of Organizations', *Geoforum* 31/4 (2000) pp.523–38.
13. Wapner (note 6) p.312.
14. For a useful analysis of conceptual problems with two main approaches to civil society, see M. Foley and B. Edwards, 'The Paradox of Civil Society', *Journal of Democracy* 7/3 (1996) pp.38–52; J.L. Cohen and A.Arato, *Civil Society and Political Theory* (Cambridge, MA: MIT Press 1992).
15. On the 'civil society argument', see M. Walzer, 'The Civil Society Argument', in C. Mouffe (ed.), *Dimensions of Radical Democracy: Pluralism, Citizenship, Community* (London: Verso 1992) pp.87–108.
16. Foley and Edwards (note 14) p.48.
17. S. Sassen, *Globalization and its Discontents: Essays on the New Mobility of People and Money* (New York: New Press 1999); Warkentin and Mingst (note 9).
18. Foley and Edwards (note 14).
19. C. McIlwaine, 'Civil Society and Development Geography', *Progress in Human Geography* 22/3 (1998) pp.145–24.
20. Foley and Edwards (note 14) p.49.
21. Ó Tuathail and Dalby (note 1).
22. G. Ó Tuathail, *Critical Geopolitics: The Politics of Writing Global Space* (Minneapolis: University of Minnesota Press 1996); P. Routledge, 'Going Globile: Spatiality, Embodiment, and Media-tion in the Zapatista Insurgency' in G. Ó Tuathail and Dalby (note 1) pp.240-60.
23. Del Casino et al. (note 12).
24. Ibid. p.526.
25. Ibid. p.535; see also S. Brunn, 'The Views of Small States: A Content Analysis of 1995 UN Speeches', *Geopolitics* 4/1 (1999) pp.17–33.
26. Price (note 12); N. Deakin, *In Search of Civil Society* (New York: Palgrave 2001).
27. Del Casino et al. (note 12).
28. Marschall (note 10).
29. Risse-Kappen (note 8).
30. S. Titscher, M. Meyer, R. Wodak and E. Vetter, *Methods of Text and Discourse Analysis* (London: Sage 2000).

31. Ibid. p.146.
32. Ibid. p.147.
33. R. Fowler et al., *Language and Control* (London: Routledge 1979); M. Foucault, *The Archaeology of Knowledge and the Discourse on Language* (London: Tavistock 1972); M. Foucault, 'Governmentality', in G. Burchell, C. Gordon and P. Miller (eds), *The Foucault Effect: Studies in Governmentality* (London: Harvester Wheatsheaf 1991) pp.87–104.
34. R. Barthes, *S/Z* (New York: Hill and Wang 1974) p.62.
35. S. Hall, 'The Determinations of the News Photographs', in S. Cohen and J. Young (eds) *The Manufacture of the News: A Reader* (Beverly Hills: Sage 1973) p.176.
36. Titscher et al. (note 30) pp.147–54.
37. American Jewish Committee, 'American Jewish Committee Confident in President Bush's Leadership to Confront Terrorism', press release, 11 September 2001.
38. Feminist Majority Foundation, 'Special Message from the Feminist Majority on The Taliban, Osama Bin Laden, and Afghan Women', press release, 18 September 2001.
39. Consider, for example, the cogent argument in J. Sidaway, 'Geopolitics, Geography, and "Terrorism" in the Middle East', *Environmental and Planning D: Society and Space* 12 (1994) pp.357–72.
40. Human Rights Watch, 'Human Rights Watch Response to Attacks on the U.S.: Civilian Must Be Respected', press release, 12 September 2001.
41. G. Evans and J. Newnham, *The Penguin Dictionary of International Relations* (Middlesex: Penguin 1998) p.485.
42. L.H. Malkki, *Purity and Exile: Violence, Memory and National Cosmology among Hutu Refugees in Tanzania* (Chicago, IL: University of Chicago Press 1995).
43. Women's International League for Peace and Freedom, 'Statement from WILPF', press release, 11 September 2001.
44. International Committee of the Red Cross, 'United States: ICRC Condemns Attacks', press release, 11 September 2001.
45. Union of Concerned Scientists, 'UCS Statement on the Response to the Terrorist Attack of September 11, 2001', press release, 27 September 2001.
46. Campbell (note 11) pp.6–8.
47. Risse-Kappen (note 8).
48. Campbell (note 11); Deakin (note26); Marschall (note 10); McIlwaine (note 19).
49. G. Picco et al., *Crossing the Divide: Dialogue among Civilizations* (South Orange, NJ: Seton Hall 2001).
50. See especially the discussion of the 'anti-geopolitical eye' in Ó Tuathail, *Critical Geopolitics* (note 22) p.221.
51. Price (note 12).
52. Ibid., and see, for example, Gordenker and Weiss (note 12); McIlwaine (note 19).

Abstracts

The Meaning of 11 September and the Emerging Postinternational World
Richard W. Mansbach

This essay analyzes the murderous attacks on New York's World Trade Center in New York and the Pentagon in Washington in terms of what they reflect about the changing nature of global politics and the theoretical demands of these changes. Among the key issues that the article addresses are the implications of 11 September for the overall role of change and the importance of history in global politics, the status of the territorial state in the field, the role of non-states in the global arena, the nature of contemporary violence and its implications for individuals, the declining role of distance, the disappearing boundary between foreign and domestic affairs, and, most importantly, the central role of identity theory in making sense of the emerging world. Overall, the essay professes a 'postinternational' perspective in the tradition of James Rosenau, suggesting that the events of 11 September reflect a world in transition from a state-based international system to a far more complex political universe with similarities to the prestate world. Such a world entails a considerable remapping of conceptual and theoretical maps concerning the field.

American Hegemony after 11 September: Allies, Rivals and Contradictions
James Anderson

11 September heralded and provided a pretext for a more aggressive but increasingly contradictory American hegemony. Some of the consequences are contrary to the United States' own interests. Its new doctrine of 'preemptive strike' against other sovereign states encourages similarly belligerent behaviour by other governments, and yet more terrorism by non-state actors, the very threats which were to be eradicated by a re-asserted US hegemony. This essay focuses on three partly overlapping themes: different strategies towards allies – *multilateral and unilateral*; different forms of power – *civil and military*; and different ideologies of globalisation – *neo-liberal and neo-conservative*. It argues that while US policy may oscillate between such poles, it often combines the different elements. The overall

strategy of the Bush administration is best characterised as *unilateral multilateralism*. The main issue for US hegemonists is the ways in which their hegemony might best be exercised, maintained and strengthened *vis à vis* allies and rivals. But for a safer, more democratic world, the choice does not lie between one faction of US hegemonists and another: we need other alternatives such as cosmopolitan democracy and a genuine internationalist movement which would give it some much-needed substance.

Calling 911: Geopolitics, Security and America's New War
Simon Dalby

The events of 11 September and their aftermath led rapidly to a military response by American forces in Afghanistan. The assumption that a state of war existed was widespread and quickly became official policy, but events might have been interpreted differently. Geopolitical reasoning was crucial to the specification of matters in terms of warfare. Three major assumptions were widely prevalent in the public discussions in the United States. First was that matters could only be understood as war, second that the primary axis of conflict was directly between America and terrorism and third that detailed investigation was unnecessary as the facts of the airliner impacts spoke obviously and said that this was an attack on America. Unpacking these assumptions shows that they are not necessarily obvious and that other geographical specifications of current geopolitical realities might lead to very different conclusions. An understanding of imperial power in particular suggests both a different geography and how assumptions of autonomous states and territorial responsibilities foreclosed other possible understandings and actions.

The Naming of 'Terrorism' and Evil 'Outlaws': Geopolitical Place-Making after 11 September
Mat Coleman

In the aftermath of 11 September, techniques of spatial surveillance and processes of rebordering indicate a moment of American (re)territorialization. This said, it seems important to move beyond a simple notion of geography-as-territoriality to focus on place and the politics of identity. In the context of events following from the mid-September 2001 'attacks', I suggest that critical geopoliticians focus on the US foreign policy naming of 'terrorism' as an iconographic place-making activity. However, perhaps the more poignant question is one concerning the post-11

September invocation of evil. I suggest here that scrutiny of the place-making naming of evil makes evident the potentially unjust and inhumane constitution of state responses to 'terrorism', declared as an outlaw to justice and humanity. This is particularly relevant given the US bombing campaign in Afghanistan, the alleged poor treatment of Taliban and Al Qaeda prisoners at Camp X-Ray in Guantánamo Bay, Cuba, and the recent detainment of suspected residents in the US. I conclude with a brief thought concerning the need to contextualize the events of 11 September in a larger frame of US global geopolitical relations and histories.

Environmental Terrorism: A Critique
Shannon O'Lear

As terrorism once again makes news headlines and attracts renewed attention from scholars, the usage of terms related to terrorism may well outpace the development of sound conceptualization of these themes. A case in point is environmental terrorism about which a small body of literature has already been written. The objective of this paper is to examine the theme of environmental terrorism by applying critiques of the more developed but similarly problematic area of environmental security. Three critiques of environmental security literature argue that there is insufficient clarity on how natural resources are linked to conflict, that the term 'environment' is not sufficiently clear as a guide to or boundary of a research area, and that the term 'security' prioritizes a realist, state-centric perspective that provides a limited perspective on relationships between natural resources and conflict. In this paper, the theme of environmental terrorism is subjected to parallel critiques as a way to examine the usefulness of this concept. Environmental terrorism, as a label, may be only partially helpful as a guide to future research that would also be aided by context-specific examinations of vulnerable natural resource and energy systems.

Strategic Troping in Sri Lanka: *September Eleventh* and the Consolidation of Political Position
Margot Kleinfeld

This essay investigates the deployment of the trope of *September eleventh* in Sri Lanka from 11 September 2001 until Sri Lanka's parliamentary elections and change of government on 5 December 2001. The essay argues that *September eleventh* in the tropic form of synecdoche performed political work for both parties to Sri Lanka's long-running conflict – the People's Alliance Government and the Tamil Tigers of Tamil Eelam, and demonstrates how each belligerent used *September eleventh* and the lexicon associated with the US attacks and early global response to brand their adversary as terrorist, to recode political and conflict narratives in *September eleventh* terms, and to indicate the appropriate scale and scope of the war. The article raises important questions about the translation of geopolitical events from one domestic context to another, the representation of political violence as global terror, and the strategic power of narrative.

Tabloid Realism and the Revival of American Security Culture
François Debrix

At a time when notions like globalisation and cultural fragmentation are being used to describe the changing nature of international politics, a persistently conservative discourse of national security (re)surfaces in foreign policy literatures. The purpose of this essay is to analyse this 'new' discourse and sketch out some of its ideological intents. Referred to as 'tabloid realism', this discourse can be found in texts authored by American scholars such as Robert Kaplan, Samuel Huntington and Zbigniew Brzezinski. Tabloid realism is a discourse of geopolitics which resists the idea that territorial sovereignty and national security are currently being transformed. Imitating the narrative style of tabloid publications, tabloid realists seek to grab the attention of the public by providing highly sensationalistic and overtly panic-stricken representations of international affairs. By proliferating fear-inducing images of current realities and preparing for a soon to be anarchical future, tabloid realists hope to conservatively re-anchor the state to stabilising visions of national security, geographical borders, and economic interests.

11 September and Popular Geopolitics: A Study of Websites run for and by Dutch Moroccans
Virginie Mamadouh

In the eyes of many, the events of 11 September 2001 validated Huntington's prediction of a future 'clash of civilizations' involving Islam and the West. Accordingly, the Muslim communities in the West are seen as vanguards of a hostile civilization (and by those on the other side, as vanguards of Islam in a hostile society). The essay explores the significance of such a geopolitical script in popular geopolitics. It deals with the representations of

Muslims in Western Europe – a 'significant minority' in that context. The analysis focuses on Moroccans in the Netherlands, a Muslim community resulting from recent immigration. The first section of the essay introduces popular geopolitics and geopolitical scripts, and presents the 'clash of civilizations' as a script highly relevant to the framing of the position of Muslims in Western Europe. The second section introduces the Dutch Moroccan case. The empirical section examines two websites run for and by young Dutch Moroccans; these websites are the group's main own media and have become key public places for this first generation of Dutch-born Moroccans. It assesses to what extent the civilizational script informs their representation of the events of 11 September and the aftermath of those events, and of their own position in the Netherlands.

Editorials and Geopolitical Explanations of 11 September

Jonathan Taylor and Chris Jasparo

In the wake of the 11 September attacks, public intellectuals, editorialists and newspaper columnists began to attempt to offer largely geopolitical explanations for the attacks through editorials and op-ed pieces. In this essay we analyze some sixty editorials and op-ed pieces from a range of perspectives. We classify the editorials under five main categories of geopolitical explanation: imperialism, 'blowback', state decline, Islamism, and the 'clash of civilizations' perspectives. We then discuss each category of explanation, highlighting the arguments made, the theoretical perspectives which inform them, and counterarguments, when presented. In our conclusion we discuss the strengths and weaknesses of the categories and suggest that geographers might help provide some integration of these varying perspectives.

Reading Geopolitics Beyond the State: Organisational Discourse in Response to 11 September

Carl T. Dahlman and Stanley D. Brunn

This essay explores organizations in civil society as constituting an important sphere of social action in which alternative geopolitical worldviews are produced and disseminated beyond the state. The authors discuss the conceptual relationship between non-governmental organizations and the geopolitics pursued by states and also develop an appropriate methodological program to investigate organizational geopolitics. This is accomplished by employing critical discourse analysis methods in the examination of press releases made by notable civil society organizations in response to the events of 11 September. While most organizational responses condemned the attacks and expressed a shared sense of sympathy for the victims, there was considerable divergence in the preferred geopolitical and social response – ranging from restraint and tolerance to aggressive militarism. The findings suggest organizations are not only important sites of alternative geopolitical representations beyond the state, but may also serve to reproduce and re-circulate dominant state-centered geopolitical visions as well.

Notes on Contributors

James Anderson teaches Geography and is Co-Director of the Centre for International Borders Research (CIBR) at Queen's University Belfast. Formerly Professor of International Development at the University of Newcastle upon Tyne where he established the Centre for Transnational Studies jointly with the Politics Department. Professor Anderson recently edited *Transnational Democracy* (Routledge, 2002) and co-edited several special issues of journals and books on borders and cross-border co-operation and governance, including *New Borders for a Changing Europe* (Frank Cass, 2003).

Stanley D. Brunn, Professor of Geography, University of Kentucky, has also taught at the University of Florida, Michigan State, and briefly a dozen European and Central Asian universities. He has published numerous books, chapters and articles on various topics, including ethnic groups, political identity, technological hazards, cybergeographies, religious worldviews, peace landscapes and humane futures. His current research focuses on electronic geographies, disciplinary history, innovative cartography and visualization.

Mat Coleman is a PhD candidate in Geography at the University of California, Los Angeles. His current research explores countervailing post-11 September US trade and security policies in the US–Mexico border region, as well as the conflicting identities which underwrite these mandates. He has published in *Political Geography* and with the International Boundaries Research Unit.

Carl Dahlman is an Assistant Professor of Geography and an Associate in the Walker Institute of International Studies at the University of South Carolina. He teaches courses dealing with post-conflict and humanitarian issues, as well as regional courses on Europe, the former Yugoslavia and the Middle East. His current research focuses on the politics of identity and displacement among Kurds from Northern Iraq, and the international effort to reverse ethnic cleansing in Bosnia.

Simon Dalby is Professor in, and Chair of, the Department of Geography and Environmental Studies at Carleton University in Ottawa, where he teaches courses on environment and geopolitics. He holds a PhD from Simon Fraser University in Vancouver and is author of *Creating the Second*

Cold War (Pinter and Guilford, 1990) and *Environmental Security* (University of Minnesota Press, 2002) and coeditor of *The Geopolitics Reader* and *Rethinking Geopolitics* (both published by Routledge in 1998).

François Debrix is Assistant Professor of International Relations at Florida International University. He is the author of *Re-Envisioning Peacekeeping: The United Nations and the Mobilization of Ideology* (Minnesota, 1999) and the editor of *Language, Agency, and Politics in a Constructed World* (M.E. Sharpe, 2003). His latest book, *Rituals of Mediation: International Politics and Social Meaning* (Minnesota, 2003; co-edited with Cynthia Weber), is a critical consideration of the place and meaning of transnational cultural interactions today. He is currently working on a new project which examines the interplay between the politics of fear and media representations in an international context.

Chris Jasparo is a cultural and political geographer specializing in environmental and transnational security issues, Asia–Pacific geopolitics and development studies. Currently conducting research on linkages between environmental and transnational security problems and globalization in Asia. Recent publications have appeared in *Geographical Review of Japan, Jane's Intelligence Review*, and *Regional Development Dialouge*.

Margo Kleinfeld is a PhD candidate at the University of Kentucky, and was recently appointed as Assistant Professor of Geography at the University of Wisconsin – Whitewater. Her research interests focus on children and geopolitics, scale and international organisation, and the strategic importance of narrative.

Virginie Mamadouh is Assistant Professor of Cultural and Political Geography at the University of Amsterdam and is currently affiliated with the Amsterdam Study Centre for the Metropolitan Environment (AME). Her fields of interest are geopolitics, European integration, scale politics, (urban) social movements, transnational networks, language issues, and the new media. She is a co-editor of *The Theory and Practice of Institutional Transplantation: Experiences with the Transfer of Policy Institutions* (2002) and an associate editor of *The Arab World Geographer*.

Richard W. Mansbach is currently Professor of Political Science at Iowa State University. He is the author, co-author, or editor of eleven books on international-relations theory, including *Polities: Authority, Identities, and*

Change(1996), *The State, Conceptual Chaos, and the Future of International Relations* (1989), *The Elusive Quest: Theory and International Politics* (1988), *In Search of Theory: Toward a New Paradigm for Global Politics* (1981) and *The Web of World Politics: Nonstate Actors in the Global System* (1976). He is also the author of several texts including *Structure and Process in International Politics* (1973) and *The Global Puzzle: Issues and Actors in World Politics* (2000), as well as co-editor of *Global Politics in a Changing World* (2001). Professor Mansbach is presently co-editor of the *International Studies Quarterly*, the flagship journal of the International Studies Association.

Shannon O'Lear is an Assistant Professor in the Geography Department at the University of Illinois at Urbana-Champaign. She is a political geographer interested in environmental and political issues in former Soviet republics. Her current work focuses on resource conflict in the Caspian Sea and Caucasus regions. Her work has been published in *The Professional Geographer, Post-Soviet Geography and Economics, Geographical Review* and *Global Environmental Change*.

Jonathan Taylor is a political and environmental geographer, and has been an Assistant Professor of Geography at California State University, Fullerton since 2000. His doctoral degree is from the University of Kentucky. His major research interests are the interface between politics and environmental change, especially in the Pacific Rim and Middle East. He has published articles in *Political Geography, Ecological Economics, Geographical Review, Journal of Geography, Post-Soviet Geography and Economics, Regional Development Dialogue*, and other journals as well as book chapters on a number of topics in human and political geography.

Index